EDMUND RICE AND THE FIRST CHRISTIAN BROTHERS

Edmund Rice. Engraving attributed to W. McDowall
after an original by Richard Kennedy (fl. 1846–), NLI.

Edmund Rice
and the first Christian Brothers

DÁIRE KEOGH

FOUR COURTS PRESS

Set in 10.5 pt on 14 pt Minion for
FOUR COURTS PRESS LTD
7 Malpas Street, Dublin 8, Ireland
e-mail: info@four courts press.ie
http://www.four courts press.ie
and in North America for
FOUR COURTS PRESS
c/o ISBS, 920 N.E. 58th Avenue, Suite 300, Portland, OR 97213.

A catalogue record for this title
is available from the British Library.

ISBN 978-1-84682-120-2

Printed in England
by MPG Books, Bodmin, Cornwall.

Contents

Illustrations

Acknowledgments

I WOULD LIKE TO EXPRESS my gratitude to the host of friends and colleagues who have helped me in the preparation of this book. First, and foremost, I would like to thank my colleagues at St Patrick's College, Drumcondra: the president, Pauric Travers, and the members of the History Department; Carla King, Diarmaid Ferriter, Marian Lyons, Gillian O'Brien and Matthew Stout for his cartography, and James Kelly who offered excellent encouragement and advice. I am grateful to the dean, Mary Shine Thompson, and the generous support of the Research Committee. Other colleagues were very supportive, too: Eileen McDevitt, Sharon King, Maura Sheehan, Philomena Donnelly, Therese Dooley, Sean MacLiam, Gordon Kennedy, Conor McNamara, Ray Topley and Ann Louise Gilligan.

This project began in response to a commission from the Christian Brothers. In that context, I wish to express my appreciation of the support of Brothers Mark McDonnell, Kevin Mullan, David Gibson and Michael Murray. The Brothers' archivists have been especially helpful: Brothers Peter Fogarty and Neville Thornton in Rome, and Karen Johnson and Michelle Cooney in Dublin. Other archivists have assisted me, too: Brother Jaime Dalumpines, De La Salle Archive, Rome, Vera Orschel, Pontifical Irish College Archive, David Sheehy and Noelle Dowling in the Dublin Diocesan Archive, Brother Connolly and his colleagues at the Brother Allen Library, Dublin, and the staffs of the National Library of Ireland and the Cregan Library, at St Patrick's College.

Members of the Edmund Rice networks have also offered me great encouragement: Ian Robertson, Peter Casey, Ted Magee, Gerry Brady, Mary Murphy, Laurie Needham, Peter Clinch, Elvina Fitzpatrick, Peter Dowling, Paul Robinson, the late Norman Gilles, Amelia Bresanello, Joe Lauren, John Dornbos, Jim Donovan, Peadar Gleeson and Andy and Kylie Kuppe. I am especially grateful for the hospitality of the Superior General Brother Philip Pinto, the community at Marcantonio Colonna and Signora Loretta Bonomi; to Father Patrick Burke, Andy Devane and Maurizio and Milena Rosati; to Monsignor Liam Bergin, rector of the Irish College, Rome, and to Father Albert McDonnell for providing a home from home in the Eternal City, as did the Schotts in

Indianapolis. Jack Burtchaell, Pat Grogan and the Waterford Historical Society introduced me to the complexities of Rice's origins, while, in Cork, Brothers Martin Kenneally, Andrew Hickey, Bede Minehan, Matthew Feeney, Donatus Brazil and Sister Pius O'Farrell welcomed me to the Presentation tradition.

I am in debt to decades of scholarship among the Christian Brothers: to the late Brothers David Fitzpatrick, Ambrose O'Hanlon and Columba Normoyle; to John E. Carroll, Frank Keane, Barry Coldrey, Dan Kelleher and Regius Hickey but especially to the Postulator of the cause of Edmund Rice, Donal Blake, for his counsel and support. John Kent's research opened a range of discussion, while Denis McLaughlin shared insights and drafts of his *Price of Freedom*. Others, too, have offered excellent advice: John Logan, Tom Dunne, Marianne Elliott, David Dickson, L.M. Cullen, Tom Kselman, Father John W. O'Malley SJ, Anthony Malcomson, Bob Schmuhl, Father Hugh Fenning OP, Father Padraig Daly OSA, Father Thomas O'Connor, Father Tom Morrissey SJ, Father Jim Wilmoth, Brother Peter Gilfedder FSC and Father David Kelly OSA. Friends and colleagues very generously read earlier drafts, John Coolahan, Nigel Yates, Eugene Broderick, Owen Dudley Edwards, Brian Lynch, Father Sean McGraw, Ciarán MacMurchaidh, Fionnuala Waldron and Tom Bartlett. Ian Hazlett, Edmund Garvey and Paul Caffrey have been constant in their support, but the project could not have been completed without the friendship and assistance of Brother Greg Wall.

I was fortunate to secure an IRCHSS Government of Ireland Senior Research Fellowship which allowed me complete this study and prepare the groundwork for a successor, which will assess the history of the Christian Brothers from 1850 to 1968. I am very grateful to Michael Adams and his colleagues at Four Courts Press. My greatest debt, of course, is to my family and to Katie and the children, John, Cora and Monica, for their patience and love. Perhaps I should chalk that miracle to Edmund Rice!

Abbreviations

APF	Archives of Propaganda Fide, Rome.
Arch. Hib.	*Archivium Hibernicum.*
CBGA	Christian Brothers General Archive, Rome.
CBER	*Christian Brothers Education Record.*
CDA	Cashel Diocesan Archive.
DDA	Dublin Diocesan Archive.
DLSGA	De La Salle General Archive, Rome.
IDA	Irish Dominican Archive, Tallaght.
IER	*Irish Ecclesiastical Record, 1865–1968.*
IHS	*Irish Historical Studies.*
LDSC	APF, Lettere e Decreti della Sacra Congregazione.
Memories	M. C. Normoyle (ed.), *Memories of Edmund Rice* (Dublin, 1979).
PBGA	Presentation Brothers, General Archive, Cork.
PICR	Pontifical Irish College, Rome.
Positio	*Positio super Virtutibus: Cause for the canonisation of Edmund Ignatius Rice* (Rome, 1988).
SORCG	APF, Scritture Originali Riferite nelle Congregazioni Generali.
SCRI	APF, Scritture Riferite nei Congressi, Irlanda.

Introduction

THE LIFE OF EDMUND RICE (1762–1844) spanned a crucial era, from the dawn of Catholic Emancipation to the eve of the Great Famine (1845–50). These were vital years in the formation of Irish Catholic consciousness, marking the emergence from the penal era and the establishment of the modern Church. Rice made a radical contribution to this process, fostering confidence and helping to create a literate modern society through the revolution in Irish education that he initiated.

No religious congregation in Ireland has attracted more attention than the Christian Brothers. Yet for all that has been written, we lack a satisfactory account of their origins and founding character. And even though Rice has been the subject of at least eight biographies, the details of his life and motivation remain vague.[1] Until recently, these studies were written by Brothers for Brothers and their devotees. This, of course, is not unusual in religious history; John O'Malley observed in his acclaimed history of the *First Jesuits* the tendency to write congregational history in terms which are 'familiar and familial' and with little regard for the new historiography. It must be acknowledged, however, that the biographies by McCarthy (1926), Fitzpatrick (1945) and Normoyle (1975) were written in advance of the historiographical achievement associated with Louis Cullen, and his circle, which greatly advanced the pioneering work begun by R.E. Burns in the 1950s.[2] Similarly, lay commentators have focussed upon the state-building role of the Brothers. Within this context, many have taken their lead from Br Barry Coldrey's *Faith and Fatherland* (1988) and, focussing more on the title than the content of this seminal study, have overstated the Brothers' commitment to Irish nationalism, while paying scant attention to their religious inspiration and educational priorities.[3] Within this reading, the Brothers are remembered primarily as 'the most indefatigable and explicit carriers' of the national ideal.[4]

The result of both tendencies has been studies which, although technically accurate, are imbalanced and tend towards hagiography rather than history. There are, of course, several factors which have frustrated attempts to interpret the world of Edmund Rice and the first Brothers. Not least of these are the difficulties associated with the traditional historiography of eighteenth-century Ireland, which tended to exaggerate the nature and duration of the penal laws.[5] Histories of the Christian Brothers have been written in accordance with the Catholic, and nationalist, interpretation of the laws which emphasised the elements of the popery code which applied to the practice of religion, but avoided the essential security considerations which inspired the laws. As a consequence, the penal era (1691–1829) is portrayed as an age of unrelenting persecution in which Catholics suffered uniformly under an alien government intent on eliminating the faith of their fathers. This has distorted the realities of eighteenth-century Ireland and the world of Edmund Rice and his contemporary religious reformers. Recent scholarship, offering a more nuanced interpretation of the penal age, engages not merely with the persecutions of the period, but also with the creative ways in which the Catholic community responded to the challenge of the laws, in a process of 'endurance and emergence' which is immediately apparent in the fortunes of the ambitious Rices of Callan.[6]

Allied to this is the increased understanding of religious practice in pre-Famine Ireland. Visitors to the island were struck by the devotion of the people; for example, the German Lutheran, Johann G. Kohl, described the Irish as 'the most genuine Catholics in the world' in 1844.[7] Yet, David Miller's research indicates that Mass attendance rates were poor, particularly in areas of the north and west, where they were as low as 40 per cent.[8] While it would be wrong to conclude from such statistics that the Irish were largely 'un-churched', these realities provoked Edmund Rice and his circle to follow the example of Nano Nagle, who was not content to 'bewail the evils of ignorance and irreligion', but laboured 'zealously to … counteract them'.[9] Within this context, the Brothers and the teaching Sisters played a vital role in 'Trenting' the Irish, decades before the so-called 'Devotional Revolution'.[10]

This evangelical imperative has been obscured by the emphasis placed on Rice's expansive charity, and the extent to which he sought to 'raise the poor'.[11] Certainly, he urged his disciples to 'give to the poor in handfuls', but it is clear that his purpose was not merely philanthropic, but that he sought at the outset to embrace the religious life.[12] Dom Eugene Boylan (1904–64), the author of a number of spiritual classics, described this more poetically as his quest for God and desire to 'abide in Christ'.[13] In this sense, the schools were the *ministry*, rather than the *raison d'être* of the first Christian Brothers. In terms of education, too, tradition asserts that Edmund launched his mission 'to give education to the poor of Waterford when they had no one to educate them'.[14] Waterford was, in fact, Ireland's third most literate city and well served for schools. Quite clearly,

Rice's focus was not merely schooling, but the provision of an *alternative* Catholic education, along the lines of the pedagogy developed by Jean Baptiste de la Salle (1651–1719) in continental Europe. Yet while Rice's priority was the evangelisation of youth, the Brothers' schools were vital to the modernisation of Irish society and the creation of a respectable urban working class, by instilling in the boys the virtues of discipline, hard work and sobriety.

Edmund Rice is a difficult subject for a biographer. The absence of a diary, memoirs or a contemporary biography makes him an elusive subject, and our images of the man's personality are restricted to mere glimpses. Indeed, during the celebrations to mark the centenary of Rice's death, one Presentation Brother, intent on reclaiming him as the founder of his congregation, asserted that the extent of our knowledge could be written on an envelope.[15] Rice's modesty was renowned; he declined to give evidence to the Royal Commission on Education in 1825, sending his deputy instead. He rarely met school inspectors; few of the 'tourists' who celebrated the Brothers' schools met the founder, and his name was seldom mentioned in the Waterford newspapers, except in connection with the Mendicity Asylum.[16] As a result, his contemporaries appear to have been unaware of the most basic details about his early life including his short marriage and the identity of his wife. This may be attributed to the cult of anonymity within the Christian Brothers, but his archive is extremely limited and the earliest extant letter is dated from 1810, eight years after he founded his Brotherhood.[17] The bulk of the remainder is of a business nature with little by way of personal comment or reflection. There are no letters in Rice's archive to compare with the detailed correspondence of Nano Nagle, his contemporary and inspiration, who has left for posterity a window into her spirituality and the workings of her soul.[18] Even his closest collaborator, Br Austin Dunphy, lamented that 'very little is now known of his early life', since all his contemporaries had 'long since been gathered to their forefathers'.[19]

In an effort to compensate for this lacuna, the Christian Brothers' general chapter of 1910, which voted to promote the cause of their founder for canonisation, launched an ambitious oral history project which aimed to collect recollections and memoirs of Edmund Rice; a selection of these was published by Br Normoyle (1979) and I refer to them in the text as *Memories*.[20] This folklore project has influenced subsequent biographies, from Br McCarthy's monumental study (1926) up to and including Denis McLaughlin's most recent assessment of Edmund Rice's educational philosophy and achievement.[21] As a historical source, however, many of these *Memories* are of limited value. Neither can the collection properly be described as 'folklore', since the project was conceived with an obvious agenda – the promotion of the canonisation of 'the Founder', or perhaps more precisely, the promotion of the congregation of Christian Brothers itself. Many of these recollections provide, therefore, a twentieth-century perspective on Edmund Rice, which describes not so much his heroic virtue as the Catholic values of Independent Ireland. Of course, this reflects the double dynamic at the heart of the canonisation process. It is not sufficient to display 'heroic virtue' in one's own lifetime, but your actions must satisfy the expectations of the generation which declares you a saint.[22] At another level, too, the hagiography has tended to demonise those who opposed 'the Founder' during his lifetime, treating them as bitter, self-centred and antagonistic.[23] As a result, the valuable commentary that the extensive correspondence of Br Joseph Leonard offers on the first generation of Christian Brothers and their mission has been largely neglected. Both realities, the paucity and the selective use of archival evidence, have allowed subsequent generations of commentators to 'remake' Rice in order to satisfy contemporary agendas. Thus he has been presented variously as Br Ignatius Rice the religious brother, Edmund the married father, Edmund Rice the ethical business man and so on.

This is an attempt to overcome these difficulties and to understand Edmund Rice and the first Christian Brothers as they understood themselves. It is not a biography, but it seeks to interpret the early Brothers in their historical context, the piety which animated them, and the community which they served and shaped. Rice and his disciples were of their time, and their cares were those of their contemporaries. Consequently, the Brothers manifest their age to an extent that their story is that of the emergence of the Church from the penal age.

CHAPTER ONE

The context: the Church in the catacombs?

I N A SMALL CONVERTED STABLE in Waterford, Edmund Rice launched an educational apostolate which in time would spread not only throughout 'the kingdom', as he desired, but to the four corners of the earth.[1] The timing of that initiative was crucial to its success, since the previous decades had brought a thaw in the penal laws which afforded unprecedented opportunities for the Catholic community to rebuild its Church. Within this process, Edmund Rice played a vital part, bringing his acumen and energy to a project which involved not simply the restoration of the Church, but the creation of a modern literate nation.

I

This 'thaw' in the penal laws reflected changing circumstances in Ireland, but it was also an indication of the nature of the legislation.[2] Raised on the memories of the Ulster rebellion and massacres of 1641, Irish Protestants believed that they remained dangerously exposed to the threat of a renewed attack from a formidable Catholic enemy, at home and abroad. The Williamite Wars (1688–91) reinforced these fears, while the generous terms of the Treaty of Limerick (1691) which concluded the conflict, left the defeated Catholics in a stronger position than might have been expected. The promise of religious toleration, the retention of the estates of those surrendering in arms, and (incredibly, given the ongoing wars with King Louis XIV) affording combatants passage to France – all this left the victors with the sense that they had won the war but lost the peace. Within this context, the penal laws, which aimed to secure the kingdom from future threat, stemmed from a deep insecurity rather than from 'vengeance [or the] unbridled licence of triumph'.[3]

The Protestant nation owed its existence to the destruction of Catholic power, which implied, as the archbishop of Dublin, William King (1650–1729), put it, 'either they or we must be ruined'.[4] The penal laws were rooted in these sentiments, and rather than representing a systematic 'code' were in fact a collection of measures enacted in an *ad hoc* fashion over half a century in response to a variety of immediate pressures and grievances.[5] In this sense, the introduction of laws and the extent to which they were applied may be represented as a crude barometer of Protestant security in eighteenth-century Ireland. Significantly, the first of the laws, enacted in 1695, which forbade Catholics from keeping arms or a horse worth more than £5 with cavalry potential, addressed immediate security concerns (7 William III c. 5). So too did the 'Act to Restrain Foreign Education' (7 William III c. 4) which aimed to limit communication between Irish Catholics and potential allies among their continental co-religionists. This act prohibited 'any child or other person … to be trained in any popish university, college or school, or in any private popish family'. A further clause of the same law reflected the subversive nature of education within a colonial context, in which the schoolmaster was a critical cultural influence:

> Whereas it has been found by experience that tolerating papists keeping schools or instructing youth in literature is one great reason of many of the natives continuing ignorant of the principles of the true religion, and strangers to the scriptures, and of their neglecting to conform themselves to the laws of this realm, and of their not using the English habit and language, no person of the popish religion shall publicly teach school or instruct youth, or in private houses teach youth, except only the children of the master or mistress of the private house, upon pain of twenty pounds, and prison for three months for every such offence.[6]

So, rather than intending to condemn Catholic youth to ignorance, this law attempted to secure a Protestant control over education by curbing the political influence of the schoolmaster.

The penal laws, then, are best understood as an attempt by the Protestant state to protect itself against 'popery', the dangerous political system which Catholicism represented, not the Catholic religion itself; this accounts for the focus of the laws upon land, the legal profession and the exercise of religious authority. In an eighteenth-century context, land lay at the heart of all political power, so the most determined of the laws were directed against property. As Corish has noted, 'here the penal code was meant to bite and made to bite, to reach what Edmund Burke (1729–97) was to call its "vicious perfection".'[7] Certainly, the 1704 Act 'to prevent the further growth of popery' (2 Anne c. 6), represented a formidable attempt to complete the destruction of the Catholic landed interest which the Treaty of Limerick had left largely intact.[8] Its provisions prevented land passing from Protestants to Catholics by prohibiting a

1.1 Engraving by Edouard Gamier depicting the visit of James II,
accompanied by Cardinal de Noailles, archbishop of Paris, to
Jean Baptiste de la Salle at the school which the exiled king had endowed
for the sons of Irish émigrés in the French capital (*c.*1700), DLSGA, Rome.

Catholic from buying land or leasing it for more than thirty-one years; leases of the permitted length had to be held at a prohibitive rent of at least two-thirds of the yearly value. The notorious gavelling clause demanded the division of the estate among all male heirs on the death of the proprietor, unless the eldest son conformed to the Church of Ireland, in which case he would inherit the entire estate; if the son conformed in the father's lifetime, the father became his 'tenant for life'.

Catholic land ownership was greatly reduced as a consequence of this legislation. At the start of the eighteenth century, Catholics held an estimated 14 per cent of the land, illustrating the great transfer of land which had taken place as a result of the Cromwellian settlement, but by 1776 Arthur Young believed that the figure had fallen to 5 per cent.[9] This dramatic reduction in Catholic fortunes has traditionally been accepted as evidence of the success of the penal laws, but the figures need qualification as there were dramatic regional variations in the application of the laws and there were many ways in which penalties could be avoided. In this sense, the stark implications of Arthur Young's figures represent what one commentator has called a 'statistical trap'.[10]

Recent research has emphasised the degree to which Catholics relied on trustees. Moreover, conformity to the established Church of Ireland was often nominal, or strategic, and there existed a large 'convert interest' of land-owning families like the Brownes of Westport or the Lynches of Galway who could shield their Catholic relatives from the rigours of the law.[11] A distinction must also be made between ownership and leasehold: when property in the form of leasehold and livestock is taken into account, Catholic personal property amounted to half the total by the end of the eighteenth century. Furthermore, since no concerted effort was made to exclude Catholics from trade, especially the provisions trade, they came to possess great economic strength in the commercial classes, particularly in Munster and Leinster.[12] It is a combination of factors like these, which explain the relative prosperity of the Rices of Westcourt, sheltered in the heart of Butler territory in County Kilkenny.

Similarly, the religious clauses of the code were concerned more with the exercise of religious authority than the practice of religion itself. In the 1960s, R.E. Burns wrote that the laws intended that 'the whole nation would be Protestant', but, as Maureen Wall argued subsequently, mass conversion could never have been the intention of legislation that aimed essentially at the preservation of a status quo rather than a dilution of the Protestant interest.[13] Because the primary concern of the penal code was the preservation of property and power, there were significant ambiguities with regard to religious practice.[14] In

1697, for example, an 'Act for Banishing all Papists exercising any ecclesiastical jurisdiction, and all regulars of the popish clergy' (9 William III c. 1), targeted clerics not on account of their priesthood, but because of their prominence in the political upheavals of the seventeenth century:

> the late rebellions in this kingdom have been promoted by popish bish-
> ops and other ecclesiastical persons of the popish religion, and foras-
> much as the peace and publick safety of this kingdom is in danger by
> the great number of said the clergy now residing here, and settling in
> fraternities contrary to law, and to the great impoverishing of his
> Majesty's subjects who are forced to maintain them, and said clergy do
> not only endeavour to withdraw his Majesty's subjects from their obe-
> dience, but do daily stir up and move sedition and rebellion.

Four hundred and twenty-four regular priests were transported in 1698, mainly to France. Many more remained in Ireland passing themselves off as secular clergy, while others returned once the initial commotion had died down. The position of the Catholic hierarchy in 1698 was already extremely weak. There were no more than eight bishops in the country, out of a possible twenty-six, and three of these left under the terms of the Act.[15] Had the terms of this 'Banishment Act' been strenuously implemented, the Catholic Church in Ireland could have been eliminated in two generations. The entry of priests from abroad was forbidden and there could be no ordinations without bishops; without priests there would be no sacraments and without the sacraments there would be no Church.

In 1703–4 further legislation was introduced to reduce the perceived threat posed by the hundreds of diocesan clergy who remained in the kingdom. Under the terms of the 'Act for Registering Popish Clergy' (2 Anne c. 7) priests were com-pelled to appear before the court of sessions and to provide vital details, includ-ing the date and place of their ordination and the name of the ordaining prelate. Attempts were also made to reduce clerical numbers by authorising only one sec-ular priest per civil parish. Priests were confined to their own county, forbidden from keeping a curate, and obliged to present two securities of £50 as a guaran-tee of their 'good behaviour'.[16] Added to this, further penalties were introduced to punish bishops and friars who had returned illegally to the country. Almost 1,100 priests registered under the terms of this Act, and far from leading to the extinc-tion of the Church it actually facilitated its re-emergence, since it granted legal recognition to the Catholic diocesan clergy. Registered priests were free to say

Mass and administer the sacraments, churches remained open, and the act contained sufficient loopholes to allow for creative exploitation, often with the collusion of compliant magistrates. Many regulars — members of religious orders — registered as diocesan clergy and bishops masqueraded as parish priests.

Additional measures were introduced in the aftermath of a failed Jacobite landing in Scotland in March 1708. In a context where the Vatican continued to recognise the legitimacy of the exiled Stuart kings, who retained the right to nominate Catholic bishops, and where the clergy openly avowed their support for James III, parliament attempted in 1709 to extract an oath of abjuration from diocesan clergy, rejecting the Pretender's claim to the throne and the supposed power of the pope to depose heretical monarchs (8 Anne c. 3). A mere thirty-three priests swore the oath of abjuration, and this rendered the status of the remainder illegal. These non-juring priests were deprived of the protection of the 'Registration Act', without which they were vulnerable to the attention of the 'discoverer', who was rewarded for information leading to the arrest of illegal clergy or schoolmasters (8 Anne c. 3).

Bishop Hugh MacMahon (whose uncle had been chaplain to James II) described for his Roman superiors the consequences of this legislation in his Ulster diocese of Clogher:

> the open practice of religion either entirely ceased or was considerably curtailed according as the persecution varied in intensity. During these years a person was afraid to trust his neighbour lest, being compelled to swear, he might divulge the names of those present at Mass. Moreover, spies were continually moving around posing as Catholics.[17]

The same report contains an evocative description of the clandestine celebration of Mass in theses episodic periods of intense persecution:

> Greater danger … threatened the priests … with the result that priests have celebrated Mass with their faces veiled … At other times Mass was celebrated in a closed room, with only a server present, the window being left open so that those outside might hear the voice of the priest … and herein the great goodness of God was made manifest, for the greater the severity of the persecution, the greater the fervour of the people.
>
> Over the countryside, people might be seen, meeting, or signalling to each other on their fingers, the hour Mass was due to begin, in order that people might be able to kneel down and follow mentally the Mass

which was celebrated at a distance. I ... have often celebrated Mass at night with only the man of the house and his wife present. They were afraid to admit even their children so fearful were they.[18]

The bishop's report reflects hostile local circumstances, however, it belies attempts to minimise the extent of the penal persecution, or to reduce such memories to a 'grotesque popular reputation' of the penal era.[19]

Yet, while the penal laws were motivated primarily by considerations of security, and were not against the Catholic faith *per se*, it was an implicit intention of the legislation to advance the 'Reformation' of Ireland. The Williamite parliament, for instance, attempted to reform the religious calendar and the celebration of 'holy days':

> Whereas many idle persons refuse to work at their lawful calling on several days in the year, on pretence that the same is dedicated to some saint, or pretended saint, for whom they have or pretend to have reverence, and chuse to spend such days in idleness, drunkenness, and vice, to the scandal of religion, no other day except those days listed herein ... shall be kept holy.[20]

Other legislation sought to end traditional pilgrimages, which attracted 'vast numbers' to Lough Derg, in County Donegal, and holy wells across the country (2 Anne c. 6). More significantly, the same Act offered an annual pension of £20 to 'every popish priest who shall convert and conform to the Church of Ireland as by law established'.[21] This 'reforming' tendency of parliament became more explicit thirty years later, when the Church of Ireland primate, Hugh Boulter (1662–1742), extended the scope of government education measures by giving them an evangelical character, based upon his sense that:

> It is of the utmost consequence to bring [the papists] over by all Christian methods to the Church of *Ireland* ...The ignorance & obstinacy of the adult papists is such that there is not much hopes of converting them. But we have hopes if we could erect a number of schools to teach their children the *English* tongue, & the principles of the Christian religion, we could do some good among the generation that is growing up.[22]

Such sentiments provided the inspiration for the foundation of the 'Charter Schools' (1733), which Thomas Wyse (1791–1862), the liberal MP, claimed 'out-

Churched the Church' and were hated by Roman Catholics on account of their proselytism.[23]

Ironically, the Primate's anxiety and the 'Charter School' initiative was sparked, in part, by a sense among Protestants that the penal laws had failed. Indeed, in 1727 Archbishop William King had observed that the Catholics had 'more bishops in Ireland than the Protestants … and twice as many priests. Their friaries and nunneries are public.'[24] This sense was confirmed by the returns made in the 'Report on the state of Popery', presented to the Irish House of Lords in 1731, which indicated the extent to which the Catholic Church had begun to reorganise; almost every diocese had a bishop, clerical numbers were rising, Mass houses continued to be built and a rudimentary educational system, with '549 Popish schools' was in place.[25] This Catholic recovery continued throughout the eighteenth century, but there were sporadic reminders that this 'passive toleration' could not be taken for granted.[26] Just as Mass houses had been closed during the invasion scares of 1709, moments of international or domestic crisis usually brought a renewed application of the penal laws. This happened in 1715, 1720, 1745 and during the war of the Austrian Succession (1740–8). There were occasions during the Seven Years War (1756–63), too, when victims of such persecution included Bishop Nicholas Sweetman of Ferns, who was accused of enlisting men for foreign armies in 1751; Archbishop Michael O'Reilly of Armagh, who was detained along with eighteen of his priests in 1753, and Fr Nicholas Sheehy, who was judicially murdered in the anti-Catholic frenzy of 1766.[27] It was incidents such as these which justified Luke Gardiner's claim, in 1782, that 'the papists were safe from the penal laws so long as the generous and merciful disposition of their countrymen disdained to put them into execution'.[28]

II

By the middle decade of the eighteenth century the threat of Jacobitism had passed. In 1760, two years before Edmund Rice was born, Catholics greeted the accession of King George III with 'effusive declarations of loyalty', while Pope Clement XIII's failure to recognize Charles Edward, on the death of the Old Pretender (1766), removed a great deal of suspicion of Catholic loyalty and allowed the Church to emerge 'from the catacombs'.[29] Kevin Whelan has identified a 'Tridentine surge' in the following decade, but while contemporary travellers such as Arthur Young and Thomas Campbell were struck by the vitality of the Irish Church in the 1770s, it would be some time before it achieved the exacting

LAVDAT TENTAT VINCIT

John . Thomas Troy
OSSORY

1.2 Book plate of John Thomas Troy, bishop of Ossory (1776–86).

standard required by the Council of Trent (1545–63).[30] The dislocation caused by
the penal laws inevitably led to a weakening of institutional structures within the
Church, and in many areas conditions remained much as they had been in 1542,
when the first Jesuit mission under Alfonso Salmerón, one of St Ignatius' original
companions, arrived in Ireland.[31] Yet ironically while persecution prevented the
full implementation of the reforms of the Council, the persistent prescription of
the faith fostered an enthusiasm which may have actually facilitated the process
of evangelisation and pastoral rejuvenation once the restrictions were lifted.[32]

The second half of the century witnessed a significant attempt by reform-
minded bishops to correct the general laxity which characterised the Irish
Church. Surviving visitation reports from the 1750s indicate that this process
was in train in the dioceses of Ferns and Cashel, while in 1776 Bishop John Troy
launched an ambitious reform programme in the diocese of Ossory.[33] In the
Dublin diocese, Archbishop John Carpenter initiated a renewal, on his appointment in 1770, which would be followed by his confreres throughout Ireland.[34]

The Dominican historian Hugh Fenning has likened the archbishop to the great reforming popes Gregory and Leo, but a comparison with Charles Borromeo (1538–84), the aristocratic and austere archbishop of Milan, might be more instructive.[35] His administration set the standard for early modern bishops, which Carpenter sought to extend to Ireland. He maintained exact administrative records; he published provincial constitutions and a large collection of 'Instructions and Admonitions' intended to be read from the altars of his diocese.[36] Above all, the archbishop sought to reform the habits of his priests. At clerical gatherings, he preached sobriety and strove to curb the 'fondness for liquor ... the fatal rock' upon which too many of his priests were 'unhappily shipwrecked'.[37] He sought to rouse the 'indolent and slothful', but, while his preference was to 'try first every gentle method', he was not averse to applying the most severe canonical sanction.[38] In 1772, he suspended the parish priest of Blessington, County Wicklow, 'for having abandoned his flock'. Similarly, he threatened to excommunicate the parish priest of Castledermot, the 'Rev but unhappy Randolph Byrne', for unspecified 'scandalous behaviour'.[39]

In the neighbouring diocese of Meath, Bishop Patrick Joseph Plunket (1738–1827), a former professor at the Lombard College, Paris, launched an ambitious programme of renewal which is documented in his visitation reports, the fullest of their kind to survive from the period. It is not unreasonable to assume that the conditions he encountered on his first visitation (1780) were replicated in rural parishes across Ireland. Indeed, the early Redemptorist missioners noted very similar conditions in the poorer parts of Connaught and Ulster in the 1850s.[40] At Kilkskeer, in the barony of Upper Kells, Plunket reported that 'the altar step, and the place about the altar, [were] by no means clean or orderly:

> The crucifix too bad. A cruet or small phial for the wine absolutely wanting. The chapel not closed, and therefore exposed to dirt and profanation. A clerk absolutely necessary to keep up some little decency in the house of God.[41]

Likewise at Oldcastle, County Meath, his observations suggest the poverty of the parish liturgy in the rural areas of the diocese:

> Neither order nor decency about the altar. The altar steps too low. The priest cannot properly convey his words when he stands almost on a level with the people. It is a shame that there should be but one set of altar linen and one rusty suit of vestments in such a considerable parish.

A black pewter chalice, greatly impaired, is absolutely unfit for the celebration of the divine mysteries, and must be dishonourable to a respectable congregation.[42]

In almost every parish, Plunket complained of the poor quality of the vestments, the sacred vessels and the irregularity of the sanctuary. Of greater concern to him, however, were the lax liturgical practices of priests who failed to preach on Sunday or who were ignorant of the decrees of the Council of Trent. At the parish of Turin, Plunket wryly commented that 'every face seemed to wear visible marks of dissatisfaction at the pastor's unpastoral conduct'.[43]

Plunket's concerns, and the demands he made upon his clergy, reflect the renewed vigour of the episcopacy in the late eighteenth century. Throughout the country, younger bishops engaged in regular visitations of their dioceses; many parishes were visited annually and complaints were carefully investigated and followed through. The ignorance of the laity was of special concern, and the priority of catechesis is reflected in almost every episcopal report to Rome in the period 1782–1803; congregations showed little respect during the Mass and it was common for bishops to refuse Confirmation on account of poor preparation. At Kilkskeer, in June 1780, Bishop Plunket noted: 'the children in general ignorant of the essential parts of the Christian doctrine, and not understanding what they say ...'[44]

While there was a basic parish school system in place by the 1730s, these 'hedge schools' excluded all those unable to pay fees. As an interim solution to the problem of Catholic education, reforming bishops relied on the assistance of educated parishioners formed into the Confraternity of Christian Doctrine to assist in the task of evangelisation.[45] Its members gave instruction to the children for one hour after the last Mass each Sunday. The societies were governed by a priest, who was assisted by a committee elected annually from the predominantly female membership. A surviving register of the Confraternity of the Blessed Sacrament and Christian Doctrine established in Mary's Lane, Dublin, in 1798, illustrates the nature of its apostolate:

> 11. The children should be divided into different classes according to the following order; 1st Class – Prayer including the Acts of Faith, Hope and Charity. 2nd Class – Small Catechism. 3rd Class – Abridgement of the General Catechism. 4th Class – General Catechism. 5th Class – Fleury's Historical Catechism, but to this last lesson no one is to be admitted but such as shall be declared fit by some priest of the Chapel ...

15. That the members do recite each day some one of the following devotions, viz.: the Office of the Blessed Sacrament, or the *Pange Lingua* ...[46]

Such schemes demonstrated efforts to promote orthodoxy and the devotions associated with the Council of Trent. As part of this process, a considerable amount of religious and devotional material was printed in the period. This included Carpenter's altar-missal which the archbishop claimed was the first to have been 'published in these Kingdoms'. It contained the feasts of the Irish saints and represented an important milestone in Ireland's devotional revolution.[47] By 1782, Archbishop James Butler's *General Catechism* had gone through eleven editions in the seven years since its publication, including a Dublin edition, published anonymously by Archbishop Carpenter as a *Catechism for the instruction of children* (1777). Of the limited devotional material available in the Irish language, the most significant was the *Sixteen Irish Sermons in an Easy and Familiar Stile* (1736), published by Bishop James Gallagher of Raphoe (1725–37).[48] Significantly, Archbishop Carpenter's *Ritual* (1776) included as an appendix, an Irish translation of his 'Instructions and Admonitions' made by Charles O'Conor of Belanagare, an accomplished scholar and founder of the Catholic Association.[49]

Reform-minded bishops were also determined to address the shortcomings in clerical formation, without which there could be no improvement in the religious life of the laity. In the absence of domestic seminaries, forbidden by the penal laws, priestly formation varied and candidates followed no set pattern. Clerical students were usually educated by the local hedge-schoolmaster, and many served a type of apprenticeship to their local parish priest, after which they would present a letter of recommendation to a bishop. Many, though not all students, were ordained before travelling to the continental colleges to commence their studies. This practice of ordaining theologically untrained young men gave rise to many abuses, and was a source of constant debate in the eighteenth century. Yet, in the absence of sufficient bursaries to support their education, early ordination was often a practical necessity since it allowed student priests live on mass stipends. A continental education, however, was not necessarily a guarantee of standards: one memorandum, from mid-century, was critical of clerics returning to Ireland 'to convert heretics who know more theology than they do themselves'.[50] Similarly, in his visitation reports, Bishop Plunkett frequently stressed the need for 'altar-cards ... that the priest may say the *credo* and last Gospel, &c., without a mistake'.[51]

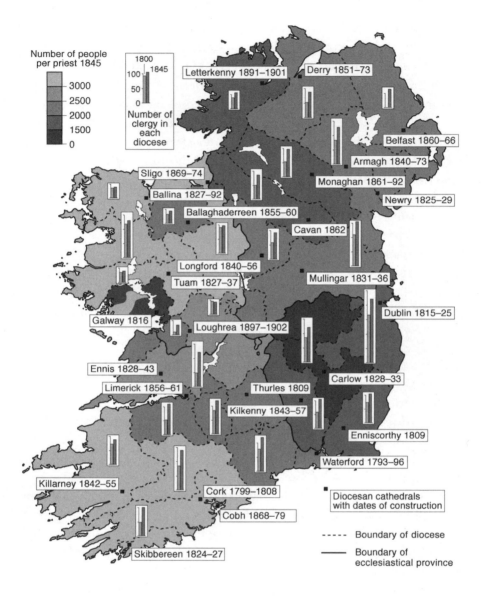

Number of people
per priest 1845

3000
2500
2000
1500
0

1800
1845
100
50
0
Number of
clergy in
each
diocese

Letterkenny 1891–1901

Derry 1851–73

Belfast 1860–66

Armagh 1840–73

Monaghan 1861–92

Sligo 1869–74

Ballina 1827–92

Newry 1825–29

Ballaghaderreen 1855–60

Cavan 1862

Longford 1840–56

Tuam 1827–37

Mullingar 1831–36

Dublin 1815–25

Galway 1816

Loughrea 1897–1902

Ennis 1828–43

Carlow 1828–33

Limerick 1856–61

Thurles 1809

Kilkenny 1843–57

Enniscorthy 1809

Waterford 1793–96

Killarney 1842–55

Cork 1799–1808

Cobh 1868–79

Skibbereen 1824–27

■ Diocesan cathedrals
   with dates of construction

- - - - Boundary of diocese

——— Boundary of
      ecclesiastical province

1.3 Priest:people ratios in nineteenth-century Ireland. *Source*: Seán Duffy,
Atlas of Irish history (Dublin, 1997). Map drawn by Matthew Stout.

To compensate for such theological ignorance, the most energetic and reforming bishops convened diocesan conferences, through which they attempted to renew their clergy, in a programme advocated by the Fathers at Trent.[52] One-day conferences were held between the months of April and October in many dioceses, and fines were imposed on those absent without reason. Bishop John Troy instituted such conferences in Edmund Rice's home diocese of Ossory in 1780. These provided a model which many of his confrères followed. Troy chose a theme for each year, and the surviving Dublin plan for 1790 reflects his meticulous approach:

January	Paschal communion—can it be deferred?
February	Viaticum for children and Mass stipends.
March	Why hear Mass, the altar and vestments.
April	The ceremony of the Mass, its language, can it be said in the vernacular?
June	Penance, what is it? Is it necessary, is it a true sacrament of the New Law?
July	Matter for penance and contrition.
August	Sacramental confession.
September	Is contrition necessary only for mortal sins?
October	The minister of penance.
November	Reserved cases, who has faculties to absolve them?
December	The sign of confession.[53]

While such initiatives were a welcome start, clerical education remained a challenge. Twenty-three years after the foundation of the Royal College at Maynooth (1795), Bishop Patrick McNicholas of Achonry complained that 15 of the 35 priests in his diocese, who had been ordained for four years or more, were theologically untrained.[54] There were indications, too, that the standard of their secular education was no better. In 1830, Br Joseph Leonard joked that the Christian Brothers 'should open a school to teach priests to spell correctly':

> Did such a school, exist it would be useful—I had letters from two P[arish] P[riests] this last month which for language and grammar I would blush to see exhibited by a third rate boy in our school [at Cork].[55]

It would be the middle decades of the nineteenth century before there were sufficient seminary places to end the phenomenon of 'half-educated and ill-formed priests', thus bringing Irish clerical formation into line with European Tridentine practice.[56]

Apart from issues of quality, the most 'ominous problem' facing the Irish Church was its inability to provide sufficient priests to deliver an increasingly ambitious pastoral programme in the context of a population explosion.[57] It was frequently claimed in the first half of the eighteenth century that the population could not support the growing numbers of clergy, and a series of rescripts were secured from Pope Benedict XIV (1740–58) to limit ordinations and to stem the number of friars in Ireland. By 1800, however, there was a universal complaint among bishops of a shortage of priests. While estimates of clerical numbers are incomplete, 1,089 priests availed of the protection afforded by the Registration Act (1704); the 1731 *Report on the State of Popery* indicated the presence of 1,445 priests in Ireland, and, in the context of the Union debate (1800), the bishops informed Lord Castlereagh that this number had risen to 1,800.[58] Analysis of these figures, however, points to a decreasing clergy:people ratio in eighteenth-century Ireland, since, between 1731 and 1800, the population increased by about 88 per cent, while the number of priests rose by just 12 per cent. There were, inevitably, great regional variations, but this roughly translates to one priest for every 1,587 Catholics in 1731, at the height of the penal era, compared to one for every 2,676 at the end of the century.[59] In Rice's Ossory, Bishops Burke, Troy and Lanigan in turn complained of a shortage of priests. While Troy ordained 23 priests between 1778 and 1785, there were only 60 priests in the diocese by 1792, but this still allowed for a ratio of one priest to every 1,600 Catholics, significantly lower than the national average.[60] But such statistics were poor consolation to Bishop Troy, who in another context noted that a scarcity of priests 'made the piety of the people grow cold'.[61]

Problems associated with popular religious expression were equally challenging. While bishops had few concerns about the religious enthusiasm of the people, there was anxiety about its unorthodox expression in the celebration of rituals which marked the rites of passage, especially 'wakes' which were repeatedly condemned from the original Counter-Reformation synods held in Ireland in the early seventeenth century. The ordinances for the province of Armagh (1618), for example, denounced 'idlers and buffoons' who introduced 'improper songs, obscene gesticulations, and ... the works of darkness' into wakes.[62] A century later, in 1748, statutes were introduced in the diocese of Kildare and Leighlin, which forbade priests saying the requiem Mass for a soul 'at whose wake such immodest songs, profane tricks or immoderate crowds are permitted'.[63] Across Ireland bishops continued to denounce 'unchristian diversions' associated with wakes: excessive alcohol, lewd entertainment, mock-sacraments and sexual games, but such sanctions produced little fruit and were largely ignored by the laity.[64]

Likewise, the celebration of festivals and 'patterns' (from 'patron' saint), were targets of the hierarchy's attempt at civilising and moralising the masses, since on these occasions, too, religious observances were often merely a prelude to secular festivities.[65] In 1782, Bishop Troy condemned such gatherings for 'wicked purposes':

> Instead of praying they wish damnation to themselves and acquain-tances with most horrid and deliberate imprecations. They profane the name of God and everything else that is sacred by most execrable oaths and finish the day by the perpetration of the grossest impurities, by shedding their neighbour's blood, by murder, and the transgression of the law.[66]

Troy was merely reiterating the sentiments of his predecessor, Thomas Burke, who in 1761 condemned the 'robbing, riding, cursing, swearing, thieving, exces-sive drinking, and other great debaucheries' practised at St John's Well.[67] Yet in spite of the determined efforts of the episcopate, such patterns survived into the middle of the nineteenth century. Amhlaoibh Ó Súilleabháin's (Humphrey O'Sullivan) description of the pattern at St James' Well, in Edmund Rice's Callan, in 1829, illustrates the attraction of such occasions:

> There were gooseberries and currants and cherries for the children: ginger bread for grown girls: strong beer, and maddening whiskey for wranglers and busybodies: open-doored booths filled with lovers: bag-pipers, and 'riosp-raspers' [fiddlers] making music there for young folks: and pious pilgrims making their stations around the well.[68]

The ultimate solution to these excesses was to move indoors into a clerically marshalled space, to achieve the goal of parochial conformity, where devotions could be celebrated in a more 'becoming manner', at the parish chapels in accor-dance with the norms of Trent.[69]

This movement reflected the 'social-disciplining' of the age and the increas-ing degree of social control exercised by the clergy. They have also been inter-preted in terms of a conflict between Tridentine Catholicism and Ireland's so-called 'Celtic Christianity'. Such conclusions, however, overstate the reality of a religious expression which was less 'Celtic' than pre-modern. In an Irish context, the survival of such practices were a product of the troubled history of the Catholic Church, the disturbance of the Protestant Reformation and the subsequent penal laws which had frustrated the modernisation of religious devotion along continental lines. However, the transformation effected by Carpenter and his successors should not be interpreted as the imposition of *foreign* discipline on a native religious expression. The process reflected not so much the 'Romanisation' of Irish Catholicism, but rather the 'victory of one indigenous Catholic culture over another'.[70] In essence, this clash between popular and elite Catholic culture mirrored the increasingly dominant influence of the merchant and professional classes within Irish Catholicism, which Rice would advance in his schools. Within this context, Cardinal Cullen's conscious decision to consecrate the church of the Sacred Heart, Donnybrook, on the old fair day (1866), presents a graphic illustration of the hierarchy's determination to effect a moral-reformation of Irish Catholics in accordance with the bourgeois values of their own class. Indeed, the new church at Donnybrook was celebrated as such and as an atonement for the wickedness of the fair, which the 'Apostle of Temperance', Fr Theobald Mathew, had described as a 'moral plague-spot'. The contemporary press, too, celebrated the church as 'a great landmark' which marked the spot 'where vice and immorality were vanquished'.[71]

The possibility of replicating this victory elsewhere, however, was predicated on the provision of appropriate chapel accommodation and would take some time to achieve nationally.[72] Chapel-building became an absolute priority of the clergy. Indeed, the Church's ambitious building programme represents the most tangible manifestation of the revival which the Church experienced in Edmund Rice's lifetime. The progress of chapel-building began in mid-Munster/south Leinster and filtered slowly into the poorer regions of Ulster and north Connacht. This reflected the regional fortunes of Catholicism as an institutional force, which was more firmly established in the richer areas, among the upper social classes and in the English-speaking towns. While this phenomenon is contrary to the received image, it is not surprising, given the historic Norman/Old English influence in the region and their enthusiasm for the Counter-Reformation.[73] The city of Waterford, for example, had three Mass houses in 1746, including St Patrick's where the young merchant Edmund Rice would worship forty years later. In 1746, Charles Smith described the chapel as 'a fine modern building':

> The aisles supported by stone pillars, the panels of the wainscots carved and gilded and the galleries finely adorned with paintings. Besides the great altar there are two lesser, one on either hand, over each of which

there are curious paintings. Facing the great altar is a large silver [sanctuary] lamp and chain of curious workmanship; round the house are niches filled with statues of saints.[74]

In these urban chapels, while the Mass was the central act of worship, the reformed Catholic devotions were also well developed. Greater devotion to the Eucharist was promoted by the Archconfraternity of the Blessed Sacrament, and sodalities of the scapular were introduced by the friars in the 1720s. The rosary, too, was promoted with great effect; it served not merely as a symbol of traditional loyalty, but as an instrument to bring the practice and doctrine of the Counter-Reformation into the heart of the Church.[75] In Wexford, the Franciscans promoted the 'Stations of the Cross' in 1749, while the Jesuits in Dublin encouraged devotions to the Sacred Heart of Jesus and conducted novenas to St Francis Xavier (1506–52), who personified the spirit of the Catholic Reformation.[76] Exposition of the Blessed Sacrament had been common in Order churches from about 1720, while many chapels performed benediction or sung vespers on Sunday afternoons.[77] There is evidence, too, that these solemn liturgies were of the highest standard. Catholics in Waterford possessed a magnificent set of fifteenth-century vestments; once believed to have been a gift of Pope Innocent III. (1161–1216), their use must have contributed greatly to the solemnity of the liturgy in Edmund Rice's adopted city.[78]

Such devotions were not possible in poorer, rural parishes. While the 1731 *Report on the State of Popery* indicated the survival of Mass rocks, particularly in Ulster, where it was more usual for Catholics to worship in 'some sort of shed', converted stables or 'mean thatched Cabins; many or most of them open at one end'.[79] As time passed, these older chapels were replaced, and even in Ulster, by 1766, Alexander McAuley noted considerable advances:

> Till within these few years, there was scarce a Mass house to be seen in the northern counties of Ulster. Now Mass houses are spreading over most parts of the country. Convents, till of late were hid in corners. Now they are openly avowed in the very metropolis. From the Revolution[1688] till a few years ago, Mass houses were little huts in remote and obscure places. Now they are sumptuous buildings in the most public and conspicuous places.[80]

Few contemporaries failed to be impressed by the material improvement of chapel buildings, although 'sumptuous' was certainly an overstatement.[81] The

1.4 Tullyallen Mass house, County Tyrone, built 1768. The presence of the hearth in the west gable points to the building being used as a school during the week. The chapel was reassembled in the Ulster American Folk Park, Omagh, County Tyrone.

penal chapels of the eighteenth century were basic, resembling the descriptions contained in Bishop Plunket's visitation diary outlined above. The older rural chapels were generally between 50 and 60ft long and half as wide, with a mud floor and a low, thatched roof. These barn-like structures were built by local craftsmen, using local materials; with whitewashed mud or stone walls, there was a window on either side of a simple raised altar and a door at the back of the chapel. There were no galleries or furnishings, congregations stood or knelt during Mass, and chapels were almost without decoration, apart from a cruci-fix behind the altar.[82] The penal Mass house, *teach an phobail*, was often the focal point of the community, serving as church, school, and meeting place; on occasion it was even used for threshing corn. As late as 1828, the Cashel provincial statutes laid down that 'it is not permissible without leave from the bishop' to keep school in a chapel, and that under no circumstances were cattle to be found in any place of worship, 'nor is it to be profaned [with] threshing or any other servile work'.[83]

The new churches, or 'barn chapels' of the late penal years, were grander in scale, built of stone and with a pitched, slated roof; steeples and bells, however, were still forbidden under the penal laws. The chapels remained simple in decoration, but efforts were made to improve the sanctuary, the altar and the quality of the vestments and altar plate. From the barn plan, they evolved to an L-shape and the more common cruciform plan. Floors were generally flagged, and galleries, often with pews, accommodated the larger congregations.[84] The level of building is recorded in the episcopal reports, the *relationes status*, sent to Rome. In prosperous Munster, where church-building proceeded faster than elsewhere, Bishop Matthew McKenna built eleven new churches in Cloyne in the ten years after 1775, and James Butler II spent one thousand guineas building a house and improving the church in Thurles. Francis Moylan boasted that the churches of Tralee and Killarney, which he had built, surpassed any Protestant church in the diocese in size and workmanship.[85] The new cathedrals, too, in Waterford (1793) and Cork (1799) spoke volumes about Catholic confidence and pretensions. More than this, they were a witness to the re-emergence of the Catholic hierarchy. In the early decades of the century, bishops communicated with their flock from their 'refuge' (*'in loco refugii nostri'*); Archbishop Christopher Butler of Cashel, for instance, lived outside his diocese with his cousins at Westcourt, in County Kilkenny, for much of his long episcopate (1711–57).[86]

By the early 1790s, although penal legislation was still in place, the bishops had conspicuously re-established themselves in the principal town of their diocese; yet, even the larger chapels proved inadequate given the population explosion and the more elaborate scale of public liturgies. The consecration of Edmund Rice's confidante, James Lanigan, as bishop of Ossory, in 1789, is indicative of the level to which the Catholic establishment had emerged from the restrictions of the penal era. It demonstrates, too, the difficulties the Church faced in accommodating larger congregations. On that occasion three bishops were present in the sanctuary along with seventy-two priests, but one witness remarked that 'the chapel was so crowded that the gallery began to give warning of some danger'.[87] Ironically, then, while reforming bishops, like Carpenter, Troy and Plunket, attempted to move religious practice into clerically supervised 'sacred spaces', the shortage of chapel accommodation dictated that outdoor celebration remained a feature of Irish Catholicism until after the Great Famine (1845–50). Emmet Larkin has concluded that the revival, indeed the survival, of the Church was only possible because of the 'stations', which had emerged in the penal era.[88]

Twice a year, priests travelled through their parishes in preparation for Christmas and Easter, celebrating Mass and hearing confessions in family homes, thus allowing the faithful to complete their annual obligations.[89]

By the last quarter of the eighteenth century, the Catholic Church in Ireland had begun its emergence from the 'catacombs' of the penal age. This revival was the initiative of an energetic episcopate; but by the end of the century the limitations of that programme had become apparent; as the *Waterford Chronicle* observed, 'necessity' of material resources rather than any legal obstacle impeded its advance.[90] The baton then passed to a prosperous Catholic laity, who provided not simply the means to complete the project, but the confident and uncompromising vision that became the hallmark of nineteenth-century Irish Catholicism. Foremost among these was Edmund Rice, Waterford merchant and 'herald of a new age of Irishmen'.[91]

CHAPTER TWO

The Rices of Callan

I N 1900, AS THEIR CENTENARY APPROACHED, the Irish Christian Brothers
launched an ambitious campaign to build a 'Mother House', novitiate and a
teacher training college in Dublin. The site chosen was 'Marino', the north Dublin
home of the eighteenth-century patriot, James Caulfeild (1728–99), Lord
Charlemont, 'the Volunteer Earl'.[1] The climax of that monumental effort was a
great bazaar held at the Rotunda Gardens, in Dublin, in the summer of 1903. In
preparation for the occasion, the Brothers published *Juverna*, a short-lived newsletter which elicited support from the congregation's schools across the world. No
opportunity was lost to promote the project, including the situation of the
campus, on the fields of Clontarf, where Brian Boru, with crucifix in hand, had
died in 'defence of creed and country' on Good Friday, 1014. Righteously inspired,
readers were duly urged 'to emulate the zeal of Brian in promotion of Christian
education' through their contribution towards the noble project at Marino.[2]

Significantly, the same publication contained what might be considered as
the first biography of their founder published by the Christian Brothers. In just
under two thousand words, readers were presented with a 'Brief sketch of the
life of the Rev. Bro. Edmond [*sic*] Rice … Christian educator of God's poor' and
founder of 'a loved and distinguished IRISH RELIGIOUS CONGREGATION'.[3] Yet, just
as *Juverna* had taken liberties with the story of Brian Boru, the 'last High King',
its account of modern Ireland's first Brother was equally self-serving. The treatment of Rice's youth was particularly unsatisfactory, not least on account of the
absence of detail:

> EDMOND RICE, Founder of the Christian Brothers, was born in June,
> 1762, in Callan, Co. Kilkenny, where the early years of his life were spent
> innocently and happily in a highly respectable, but simple and edifying
> family circle. Affectionate, dutiful, pious and devoted to study—he
> passed his youth in uneventful quiet.

More importantly, this emphasis on simplicity and tranquillity created an
impression greatly at odds with the complex realities of eighteenth-century
Ireland, and of County Kilkenny in particular. In a sense, however, this descrip-

2.1 'Kilkenny Castle, seat of the Marquis of Ormonde', *Illustrated London News*, 12 August 1848, NLI.

tion of Rice's youth was of its time and reflected Catholic understanding of the penal era which would find its clearest expression in Daniel Corkery's emotive *Hidden Ireland* (1924), which influenced the historical orthodoxy of the newly established Irish Free State.[4] At its simplest, this reading of the eighteenth century presented a stark contrast between the arrogant world of the 'Protestant Ascendancy' and the 'hidden Ireland' of Catholics smarting uniformly under the unrelenting persecution of the penal laws. Not surprisingly, this paradigm has dominated Edmund Rice studies, but the reality was altogether different from this crude black and white analysis of the penal laws and their practical application as outlined in chapter one.

I

At one level, Rice's native Callan does reflect the 'Gaelic survival' described by Corkery, himself a product of Edmund Rice's Presentation Brothers. Callan lay in the centre of 'a cultural reservoir', spanning north Tipperary and south Kilkenny.[5] Here the remnants of the Ormond family and the Catholic Butlers, who had benefited from the terms of the Treaty of Limerick (1691), retained a great deal of their influence and were able to shelter the region from the worst excesses of the penal laws. Superficially, the 'Gaelic survival' was revealed in the extent to which the Irish language remained the vernacular in south Kilkenny. In all probability, Irish was the language of the Rice home at Westcourt, where Rice would have been called 'Éamann' by his family.[6] William Tighe noted how the 'common people' seldom spoke any other language, while at Mass the priests 'preached alternatively in Irish and English', but always in Irish when determined to be understood.[7] In 1775, Bishop Thomas Burke of Ossory published a cate-chetical *Summary of the Christian Religion* in Irish, while, later still, Bishop Kyran Marum (1814–27) commissioned Irish translations of *The Eternity of the Soul* and other devotional texts because significant numbers of Catholics in the south of his diocese could not speak English.[8]

The benevolence of the Butlers was a significant factor in the survival of the Catholic Church in the region. The choice of three successive Butlers as archbishops of Cashel in the eighteenth century was an acknowledgement of that favour, but their presence also afforded continuity and local political influ-ence.[9] In 1704, for instance, at the height of penal persecution, the parish priest of Callan used a house belonging to the Ormond's as a chapel.[10] Later in the century, Archbishop Christopher Butler (1711–57) was sheltered by his cousins at Callan and there is a tradition that he used to recite the rosary *in Irish* beneath the trees at Westcourt, beside the Rice home.[11] Throughout the cen-tury, Callan was well served for priests. When Bishop Thomas Burke com-plained of clerical shortages in 1766, there were three secular priests and four Augustinians in town.[12] The parish church beside the Green was typical of many penal chapels with its stone-walls, trampled clay floors, rustic benches and a spartan wooden altar. The friars meanwhile lived in a thatched cottage on Clodeen, or 'Clothier's' Lane, and two neighbouring cottages, joined together, served as their chapel.[13]

On the land, too, the existence of local patrons enabled Catholics to avoid the rigorous application of the penal laws. Catholics could preserve their land-holdings by relying on trustees, nominal conversion to the Established Church and the presence of large 'convert interest' of land-owning families like the Protestant Butlers who had Catholic relatives and sympathies. In this sense, contrary to the traditional historiography, many conversions to the Established Church reinforced, rather than weakened, the Catholic position. Catholics relied on these converts for their protection in the legal profession too, where former Catholics were a significant presence. In the Irish parliament, likewise, their cause was defended by sympathetic members like Lucius O'Brien (1733–95) and Anthony Malone (1700–76), while at Westminster Edmund Burke

(1729–97), a cousin of Nano Nagle, foundress of the Presentation Sister, championed their cause.[14]

A large portion of the land in south Kilkenny and north Tipperary remained in Catholic hands due to the sympathetic influence of the Ormond family and their Butler cousins. This Catholic branch of the family owned considerable land in Tipperary, including a large estate at Cahir and another at Kilcash. On their Cahir estate alone, 97 of 141 leases in the period 1720–50 were to Catholics like the Sheehys, Nagles and Prendergasts.[15] These prosperous families, farmers engaged in grazing and dairying, were vital in the preservation of the Gaelic culture celebrated by the Munster poets of the time. They were, in Whelan's phrase, 'the tradition bearers, who survived *in situ* through national upheavals to provide the backbone of a cohesive, if secretive, culture'.[16] In Callan, the leading Catholic families were the Butlers of Westcourt Castle, where Colonel John Butler, a nephew of the first duke of Ormond, had settled at the old manor house, and the Smyths of Damagh, at Callan Lodge which they had acquired in the 1730s. Beneath this sub-gentry there was a layer of strong farmers who had advanced socially from the small-farm ranks in the expanding economy of the eighteenth century. Included in this group were the Rices of Westcourt.

The Rices had no great social standing among the old families of Kilkenny, but their rise to the petit-bourgeois level of their town was reflected in the appointments, by the strongly Protestant corporation of Callan, of Rice's grandfather (another Edmund) as an applotter (1754) and his father as market juror (1762) for the town.[17] While the nature of these functions is unclear, the holders may have had a role in the calculation of local taxes (cess) and an arbitration, or quality control, function at the town's market. That two generations of Rices held these positions was a reflection of their business acumen, as well as an indication of the upward and downward esteem with which they were held. This was a significant achievement in a troubled town like Callan and with landlords like the Agars, a powerful ascendancy family who were a considerable force in both church and state. The earliest references to the family appear in the hearth tax rolls for 1665–6, where John Rys and Patrick, Richard and James Rice appear in the townland of Sunhill.[18] However, through strategic marriages with rising families, the Rices advanced to a point where they were 'related to all the independent farmers in the locality'.[19] The marriage of Rice's parents reflected this pattern; his mother, Margaret, was one of the Tierneys, an 'old Catholic family of gentle stock' who farmed one hundred acres at Maxtown.[20] The family were respected by and related to many of the region's prominent families, including the Smyths of Damagh and the Mahers of Tipperary. Among the clergy, too, the

2.2 Westcourt, Callan, County Kilkenny, birthplace of Edmund Rice, 1762. Photo
*c.*1960 © CBS European Provincial Archive, Dublin.

family had an established presence, and several members held office at the
Augustinian friary in Callan. Fr Daniel Tierney established a novitiate there in
1781, and Fr James Tierney became prior in 1791.[21]

Margaret Tierney was a widow and her marriage to Robert Rice gave him
two step-children, Joan and Jane Murphy. Together they had seven sons, including Edmund, their fourth. Sources for the history of the family are scant; there
are, for instance, no records of baptism or marriage for any of the Rices, since
parochial registers were not kept at Callan until 1821.[22] In fact, the most complete source for the history of the family is the will of Robert Rice (1787) and it
is from this that details concerning the composition of the family are drawn.[23]
Br Columba Normoyle's edition of the recollections of Edmund Rice is a useful
resource, but the memoir genre is not without limitation and must be read critically, since many of the recollections tend towards hagiography.[24] Martin Ryan,
for example, in his submission (*c.*1912), recalled that Rice 'from his youth
upward he had an inclination towards piety. I heard the people say that since

2.3 Augustinian Abbey, Callan, County Kilkenny (*c.*1791). Completed
by the Augustinian Friars in 1471, it was suppressed in 1540 during
the Tudor Reformation. NLI.

he was a boy barely able to walk … he frequented Holy Mass at the Augustinian
Church'.[25] In fact the inherent weakness of such recollections was recognised
by Br Mark McCarthy, the author of Rice's first major biography (1926), who
acknowledged that:

> the memory of his virtue became a cherished tradition … and to have
> known Edmund Rice, or to be able to say that one's father or mother
> knew him and conversed with him, was regarded as an honour by the
> older people of Callan, so great was the veneration inspired by his early
> virtues and subsequent works of zeal and charity.[26]

It is possible, however, to reconstruct an impression of the lifestyle of the family,
from contemporary descriptions of the south Kilkenny region.

The Rice home at Westcourt was similar to many owned by their class. It
was a long, low cottage with a deep thatch; warm in winter and cool in summer.
It had four bedrooms, each 10ft by 9, a parlour and kitchen, both 17ft by 12, and
a hall way. In keeping with most large Catholic farmers, their lifestyle was frugal,

as is reflected in William Tighe observations on the simplicity of the Aylwards, a prosperous family in the county:

> They slaughter their pigs generally at home and eat the offal which is the only animal food they usually make use of, living principally on potatoes and some griddle bread. Their incomes are probably not less than £600 or £700 a year.[27]

This modest lifestyle and frugality was a prized virtue, but in the longer term it was the key to the strength of rising families like the Rices. With small outgoings, the families were able to endure hard times, but during the agricultural boom in the last quarter of the century they were in a position to accumulate capital, which allowed for education, commercial investments and the provision of all important dowries.

The Augustinian friars, who had been in the town since 1467, were frequent visitors at Westcourt, and the Rices received their early education from one of their number, Patrick Grace (1747–1830). The 'Bráithrín Liath' (the little grey friar) as he became known on account of his premature greyness, was a wandering schoolmaster before he joined the Order in 1774. It was at this time that he was employed by the Rices to give instruction to their children. This young man made an enormous impression on the boys, and it is to his influence that John Rice's vocation to the Augustinians has been attributed, while the 'well disposed Edmund Rice was deeply moved by his mentor'.[28] Grace returned to Callan after his ordination in Rome in 1783 and spent the remainder of his life among his native people. The subject of significant folklore, one tradition recalls that in 1810 the thatch of the old penal chapel at Clodeen Lane collapsed while Grace was at the altar, but that the congregation held the roof aloft until the friar completed the prayers of Consecration.[29]

In time, Rice attended the local 'hedge school' in Moat Lane. For a population of almost 3,500, Callan was poorly served for schools, with a 'hedge school' and a second conducted by the Protestant rector. One of the earliest Christian Brothers, Edward Francis Grace (1782–1859), has left us a description of the hedge school he attended as a boy in Callan, twenty years later. It was a small, one storied building which catered for thirty students; it is tempting to surmise that this was the school attended by the Rices:

> The Academy ... consisted of a small antique structure covered with a verdant coat of thatch. The door was the only lateral aperture, and the

remains of what were once windows were securely closed ... When a 'new boy' presented himself for admission he was approached in somewhat courtly style by the master, a portly man, attired in frieze bodycoat, knee-breeches, and woollen stockings, and cordially greeted with the pious salutation, 'God save you' ... This established confidence and led to the business part of the reception, during which the aspirant to participation in the benefits of the 'Academy' was informed that the terms were four pence a week and a half-penny for dancing, which was practised on the door of the 'Academy' laid flat on the clay floor. Thus the door, like Goldsmith's bed by night and chest of drawers by day, had "its double debt to pay".[30]

Students were taught individually and the greater part of the day was spent 'writing', copying headlines and 'rehearsing' or learning facts by heart. In time, Rice graduated from the 'Academy' to a school in Kilkenny, possibly the predecessor of 'Burrell Hall', established by Bishop Troy as the first diocesan college in Ireland (1782). Rice was the first of his family to be educated to this level. This was perhaps an indication of his ability, but more likely a reflection of the improved financial position of his family. The Rices paid £20 per year for their son to board at Mr White's school (the equivalent of the Master's income at Callan), which stood on the site now occupied by St Mary's Cathedral in the city. For this he received a classical education. The range of subjects taught in such schools usually included: English, writing, grammar, globes, maps, drawing and sometimes Latin.[31] Such schools provided a thorough grounding in commercial subjects, mathematics and bookkeeping, and relied heavily on the textbooks of the Quakers Elias Voster (1772) and John Gough (1790), best-sellers which were used, in turn, by Rice in his own schools.[32] With its practical emphasis on business and bookkeeping calculation, this education fitted Rice for his subsequent apprenticeship to his uncle Michael Rice, a prosperous merchant in the city of Waterford.

II

'Thus, happily and peacefully, in the sanctuary of a model Catholic home, the child's love of God and his holy religion grew as he advanced in years', so Br McCarthy described Edmund Rice's youth in Westcourt.[33] Yet just as the *Juverna* biography accentuated the tranquillity of the age, so too does this account ignore the realities of Callan, which was known as *Calainn a' Chlampair,* or 'Wrangling Callan', for good reason. Indeed, an old adage went, 'Walk through any town in Ireland, but run through Callan'. Evidence suggests a radical disparity between the comfortable lifestyle of the Rices and the experience of the majority in the town, which was characterised by tension and distress, and illustrates clearly the folly of simple notions of a 'penal consensus', depicting Catholics uniformly languishing in a sea of undifferentiated poverty.

Kennedy's thorough study of the economy of Callan points to the misery of the town.[34] Documentary evidence for eighteenth-century Callan is scarce, but travellers who visited described it invariably as 'a poor dirty town', or a 'wretched village' of 'mean appearance'.[35] One such commentator, Rufus Chetwood, an English visitor, has left us a fine description of the town in 1748:

> This place seems to lie in the ruins Oliver [Cromwell] left it [in 1649]. You see the remains of three castles, and an old church of the Gothic building [old St Mary's] on the right as you enter the town, but the roof is gone and all the rest a mere anatomy ... The situation of this place is very agreeable, upon a stream called the King's River, dividing in two branches above the town ... The main stream runs under a bridge of four arches, and the small one (after driving a mill) under two ... Upon this stream about a mile below Callan, is a very famous iron mill, that brings great profit to the proprietors. The town is built in the form of a cross, and in the centre a cross is erected, with a square glass lantern, that gives light in the night to travelers that come from the four cardinal points of the compass. One would imagine this town should be in a more thriving condition since the two great roads of Cork and Limerick go through it.[36]

The economic condition of the town declined even further as the century progressed. The population of the civil parish increased rapidly, from 1,300 in 1731 to around 3,500 by the end of the century, but there were few employment prospects: the iron mill closed in 1788 on account of a timber shortage, and James Agar's weaving industry never matched expectations. In 1845 the *Parliamentary Gazetteer* described the town as 'the very impersonation of Irish poverty and wretchedness'.[37] With such bleak prospects, many had no option but to join the large numbers emigrating to Newfoundland; included in this flow was Rice's eldest brother, Thomas, who left Callan with his family in 1825.[38] Whatever prosperity the town enjoyed arose out of its role as a parliamentary

borough and market town for the surrounding countryside. There were two
market days per week, Wednesday and Saturday, and three fairs were held annually; in 1790 that number was increased to four. The local schoolmaster/shop-
keeper Amhlaoibh Ó Súilleabháin described the scene of one undistinguished
fair day in 1827:

> A bright sunny morning: a bracing south-west wind: seven o clock, the
> clouds lying on the mountains: the day growing dark: two cows and
> nine or ten pigs on the fair green: a tent being put up: eleven o clock,
> small pigs dear being sent to England: sucking pigs dear: if a low price
> were asked for a yearling it could be sold: no demand for any other kind
> of cattle: plenty of calves and yearlings there, but little demand for them
> … little business at the one tent which is on the fair green: no business
> being done by the small traders, alas! 'Better crossness than loneliness.'
> It is a 'mock-fair' unquestionably.[39]

Yet, while the fair brought cash into the town, it did little to relieve the crushing
distress, which was reflected in the poor quality of housing; of a total of 530
dwellings in 1800, only 39 paid hearth tax and 46 window tax.[40] Another
contemporary has left a vivid picture of the misery of the village which stands in
stark contrast to the 'sanctuary of [Rice's] model Catholic home' described above:

> Like too many of the peasants in the south of Ireland, they are miser-
> ably lodged; there are numbers of them who have not a bedstead, not
> even what is called a truckle-bed frame; a pallet to sleep on is a comfort
> unknown to them; a wad of straw or perhaps heath laid on a damp
> floor forms their resting place; but very few of them have anything like
> sheets; their blankets are generally wretchedly bad; in short the bed
> clothes are ragged and scanty; they put their coats and petticoats over
> them in aid of their blankets in cold weather, too often they are still
> damp having been put imperfectly dried by a miserable fire after they
> were worn at work in the rain. [41]

Ironically, too, the repeal of several of the penal laws in 1778 and 1782, rather
than advancing the plight of the dispossessed actually served to accentuate their
sense of social exclusion.

The first of these 'relief' measures, as they were known, was introduced by
Luke Gardiner MP and formed part of the government's military recruitment

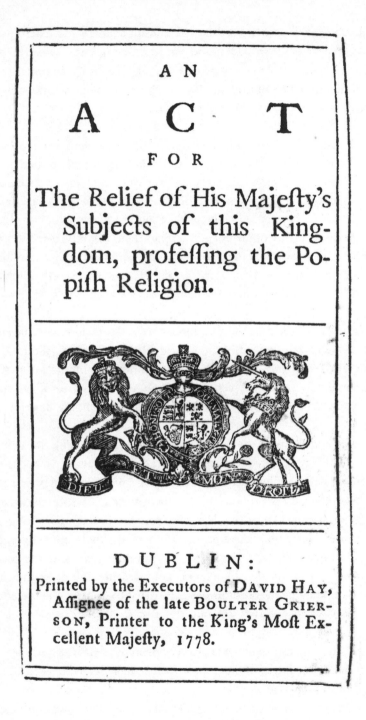

AN

A C T

FOR

The Relief of His Majeſty's Subjects of this Kingdom, profeſſing the Popiſh Religion.

DUBLIN:

Printed by the Executors of DAVID HAY, Aſſignee of the late BOULTER GRIERSON, Printer to the King's Moſt Excellent Majeſty, 1778.

2.4 Title page of the Catholic Relief Act (1778).

drive in the context of the American War of Independence (1775–83). The Act dealt almost exclusively with landed property; it allowed Catholics to hold land on equal terms with Protestants and the hated gavelling law was removed. Ultimately, the importance of the act lay not so much in its content as in the principle which it established, which Edmund Burke correctly predicted would 'extend further' in time. Forty years later, in the wake of O'Connell's 'revolution', Thomas Wyse vindicated Burke's confidence, arguing that Gardiner's Relief Act 'was the first step which really emancipated'.[42] The 1778 relief measures left intact all the restrictions on the Catholic clergy and worship, but towards the end of the war in 1782, the government sponsored a second relief act which was much more sweeping than the first. The remaining disabilities relating to land were removed and the secular clergy were freed to perform ecclesiastical functions legally. Of paramount importance in the context of Edmund Rice's subsequent vocation, the Act also allowed the establishment of Catholic schools, on receipt of a license from the Church of Ireland bishop, but endowment of such schools was forbidden.[43]

These measures represented an unprecedented opportunity for Irish Catholics, to the extent that their legal position was 'transformed as to merit the use of the word revolution'.[44] From the perspective of the clergy, the relief measures removed the legal obstacles to the Catholic revival, described in chapter one, and it is from the 1780s that we can see the 'Tridentine surge' in earnest.[45] In Callan, however, that revival was impeded by the presence of an ineffectual parish priest, Darby Murphy, who had been appointed to the town in 1768. Twenty years later he was suspended by Bishop John Dunne (1788) and was subsequently excommunicated for resisting the sentence. There is no record of the cause of his suspension, but Carrigan, the diocesan historian, perhaps euphemistically attributes it to 'the neglected condition in which he kept the parish chapel', which he failed to rectify despite repeated warnings from his bishop.[46] From the point of view of the laity, the relief measures created a climate of unprecedented opportunity. This springtime was especially welcomed by ambitious, rising families like the Rices, whose frugal lifestyles had allowed them accumulate capital. Once the penal laws were dismantled from 1778 onwards, these families were no longer restricted to acquiring land on leases of thirty-one years, and often outbid their more ostentatious Protestant neighbours in the acquisition of land. By his death in 1787, Robert Rice had assembled a farm of 182 acres, 55 of which were at Westcourt and the remaining 127 at Ballykeefe.[47]

Yet the advance of such large tenant farmers was not made without serious consequences, and increasing land-hunger led to heightened social tensions in the county as the cleavage widened between them and the swollen ranks of the poor. Significantly, several of the recollections of Edmund Rice comment on the notorious ambition of the family who made every effort to consolidate and enlarge their holding, even when this verged on land grabbing. The Rices, according to one testimony, were 'ambitious for land and were anxious to get rich quick'. A second reminiscence claimed that they 'were considered to have been ... endowed by a too keen sense of business', and again that 'they were fond of land and were always anxious to secure a good place'.[48] Perhaps more significantly, one contributor believed that Rice was not untouched by the avaricious nature of his family, and drew the hard-hitting conclusion that his charity may have been funded by the fruits of land-grabbing:

> I heard some old people refer to the fact that Edmund Rice took farms which some less prosperous people were unable to hold. He re-set these farms and from the proceeds financed his schools. Some of the descendants of the people who had lost their holdings in the Minauns area of Callan were rather critical and embittered against Brother Rice.[49]

Such images are greatly at odds with traditional representation of Westcourt as a merry haven, a place where 'the poorer children gathered ... [and] where Rice's mother saw that they had plenty to eat'.[50] Such conflicting memories, however, are not necessarily mutually exclusive.

Tension and dispossession gave rise to agrarian violence, such as found expression in the 'Whiteboy' and subsequent 'Rightboy' movements.[51] These emerged initially in protest against the enclosure of common land in Tipperary in 1761, but the violence and 'levelling' of the Whiteboys eventually spread through much of Munster and south Leinster, threatening the security of the region, within the wider international context of the Seven Years War (1756–63). In time the Whiteboys widened their agenda to oppose high rents, cess, evictions and, above all, the hated tithes paid to the Anglican clergy. It was in the context of these disturbances that Fr Nicholas Sheehy was executed at Clonmel (1766), twenty miles from the Rice homestead, in what many Catholics concluded was a judicial murder which demonstrated the potential of 'arbitrary repression' at a time when the formal application of the penal laws was on the wane.[52]

Simple sectarian interpretations cannot be applied to this agitation, which illustrates clearly the complexity of late eighteenth-century Irish society. Indeed, in Butler territory, where many of the landlords were Catholic, a great deal of its attention was directed against avaricious Catholic farmers. In 1775,

Archbishop James Butler II was incensed at the ingratitude of the people towards their traditional protectors, and denounced the Whiteboys for their assault on Ballyragget, 'a town belonging to a Butler'.[53] Whiteboy violence was condemned by the Munster bishops in a series of pastorals, but the archbishop of Cashel took measures further. He organised the people of Ballyragget into a vigilante-style league, sworn at their chapel by a justice of the peace to defend their landlord, his brother Robert Butler (1774).[54] At the other end of the social scale, migrant workers were intimidated because they represented an economic threat to the poor of Callan, who themselves relied on casual and seasonal work on the local farms. Occasional skirmishes took place in Callan, but in time these migrants, or '*spailpíní*', became targets for organised Whiteboy aggression. Tipperary men working in Ballyragget, Urlingford and Johnstown were attacked and made swear never to work in Kilkenny again, while, in 1779, rumours were spread that press gangs were operating at the hiring fairs in Kilkenny to frighten off would-be labourers from outside the county.[55]

It was against this troubled background that Bishop Troy delivered his excommunication of the Whiteboys in 1775, and again in 1779, condemning them to 'everlasting Hell':

> When they shall be judged, may they be condemned … may their posterity be cut off in one generation. Let their children be carried about as vagabonds and beg and let them be cast out of their dwellings. May the usurers search all their substance and let strangers plunder their labours. May there be none to help them, nor none to pity their fatherless offspring. May their names be blotted out … let their memory perish from the earth. Let all the congregation say Amen, Amen, Amen.[56]

The Catholic Church increasingly aligned itself to propertied interests and the preservation of the *status quo* in the face of such social challenge. In August 1778, a great number of 'the most respectable Roman Catholics' of the city and county of Kilkenny took the oath of allegiance to King George III.[57] Rice's father, Robert Rice, joined that number in the following year.[58] So too did the clergy of Ossory, led by their bishop, who accepted the oath as a 'condition *sine qua non* of our establishment in this Kingdom'.[59] However, this alignment had detrimental consequences and the period witnessed a dramatic rise in anti-clericalism, which resulted in the increasing alienation of the 'faithful' poor from the emerging institutional Church. The violence of the Rightboys, directed at the clergy, was a manifestation of this. In one instance, the aged Bishop Michael Peter

MacMahon of Kilalloe, attempted to calm the disturbed parish of Castleconnell in 1786, but his pleas produced an exodus from the chapel, by the 'people would not listen to a word from him'.[60] Closer to the Rice home, Fr Michael Darcy was attacked on the altar by a band of Rightboys as he celebrated Mass at Mullenaglock near Ninemilehouse, on the Kilkenny–Tipperary border.[61] It was not without reason then, that in 1786, Bishop Denis Conway of Limerick predicted 'a total overthrow of Religion in the Province [of Munster], if the Almighty does not stretch forth his powerful Arm to avert it'.[62]

This was the real 'hidden Ireland' of Edmund Rice's youth. Not the tranquil oasis described in *Juverna*, but rather a complex society marked by intensified levels of class conflict, social tensions and stark divisions within the Catholic Church. Far from the accepted notions of the conflict between the 'big house' and the great mass outside the gate, it was there that the real struggle took place as Catholics jostled for position in a rapidly evolving society. It is among this conflict that Edmund Rice is best understood, rather than in a mythical 'penal consensus' or misleading sense of '*muintearas*' (friendship/community), which serves only to obscure the radicalism of his subsequent religious conversion.[63]

CHAPTER THREE

The Waterford merchant, 1779–1802

WHEN EDMUND RICE MADE HIS WAY TO Waterford in 1779, there was no bridge across the Suir. The young apprentice stood on the Kilkenny side of the river and waited for the ferry which carried him the distance to his new life beyond. The next twenty years were to be the most eventful in his life; these years brought him commercial success beyond expectation. They also brought unforeseen personal tragedy which changed the course of his life. His was a classic conversion experience, not dramatic in the sense of St Paul's, but his years in business were marked by a number of well-defined steps which chart his transition from merchant to founder.[1]

I

Michael Rice, Rice's uncle, had a provisioning business near the Quay in Waterford. Like other merchants in the city, he benefited greatly from the agricultural boom in tillage and dairying which brought prosperity to the southeast in the second half of the eighteenth century. Waterford, with a population of 30,000, was ideally placed to reap the benefits of this economic success. A great deal of the agricultural surplus from the rich lands of its hinterland was shipped along the three rivers, the Suir, the Nore and the Barrow, to be processed in the city, where the rivers converged. Waterford developed flour-milling, brewing, distilling, bacon-curing, tanning, soap-making and other industries whose products were exported through its fine port. These goods went to England, Spain and Portugal, but fortunes were also made servicing the triangular trade with the West Indies and North America. Charles Smith (1746) has left a dramatic impression of this vibrant city:

> The Quay is about half a mile in length and of considerable breadth, not inferior to but rather exceeds the most celebrated in Europe. To it the largest trading vessels may conveniently come up, both to load and to unload, and at a small distance opposite it may lie and constantly afloat. The Exchange, Custom House and other public buildings, ranged

3.1 Waterford, *c.*1800.

along the quay are no small addition to its beauty, which together with a number of shipping afford an agreeable prospect. The whole is fronted with hewn stone, well paved and in some places it is forty feet broad. To it are built five moles or piers which stretch forward; at the pier heads ships of 500 tons may load and unload and lie afloat. In the road before the Quay the river is between four and five fathoms deep at low water where sixty sail of ship may ride conveniently, clear of each other in clean ground.[2]

The last quarter of the century brought further expansion. During the period 1770 to 1800, beef exports to Britain quadrupled, butter doubled and pork increased fourfold. By the end of the century 130,000 pigs were slaughtered annually in Waterford and, with guaranteed navy contracts, Bishop Hussey believed this brought as much as £520,000 to the city of Waterford.[3] The French Wars (1793–1815), too, increased trade. Between 1790 and 1810 it is estimated that

3.2 Catholic Cathedral, Waterford. Engraving by Newman, Watling Street,
London (*c*.1860), NLI.

as many as 1,000 ships, averaging 900 tons each, visited the port annually. In
addition, Waterford had a fishing fleet of eighty vessels which gave rise to a local
fish-curing industry.[4] The Rices shared in the prosperity of Waterford where
Catholics made up one-third of the merchant numbers in the early nineteenth
century.[5] Michael Rice engaged in extensive home and foreign trade and appears
to have specialised in livestock, slaughtering, packing and exporting meat to
Bristol. In addition he had lucrative contracts with the army, the Admiralty and
shipping companies. A significant portion of his trade was with Newfoundland,
exporting meat and importing the dried 'lander' fish which formed an important part of the Waterford diet.[6]

Rice lived with his uncle at his home in Arundel Place, off Barronstrand
Street. He worked alongside his cousins Patrick and Robert, but neither of these
appears to have had an inclination or aptitude for trade and in time he bought
their share of his uncle's business.[7] In 1788, John Rice joined his brother Edmund
in Waterford; having learned the details of the export trade, he was sent to Cadiz
to oversee the Spanish section of the business.[8] The mobility of families like the

Rices in the south-east is quite remarkable. Cullen believes that it is not present
on such a scale in any other part of Ireland, outside the Presbyterian community of the north. He attributes this to 'a combination of social pressures and
aspirations which predisposed even the lower classes to mobility', with as many
as 5,000 crossing the Atlantic annually in search of seasonal labour in
Newfoundland.[9] A more recent commentator has identified this mobility as a
contributory factor in the Catholic re-emergence in the region. Kevin Whelan
has pointed to essential links between the surviving gentry/strong farmers group
and their co-religionists in the towns. He identifies a 'synchronisation of zones',
manifest in what he calls 'the symbiosis of town and country', the integration
of marriage fields and the constant replenishment of town families by rural
recruits.[10] All of these features are illustrated in the case of Edmund Rice.

Under the direction of his uncle, Rice honed his intuitive business skills.
There are few recollections of him from this time. The earliest description comes
from Br Austin Dunphy (1785–1847), a native of Callan who would become his
Assistant, which attests to his standing as one of Waterford's leading merchants:

> He was unquestionably a very remarkable man. The first time I saw him
> was in the year 1796. He was then a very fine looking man, and bore a
> high character among the Catholic people and mercantile classes of the
> country. Indeed, he was respected and trusted by men of all creeds and
> classes …[11]

Almost all of the recollections collected by Br Hill and his successors in the folklore project are in agreement on Rice's keen business sense. His commercial
integrity was noted, too, in terms which are at odds with the land-grabbing
accusations made in several of the rural reminiscences:

> In his dealings with others, in buying and selling Br Rice's probity and
> uprightness could be noticed, as in these particulars he seemed to stand
> on a higher level than others. When buying he offered the full value
> without huckstering.[12]

Such a reputation, however, was paramount in a trade based entirely on trust,
where there were no written contracts, and where business was conducted by
verbal agreements, sealed by handshake, more often than not, over a drink. In
this context, Rice learned that a man was as good as his word, a maxim which
would direct his life, but would blight his old age as he became embroiled in a
bitter dispute involving a mortgage. More of the *Memories* refer to his sense of

3.3 Ballybricken Fair, Waterford (*c.*1900). Poole Studios, NLI.

humour, a vital asset in trade; other recollections recall his piety and how the young merchant would say his rosary as he travelled to fairs.[13]

If there was a criticism of Rice in this period, it was that he became very self-conscious.[14] Several of the *Memories* recall that he was 'too fastidious about his dress', echoing an observation by John Shelly, a native of Callan and member of the Royal Irish Academy, in 1863:

> Mr Rice was, in his early days, of a gay and worldly disposition. Whilst on a visit one time with his uncle to Callan, he was met by the [local] poet [James Phelan of Coolagh] on entering the house of God. The poet was struck by his gaudy dress and the levity of his manners, so totally

unfit for a worshipper in the house of prayer. On Mr Rice's coming out, the poet addressed him in our ancient language and in words of much religious fervour of the impropriety of his conduct. The words of the poet made a deep impression on him, and from that time he was noticed to be an altered man.[15]

Clearly, Rice enjoyed the lifestyle prosperity brought him and his bustling social circle at Waterford included the Aylward and St Leger families, as well as Edward Shiel, who amassed a fortune in Cadiz, and who was the father of Richard Lalor Shiel (1791–1851), the politician and Catholic activist. There is a tradition among the Brothers, too, that Rice was acquainted with the poet Tadhg Gaelach Ó Súilleabháin (1715–95). In cultural terms, the existence of such a friendship would point to Edmund Rice's inclusion in the Gaelic survival of Munster, but the sincerity of Tadhg Gaelach's religious conversion, as reflected the spiritual poetry of his *Pious Miscellany* (1804), may have influenced the young merchant in his own quest.[16]

Ironically Rice's most intimate relationship is the one about which we know the least. It was about this time, possibly in 1785, that he married, but no details of his short-lived marriage survive other than the newspaper announcements of the tragic death of his wife in January 1789:

Died at Ballybricken the wife of Mr Rice.[17]

This apart, the sources are silent about the wife of Edmund Rice.[18] Nor do we know much more about the couple's daughter Mary, who was 'delicate' or hand-icapped in some way.

This absence of information about his brief marriage may be attributed to nineteenth-century attitudes towards religious life, particularly the tendency to exalt consecrated virginity above the married state. Sandra Schneiders has developed the concept of 'born-again virgins' within the early Church, in so far as widows embracing religious life could start anew.[19] There was however no such latitude within nineteenth-century Irish Catholicism, which, like the prevailing European spirituality, has been characterised as cerebral, 'disembodied and anti-incarnational'.[20] Edmund Rice himself was coy about his past. Writing to the Superior of the Presentation Convent in Waterford, on the occasion of the death of a mutual friend, he made a significant observation to Mother Keeshan, who had been his ward and who was herself a widow:

O what Thanksgiving should we not give to God for calling us into Religion, and to have us divested from the cares of providing for husband, wife or children. May He be blessed and praised for ever and ever. Amen.[21]

Br McCarthy's biography of Edmund Rice (1926), which runs to 535 pages, treats the marriage in just one paragraph. The absence of information is curtly excused by the fact that 'the early brothers, with a delicacy of feeling which is commendable, seldom refer to it', in a reflection of his contemporary attitudes among religious towards the lesser married state.[22] Almost nothing is known about Mrs Rice, although McCarthy confidently casts her as a 'model wife', similar to those which the Brothers' *Our Boys* magazine recommended to the pupils of independent Ireland.[23] Accordingly, he assumes that,

> a gentleman of his kindly nature and virtuous habits must have been an ideal husband, and that one of his strong character, practical sense, and religious principles made a wise selection in choosing the lady who was to be the mistress of his home.[24]

The first time Rice's wife is named is in the memoir of Martin O'Flynn collected 160 years after her death. This was the only one of the 250 memoirs published by Br Normoyle which offered a name and a surname. Yet even this informant was unsure, as she is described as 'Mary or Bridget' Elliott, the daughter of a Waterford tanner.[25] This is most likely, since Rice began his first school in 'Elliot's Yard' in Waterford. More recently it has been asserted that Mrs Rice was 'Maria Ellis', whose family had a livery yard in New Street.[26] This echoes information gleaned by Br Berchmans Cullen, who conducted extensive research on Rice's Waterford connections, in the course of which it was suggested to him that Rice's wife was an 'Ellis', possibly a sister of Br Patrick Ellis, one of the early Brothers.[27] There is a tradition, too, that Mrs Rice may have been a MacElligott from Annestown, County Waterford.[28] If this was a corruption or gaelicization of 'Elliott', it might explain why the seaside village became Rice's favourite place for peace and relaxation during the trials of his later life.

The search for Mrs Rice is frustrated by the lack of parochial registers for the period in the diocese of Waterford and Lismore. However, the absence of such information is not at all unusual before the introduction of state legislation requiring the registration of births and deaths (1863) and the establishment of the General Register Office in Dublin in the following year. In fact, the wives of many prominent individuals in nineteenth-century Ireland are virtually unknown. Nothing, for instance, is known about the wife of Rice's contemporary Edward Hay (c.1761–1826), the historian and Catholic activist who O'Connell described as 'the servant of eight million people'.[29] In a sense, too, the problem was compounded by marriage which deprived women of their Christian and maiden names; most were remembered by their new identity as wives, as in the case of Mrs Edmund Rice.[30]

In the absence of such hard information, creative interpretations have been offered for her identity. Br Liam Ó Caithnia flew a number of kites, one of which suggested that she may have been a Protestant, or that the couple were married in the Protestant church.[31] Such a proposition cannot simply be dismissed; Edmund Rice was on good terms with the leading Protestants of the city, where inter-church relations reflected the mutual toleration and co-operation which characterised the latter decades of the eighteenth century.[32] Nevertheless, once that relative ecumenism gave way to the open hostility of the 'Second Reformation' in the 1820s, it was likely that such a mixed-marriage would have been flaunted by the Brothers' Protestant enemies in the 'Bible Wars'.[33]

In his recent study of the education charism of Edmund Rice, Denis McLaughlin has broadened the debate on Mrs Rice, challenging the assumption that she was 'a lady of a well to do family'. Instead, he suggests that her people may have been 'relative nobodies', or modest farmers, from whom Rice purchased pigs at local fairs or markets.[34] This thesis is offered on the basis of a number of observations, and circumstantial evidence, but chiefly on her willingness to live with Rice at Ballybricken, 'a part of the city where vice and ignorance prevailed to a greater extent than elsewhere'.[35] From this he assumes that Mrs Rice cannot have been 'too precious to live among the common folk'. Moreover, 'this fun-loving ... hospitable teenager shared Rice's sensitivity and compassion for the poor', to the extent that one of the Memories has described their Ballybricken home as Rice's first school, where the couple fed and clothed poor children, fifteen years before he started his enterprise in Mount Sion.[36]

This is an attractive scenario which suggests that 'Ricean education' was 'conceived within a loving family dynamic', but it cannot be substantiated.[37] Ballybricken was not a mass of undifferentiated poverty. It is true that the most prosperous areas of the city were nearest to the quay, but Ballybricken was an exception. The area was the centre of the livestock trade, with its associated conditions, but the housing stock reflected the full range from the homes of prosperous merchants through to those of the urban poor. That Ballybricken was a hub of activity is reflected in the presence of thirty pubs in the district. These were effectively the exchanges or 'bourses' of the city; it was there deals were made and labour hired. For a merchant like Edmund Rice not to have a presence in Ballybricken was unthinkable.[38]

Significantly, too, given the Rice family's famed ambition, it is probable that he would have made a strategically advantageous marriage. Besides, the marriage patterns of families such as Rice's were 'carefully controlled to nurture family interests'.[39] More crudely, it has been argued that within an eighteenth-century context, the requirements for such marriages were virginity and a dowry; without both any union was inconceivable.[40] For all these reasons, it is unlikely that Rice would have married below his class. Significantly, too, the appearance of her death notice in no less than four national newspapers suggests categorically that she, or at least he, was already a person of consequence and standing within the social hierarchy of Waterford.

The marriage ended with Mrs Rice's sudden death in January 1789, leaving Rice as a 27-year-old widower and father of an infant daughter. Family tradition, related by Sr Josephine Rice of St John's, Newfoundland, in 1929, holds that Mrs Rice died in a riding accident:

> The Founder had been married to a lady of a well-to-do family who was fond of the hunt as most wealthy people were in those days. When she was well-advanced with child, she was riding and was thrown from her horse, dying as a result of the accident. The doctor managed to save the child who had evidently been injured by the fall and hence did not develop normally. This was the child he provided for when he began his work.[41]

This account has been convincingly challenged by Ó Caithnia.[42] As a folklorist he questioned the reliability of the transcription: why would Sr Josephine refer to Edmund Rice as 'The Founder'? Apart from this and other textual criticisms, he speculates on how this tradition could be preserved for 140 years by the Newfoundland Rices when not one of the 250 interviews contained in Normoyle's *Memories* refers to the event? Ó Caithnia rejects this riding accident thesis and instead accepts the tradition that Mary Rice died in the fever which swept Europe in 1789; that 'dreadful fever' which Dorothea Herbert claimed, 'raged all over the World … and carried off Millions in every quarter of the Globe'.[43]

The veil of secrecy which surrounds Mrs Rice also cloaks Rice's daughter Mary. In fact, the invisibility of the mother may have contributed to the rumour that his daughter was illegitimate.[44] (This contention may have fuelled the accu-

3.4 No. 3 Arundel Place, where Edmund Rice lived with his daughter after the death of his wife in 1789.

sation made in 1818 that Rice had fathered 'many a bastard child' in the city of Waterford.)[45] Little is known about Rice's daughter, although the *Memories* indicate a general awareness of her existence, and several of these recollections recall her presence at Westcourt.[46] A contemporary Brother described her as 'weak-headed', while some of the memoirs refer to her as 'delicate'.[47] The nature and extent of Mary Rice's illness is unclear. On the basis of the memoirs he collected at Callan, Berchmans Cullen was emphatic that she was 'not of unsound mind, unbalanced, crippled or deformed', but it is usually assumed that Mary Rice was mentally handicapped.[48] In this context, Ó Caithnia believes that the story of the fall from the horse is more correctly related to the child's condition and not the mother's death. Similar motifs were often invoked to account for handicap or mental weakness in order to protect 'the good name of the family'.[49]

Following the death of his wife, Rice moved from Ballybricken to Arundel Place, where Joan Murphy, his half-sister, assumed the responsibility of maintaining his household and caring for Mary.[50] When, in 1802, he embarked on his mission he entrusted his now teenage daughter to Patrick Rice, his brother at Westcourt. On his death in 1833, Mary moved to Carrick-on-Suir,

County Waterford, where she remained in the care of her D'Alton cousins until her death in January 1859.[51] Throughout his life Rice paid for the care of his daughter; we might speculate whether he visited her at Callan or subsequently at Carrick, where he called frequently to the Brothers' monastery. What is beyond doubt, is that he provided adequately for her physical welfare, and his accounts for 1826 reveal that she was maintained at a considerable expense of £16 per annum, which was the equivalent of a teacher's salary.[52] The Brothers continued to support her after his death, but the level of maintenance decreased dramatically; in some years recorded payments are as little as £3.[53] However, the correspondence of Rice's trustees reflects the limited extent to which he had informed even his closest confreres about the details of his family and daughter. In 1850, Br Ignatius Kelly wrote to the assistant superior general of the congregation:

> There is an impression on my mind that about the year 1836 I heard Br Ign[atiu]s Rice make some statements about those poor relatives in Callan … as if there was something due to some of them, but of this I am quite uncertain, but I suppose there are many of them there, and why this person in particular should, for so long a time, receive so much, does not appear, and it might be worth enquiring into … If it were that weak-headed creature, the d[aughte]r, I should feel ourselves bound to support her.[54]

That Br Ignatius, one of Rice's closest friends, was ignorant of these personal details is an indication not only of Rice's reticence but of the extent to which the founder's married years had been forgotten or perhaps avoided. It is difficult to credit that in a small city such as Waterford, that no one would recall this crucial episode in the life of the city's most illustrious adopted son and his wife, about who all we can say is: 'Died at Ballybricken the wife of Mr Rice'.[55] In the absence of additional sources, anything more is simply conjecture.

II

Rice's desolation at the death of his wife can only be imagined. Of a friend in similar circumstances he later wrote, 'May the Lord help her, she is now [in] the dregs of misery and misfortune. I pity the poor Mother, it will break her heart.'[56] Yet this double tragedy was to play an enormous part in his conversion, and it is possible from this period onwards to identify a heightened religious and social conscience coupled with a growing sense of a religious vocation.

We have already noted the so-called 'Tridentine surge' which took place in the last decades of the eighteenth century; in the city of Waterford the process was lead by Thomas Hearn, vicar general of the diocese and parish priest of Trinity Within. This revival was manifested in many ways, chapel building being perhaps the most obvious, including the cathedral of Waterford completed in 1796. The first Catholic cathedral to be built in Ireland since the Reformation, it was designed by local architect John Roberts, a Protestant, who was also responsible for the Church of Ireland cathedral built in the city in 1774. In a significant reflection of the status of Catholics in Waterford, their new cathedral was erected at a cost of £20,000, whereas the Anglican one had cost less than £6,000.[57] There were, however, more dynamic aspects of this renewal, and these were reflected in the increased levels of devotional printing as well as the growth of pious confraternities in the city, including the sodalities of the Sacred Heart and the Blessed Virgin. Edmund Rice was part of this revival and enthusiastically embraced the exacting spirituality of the Catholic Reformation, which was characterised by sacramental devotion, meditation, prayer, and the exercise of good works.[58]

About the year 1790, at the age of 38, he joined a number of young men in Waterford who formed a pious association, under the influence of Jesuits who had remained in the city following the suppression of their congregation by the pope in 1773. This was to be a particularly formative period in Rice's life; it was within this circle that he was introduced to the wealth of Jesuit spirituality. The Waterford group met in St Patrick's, the 'Little Chapel' in Jenkin's Lane, and its members were committed to living more active Christian lives, along the lines promoted by St Ignatius and his early companions. Among the various duties they promoted were: private prayer, spiritual reading, the practice of charity and the frequent reception of the sacraments of the Eucharist and Confession, which the Jesuit Peter Faber (1506–46) had advocated 'more than anything else' as the foundation for a happy life.[59] This was a radical commitment since frequent communion was then uncommon; in 1829, for instance, Bishop James Warren Doyle (JKL) reported that only 10 per cent of the faithful of Kildare and Leighlin were regular monthly communicants.[60] Frequent communion was not particularly stressed by the Church until the pontificate of Pius X (1903–14), yet Rice was a daily communicant since this time, and devotion to the Blessed Sacrament remained the defining hallmark of his spirituality.[61]

In spite of his limited education, Rice immersed himself in the spiritual classics as he sought to bring meaning to his apparently unfulfilled life. He delighted
in *The Imitation of Christ*, by Thomas à Kempis (1379–1471), a book to which he
remained devoted throughout his life. It, too, encouraged frequent Communion
and Confession. At its simplest, *The Imitation* was a call to inwardness and
reflection. It was not abstract or simply intellectual, but, in O'Malley's phrase,
'it spoke to the heart from the heart'; it was a call to conversion, 'to personal
appropriation of religious truth in holiness of life'.[62] In addition, Rice's name is
present on subscription lists for several religious imprints, including a 1793
Waterford edition of *The Spiritual Combat* (1593), a translation of Lorenzo
Scupoli's (1530–1610) classic devotional work, which St Francis de Sales described
as his 'golden book'. Its sixty-six chapters presented a 'battle plan' or strategy for
achieving perfection and salvation: they were to the Theatine Order (founded
in 1524) what the *Spiritual Exercises* were to the Jesuits. This was an influential
handbook and its importance at this stage of Edmund Rice's spiritual development can hardly be over-estimated. A recent edition of the classic has grouped
Scupoli's reflections into eleven chapters, the titles of which have immediate resonances with Rice's spirituality:

> Understand the means for attaining Christian perfection; Distrust your-
> self; Trust God; Use trustworthy spiritual methods; Pray; Rely on the
> Eucharist; Persevere in spiritual combat; Govern your heart; Give your-
> self to God; Do not yield to discouragement; Learn to preserve your
> inner peace.[63]

As Rice's spiritual biographer has observed, in Scupoli he 'had to hand an
approved manual of perfection which provided a methodical approach to the
spiritual life congenial to his ordered business mind'.[64]

The most significant step in Rice's spiritual development came in 1791 when
he subscribed to a Dublin imprint of the Douai Bible.[65] This was the critical
moment in Rice's formation, for he accepted literally his Saviour's invitation to
make his words his home. The surviving Bible is not only heavily thumbed, but
it also contains his original annotation and twelve scriptural texts which he tran-
scribed under the heading 'Texts against Usury' inside the flyleaf:

> Exodus 22:25 If you lend money to any of my people that is poor, that
> dwelleth with thee: thou shalt not be hard upon them as an extortioner,
> nor oppress them with usuries.

Leviticus 25:35–6 If thy brother be impoverished, and weak of hand, and thou receive him as a stranger and sojourner, and he live with thee: Take not usury of him nor more than thou gavest. Fear thy God, that thy brother may live with thee.

Deuteronomy 23:19 Thou shalt not lend to thy brother money to usury, nor corn, nor any other thing.

Psalm 14:5 He that hath not put out his money to usury, nor taken bribes against the innocent; he that doth these things shall not be moved for ever.

Psalm 54:11–12 Day and night shall iniquity surround it upon its walls; and in its midst thereof are labour and injustice. And usury and deceit have not departed from its streets.

Proverbs 22:16 He that oppresseth the poor, to increase his own riches, shall himself give to one that is richer, and shall be in need.

Proverbs 28:8 He that heapeth together riches by usury and loan gathereth them for him that will be bountiful to the poor.

Ezra 18:31 That grieveth the needy and the poor: that taketh away by violence: that restoreth not the pledge: and that lifteth up his eyes to idols: that committeth abomination: that giveth up usury and that taketh an increase; shall such a one live? He shall not live.

Ezra 18:31 Cast away from you all your transgressions, by which you have transgressed, and make to yourselves a new heart and a new spirit: and why should you die, O House of Israel?

2 Ezra [Nehemiah] 5:11 Restore ye to them this day their fields, and their hundreth part of the money, and of the corn, the wine and the oil, which you were wont to exact from them, give it rather for them.

Matthew 5:42 Give to him that asketh of thee; and from him that would borrow of thee turn not away.

Luke 6:35 But love ye your enemies; do good and lend, hoping for nothing thereby; and your reward shall be great and you shall be the sons of the highest for he is kind to the unthankful and to the evil.

A literal analysis of the selection may suggest a concern with his business practice to date. Some Catholic merchants added to their fortunes by money-lending. While there is no proof that Edmund Rice engaged in the practice, given the recollection that the Rices were 'endowed by a too keen sense of business', it is not improbable that he did.[66] Besides this, there was rumbling controversy among the Catholics of Munster throughout the eighteenth century on the morality of lending at interest. As late as 1824 Bishop Coppinger of Cloyne declared that he was 'fully aware that many worthy ecclesiastics have their scruples upon legal interest'.[67] In some respects, however, the emphasis given the 'Texts against usury' has distracted attention from the possibility that the transcriptions may provide a key towards an understanding of Rice's spirituality. Indeed, Carroll has argued that they reflect his image of God, and the appeal of the notion of the covenant between Yahweh and his people, 'a merchant concept: a bargain, a contract that he could understand'.[68]

At a broader level, this engagement with the Scriptures is suggestive of the extent to which Rice accepted the radical challenge at the heart of the Gospel. It is tempting to speculate about his reading the story of the 'Rich Young Man'. He was particularly struck by the inseparable connection between the love of God and the love of neighbour. He was fired by the concept and his subsequent life was driven by a desire to fulfill the imperative presented in chapter twenty five of St Matthew's gospel, where Jesus delivers the parables of the ten virgins, the talents, and the description of the last judgment:

> 25:34–40. Then the King will say to those on his right, 'Come, you who are blessed by my Father; take your inheritance, the kingdom prepared for you since the creation of the world. For I was hungry and you gave me something to eat, I was thirsty and you gave me something to drink, I was a stranger and you invited me in. I needed clothes and you clothed me, I was sick and you looked after me, I was in prison and you came to visit me.' Then the righteous will answer him, 'Lord, when did we see you hungry and feed you, or thirsty and give you something to drink? When did we see you a stranger and invite you in, or needing clothes and clothe you? When did we see you sick or in prison and go to visit you?' The King will reply, 'I tell you the truth, whatever you did for one of the least of these brothers of mine, you did for me.'

This parable demonstrates the essential Christian understanding of *caritas*; in a very striking way Matthew 25 became the constant yardstick, as it had for St Vincent de Paul, against which Rice measured his actions. The text is not annotated in his Testament, nor is there documentary evidence that this was so, but its spirit is implicit in the most frequently quoted of Rice's expressions in which he reminded a friend that:

> Were you to know the merit and value of only going from one street to another to serve a neighbour for the love of God, we would prize it more than gold or silver.[69]

Moreover, an extrapolation of his behaviour suggests the text provided a moral checklist which he conscientiously observed as he strove to exercise the corporal works of mercy.

Rice's commitment to the poor was evident in his involvement in a number of the charitable societies in Waterford. In the absence of a formal mechanism for state intervention prior to the passage of the poor laws in the 1830s, the alleviation of distress was left principally to private charity. Waterford had a number of Catholic charitable societies. In 1771 the Butler and Fitzgerald charities established two hostels each; in 1779 the Wyse charity provided a further three. In 1793 Edmund Rice was among the founding members of the Trinitarian Orphan Society, which maintained the large Congreve mansion on New Street where one hundred boys and girls were housed and educated.[70] In the following year, during a time of particular famine and distress in the city, Rice was among the founders, if not the initiator, of the 'Waterford Society for visiting and relieving distressed room-keepers', a group not unlike the St Vincent de Paul Society.[71] He had also particular concern for the plight of prisoners, as advocated in Matthew 25. There was little long term incarceration in the eighteenth century and prisoners tended to fall into two categories; debtors or those awaiting sentence, execution or transportation.[72] Rice visited the prisons and assisted the inmates materially, providing them with food and small funds to help relieve the misery of hunger and overcrowding. This was to be a constant feature of his life and special apostolate of the early Christian Brothers; on his arrival in Australia, too, Ambrose Tracey (1868) initiated a ministry to prisoners at Melbourne.

There are two striking accounts of individual beneficiaries of Rice's charity to the stranger. The first concerns the young Italian immigrant, Charles Bianconi, who was introduced to Rice by Brother Joseph Cahill, in 1806.[73] This was a fortuitous encounter. Rice taught him English, and his interest and advice deeply affected the young man's life. The Scottish author and reformer, Samuel Smiles (1812–1904), has described the effects of that friendship and tutelage, which 'set and kept Bianconi's life in the right road':

[He] was no longer a dunce as he had been at school, but a keen, active, enterprising fellow, eager to make his way in the world. Mr Rice encouraged him to be sedulous and industrious, urged him to carefulness and sobriety, and strengthened his religious impressions. The help and friendship of this good man ... could not fail to exercise—as Bianconi always acknowledged they did—a most powerful influence upon his whole life.[74]

Rice's assistance went beyond simple counsel and he helped him secure a business premises in Clonmel (1808).[75] In time, Bianconi developed an extensive transport system; he was twice elected mayor of Clonmel, and he played a prominent role in the establishment of the Catholic University in Dublin (1854). His friend, Anthony Trollope, commented in 1857, that 'perhaps ... no living man has worked more than he has for the benefit of the sister Kingdom', Ireland.[76] But he never forgot Edmund Rice, who he described as 'a true benefactor to his country'.[77] Each year he sent £50 and twenty suits of clothes for poor boys. His appreciation for the 'good friend who took a kindly interest' in him was reflected in a clause of his will which ran 'failing direct issue, I bequeath to the Christian Brothers the reversion of my property'. Bianconi was survived by a daughter.[78]

The second beneficiary was a black slave boy whom Rice saw on the deck of a vessel at the quay in Waterford. Rice bought the boy from the ship's master and entrusted him to the care of the Presentation Sisters on Hennessy's Road. When the boy grew, he worked as a messenger for the sisters, and later Rice helped him purchase premises at Gracedieu in the city. In time 'Black Johnnie', whose legal name was John Thomas, succeeded in business, and on his death his property, consisting of two houses, was left between the Christian Brothers and the Presentation Sisters.[79] Traditional accounts of this history have presented the details of this encounter in a pious and sentimental fashion, stressing 'Black Johnnie's' industry and piety learned from his benefactor, repeating, for example the adage that in death his soul was as white as his skin had been black in life.[80] In its historical context, however, Rice's actions in freeing the boy mirror the sentiments of the abolitionist William Wilberforce; it anticipated the abolition of the slave trade by almost a decade (1807), and the emancipation of British slaves by thirty years (1833). The liberation of a slave by a merchant who had benefited greatly from the trans-Atlantic trade, so dependent upon slavery, is indicative of Rice's full and radical conversion and serves as a metaphor for the liberty he would later bring to the poor of Waterford through the power of education.

Of course, Rice's contemporaries in Waterford were more concerned about what from the mid 1790s was called 'Catholic Emancipation'. Rice did not hesitate to lend his support to that campaign either. After 1778 and 1782, the bulk of the religious and economic disabilities of the penal era had been removed, but the political restrictions remained on the statute book. Since the middle of the century, Catholic interests had been represented by an ineffectual Catholic Committee. Already by the 1780s, tensions had begun to develop within this body as the confident new middle class began to challenge the aristocratic and episcopal leadership. In the past the Committee had been content to seek relief from their 'gracious sovereign' in deferential terms, but under the influence of French Revolutionary ideology this more aggressive faction demanded redress for Catholic grievances as a right.

Waterford played a prominent role in Catholic politics of the eighteenth century; in the 1750s the leadership of the Catholic Committee was largely provided by Thomas Wyse, one of a wealthy mercantile family with continental connections. It was understandable that ambitious, prosperous Catholics would turn their attention to political disabilities, and Edmund Rice was no exception. In 1792 the Irish parliament passed a relief bill which granted only minor concessions to the Catholics. The heated parliamentary debate generated considerable resentment within the Catholic community, and there was particular bitterness among the Catholic Committee at the insults hurled in their direction. The Committee was dismissed in parliament as 'shop-keepers and shop-lifters', 'men of very low and mean parentage'. Theobald Wolfe Tone, its secretary, was particularly incensed at the depiction of the Committee as a 'porter-drinking' rabble meeting in 'holes and corners'.[81]

These attacks placed the Committee on the defensive, but resentment quickly gave way to anger. In March 1792 it published a 'Declaration', demonstrating that the principles of Catholicism were in no way incompatible with the duties of citizens or 'repugnant to liberty, whether political, civil or religious'. The declaration answered many of the questions levelled at Catholics during the parliamentary debates; it renounced all interests in forfeited estates, and declared that, if restored to the elective franchise, they would not use the privilege to 'disturb and weaken the establishment of the Protestant religion or Protestant government' in the country.[82] The Committee decided to muster as much support for this Declaration as possible. Chapel meetings were held around the country to garner support and gather signatures. Significantly, Edmund Rice's presence, together with Bishop Egan and Dean Hearn, among the one hundred leading Catholics of Waterford who signed the declaration, is an indication of the extent to which he belonged to the city's elite.[83]

The Committee mounted equally forceful campaigns in 1793 and again in

1795, but on these occasions Rice's name was absent from the Waterford Addresses. Nor was he among the 209 signatories of the memorial of the Catholics of Waterford in favour of a legislative union in 1799. This may be accounted for by the bitter and acrimonious nature of the Union debate in the city, and the involvement of the Church of Ireland dean, Christopher Butson, in the Catholic agitation in defiant opposition to the anti-Union stance of his bishop, Richard Marlay.[84] More importantly, Rice's mind was turning increasingly from political to religious matters, as he sought to give his religious convictions concrete expression. His brother John had returned to Ireland in 1792 to join the Augustinian Order at New Ross. Rice supported his brother financially, and it appears that he was contemplating a similar course.[85] Circumstances, however, would direct the expression of his vocation in a different and novel direction.

CHAPTER FOUR

'The Summons of Grace'[1]

IN 1975 A CONTRIBUTOR AT A Christian Brothers' spirituality conference spoke of 'the providential death of Mrs Rice in 1789'.[2] Thirty years later such sentiments may be politically incorrect, but the import of the statement stands in so far as the desolation of his bereavement was a pivotal moment in the vocation of Edmund Rice. From this point, his priorities changed perceptibly and the alleviation of the misery of others became a primary concern. While initially he considered a classic 'flight from the world', the chronic poverty of Waterford city and a critical confluence of circumstances convinced him that it was there he belonged, rather than in the seclusion of a cloistered life.

I

As a widowed father, the obvious option for Edmund Rice was to remarry, just as his mother had done following the death of her first husband. Rice chose otherwise and contemplated a religious life, but it was not clear how that would be expressed. For a decade he engaged in a complex process of what religious writers call 'discernment', a searching for direction which, in Rice's case, Archbishop John Charles McQuaid characterised as 'an obscure groping towards his vocation'.[3] Initially, he appears to have considered joining the Augustinian order. This was an obvious choice; he had worshipped in their chapel at Callan, while his first teacher, Patrick Grace, and several of his mother's family were Augustinians. His brother John entered their novitiate at New Ross in 1792, but tradition asserts that he discouraged Rice from this path.[4] The spirituality of the Jesuits, too, appealed to him greatly, but the order had been dissolved by Pope Clement XIV (in 1773), in response to pressure from European monarchs. The suppression was an unmitigated disaster for the Church; the pope acknowledged that he had 'cut off his right hand', but for Edmund Rice it ruled out a vocation within which he might have been perfectly content.[5] It would seem, too, that he was attracted by the contemplative life and the thrust of much of his spiritual reading tended towards monasticism. The *Imitation of Christ,* to which he was so devoted, extolled the 'solitary sweetness of the monk's cell' and placed little importance on apostolic activity.[6] Tradition asserts that Rice considered a life of seclusion at the Cistercian monastery at Melleray in Brittany.[7] Yet neither was this a possibility, since French monasteries had been suppressed by the revolutionary government in 1791.

This was the range of options available to Rice, and it is significant that none of the traditions or *Memories* suggest that he gave any thought to the possibility of being ordained as a priest for the diocese, in order to serve in the parishes of Waterford. Clearly his inclination was towards a life in a religious community. Characteristically, Rice weighed his various options carefully, but his important decision was not made alone. Throughout the process of discernment he drew on a close circle of trusted friends and advisors. In the first instance, he drew on the counsel of his peers within the pious association centred on St Patrick's chapel. There he enjoyed the direction of the Jesuit priests, and the manner and form in which Rice isolated and annotated the twelve scriptural texts in his Douai Bible suggest the influence of a spiritual director at this critical period of his spiritual formation.[8] Rice's companions made an annual retreat. In all probability, too, they followed an adapted form of the *Spiritual Exercises*, the rigorous programme of meditation and self-reflection composed by St Ignatius with the express purpose of 'disposing the soul ... to seek and find' God's will and ordering one's life accordingly.[9] Among his circle of friends, Fr John Power, subsequently bishop of Waterford, was a considerable influence, although it was his sister, remembered simply as 'Miss Power', who is traditionally credited with Rice's ultimate decision to dedicate his life to God in the service of the poor of his adopted city.[10]

McCarthy's description of Miss Power's spirited intervention in Rice's resolution reflects the orthodox interpretation of his conversion and the way in which his hagiography has been constructed. In McCarthy's re-creation of the encounter, based upon the recollections of the Presentation Sisters in Waterford, Miss Power confronted the merchant, reprimanding him for his intention of leaving 'his native country' to enter religious life abroad:

> It would be a strange and inconsistent thing for you to travel leagues of land and sea, and shut yourself up in a monastery in some distant place, while the sons of your poor countrymen at home are, owing to untoward circumstances, utterly unacquainted with the rudiments of divine or human knowledge, and running wild through the town, without a school, or a teacher, or any possible means of acquiring the most elementary education ... Would it not, Mr Rice ... be far more meritori-

ous work, and far more exalted, to devote your life and your wealth to the instruction of these neglected children in the principles of religion and in secular knowledge, than to bury yourself in some Continental Religious House, where you will have no scope for the exercise of active benevolence?[11]

Miss Power touched a nerve in Rice, but his dilemma remained, since none of the traditional orders in Ireland appealed to him. Nevertheless, retreat to a monastery was not an option, not least on account of the likely consequences, which she had identified, of his departure on the fledgling charities, the Orphan Society and the Distressed Roomkeepers, which he helped establish in the city.[12]

The earliest historical record of the foundation of the Christian Brothers identifies 1793 as a key year in the resolution of Edmund Rice's decision. This forty-page manuscript, entitled 'An Account of the Origin, Rise and Progress of the institute of the Society of Religious Brothers' (referred to here as 'Origin'), describes the first twenty years of its history from its foundation in 1802, through to the general chapter of 1822.[13] It has been attributed to Br Austin Dunphy (a confidante and member of Rice's general council, 1822–9), and dated to 1829; it provides the first account of Rice's decision to teach the poor:

> In the year one thousand seven hundred and ninety three, Mr Edmund Rice of the City of Waterford formed the design of erecting an Establishment for the gratuitous education of poor boys. In the fol-lowing year he communicated his intention on the subject to some friends, and particularly to the Right Reverend Doctor James Lanigan, Roman Catholic Bishop of Ossory, who strongly recommended him to carry this intention into effect; and assured him that in his opinion it proceeded from God. From this time forward Mr Rice did not lose sight of the object he had in view; though from various causes, he did not commence the building till the year 1802.[14]

The 'various causes' which delayed the enterprise may have included Rice's desire to care for his daughter Mary, but politically, circumstances militated against such an initiative. Europe had been convulsed since the outbreak of the Revolution in France in 1789. While foreign observers initially looked on with a mixture of horror and delight, the advent of war between Britain and France, in February 1793, removed the security afforded by distance from the conflict. Moreover, events in France radicalised Irish politics. And while Theobald Wolfe

4.1 'Surrender of French General Humbert to General Lake
at Ballinamuck, 8 Sept. 1798' (c.1798), NLI.

Tone welcomed the Revolution as the 'morning star of liberty for Ireland', the Catholic establishment saw it as an assault on Christianity itself.[15] Sections of Presbyterian opinion assessed the Revolution in equally apocalyptic terms, and interpreted the burning of papal effigies in France as the demise of the anti-Christ, and a prelude to an imminent providential intervention if not the Second Coming.[16]

As Tone observed, the French Revolution quickly became the test of every-man's political creed. We have no documentary evidence of Rice's stance, but it is significant that while he signed the early declarations of the Catholic Committee, he appears to have withdrawn from political activity by 1793.[17] It is probable that he shared the caution of the Catholic propertied classes, and as a merchant involved in the provisioning trade he was heavily dependent on con-tracts from the Admiralty and the army which he was unwilling to jeopardise. In the context of Rice's vocation, more practical considerations might have effected his decision to remain in business in the short term at least. The war with France created a boom in agricultural trade, which brought prosperity to Waterford and its merchants. Such considerations could not have been ignored by Rice who would have seen these profits as the means to fund his philan-thropic mission.

I use the word 'philanthropic' consciously, because while it has been argued that Rice had decided upon his vocation by 1793, the manuscript history cited above suggests otherwise.[18] The 'Origin' refers to Rice's 'design of erecting an *Establishment* for the gratuitous education of poor boys', but it does not claim that by 1793 he had considered the foundation of a religious congregation. Similarly, with reference to the postponement of the project, Dunphy says noth-ing of Rice's vocation but states explicitly that 'he did not commence the *build-ing* till the year 1802'.[19] Perhaps at this early stage, then, the educational initiative may simply have been just another philanthropic project which Rice aspired to add to his care of the poor, the sick and the orphans of Waterford.

II

It is clear that Edmund Rice was animated by the education question. Among his surviving correspondence there is little by way of social commentary or political analysis, but in one letter to Frère Guillaume, the superior general of the De La Salle Brothers in Paris, he outlined the detail and consequences of the education clauses of the 'Popery Code':

Among the many cruel penal laws which were enacted against the Catholics of Ireland since the Reformation, there was one which forbade any Catholic to teach school or even to be a tutor in a private house under pain of transportation for life! His being detected in the act of teaching any one subjected him to this terrible punishment without even the formality of a trial … It was in force for an entire century, and you will judge, it must have great power in demoralising the people.[20]

The penal laws, it will be recalled, were rooted in Protestant anxiety in the wake of the Williamite Wars, and were therefore concerned with national security. Within this context, the initial intention of the educational aspects of the legislation was not to reduce Catholics to ignorance, but rather to 'restrain foreign education' (1695), in order to limit contact with potential allies in Catholic Europe. But no matter how the laws began, in time the provisions were extended to a point where Catholic schools were theoretically outlawed. The 1709 amendment to the 'Act to prevent the further growth of popery' (8 Anne c. 3), for instance, decreed that:

Whatever person of the popish religion shall publicly teach school, or instruct youth in learning in any private house within this realm, or be entertained to instruct youth as usher, or assistant by any Protestant schoolmaster, he shall be esteemed a popish regular clergyman, and prosecuted as such … and no person, after November 1, 1709, shall be qualified to teach or keep such a school publicly or instruct youth in any private house, or as usher, or assistant to any Protestant schoolmaster, who shall not first … take the oath of abjuration, under a penalty of £10 for every such offence—a moiety to go to the informer.

There is good evidence that this legislation was enforced, at least in the first quarter of the century, but P.J. Dowling's comparisons of eighteenth-century education to 'a kind of guerrilla war' where the teacher, like the priest was frequently on the run, is an overstatement.[21] It was easier for schoolmasters to avoid prosecution than priests, but there are numerous instances of masters being punished. In his study of the penal era Corcoran lists nineteen indictments against popish schoolmasters brought before the Limerick grand jury alone between 1711 and 1722.[22] In reality, however, the educational restrictions, like the other provisions of the penal laws, were relaxed outside of times of international crisis and political threat.

So rather than ending Catholic education, the effect of the legislation was to drive such schooling underground, producing in the process the celebrated 'hedge schools'.[23] Much has been written about the hedge schools and they have become the subject of great lore. Many accounts are excessively laudatory and others dismiss them as places of squalor. The truth lies somewhere in between, as *The Nation* acknowledged in 1847, when the Young Ireland newspaper concluded: 'say what you like of them, [the 'hedge schools'] did good not easily measurable!'[24] Catholic teachers operated outside the law, but after 1730 they were largely left undisturbed. In 1731 a House of Lords committee was appointed under Archbishop Hugh Boulter to enquire into the state of popery, and it reported the existence of over 550 popish schools. Some areas were better served than others: the bishop of Clonfert had one school in every parish, while in the diocese of Ferns there was no 'Popish schoolmaster' in or near the town of Wexford.[25]

The Charter Schools were established in the wake of Boulter's report in an effort to promote English Protestant education in Ireland, and as such were hated by many Catholics; one later commentator described them as an attempt 'to carry the nation by a *coup de main*'.[26] This state-sponsored initiative coincided with the visitation of Ireland by Fr John Kent, a native of Waterford, who reported to Pope Benedict XIV on the condition of the Catholic Church in Ireland.[27] Kent's investigations were minimal, and critics alleged that he had only seen as much of the country as could be observed from the window of the coach which carried him from Waterford to Dublin.[28] Nevertheless, his recommendations to Rome and the intensification of proselytism with the establishment of the Charter Schools prompted the Catholic clergy to systematise their schooling, so that by the second half of the century, there was an effective parish school system over much of the country. In many cases the Mass house served as a school during the week and this strengthened the renewed parish structures. The close links with the parish is also reflected in the priority given to education and catechesis in episcopal visitations of the period. Archbishop Butler's reports from Cashel in the 1750s illustrate the important part played by the schoolmaster in parish life. In most cases masters were required to teach catechism and were reprimanded for failure to do so. At Templemore, for instance, Archbishop Butler directed the pastor to recommend the 'schoolmaster to teach Christian doctrine and instruct … midwives concerning baptism'.[29]

In the latter years of the eighteenth century, the number of schools increased rapidly; by the turn of the century, it is estimated that there were over 7,000 hedge-schools accommodating as many as 400,000 pupils in Ireland.[30]

The essential point, in this instance, is that these schools, like 'The Academy' at Callan, attended by Rice, were pay schools. As one recent commentator has argued 'hedge schools' were in fact private schools established on teacher initiative which survived as long as they proved financially profitable.[31] As such, they excluded those who were unable to pay fees and, as late as 1824, it is estimated that approximately 60 per cent of school-age children in Ireland were not attending school, due to a combination of poverty and lack of schools.[32]

Waterford, however, was well served for schools.[33] The common perception is that Rice founded his Brotherhood in Waterford in order to care for the poor boys of the city for whom nobody else cared. The reality, however, was quite the contrary; rather than lacking educational provision, Waterford was the third most literate city in Ireland after Belfast and Dublin (table 4.2). Moreover, an extrapolation of the statistics contained in the census of 1841, suggests that the foundation of Edmund Rice's schools brought no dramatic increase in the levels of literary attainment in Waterford.[34] This would indicate that Rice was not simply concerned with the provision of education, but rather of an emphatically Catholic education, as an alternative to the schooling on offer in the city.[35]

4.2 Extrapolation of literacy levels for males in Waterford, 1841[36]

Age group in 1841	46–55	36–45	26–35	16–25
Attended school in decade	1791	1801	1811	1821
Could read and write	62%	67%	70%	70%

Analysis of 1841 Census, in J.E. Kent, 'The educational ideals', p. 56.

In 1791, there were ten pay schools in the city of Waterford. Two of these were under Catholic management: one conducted by Fr Ronayne and the other by Mr Waters, whose school was attended by Catholics and non-Catholics alike. In these private schools, the annual fee was 6gns. for day pupils and 30gns. for boarders; such charges automatically excluded the children of the poorer classes. There were no Erasmus Smith or diocesan schools and a mere eight parochial schools were attended by 235 pupils, paying minimal fees. There are no statistics to indicate the numbers of children educated by private tutors, going from house to house throughout the city. Free education was provided by a small school adjacent to St Patrick's chapel; funded by the Valois bequest, it catered for 33 boys. There were, in addition, three endowed schools, these were: the

4.3 Thomas Hussey, bishop of Waterford and Lismore (1797–1803).
Engraving from the original by C.F. Von Breda (*c*.1797), NGI.

Charter School at Killotran which had between 50 and 60 students; the Blue Coat School for poor girls had 34 pupils in residence and the Bishop Foy School, founded in 1707, catered for 75 boys.[37] These schools became the focus of a bitter debate in 1797, following the publication of a pastoral address by Bishop Thomas Hussey. That pastoral has been considered seminal to the ultimate decision of Edmund Rice to establish his 'Society of the Presentation'.[38]

Thomas Hussey became bishop of Waterford and Lismore in December 1796.[39] Born in County Meath in 1746, he had an international career as chaplain to the Spanish ambassador in London. This position placed him at the centre of a bustling social scene in the city and his friends included Dr Johnson, Edmund Burke and many of the leading Whigs. After 1793, he played a crucial role in the negotiations with the lord lieutenant leading to the establishment of St Patrick's 'Royal' College, Maynooth, and he was rewarded with the presidency in 1795. Described by Bowen as 'a proto-ultramontanist', he was willing to oppose the Protestant Ascendancy in church and state.[40] This, however, was not immediately apparent; if anything his appointment as bishop was due to his previously impeccable loyalist credentials and willingness to work with the Dublin Castle administration.[41] Nevertheless, Hussey's episcopate was characteristic of the new confidence enjoyed by the Catholic Church in the period; in Richard Lalor Shiel's expression, unlike his predecessors, 'there was nothing servile, timorous or compromising in his demeanour'.[42] From the outset his administration was in stark contrast to the reserve of the penal era. While the previous bishop of Waterford William Egan was consecrated in secret in his sister's house at Taghmon, County Wexford, in 1771, Hussey's episcopal ordination took place in Francis Street chapel, Dublin on 26 February 1797. The ordaining prelate was Dr John Troy of Dublin, and he was assisted by the archbishop of Armagh and Bishops Moylan of Cork, Tehan of Kerry and Delaney of Kildare and Leighlin. In a radical breach with the past, the consecration was marked by the presence of a military guard of honour.

Hussey was the first Catholic bishop to reside in the city of Waterford since the time of Bishop Comerford, who had died in France in 1652.[43] Following his arrival in Waterford, the new bishop made a formal visitation of his diocese. His initial observations are contained in a letter to Edmund Burke, written in May 1797.[44] Hussey devoted considerable attention to a description of the schools of the diocese. Within two months of his arrival, the bishop boasted that he had been able to establish a charity school in the principal towns of the diocese in order 'to instruct the children of the poor, gratis, in reading, writing and accounts'. The bishop was particularly concerned at the proselytising activities

of the free schools of Waterford where 'the clergy of the establishment wanted
to have no catechism taught but the Protestant one, and seemed inclined to
assimilate them to the Charter schools'. Hussey noted that his opposition was
shared by the Quakers of the city, the most numerous branch of Protestants and
'the most regular and industrious sect'.

The bishop revisited this theme in a controversial pastoral address to the
clergy of his diocese in the following year.[45] The pastoral, which dealt with a wide
spectrum of diocesan concerns, began with the rhetoric normally associated
with the hierarchy, but very suddenly changed its tone:

> In these critical and awful times, when opinions seem spreading over
> this island, of a novel and dangerous tendency—when the remnants of
> old oppressions and new principles which tend to anarchy, are strug-
> gling for victory, and which in collision may produce the ruin of reli-
> gion—when a moral earthquake shakes all Europe, I felt no small
> affliction and alarm, upon receiving the command of the Head of the
> Church to preside over the Catholics of these united dioceses.[46]

Hussey's allusions to the French ideology, the politicisation of the United
Irishmen and the impending rebellion were stark, but it was the reference to
'the remnants of old oppression', the remaining penal laws, which excited the
alarm of Protestants. This double-edged approach characterised the pastoral
and gave rise to much ambiguity as the bishop continually contrasted the present with the 'forgotten' past.

Bishop Hussey publicly challenged the proselytising schools and commanded his priests to resist their efforts:

> Stand firm against all attempts which may be made under various pre-
> texts to withdraw any of your flocks from the belief and practice of the
> Catholic religion. Remonstrate with any parent who would be so crim-
> inal as to expose his offspring to those places of education where his
> religion, faith or morals are likely to be perverted ... If he will not
> attend to your remonstrances, refuse him the participation of Christ's
> Body; if he should continue obstinate, denounce him to the Church in
> order that, according to Christ's Commandment, he be considered as a
> heathen and a publican.

The priests of the diocese were urged to make their flocks aware that they were
members of 'the Catholic communion', not a 'small sect, limited to that coun-

try where that sect itself was formed'. They were members of a great Church which had lasted 1700 years, thrived in every part of the world and would 'flourish until time shall be no more'. Consequently 'they should not be ashamed to belong to a religion, which so many kings and princes, so many of the most polished and learned nations of the world glory in professing'. The pastoral also included an uncompromising condemnation of the practice of compelling Catholic soldiers to attend Protestant religious services under pain of flogging.

Understandably, given the tense political atmosphere of the period, the pastoral met with a barrage of criticism. At least five pamphlets appeared criticising its content and questioning its motives. At very best it was a 'saucy contemptuous challenge – daring us to enter anew … the rancorous field of controversy'.[47] The conservative firebrand Dr Patrick Duigenan believed that it was 'as seditious a publication as any which has appeared in modern times, provoking the Irish Romanists to insurrection'.[48] The more moderate Anglican bishop of Meath, Thomas Lewis O'Beirne, a convert from Catholicism and a former seminarian, reacted strongly to Hussey's advocacy of segregated education and declared that 'the worst enemies of Ireland could not devise a scheme more effectually calculated to keep this distinction of the King's subjects a distinct people forever, and to maintain eternal enmity and hatred between them and the Protestant body'. He was convinced the bishop intended to erect a spiritual wall to replace the civil barriers which were being dismantled.[49] Dr Troy, the Catholic archbishop of Dublin, too, criticised the pastoral believing it contained 'too much vinegar … not sufficiently tempered with oil', and noted that there was opposition to it from the poor of Waterford who believed that Hussey's sentiments might jeopardise their chances of employment in Protestant households and businesses.[50] In a very telling comment, however, America's first bishop, John Carroll of Baltimore, whose instincts were closer to Hussey's than his cowed confreres, confessed that he had read it with 'pleasure and approbation'.[51]

Hussey's intervention was welcomed by Edmund Rice and it provided the impetus needed to confirm his choice of vocation. Indeed, this was acknowledged in Rice's panegyric, when his confessor alluded to the influence of the 'enlightened and apostolic bishop' Thomas Hussey, who 'in troubled times and at considerable risk … hesitated not to vindicate the cause of free religious education'.[52] A century later his biographer spoke of 'the natural kinship between the minds and characters of these two men' which 'helped considerably in bringing to fruition the divinely inspired purpose of Edmund Rice'.[53] In this respect, however, it is important to see Hussey not as a bigot as described by Patrick Duigenan, but as a liberal Catholic, who had once served as ambassador of King

George III. In fact the pastoral aroused the anger of the establishment precisely because it questioned the legal legitimacy of the Church of Ireland and challenged the basis of Protestant Ascendancy in Ireland.

Acknowledging the influence of Hussey's 'incendiary' publication, however, does not imply that Edmund Rice was motivated by an aggressive desire to combat proselytism, as his earlier biographies have recently been interpreted.[54] Such an interpretation is anachronistic and reflects more the altered attitudes of the 1820s; the issue at stake in the 1790s was not one of combat, but rather of offering opportunities and alternatives to Catholic children. Rice was neither reactionary nor sectarian and his ecumenism was evident in his interdenominational friendships and his service with members of other denominations on the boards of various charities. In responding to Hussey's clarion, Rice sought to offer an alternative to the endowed schools; gratuitous Catholic education which was formerly unavailable in the city. In a sense, he demonstrated liberal sentiments similar to those articulated by Daniel O'Connell twenty years later. In the context of the 'Second Reformation', and debates on the system of National Education, the Liberator declared: 'let Protestants educate their own children as they choose. All that Catholics ask is to be allowed the same privilege.'[55]

III

Edmund Rice's objective was not merely to provide schooling but to offer a 'special kind of education, even a special kind of Catholic education'.[56] Clearly, too, he was not content to remain a philanthropist, but sought to embrace the religious life. The difficulty was how the two ambitions could be reconciled within the constraints of the traditional male religious orders in Ireland, which would not allow the kind of apostolate he had in mind. The manuscript history, 'Origin', suggests that Rice discussed his intentions with James Lanigan, bishop of his native Ossory, in 1794.[57] That Lanigan was supportive is no surprise. He was an enthusiast of Catholic education and in the previous year he had expanded 'Burrell Hall' in Kilkenny (the successor to Rice's *alma mater*) to make it Ireland's first diocesan seminary.[58] As a graduate and former professor at the University of Nantes, Lanigan would have had first hand experience of the De La Salle Brothers and may have shared his thoughts on the concept of a religious brotherhood with Rice.[59]

The 'Origin' expresses Lanigan's support for his planned 'Establishment'. In 'his opinion it proceeded from God', but it is surprising that if this was so that neither the bishop, nor any of his successors until 1859, invited either the Presentation or Christian Brothers into his diocese.[60] It was claimed, too, by Br Bernard Dunphy, in evidence before the Education Commission of 1825, that Rice had submitted his proposals to Pius VI in 1796 and that the pope had 'encouraged Mr Rice to proceed'.[61] Such an approach is difficult to substantiate, given the Napoleonic annexation of the most prosperous of the Papal States, the Legations of Ravenna and Bologna, and the subsequent humiliation of the 'Citizen Pope' in the spring of that year.[62] In any event, the solution to Edmund Rice's dilemma was closer to hand and in this instance, too, the influence of the Power family was critical.

Tradition attributes the arrival of the Presentation Sisters in Waterford to a chance encounter between Fr John Power and a young servant girl. Having heard her confession, the priest enquired where she had received her schooling, she replied that she had been educated at the Presentation Sisters in Cork.[63] This was a teaching congregation founded in 1775 by Nano (Honora) Nagle. A native of Ballygriffin, near Mallow, the Nagles were a Catholic sub-gentry family; steeped in the Gaelic traditions of the Blackwater Valley.[64] The family had been prominent in the Jacobite cause and was seriously disadvantaged by the penal laws.[65] Nevertheless, Nagle's childhood was privileged, and her education in France, where the family had strong mercantile connections, illustrates the ability of those with wealth to evade the rigour of the laws. On her return to Ireland, in 1746, she was struck, not only by the poverty of the people, but by their ignorance of religion and their gradual decline into superstition and vice:

> she was afflicted to perceive that these poor creatures were almost strangers … [to the business of Salvation, our duty to God, and the great mysteries of Religion]. Under a misconception of their obligations, they substituted error in the place of truth: while they kept up an attachment to certain exterior observances, their fervour was superstitious, their faith was erroneous, their hope was presumptuous, and they had no charity. Licentiousness, while it could bless itself, and tell the beads, could live without remorse, and without repentance; sacraments and sacrilege went hand in hand, and conscience was at rest upon its own stings.[66]

Her first biographer, Bishop William Coppinger, interpreted this reaction in terms which echoed the anxiety of his contemporary reformers at the alienation of the lower classes from the institutional Church and their more general preoccupation with the task of moral reformation:

4.4 Nano Nagle (1718–84), foundress of the Presentation Sisters.
Engraving by Charles Turner, London 1809, British Museum.

By the plainest analogy she had every reason to fear, that the evil was not confined to the poor immediately around her. She turned the matter in her thoughts, she meditated fondly upon it, she traced it to posterity through all its consequences. Idleness, dishonesty, impiety, drunkenness, like specters stalking before her; but for the present she could only sigh at the prospect.[67]

Significantly, too, the bishop's description of Nagle's moment of conversion served as a model which Rice's biographer borrowed in his analysis of the critical moment in Rice's spiritual journey. This is especially true in his narration of Rice's decisive encounter with Miss Power and her challenge which settled his mind on a vocation as a teaching Brother.[68]

There were, however, striking resonances in the conversion narratives of both founders. Like Rice, Nagle's process of discernment was tortuous. Initially she joined a convent in France, but her Jesuit confessor advised that 'her duty was to return to her native land to instruct Irish children, to disobey this inspiration, he warned, would imperil her soul's salvation.[69] In recounting this exchange, Bishop Coppinger, constructed her hagiography with a conscious allusion to that of St Patrick:

> But the poor Irish still rushed on her mind; their spiritual necessities haunted her unremittingly;—thousands of tender babes seemed to implore her assistance.[70]

On her return, she established a free school for girls in Cove Lane. As numbers grew she moved to a new building in Philpot Lane and by 1769 she had seven schools in various locations in Cork, catering for 200 boys and girls. Nagle left a description of her schools, in terms which would certainly have delighted both Fr John Power and Edmund Rice:

> At present I have two schools for boys and five for girls. The former learn to read, and when they have the Douai catechism by heart they learn to write and cipher. There are three schools where the girls learn to read and when they have their catechism by heart they learn to work. They all hear Mass every day, say their morning and night prayers, say the catechism in each school by question and answer all together. Every Saturday they all say the beads, the grown girls every evening. They go to confession every month and to Communion when their confessor

thinks proper. The schools are open at eight. At twelve the children go
to dinner, at five o'clock they leave school.[71]

As the years progressed, Nagle sought to secure the permanence of her schools
and, on the advice of her spiritual director Patrick Doran SJ and his nephew,
Bishop Francis Moylan, she began negotiations with the Ursuline Sisters in Paris,
to whose care she hoped to entrust the project. In 1771, the Ursulines sent four
Irish-born novices and a mother superior to Cork, where they established a fee-
paying school in Cove Lane, in a convent which Nagle had provided for them.[72]

Before long, however, the limitations of the Ursuline regime and ethos
became apparent to Nagle, who realised that their enclosed life militated against
her desire to reach out to the poor. As a result, she decided to establish a new
type of sisterhood, and on Christmas Eve 1775, together with three companions,
she commenced her novitiate:

> On this day these four ardent and zealous followers of the humbled and
> Crucified Jesus commenced their novitiate, delivering themselves up
> unreservedly to the practice of the most severe monastic discipline and
> to all the privations and austerities to which their future poor, labori-
> ous and annihilated life was in every shape calculated and likely to lead
> them. [73]

Nagle's decision was not made lightly and her actions raised the ire of Bishop
Moylan who violently opposed this initiative, fearing that it would undermine
the Ursuline community, of which his sister was a member.[74] Nagle, however,
was not for turning; driven by a strong social mission, in a characteristically
tenacious display, she threatened to leave Cork rather than compromise on this
matter of principle.[75] The bishop backed down and the annalist notes that 'he
remained ever after silent on the subject'.[76]

In the foundation of the Presentation Sisters, Nano Nagle had managed to
square the circle, in so far as she had created a congregation which combined
the essential elements of the religious life with her apostolic zeal. The
Presentation Sisters, however, were not the first female order to do so. The
Daughters of Charity had pioneered this lifestyle in seventeenth-century France;
where, in the words of their co-founder, Louise de Marillac (who was herself a
widowed mother), they were enclosed only by obedience and had the fear of
God as their 'grille'.[77] In England, too, Mary Ward caused a commotion when
she established a female congregation in 1603. Modelled upon the Jesuits, her

Institute of the Blessed Virgin Mary rejected traditional enclosure and, as a consequence, the sisters were dismissed as 'wandering nuns' or 'galloping girls'.[78] These communities had rebelled against the legislation of the Council of Trent, which had attempted to regulate the position of women within the Church. While the Council Fathers disciplined the priesthood through scrutiny and training, 'women were regulated by removing them from society – placing them beyond the realm of sin' contained by the security of the cloister.[79] For breaking these norms, Ward was imprisoned by the Inquisition in Germany for two months in 1731. It was not until 1749 that Pope Benedict XIV's encyclical *Quamvis Iusto* recognised the legitimacy of the institute and, by extension, in ending forced enclosure, conceded the right of women to form a new style of religious life.[80]

Nagle extended this initiative to Ireland. She had identified the ignorance of religion as the root cause of the misery of the poor, and her Sisters embraced the contemporary European 'ideology of the schools', which argued that only in childhood instruction could vice be destroyed and virtue established.[81] The young servant girl who presented in confession at St John's appeared to justify this faith and Fr Power was excited by the possibility of what could be achieved if a Presentation foundation were established in Waterford. The realisation of that dream was achieved through kinship-based co-operation which became the pattern of the diffusion of religious communities in the period. Two of the priest's family, Ellen Power, his widowed sister-in-law Margaret Power, and a companion, Mary Mullowney, travelled to Cork to make their novitiate as Presentation Sisters.[82] They subsequently returned to Waterford in 1798 to open their school at Hennessy's Road, funded from their dowries.

From the outset, the project had the eager support of Edmund Rice, who gave the sisters financial advice. In 1796, he leased a site for the sisters and the initial accounts of the convent are partly in his handwriting. He signed the wills of eleven of the early sisters; he acted as agent and business manager and provided for their financial security by affording them an annual interest of 10 per cent on their dowries, a rate in excess of any offered by a commercial bank. As late as 1825, such mundane details as a supply of cocoa appear in his writing in the sister's cash book.[83] His interest however was not purely commercial and it appears that, at last, the novelty of the Presentation life provided the resolution of his agonizing search.

Revisionist interpretations, beginning with Br Ambrose O'Hanlon in the 1970s, have rejected the traditional emphasis upon the extent to which Rice was moved by Nagle's example and the sense in which he was inspired to do for the boys of Waterford what she had done for girls in Cork.[84] Yet Rice's confessor, preaching his panegyric, stressed this influence, and the 'noble example' of the Ladies of the Presentation which 'stimulated the man whose memory we this day honour, to share in their meritorious labours'.[85]

Moreover, of the few anecdotes of Edmund Rice which survive from the period, one describes a seminal encounter between himself and a friar when they shared a room at an inn, in some unidentified market town.[86] The friar prayed throughout the night, and the merchant was so deeply affected by this experience that it has been identified as a crucial breakthrough in his spiritual development. Indeed, David Fitzpatrick has described Rice's account of this Emmaus encounter as 'the only recorded occasion when he disclosed the inner workings of grace in his soul'.[87] In his spiritual biography, O'Toole has suggested that the 'pious friar' may have been Lawrence Callanan (1739–1818), Nano Nagle's Franciscan confessor who had been invited by Bishop Moylan to write the rule and constitutions for the Presentation Sisters in 1791.[88] The friar was eminently suited for this task, since in 1786 he had been appointed apostolic vistor to the Irish Franciscan foundations on the Continent, with a special brief to study educational methods.[89] If Callanan was indeed the friar, this stimulating encounter may have prompted Rice towards his ultimate vocation and a resolution of his quest.

Recognition of this Presentation influence, however, is not to suggest that Edmund Rice 'joined a spiritual movement that was both middle class and feminine', or that the Brothers could 'legitimately be described as "male nuns"'.[90] It shows rather how a confluence of circumstances gave shape to Rice's mission as founder of a congregation of teaching brothers. Moreover, rather than being possessed of an exclusive vision, the merchant's vocation was honed within the dynamics of an influential founding circle, which included bishops (or future bishops) Hussey, Lanigan and Power; colleagues and collaborators, John Rice, 'Miss Power', the Jesuit society centred upon St Patrick's and possibly the 'pious friar' Lawrence Callanan.

CHAPTER FIVE

'Poor Presentation monks', 1802–22

T HERE WAS NO DRAMATIC EPIPHANY in Edmund Rice's groping towards discernment, but the example of Nano Nagle, her life and the hybrid congregation which she had created, served as a prism to direct what had previously appeared as the irreconcilable attractions of a religious vocation and the care of the poor. Inspired by her example, and galvanised by Bishop Hussey's advocacy of Catholic education, Rice put ideas of a contemplative life behind him and embarked on his mission to do for the neglected poor Catholic boys of Waterford what Nano Nagle had done for the girls of Cork.

I

A combination of good fortune and business acumen had allowed Rice amass a considerable fortune. He benefited greatly from the agricultural boom, and in 1787 acquired the family holding at Ballykeefe on the death of his father. Seven years later he inherited his uncle's thriving mercantile business in Waterford. The young merchant was thus ideally placed to reap the benefits of the economic miracle, and by 1802 he possessed what Fr John Power later described as a 'large private fortune'.[2] Like so many of his class, Rice had a deep mistrust of the banking system and was nervous about the hugely increased volume and variety of paper money in circulation.[3] The gradual repeal of the penal laws, however, allowed him to invest his profits in landed property. A deed of conveyance drawn up in 1815 indicates that he held house property and as much as 1,500 acres in his own right spread over the counties of Kilkenny, Tipperary and Laois. In addition, he owned the Garter Inn at Callan, ten houses in Waterford, and three on St Stephen's Green, Dublin.[4] This property had a capital value of £50,000 and rent alone could earn its owner as much as £5,000 each year, the equivalent of one quarter of the total spent by the Catholics of Waterford building their magnificent cathedral.[5]

Booming demand for agricultural produce, however, increased social tensions throughout the south of Ireland. Rents rose, and this in turn created land hunger and all the associated grievances opposed by the Whiteboys and

5.1 Arundel Square, Waterford (*c.*1900). Poole Studios, NLI.

Rightboys in the 1780s. Yet for Edmund Rice the period had brought prosperity, and he benefited greatly from his extensive contracts with the Admiralty, particularly since the advent of war with France in 1793. During the rebellion of 1798, these government connections guaranteed his geographic mobility, and he was one of the few allowed to pass unchallenged at all the military posts in Carrick, Waterford, Clonmel, Tipperary and Limerick.[6] Nevertheless, Rice must have been struck by the misery inflicted during the summer of 1798, when upwards of 30,000 perished in the violence.[7] Fortunately he was in a position to save from execution John Rice, the husband of his half-sister Jane Murphy. Known as 'the Wild Rapparree', he had fallen foul of the authorities during the rebellion. Edmund Rice hid him in his home until an opportunity arose and then he was smuggled in a barrel to Newfoundland. Many others were less fortunate and, in the following year, Rice witnessed the grisly execution of a nephew of his friend, Thomas Hearn, vicar general of the diocese and architect

of the Catholic revival in Waterford and Lismore.[8] Young Francis Hearn had
been a seminarian at Maynooth, but was expelled in the purge of radical students in May 1798. He joined Carlow College, but was taken up in the white
terror which followed the suppression of '98, on charges of United Irish membership, swearing, and organising rebellion as late as September 1799. His arrest
was seized upon as further ammunition by propagandists in an effort to blacken
the reputation of Maynooth and the Catholic clergy in general. His execution
in Waterford became a public spectacle; on the scaffold before a large crowd he
was interrogated by Fr William Power, of Ballybricken, in an effort to demonstrate the loyalty of the Church. The unfortunate Hearn lamented ever having
seen the United Irishmen who swore him, and declared them unfit persons to
live in society.[9] There was no mercy, however, and the seminarian's confession
served only to undermine further the reputation of Bishop Hussey and added
fuel to the bitter sectarian polemic then raging.[10]

Thomas Hussey had left Ireland in the tumult that followed the publication
of his controversial pastoral, so it fell to the dean to implement the bishop's
ambitious plan for the erection of a diocesan system of elementary schools.
Dean Hearn was among the influential circle whose example inspired Rice to
embrace the cause of education. In September 1799, Hearn had called a meeting of the leading Catholics in Waterford to establish a fund to build schools
across the diocese. It is probable that Rice was included in the group assembled
by the dean and, no doubt, the enthusiasm of the gathering served to confirm
his resolution to devote his life and resources to the provision of Catholic education. As a consequence of the meeting, Hearn rejoiced that 'we are busy now
in procuring schoolhouses for the poor children of both sexes'. It is within this
context of a diocesan campaign, then, rather than in isolation, that Rice
embarked upon a course which would produce a revolution in Irish education.

II

Edmund Rice was no St Francis. He was not a founder who gave up all to follow
Christ, but rather he retained his considerable property and investment, and
with these financed his schools.[11] This may have justified the bitter folkloric recollection that he had 'financed his schools' from ill-gotten gains.[12] Or, indeed,
the criticism of his bitter enemy, Bishop Robert Walsh, that his Brothers went
'to the fairs and markets, buying and selling cattle and collecting rents and exe-
cuting seizures, like common landlords, against the poor to exact rent'.[13]

Moreover, this failure to surrender his property to the congregation caused very significant conflicts in his latter years. Rice sold his provisioning business to his friend Thomas Quan, who from 1790 had been a fellow member of the confraternity in Waterford. The proceeds from this sale financed the purchase of a three-acre site at Ballybricken and part of the £3,000 spent on the construction of a new school.

In theory, at least, the penal restrictions on Catholic education had been repealed by the time Edmund Rice began his great project. In practice however, there were still obstacles and prejudices to be overcome. The Relief Act of 1782 declared Catholic schoolmasters legally free to teach on the condition that they took an oath of allegiance and obtained a license from the local Protestant bishop. Hercules Langrishe's Relief Act of 1792 made the latter requirement unnecessary, but the benefits of this concession were removed in 1799 by the imposition of a hefty window tax which applied to non-licensed schools. It seems likely that Edmund Rice received a licence for his new school. In many cases application was a mere formality, but attitudes varied. In 1799 Anastasia Tobin, foundress of the Ursuline convent in Thurles, was granted a licence; in the same year the Presentation Sisters of Waterford made a successful application to Bishop Marley; but as late as 1814 a licence was refused to Fr Peter Kenney SJ for his school at Clongowes Wood in County Kildare.[14]

Further complications threatened Rice's project. After 1782 the endowment of Catholic schools was forbidden by law, while the third clause of the 1791 Relief Act forbade the foundation of any association or society bound by religious or monastic vows. The latter restriction, like so many of its kind, was more than likely a dead letter from its enactment. It may indeed have been included simply to placate the bitter opposition to Catholic relief from the ultra-loyalist faction within the Irish parliament. The question of endowment was a more serious obstacle, which was further complicated by a clause in the 1793 Relief Act which forbade the establishment of schools and colleges *exclusively* for Catholic education. In the short term, however, Rice could afford to ignore these impediments. He had not yet considered religious consecration and the schools would be financed from his own purse.

Without waiting for the completion of a permanent school, Rice began teaching in an old stable in New Street. This building, known for many years as 'Elliott's Yard', may have been inherited from his wife 'Mary Elliott'; if so, no location could have been more appropriate for his mission to begin. Rice moved from the comfort of Arundel Place, and his half-sister Joan returned to Callan, along with his daughter Mary, who was by then in her late teens. Rice lived above the stable, where three ground-floor rooms were fitted out for school. Conditions were primitive; furniture was sparse, and benches were borrowed each day from Buggy's pub in Barrack Street nearby.[15] Br McCarthy has left us with an idealised description of the master and his first pupils in 1802:

> Very soon the rooms were filled with boys, poor lads utterly ignorant of even the first notions of religious or secular knowledge. They were rude and rough in manner and not all amenable to the salutary restraints of school discipline. But Edmund Rice, joining to a commanding presence an agreeable and winning manner, gained the confidence of the most wayward, and soon established regularity and discipline in the school.[16]

The reality, however, was less spectacular. Initially he was assisted by two paid assistants, but these soon abandoned him, leaving him to his own devices. Nevertheless, from a modest start – with as few as six pupils in a night school – the rooms were soon so thronged that he was forced to open a second school in Stephen Street nearby. Gradually Rice assembled strips of land at Ballybricken, where he intended to build a school. Through the influence of friends in the Wyse Trustees, he was able to acquire the site of the old Faha chapel and, in a reflection of his close bonds with the Presentation Sisters, he purchased a small passageway to their convent on Hennessy's Road so he could attend Mass there.

At the beginning Bishop Hussey was an ardent supporter of Edmund Rice's plan. His controversial pastoral had prompted Rice to take the great step, and he laid the foundation stone of the new school in June 1802. During that year, however, a strange coolness developed between the two; the bishop lost interest in the school and appears to have become quite hostile to the project. The explanation for this unexpected change is unclear, but it may be attributed to two factors that surfaced frequently in Edmund Rice's life – human jealousy and the vexed question of episcopal authority.

Jealousy needs no explanation (Rice could certainly excite that emotion), but the exercise of episcopal authority was more problematic. A combination of his own character and circumstances made Rice's venture extraordinarily independent and open to misunderstanding. He had supplied both the initiative and the finance, and in this way was answerable to no one, least of all the local bishop. This was complicated further by the fact that the Faha site was ecclesiastical property, leased to Rice by Dean Hearn acting for the diocese in the absence of the bishop.[17] Thomas Hussey was a prickly individual; his service in the Spanish embassy in London had made him extremely conscious of protocol, and he jealously guarded what he regarded as the episcopal prerogatives. Unwittingly, Edmund Rice may have offended the bishop's sensitivities; he had stepped beyond the acceptable limit, establishing a Catholic school free from clerical supervision (this was not unlike the conflict that developed between Bishop Francis Moylan and Nano Nagle following her initial foundation at Cove Lane, in Cork). Fr John Power, one of Rice's oldest friends, suggested a way out of this delicate situation.[18] He advised Rice to draw up a deed of assignment handing the site over to the bishop, reserving only a life-interest for himself. In this way, Power believed, he would 'prove [his] submission to his Lordship and the baseless character of the stories he has been told, as well as the vileness of the motives ascribed to [him]'.[19]

It is idle to speculate on the nature of these rumours or the vile motives attributed to Edmund Rice, but throughout his life critics were never slow to allude to less attractive aspects of his personality and to sins of his youth. Twenty years later, for instance, in a vitriolic attack clerical enemies in Waterford castigated him as 'a common Butcher' and father of several 'bastard' children.[20] In 1802, it appears that there were those in the city who remained cynical about Rice's conversion, not surprising if he had been engaged in money-lending and aggressive property speculation, as it has been alleged. Fortunately, Hussey was content with Rice's gesture in regard to the Faha site, which was a very significant move, since the bishop could have made no claim, either civil or ecclesiastical, on the property.[21] By this offer Rice had become not only a tenant of the bishop, but his submission to Dr Hussey was a very public and legally binding statement of his new departure. The deed was duly registered and an important milestone had been passed. Rice had brought his mission under episcopal supervision, and secured a generous benefactor in the process. Ironically, just as Francis Moylan took credit for *his* Presentation Sisters, so, too, Hussey was lauded for *his* Waterford initiative.[22]

Thomas Hussey blessed the completed residence at Ballybricken in June 1803. Commenting on its elevated site above the port, he alluded to the Holy City of Jerusalem: 'all things considered, I think a very appropriate name would be Mount Sion, and so I name it'.[23] One month later, the bishop died suddenly at Tramore, having taken a fit while swimming there. Even in death Hussey managed to rouse strong feelings, and his funeral became the scene of a violent protest. As his remains were being brought to Waterford for burial, the funeral procession was interrupted by a group of drunken soldiers returning from an Orange meeting who tried to throw his remains into the river Suir. Thomas

Hearn later described for Lord Donoughmore how this mob had 'uttered the most abusive threats to cut up his remains and his friends'.[24] Among those friends was Edmund Rice, to whom Thomas Hussey left the greater part of his estate; apart from a bequest of £2,000, five masters were each to be paid £20 per annum, Rice was to receive a salary for life and funds were provided to clothe poor boys.[25]

III

For Edmund Rice, the provision of education was simply an apostolate; his desire was to live the life of a religious. Others shared his vision and within months of opening his school in New Street he was joined by two Callan men, Thomas Grosvenor and Patrick Finn. Together they formed a religious community which prayed together, attended daily Mass and devoted time to spiritual reading. Bishop Hussey's last report to Rome in June 1803 contained a description of this fledgling congregation:

> some few men have been formed into a society who eagerly desire to bind themselves by the three solemn vows of chastity, poverty and obedience under the rules similar to those of the [Presentation] Sisters, and already a convent has been built where four holy men reside who seek approbation of their rules whenever it will be deemed advisable by the Holy See.[26]

In his will, too, Hussey referred to Edmund Rice not by location but, 'of the Society of the Presentation', even though the Brothers had as yet no canonical status.[27]

From the beginning, then, Rice and his companions followed the vision which would later be enshrined in the first chapter of the constitutions of his society:

> The end of the Institute is that all its members labour in the first place for their own perfection and in the second for that of their neighbour by a serious application to the instruction of male children, especially the poor, in the principles of religion and Christian piety.[28]

The annals of the Christian Brothers in Thurles, County Tipperary, expressed the purpose of the founding group more colloquially; however, both reflect the Tridentine imperative of 'faith and good works', which inspired Ignatius Loyola, Angela Merici and the great religious founders in the early modern period:

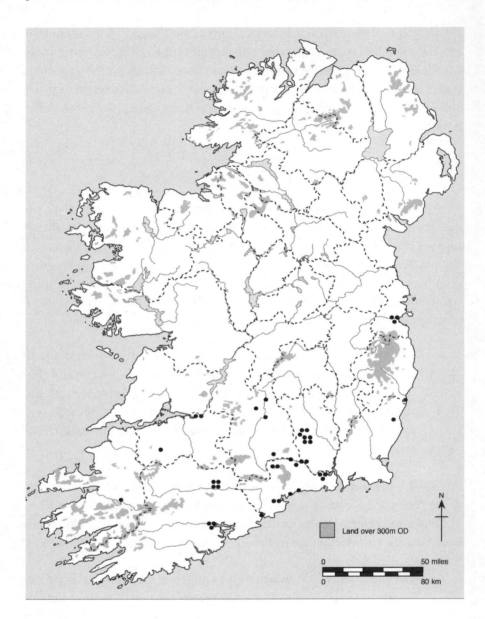

Land over 300m OD

N

0   50 miles
0   80 km

5.2 Birthplace of the Brothers of the Society of the Presentation, 1802–21.
Source: Br W. A. O'Hanlon, *The Early Brothers of the Society of the Presentation*
(Dublin, 1979). Map drawn by Matthew Stout.

Their chief object was to sanctify themselves, to give good example, to encourage others, especially the young and to teach and keep alive in the latter the principles and practice of the Catholic religion.[29]

The school at Mount Sion opened its doors and was blessed by Hussey's successor and Rice's old friend, John Power, on 1 May 1804. There were then over 300 boys on the roll and before long the accommodation proved inadequate. Additional rooms were secured and the Brothers opened a night school to educate the illiterate and instruct them in the catechism.

The Brothers' charity extended beyond the provision of education.[30] Just as the proselytising schools provided charity, or what Hussey had called 'specious pretexts', to attract the children of the poor, so Rice's school at Mount Sion attended to the physical needs of the boys.[31] A small bake house was built to provide the poorer pupils with a daily meal of bread and milk. For many years, too, a tailor was employed at Mount Sion repairing tattered clothes and distributing suits to the poor.[32] The plight of prisoners, too, remained a priority for Rice. Many of the *Memories* recall Rice's visits to the cells; how he interceded for debtors and often escorted condemned men to the gallows:

> This was a special privilege extended to Br Rice as he was credited with having a wonderful power of moving to repentance some of those hardened people who seemed callous when appealed to by the clergy even.[33]

Contemporary reports highlight the misery of the prisons, but the Brothers were 'ever to be found' administering to prisoners and alleviating their sufferings.[34] Rice's generosity to prisoners was expansive; surviving account books record that on one visit to the gaol, at Christmas 1808, he distributed 42 half-crowns to the poor inmates.[35] In the great humanitarian disasters of the age, too, the Brothers were prominent in their attempts to relieve the sufferings of the poor. In the Asiatic cholera pandemic of 1832, which claimed 25,000 Irish lives, the Brothers made their monasteries and schools available as temporary hospitals. Rice was particularly concerned at the plight of 'the very poorest class', but derived comfort from the heroic efforts of his confreres, particularly in Limerick where the annals record the death of 525 patients in the makeshift hospital established at the Brothers' school at Clare Street.[36] In the Great Famine, too, the Brothers responded to the misery around them. The annals of the North Monastery record Br John Baptist Leonard feeding 300 starving children daily in Cork during 'Black '47', while in Dublin Brothers from Francis Street attended to the fever patients in the hospital at Kilmainham.[37]

While Thomas Hussey informed the Roman authorities, in 1803, of the Brothers' desire to be bound by solemn vows, no moves were made towards a formal recognition of the 'monks', as they were called, until 1808.[38] In this sense, there was little to separate Rice's group from the pious teaching communities of laymen, or 'monks', which had sprung up in Cork, Thurles, Kilkenny and other towns in the south east. These groups, rather like the medieval Beghards, lived a semi-religious, austere lifestyle, but they were not bound by formal religious vows. Rice hoped to change this.

He 'pressed' and 'begged' Bishop Power to admit his Brothers to vows.[39] His anxiety was fuelled by religious motives, but it is certain, too, that a public profession would afford his little group ecclesiastical recognition and the prospect of permanence. Episcopal approval would also serve to dispel any lingering disquiet about Rice's character and 'the motives ascribed to [him]'.[40] Various reasons have been given for the bishop's delay: the penal prohibition on the formation of new religious orders, the question of exclusively Catholic schools, the issue of endowments, and the continuation of the war with France. None of these explanations is convincing.[41] Similarly, the timing of Rice's eventual profession in 1808 has been attributed to changing political circumstances which suggested 'the dawn of [Catholic] emancipation was on the horizon'.[42] Neither is this explanation satisfactory; the duke of Portland's administration not only sought to shelve the emancipation issue, but also fought the 1807 general election successfully on a 'no popery' platform. In these circumstances Henry Grattan's petition for emancipation had little hope of success, and the emergence of a divisive controversy on the proposed royal veto on episcopal nominations blighted future prospects.[43]

The decision to allow religious profession was more likely due to practical rather than political considerations. It was eight years since Rice had begun his mission in Elliott's yard; nine Brothers were by then living the life of Christian educators in three communities, at Waterford, Carrick-on-Suir and Dungarvan. Within the diocese, too, Rice enjoyed the support of the clergy, and Bishop John Power had been among his closest friends and supporters. The Presentation nuns in Waterford had made their solemn vows according to their new rule on 15 August 1806, while, in the diocese of Kildare and Leighlin, Bishop Daniel Delaney had received the first four members into the Patrician Brothers in February 1808.[44] All of these factors indicated that the opportune moment had arrived.

Bishop Power welcomed Rice's request for profession and it was agreed that the three communities would assemble at Mount Sion on the feast of the

5.3 First profession of Edmund Ignatius Rice and his companions,
15 August 1808, CBGA.

Assumption to make their commitment in common. On 15 August 1808 eight
Brothers made annual vows according to the rule and constitution of the
Presentation Order.[45] One of Rice's earliest followers, Thomas Brien of the
Carrick community, chose not to proceed. Despite his well-intentioned zeal, the
gruelling regime of the schools had proved too much for the 60-year-old who
returned to Waterford where he resumed his wine merchant's business.

The Brothers were now religious living in temporary vows under episcopal
'authority and jurisdiction', but all concerned were anxious that the
congregation would be placed on a more secure footing.[46] With this in mind,
Bishop Power submitted a petition to the Holy See requesting Apostolic
approval of the new institute. This appeal met with a favourable response from
Propaganda Fide, which granted provisional approval, pending the submission
of a rule and constitutions.[47] Encouraged by this development, the bishop
agreed to admit the Brothers to perpetual vows in 1809. Once more, however,
not all of his companions made this long-hoped-for profession. Br John Power
returned home, while Rice's first disciple, Patrick Finn, left Ireland to join the
Cistercian monastery at Melleray in France. He returned in 1833 and was among
the founding members of the monastic community at Mount Melleray Abbey,
County Waterford.

III

The young congregation lived an austere and regimented lifestyle according to an adaptation of the Presentation Rule, written for the sisters by Laurence Callanan OFM, the pious friar of Rice's conversion story.[48] At his first profession, Rice chose 'Ignatius' as his name in religion, and afterwards it became the practice for novices to choose the names of saints whose spirituality or heroic virtue inspired them. That choice, in preference, for example, to Kieran, patron of Ossory, or Declan of Ardmore, illustrated the extent to which his spirituality was that of the European Catholic Reformation. The original Presentation Rule embodied that spirituality, too, with its echoes of St Francis de Sales (1567–1622) and focus upon diligence in prayer, self-improvement and good works.[49] Moreover, the Rule reflected Nano Nagle's enthusiasm for the reformed devotions of the early modern Church: the Passion, the Eucharist, the Sacred Heart of Jesus and the Virgin Mary.[50] Rice accentuated that culture by his addition of John the Baptist, Teresa of Avila and Ignatius of Loyola to the litany of sixteen saints to whom the Rule urged particular devotion.[51]

John the Baptist was included as an exemplar for religious, who had attained 'the most eminent degrees of poverty, chastity and obedience'.[52] Rice's spiritual biographer has described St John as an unusual model for religious, but notes the traditional devotion to him within Gaelic society.[53] Such devotion, however, was ambiguous since St John's Eve was celebrated not so much in honour of the Baptist, but, as the pagan festival of the summer solstice, a celebration fiercely opposed by John Troy and the reforming bishops of Rice's generation. There was no such ambiguity about St Teresa, whose insertion in the Rule reflected Rice's special affection for the Spanish mystic, whose writings inspired his mature years. One of his companions, Austin Grace, provided a very intimate recollection of Rice's remarkable devotion to St Teresa:

> He kept a picture of the saint in his room, and often he would be seen pressing his lips to it. His devotion to the great saint became more remarkable as his life drew to a close, but as might be expected his devotion to the Holy Mother of God was most intense.[54]

The influence of St Ignatius was reflected throughout the Rule, not least by the banner, *Ad Majorem Dei Gloriam,* at its head. Unlike traditional religious orders, the Jesuits did not recite or chant the liturgical hours, or office, in common in order to free them for the exercise of their dynamic apostolate. In a similar way,

5.4 St Ignatius of Loyola by Peter Paul Rubens (1577–1640).

the Brothers were obliged only to recite the short Office of Our Blessed Lady, which the early Jesuits had used and promoted among the literate laity. In addition, the Presentation Rule commended 'mental prayer', meditation and contemplation, to elevate the soul, and enflame the heart with the love of God and of heavenly things'.[55] The inclusion of this injunction was a further manifestation of the influence of the Catholic Reformation, which had seen meditation refined in the writings of Lorenzo Scupoli, author of Rice's prized *Spiritual Combat*, and St Ignatius, whose successor as general of the Jesuits, Diego Laínez, prized 'mental prayer' above the recitation of the Office or other formulaic prayers.[56] The Ignatian thrust was evident, too, in chapter nine of the Rule which advocated the 'Spiritual Exercises', annual retreats, at summer and Christmas, and monthly days of recollection for the community.[57]

Rice's spirituality, like that of his patron, was Christocentric with a strong Marian aspect. Love of God and love of neighbour, as expressed in the twenty-fifth chapter of Matthew's Gospel, animated the life of the early Brothers, but they were particularly devoted to the presence of Jesus in the Blessed Sacrament. Eucharistic Devotion became the hallmark of Rice's spirituality. From the first day at Mount Sion they reserved the Blessed Sacrament in their oratory, and their Rule encapsulated the Council of Trent's teaching on the Eucharist (Session XIII, 1551):

> The most holy Eucharist having been instituted by Jesus Christ for the nourishment of our souls as well as for our sacrifice, and as in it he imparts to us the most precious pledge of his love, the Brethren shall cherish the tenderest and most affectionate devotion towards this adorable Sacrament.[58]

The daily routine was punctuated by regular visits to the oratory and, while the Brothers attended Mass every morning, they were obliged to receive Communion only on Sundays and holy days. In a further reflection of early-modern practice, too, the Brothers were forbidden from going to Communion three days in succession without the permission of the superior. The Rule also reflected Trent's emphasis upon the sacrament of Confession (Session XIV, 1551).[59] The bishop was to appoint a confessor to each community and the Brothers were to approach the sacrament each Saturday and on 'the eves of great feasts'. In this sense the lives of the Presentation communities reflected the trend within the Church towards frequent Communion and Confession. This was a radical departure from traditional Irish practice, where the sacrament of

Confession was often merely an annual preparation for the reception of Easter Communion.[60]

Every hour of the day was regulated, and since 'idleness … "teacheth much evil"', no opportunity was left for the Brothers to 'giddily [lose] their precious time'.[61] Chapter twenty of the Rule, which established the *horarium* of the community, contains not simply an account of the lifestyle of the brothers, but a succinct résumé of their spirituality and purpose:

1 The Brethren of this Congregation shall rise, every morning, winter and summer, at five o'clock, making the sign of the Cross on themselves and giving their first thoughts to God. They shall dress themselves with dignity and modesty, take the holy water, and on their knees offer themselves and all the actions of the day to Almighty God.

2 At a quarter after five, they shall assemble in the chapel for common prayer and meditation, which shall continue until six o'clock. They shall finish with the *Angelus Domini*, the litany of the Holy Name of Jesus, and a few prayers for particular intentions, such as the exaltation of the holy Catholic Church, for His Holiness the Pope, the Bishops and clergy, the conversion of sinners, and perseverance of the just; and a *Pater Noster*, and *Ave Maria*, in honour of the Sacred Heart of Jesus. Then they shall recite together the small Hours of Prime, Tierce, Sext and None, after which they shall retire to make their beds and clear up their cells.

3 At seven o'clock they shall attend at Mass, and after it, they shall say the *De profundis*, with three orations, *Deus qui inter Apostolicos Sacerdotes, Deus veniae largitor, Fidelium Deus*, etc.

4 At eight o'clock breakfast, in common; spiritual lecture if time permits. Then preparation for schools, which shall open at nine o'clock and hold till twelve.

5 At a quarter before twelve, particular examen (excepting the Brothers, who give the spiritual instructions at that time) which they shall close with the *Angelus Domini*, and the Acts of Contrition, Faith, Hope and Charity, with devotional prayers for such intentions as the Father Superior may judge proper, not exceeding five *Paters* and *Aves*.

6 At a quarter after three, dinner, before and after which they shall say the usual prayers. They shall go after dinner in procession, two by two, to the chapel to say the Psalms, *Miserere*, and the oration, *Respice, quae-*

sumus Domine super hanc familiam tuam, etc. Then recreation until five o'clock.

7 At five o'clock Vespers and Compline, after which they shall offer devotional prayers for such intentions as the exigencies of the time, or particular circumstances may require, and for this purpose, shall recite five *Paters* and *Aves*, in honour of the passion and death of our Lord and Saviour Jesus Christ. At six, the *Angelus Domini* with devotional prayers for the Bishop and priests of the diocese, and a spiritual lecture for a quarter of an hour.

8 At seven o'clock, meditation for half an hour, after which they shall recite Matins and Lauds. At eight o'clock, supper or collation, after which they shall say the usual prayers and go, as after dinner, to chapel to say the *Magnificat*, the verse, *Ora pro nobis*, and the oration *Concede*.

9 At nine o'clock, they shall assemble in the chapel for night prayers, to make their examen and to read or hear the subject of next morning's meditation. After which they shall retire in silence to their respective cells, and be in bed by ten o'clock.[62]

This was, in essence, a remarkably ascetical regime which stood out in stark contrast to the laxity which contemporaries noted in the lifestyles of the friars and older religious orders in Ireland.[63] The Brothers lived their life as an oblation to God in the service of the schools. The Rule reflected this wholehearted commitment to their new state of life, which made demands in excess of that required by contemporary apostolic congregations, including the De La Salle order which had pioneered the vocation of the teaching Brother.

Rice envisioned a humble and ascetic lifestyle for his Brothers. They had renounced the world, and their rule regulated the various communities accordingly, so as 'to cut away as much as possible what might tend to introduce its spirit'.[64] They observed a spirit of enclosure, in which the school was their cloister, and were forbidden from 'going beyond the limits marked out for them, except with the express leave' of the superior, who they were to obey, 'as having authority from God'.[65] Within the community, too, they were to observe the rule of silence, 'the ornament of religious souls and the faithful guardian of interior recollection'.[66] They were to have minimal contact with the world; restrictions on 'intercourse with seculars' would become a feature of later regulations, but in the original rule the injunctions on chastity urged the brothers to adopt the 'most guarded reserve' when 'spoken to by women of any state or profession'.[67]

This desire to shun the world was also behind successive attempts to banish newspapers from the various monasteries.[68] The Christian Brothers' chapter of 1829 restricted papers to the professed brothers, and advocated instead 'the study of historical, educational and religious periodicals'.[69] Three years later, during a reconnaissance of the De La Salle system in Paris, Br Bernard Dunphy noted that the French general had severely rebuked some of his brothers 'who had taken the liberty of reading newspapers, a practice which he declares to be very pernicious'.[70]

In their vow of poverty, the community renounced 'all property in earthly things' and this was reflected in the austerity of the Brothers' lifestyle.[71] Their clothes, made from rough cotton, were 'modest and grave'; their cells were simple and nothing about the monastery was 'superfluous, costly or rich'.[72] Meals were especially frugal, even by comparison to the French Brothers, whose diet was more generous and varied. Breakfast, at eight o'clock, consisted of porridge with bread, butter and milk. Nothing more was eaten until they returned from school; dinner, at 3.15 pm, was the last meal of the day. It consisted of 'boiled meat (rarely roast), with vegetables; no bread except on fast days' and water.[73] Rice prescribed the Lenten fasts, and throughout the year there were at least two meatless days per week. The only concession made on account of the 'arduous and laborious' duties of the schools, was that the Brothers were obliged to fast only on the days of abstinence ordered by the Church for the laity.[74]

In time, this spartan regime took its toll upon the Brothers; it contributed to the high attrition rate and the health of those who remained suffered. Within the congregation there was a desire for change, and the controversial 'general' chapter of 1829 added a simple supper of four ounces of bread and milk. Yet, despite the modesty of the change, in an age when a supper was universal, Rice was angered by this innovation, and attempted to reverse the decision by way of a circular letter which he addressed to the directors of the various houses.[75] Explaining his controversial action, he informed the superior general of the De La Salle Brothers, in Paris, that 'hitherto the quantity and quality of our food and beverages … was both wholesome and sufficient'.[76] Rice was anxious about the trend of such reforms and the extravagance of the change, within a context where postulants were being turned away, and the Order's novitiate remained unfinished for want of funds.[77] The circumstances of the chapter, however, were particularly fraught, and Rice faced significant opposition on a number of issues, as discussed in chapter ten. Yet, even though the changes initiated by the 'general' chapter were legally binding, Rice enquired of the French general whether the Brothers were obliged to live on bread and water, by virtue of their vows, 'if revenues decreased to a point where it is not possible to provide the regulation diet'.[78] This was not merely idle speculation, for the extreme poverty of the North Richmond Street schools suggest that the query related to that community.

Even in his advanced years and during periods of ill-health, Rice made great demands of himself. The Annals of the Christian Brothers recall that he was 'a mortified man, he denied himself in a variety of ways, but made no display of the acts of his virtue'.[79] There was, however, one dramatic recollection of his self-denial:

> For many years he had been a great snuff-taker. In one of his annual retreats he resolved to give up the habit completely. As if to signalise his renunciation of this luxury, he threw his snuff box into the fire and never after took snuff.[80]

On another occasion he refused to take punch for medicinal purposes unless it was made with salt rather than sugar.[81] At the chapter of 1829, too, he made an unsuccessful attempt to have included in the Rule a paragraph encouraging the use of hair shirts and other disciplines. However, one of the capitulants recalled that it took 'great effort and good management' to defeat the proposal, which was opposed by several of the older Brothers who regarded the work of the schools punishment enough.[82] Even without such formal obligations, however, many communities continued to practise various corporal austerities, including the use of hair shirts, chains and other disciplines which were an accepted part of contemporary mortification. The 1832 Rule, however, included an important caveat that no Brother would undertake any penances which would 'injure his bodily strength which is so necessary for discharging the duties of the institute'.[83]

Austin Dunphy's 'Origin', the earliest history of the congregation, described the purpose of Edmund Rice's little band in classical terms:

> Their motives, in … associating together, were, in the first place to with-draw from the dangers of a sinful world: and … to sanctify themselves by frequenting the Holy Sacraments, by prayer … and the works of mercy, especially that of instructing poor ignorant boys in the principles of Religion and Christian piety. [84]

The Presentation Rule provided the first brothers with the framework in which to live this life. Their fidelity to its aspirations won them great esteem and it was arguably the quality of their lives that caused their work to be successful.[85]

Indeed, the *Manual of School Government* (1845) reminded the Brothers that their efforts as educators would bear fruit proportionate to the pursuit of their own sanctification.[86] The founding group was in the vanguard of the Catholic revival which characterised the age. Yet while this process of renewal had begun as an episcopal initiative, by the early years of the new century the baton had passed to the new religious orders; within this context the efforts of the Brothers were recommended to Rome as 'praiseworthy and advantageous to religion'.[87] But it was in the classroom that the Brothers would make the greatest contribution to the reformation of Irish Catholicism.

CHAPTER SIX

The Brothers' schools, 1802–45

FROM A HUMBLE START IN Waterford's New Street, Edmund Rice took the first steps towards the achievement of a revolution in Irish education. Beginning with a handful of rough lads in a thatched mews, he began a process of experimentation in which he tried and tested the best practice of the age. These early days were a learning experience for the teacher as much as for the students, yet by 1810 a process of practical adaptation produced a system which remained a model for Catholic education for over a century. Through its careful implementation the Brothers effected a transformation of Catholicism and the modernisation of Irish society, by providing their pupils not merely with a 'useful education', but with a moral vision which supported the creation of a new Ireland.

I

In continental Europe, the early modern period witnessed the emergence of a distinctly Catholic pedagogy which reflected the Jesuit dictum that 'the well being of Christianity and of the whole world depends on the proper education of youth.'[1] In contrast to the spirit of the Reformation, which emphasised the relationship of the individual with God, it rooted man within an ecclesial context and was directed towards his moral formation and the salvation of his soul. Such sentiments were at the heart of the mission of Edmund Rice who was not simply concerned with the provision of education, but rather one which embraced the evangelisation of youth.[2] These priorities were expressed in the opening chapter of his Presentation Rule, which identified among the ends of the institute 'the instruction of poor boys in the principles of religion and Christian piety'.[3]

The need for such education was identified by a succession of reforming bishops whose introduction of the Confraternity of the Christian Doctrine into their dioceses had been an interim measure. In Waterford, Thomas Hussey had made education a priority of his episcopate, and his pastoral address served as a catalyst in Rice's process of discernment. In the case of Nano Nagle, too, her choice of vocation was described by her episcopal biographer in ways which reflected the anxiety of the bishops at the alienation of the poor from the institutional Church. Moreover, Bishop Coppinger's description of 'the bleak ignorance' that confronted Nagle at every turn echoed the bourgeois preoccupation with the need for the moral reformation of the lower orders.[4] The French Revolution had shown the superficiality of religious faith and practice in France, but the alarming susceptibility of Irish Catholics to the 'French disease', as conservatives described radical politics, brought home the tenuous nature of the Church's call on the loyalty of the people, who had ignored the threat of excommunication and embraced the rebel cause.

From a Protestant perspective, too, the rebellion of 1798 had demonstrated the volatility of the island and highlighted the necessity of extending popular elementary education, not merely as a safeguard against future political calamity, but as an engine of social and economic regeneration. These sentiments, which fuelled a wide-ranging debate in the first decades of the new century about the nature, range and form of education, were succinctly articulated by the English educationalist Joseph Lancaster (1778–1838) in his ambitious 'plan for the poor of Ireland' (1805):

> The feelings of the Irish Nation are strong, and their passions sometimes dangerous in the extreme. It is by informing the minds and reforming the morals of the people that Ireland will attain its proper dignity among the virtuous nations. It is possible for Ireland, by its reformation, to prove to Europe the benefits derived from education.[5]

Of course, many reformers, particularly those inspired by the evangelical revival, equated 'reformation' with conversion to the Reformed Church. Their sentiments inspired the so-called proselytising schools and were central to the educational programme of the later 'Second Reformation', which hoped to eradicate vice and, by its conversion, to make Ireland loyal and industrious.[6]

Edmund Rice lived in that 'Age of Moral Reform' and was hailed as a 'bold reformer' by the patriot Thomas Francis Meagher.[7] He embraced the modernizing ideal and the 'Protestant ethic', but he sought to achieve a distinctly 'Catholic Reformation' through the provision of 'useful education' which would benefit not only the poor, but the church and state.[8] Like his peers, he aimed to impress upon the young 'the maxims of a virtuous life', and the critical focus of his system was upon the 'moral improvement of the Scholars'.[9] He sought not just to provide a literary education but to rescue boys from idleness and to teach them how to behave as useful members of modern society. In Rice's expression, his Brothers laboured 'to train up … children in early habits of solid virtue, and to instil in their young minds principles of integrity, veracity and social order'.[10] Such motives were indicative of a social conservatism, born out of the turmoil of the 1790s, yet the implementation of his system led to the emergence of a meritocracy which in time would undermine the existing social order.

The earliest description of the Brothers' regime is contained in the oldest extant letter of Edmund Rice addressed to Archbishop Thomas Bray of Cashel in 1810 (see Appendix 2), which outlines the philosophy and structure of the education offered to the boys at Mount Sion and the schools of the fledgling congregation. Together with a letter written by one of his earliest disciples, Br Thomas Grosvenor, to the parish priest of Preston in Lancashire, it illustrates the comprehensive nature of the system which Rice had put in place within a decade of his first efforts.[11] Rice of course was not an educationalist, but a successful businessman. His own education was limited, but the routine in his schools reflects a judicious borrowing from best practice and the insights of contemporary reformers and their pedagogical innovations, including those of Edgeworth, Lancaster and Bell.

Fortunately, too, between 1806 and 1812, a Royal Commission, styled the 'Board of Education', produced fourteen reports and recommendations on Irish schooling.[12] Rice reflected on their conclusions, and on the merits of the schools conducted by the Kildare Place Society and the subsequent National Board, to produce a system which visitors to Mount Sion believed contained all that was 'most practical and useful in recent improvements'.[13] He also drew from his memories of the 'Academy' in Callan, but he radically improved the traditional teaching methods of the 'hedge schools' to satisfy the demands of the large numbers his urban schools attracted.[14] The Presentation influence was central to his project, too, not simply because of his observation of their 'little schools' in Cork and Waterford, but because the Sisters, like his own Brothers, were religious, vowed to the education of the poor.

Fr Laurence Callanan had given the Presentation Rule, which the Brothers adopted in 1802, a distinctly European character. It reflected the influence of Jean-Baptiste de la Salle (1651–1719) who had systematised the pedagogy of the Catholic Reformation. Indeed, his *Conduct of Christian Schools* was to education what the *Spiritual Exercises* were to spirituality in the period.[15] He developed the modern management and teaching methods which subsequent religious founders, including Edmund Rice, sought to emulate. In the large urban schools of France, his Frères des Ecoles Chrétiennes, prepared the chil-

CONDUITE

DES

ÉCOLES CHRÉTIENNES,

DIVISÉE EN DEUX PARTIES;

*Composée par Messire DE LA SALLE,
Prêtre-Docteur en Théologie, et Ins-
tituteur des Frères des Écoles Chrétiennes.*

Prenez garde à vous, et ayez soin d'enseigner
les autres ; persévérez dans ces exercices , car
par ce moyen vous vous sauverez vous - même,
et vous sauverez ceux qui vous écoutent.
1. *Epit.* à TIMOTH. 4 , v. 16.

A LYON,

CHEZ RUSAND , LIBRAIRE , IMPRIMEUR DU CLERGÉ.
1823.

6.1 Title page of the De La Salle teaching manual, first received by the
Christian Brothers in 1826. DLSGA, Rome.

dren for their future lives as good Christians and subjects in an increasingly industrialised society. As Sarah Curtis has observed:

> The structure of their school lives, even more than the content of their lessons, emphasised the kind of method and order that employers and notables hoped would result in a well disciplined society and polity … To them, social order and religious order were fundamentally connected. [16]

The elites of nineteenth-century Ireland were no different in their expectations and it was the Brothers' ability to satisfy their aspirations which won them enthusiastic approval.

The Irish Brothers initiated a correspondence with the De La Salle superior general in 1826 in order to learn from them what in the Jesuit context was referred to as 'their way of proceeding'.[17] Very quickly a rapport developed between the two congregations as they shared insights into the religious life and questions of pedagogy. In describing the relationship between the two groups, one attempting to recover from the devastation of the French Revolution, the other just starting out, a De La Salle historian has employed a familial metaphor, referring to the congregations as 'the older in France and its younger twin in Ireland'.[18] It was in the context of this exchange that the Brothers formally received a copy of the De La Salle teaching manual, *The Conduct of Christian Schools,* which had been copied by teaching orders across Europe.[19] Br Austin Dunphy believed the methodologies far excelled those adopted in Ireland, and sought to replicate them.[20] *The Conduct* was translated into English, under the title 'School Government', and circulated to the Brothers' schools.[21] In time, however, they departed from it in several ways, most notably by Rice's radical adoption of the 'mutual' or monitorial system which had been developed by Lancaster and Bell. Their methods were not without critics, who argued that large numbers of children herded together under the direction of an older child learned little, but they were taught discipline and the system was inexpensive.[22] This was an important consideration for philanthropists and the providers of large-scale education; Bishop Moylan's charitable committee in Cork, for one, was particularly attracted by what its minutes refer to as 'Mr Lancaster's cheap mode of instruction'.[23] The Presentation Sisters used it in their schools, but the French Brothers considered this English novelty a Protestant anathema, which would undermine the presence of the master in front of the class in the traditional 'simultaneous' system.[24] Rice's clever mixing of the simultaneous and mutual methods of teaching resulted in a hybrid system which contemporaries described as an improvement on Lancaster's methods.[25]

In time, the Brothers' innovations were institutionalised in their *Manual of School Government*, published in 1845, the year after Rice's death.[26] This programme represented an enormous advance from the schema he outlined for Archbishop Bray in 1810, but the character of his schools remained unchanged. The *Manual* was compiled in response to a resolution of the 1841 general chapter which appointed a committee of Brothers to visit each of the schools with a view to creating such a compendium of best practice for the order.[27] In Kent's expression, the *Manual* was a practical 'distillation of the accumulated wisdom' of those who had studied under Rice and operated his system for forty years.[28] It, in turn, provided the inspiration for the teaching manuals of the Sisters of Charity and other teaching orders, while in England, the first Inspector of Catholic Schools reported that the Brothers' system was the model for most of the 105 schools he inspected in 1849.[29] At another level, too, the Brothers' translation of the *Conduct of Christian Schools* was of great significance in the mediation of de la Salle's pedagogy to the Anglophone world. In 1848, two years after the French Brothers received the translation and the new *Manual* from Dublin, they established schools in Baltimore, St Louis and New York, the first foundations in a network which would include one hundred schools in the United States alone.[30]

The *Manual* outlined in the 'minutest detail' the essentials which Brothers required in order to 'discharge systematically and efficiently the important duty of instruction'.[31] Such compendia were vital to the maintenance of an efficient system of education, which prized 'perfect uniformity' above 'capricious novelty' or any deviation from the authorised standard.[32] This standardisation across the congregation facilitated the necessary, and often frequent, transfer of Brothers from one school to another. It also reduced competition and conflict among Brothers, but perhaps more significantly it made teaching easier for the weaker ones.[33] This was an important consideration given the fact that the majority of the early Brothers would not have been considered well-educated by their contemporaries.

II

Every minute of the school day, from nine to three o'clock, was accounted for in the Brothers' system, and Rice consciously placed striking clocks in each class 'to better direct [the boys] in regulating the time' as a vital preparation for the new labour habits and time-discipline of the industrial age.[34] Every detail was directed towards the end of the enterprise, which was the 'salvation of … children' and their transformation into 'good practical Catholics'.[35] Like the Brothers' own regime, no moment was allowed for idleness and the constant activity and boundless energy of the children was 'regulated and controlled' with what one inspector for the Commissioners of Education described as 'military precision'.[36] This impression of robotic obedience was due in no small degree to the Brothers' efficient use of the 'signal', or wooden clicker, which they acquired in France and used to commanded attention.[37] A contemporary report of the Liverpool schools illustrates both the effectiveness and the mechanical nature of the system:

> On entering the school … the boys were ordered to make a bow, an act which was done with great uniformity. Then at a given signal, made by a 'click' from a small instrument which the master held in his hand, the boys ranged themselves round the room. At another 'click', they all held out their hands, to show that they were clean. At another 'click', and with almost military precision they turned round to show that their clothes were clean also; and at another signal they were all in an instant upon the forms.[38]

Teachers 'spoke little and in a whispering or low tone', while the careful use of the signal facilitated the maintenance of silence and order, which was considered the sure sign of effective teaching.[39]

The boys were taught in variations of the 'two room system', depending on the size of the school, which Edmund Rice had adapted from the Presentation Sisters. In the lower room they learned 'spelling, reading and writing on slates', while the upper room was reserved for the more advanced scholars.[40] The rooms, or 'schools', were broken into 'divisions', by levels of attainment, within which boys were arranged according to their home 'districts'. An ideal 'school' room consisted of 120 boys, divided into two divisions of 60; while each division had 12 monitors and four classes of 12.[41] This represented an effective application of the factory principle of division of labour in which the master taught the monitors, who were the more advanced of the students, and they in turn taught their companions. Normally, there was more than one Brother in each room, but this was not always possible, since a shortage of Brothers stretched the congregation to a point where teacher training and novices' spiritual for-

6.2 Christian Brothers' schoolroom. Detail from 'Souvenir of Brother Gerald Griffin – Irish poet and novelist'. Guy, Cork (*c.*1897–1923), NLI.

mation was sacrificed to meet the pressing needs of the schools. In 1858, for example, a Brother in Portlaoise complained of having to teach one hundred children. In response, Br Joseph Hearn pointed out that in Richmond Street 'a Brother not yet 19' had charge of 150 boys, while in Francis Street on the south side of the city, 'a novice has 160 daily by himself'.[42]

Chapter two of the *Manual of School Government*, includes a comprehensive description of the furnishing of the schools, which demonstrates the detailed attention which the Brothers devoted to the physical requirements of the schoolroom. The Brothers had acquired sample furniture from the Da La Salle schools in Paris and studied closely their contemporary theorists who placed such emphasis on the architecture of education.[43] The detail of Chapter two provides valuable insights, not just into the physical environment in which the teachers and pupils worked, but also the educational principles which inspired the teaching space:

One large desk for the master at the centre of the upper end of the school, elevated on a platform; and two smaller desks, one at either side of the master's, for the general-monitors, with a stool to each.

Eight desks, each eighteen feet long, for the boys.

A raised stool, from which the master may give lectures and signs for the exercises. This stool should be about two feet higher than the desk-stools, and be ascended by one or two steps: a drawer under the seat might be found useful.

One leaden ink-stand for every two boys writing on paper; – a jar and a jug for ink.

A black lecture-board, three feet by two, to each class, and one of five feet by three and a half, for the master's class, with a wooden pointer and a sponge for each.

Tablet-lessons on cards to correspond with the First Reading Book, for first school, and Arithmetical Tablets on cards for second school.

A ball-frame for first school.

Large Maps of the World, Europe, Asia, Africa, America, Ireland, England, and Scotland, for each school, the first excepted, for which a map of the world will suffice. A Gazetteer, Walker's Dictionary, and models for illustrating problems in mensuration, for third and fourth schools, and a pair of globes for fourth school.

One religious picture, at least, in each school; also, pictures and objects for illustrating the lessons.

A wooden box fixed to the wall in each class of the second, third, and fourth schools; to hold the books, &c., of the class.

One hundred Reading Books to each of the schools, save the first.

Six treatises on Book-keeping in the advanced schools to lecture from.

A sweeping-brush, a duster, dust-pan, and sprinkling-pot for each school. One long-handled brush for walls will be sufficient for the four schools.

A clock, a signal, and a strap of leather thirteen inches long, one and one-fourth inch wide, and one quarter inch thick, for each school; also, a hammer, pincers, and gimlet.

A registry and muster-roll for each school, according to plan hereafter given.

A class-slate, suspended at each semicircle, for the names, &c. of the boys of the class, and ruled for recording their failures in tasks; besides 100 slates, or one for each boy, except for those of first school.[44]

These spatial arrangements reflect not just the practical need to accommodate large numbers in schools, but the institutionalisation of the panoptic principle which stressed the essential moral influence of the Brother. From his elevated platform, the teacher exercised Foucauldian vigilance and continuous surveillance which characterised early-modern schooling; with 'the master's eye upon them', the children kept to their duties and were prepared for the world of employment.[45] Yet the elaborate mechanism of the classroom structure and the supervised student activity employed by the Brothers assured that the school would run itself as a kind of self-regulating machine. Within this context, the Brother became 'a silent by-stander and inspector' and the obedience of the children was not to him personally but to the rules, thus the children were provided with a transferable respect for authority which they carried through life.[46]

In a radical departure from traditional practice, Edmund Rice and the first Brothers hoped to achieve this moral reformation of youth through a 'spirit of love rather than fear'.[47] This was an ambitious aspiration in an age where school management usually depended on the threat of punishment. Discipline in Irish schools was frequently harsh and brutal, as recorded in the *First Report of the Commission of Irish Education Inquiry* (1825), which contains instances of savage brutality in schools, including the use of horse whips by masters.[48] By contrast, the Brothers, who were motivated by Gospel values, aspired to remove 'as much as possible, everything like corporal punishment' from their schools, and relied instead on intuitive and emotional means of securing order which had been pioneered by contemporary reformers.[49] Nevertheless, while Rice banned the use of 'whipping', except for 'very serious faults' which seldom occurred, he allowed for 'slight punishments'.[50] That said, successive government reports and visitors praised the Brothers as disciplinarians, who despite their large class sizes seldom resorted to physical punishment.[51] Richard Lovell Edgeworth junior on his visit to the 'North Mon', in 1824, was 'struck with the discipline that seemed to pervade the whole school', but commented on the cheerfulness of the boys.[52] Twenty years later, the Anglican cleric, Edward Caswall, was equally positive in his observations of the Cork schools. He recorded that he had never seen 'a better managed set of schools nor more lively intelligent and well behaved boys', and he too noted 'no appearance of heaviness anywhere'.[53]

By the time the *Manual* was published, in 1845, the Brothers had developed an elaborate philosophy of classroom management which emphasised a combination of 'mildness' and 'firmness'. However, the essential ingredient in the conduct of schools remained the Brother's paternal surveillance and inspection:

> The children should respect and fear the master, and his presence
> should inspire them with seriousness and gravity; these are the effects
> of firmness. They should love their master; they should love the school,
> and the exercises of the school; these effects are produced by mildness.[54]

The Brother's influence was augmented by a system of rewards and premiums, which fostered ambition and industry, and a judicious application of what Br Patrick Ellis, in 1855, described as 'tasks and humiliations', to induce a sense of shame, which contemporary educational reformers considered essential to the development of internalised self-discipline.[55] What he meant by 'humiliations' is unclear, but there is no suggestion that the Brothers employed the elaborate methods advocated by Lancaster, which included the use of a fool's cap, confinement in a cupboard or a pillory, or even suspension in a basket from the rafters.[56] Rewards usually consisted of pennies or medals, and it appears that suits of clothes might have been given as a reward for merit and improvement.[57]

Br Ellis claimed that 'corporal punishments were generally disapproved of' among the Brothers, but he acknowledged that 'necessity required some'. On those occasions boys were punished with slaps on the hand with a *ferula*, a strap which the Brothers had received from the De La Salle Brothers in 1826.[58] Saliently, the advent of 'the leather' (which in time became synonymous with the Christian Brothers' schools) was seen as a reform by contemporaries, since it allowed for uniform punishments and the banishment of sticks and other crude instruments from the classroom. Writing to Frère Guillaume, Br Austin Dunphy noted the benefits of this innovation:

> The youth of this country are already deeply indebted to you. We have,
> from your example, banished all corporal punishment from our
> schools. Other masters are beginning to take the hint from us.[59]

Of course, in spite of the rhetoric corporal punishment was never completely banished from the schools and the constant tensions between the philosophical rejection of physical chastisement, as servile and degrading, and the tough realities of schoolroom discipline remained. In his memoir, for instance, Edward O'Flynn, who had been a student at the 'North Mon' in the late 1840s, recalled Br John Wiseman, a former civil engineer and author of several of the Brothers' celebrated textbooks, punishing a liar by chasing 'the victim round the school, caning him at the same time'.[60]

Whatever about Rice's original intention, some commentators are cynical about later claims regarding the formal prohibition of corporal punishment, which they believe were often a public relations exercise to mask its use.[61] Certainly, the De La Salle Brothers sought to obscure its use and privately acknowledged that 'correction that is merited, but given at the wrong time' could ruin the establishment.[62] The Irish Brothers were also aware of this danger; during a visit to Paris in 1832, Br Bernard Dunphy learned of the public scandal which resulted from the appearance of several French Brothers before the Commissary of Police as a result of severe punishments meted out to boys.[63] Closer to home, in 1842, a young novice in O'Connell's Schools narrowly escaped imprisonment when he beat a boy with a wooden pointer. In this instance, it was only sympathetic magistrates, including a Protestant former Secretary of the National Board of Education, who saved the Brother from six months' hard labour.[64] In the late 1830s, too, there was an incident at Sunderland, in England, where a mother abused Brothers in the street for having punished her boy. They had, she claimed, run away from the 'bogs of Ireland' to kill 'their bairns [children]'.[65] Significantly, therefore, the *Manual* (1845) forbade the punishment of any boy 'when going out of school' and directed that 'a slap should never be so heavy as to cause any marks'.[66]

Quite clearly, corporal punishment was an issue during Rice's lifetime, indeed while he was still superior general. It is misleading, therefore to suggest that abuses had crept in only after his death in 1844.[67] Moreover, successive revisions of the Brothers' Rule and teaching manuals brought a dilution of Rice's original prohibition of physical punishments, to a point where the regulations published in 1851 contained none of the exhortations found in earlier statutes that such punishment should be rare.[68] These changes suggest a philosophical shift, and may point to an increase in the use of corporal punishment within the schools. Certainly, the 1841 general chapter recommended penances for Brothers guilty of inflicting 'immoderate' punishment, while in the following decade Br Paul Riordan, second superior general, found it necessary to issue a circular letter on the subject.[69] This followed 'some very painful occurrences' which had taken place in the institute. 'Such cruel treatment', he warned, 'was against the rule as well as against humanity':

> The cases were such that, if publicly known, and prosecution instituted they would bring odium both on the brothers in fault and the Institute. Henceforth, let no Brother give any boy more than two slaps, and these with the leather strap, and only on the palm of the hand. Immoderate severity towards children defeats the end of correction, mars the effect of religious instruction, and stamps the Brothers who inflict it with a character quite repugnant to his holy profession.[70]

Such directives reflect a commendable desire to curb physical abuse in the schools, but they reveal also the extent to which the 'good name' of the institute had already assumed an importance in the priorities of the superiors. However, physical punishment remained the norm in Irish schools. In this sense the Brothers' ambition was counter-cultural. Indeed, in 1855 it was necessary to exhume the body of a child who had died following a beating in the National School at Shinrone, County Offaly.[71]

III

It was not premiums or punishments which mattered most to the parents of the children at Edmund Rice's schools, but the education the 'Monks' offered and the opportunities for advancement it afforded. The first Christian Brothers emphasised the manners, diligence and behaviour which employers expected in their workers. 'Good habits' had been a constant theme of educational discourse of the eighteenth century, but in the reforming agenda of Rice's contemporary devotees of the 'ideology of the schools' religious training assumed paramount importance. As the bishop of Cloyne observed in his oration for Nano Nagle (1794), for Christian educators, the task had an added theological significance which was of paramount importance:

> Early Christian education will make men honest, sober, temperate, and regular, it will in a great degree make Jails, Hospitals, and Poor-houses unnecessary. In one word … without an early virtuous education, it is morally impossible to enter into the kingdom of Heaven, and under the influences of such an education there are the best grounded hopes of arriving at a blessed immortality.[72]

Their ambition, therefore, was not simply to break the child's will, but to train it. They sought to shape the behavioural traits of students, but especially to develop the boys' *character*, to infuse *internalised* moral regulation and self-discipline, which would do for moral education what mechanical power had done for the industrial revolution.[73] The English tourists, Mr and Mrs Hall, on their visit to Mount Sion in 1840, noted that the masters' greatest concern was the 'training of the affections the manners and the habits' of the boys.[74] Indeed, the *Manual* reminded Brothers that this formation 'may prove of much greater advantage to them than their literary or scientific attainments', and that without it boys would remain 'unfit for the commonest duties of society'.[75]

Developing such habits, however, would be no mean feat among students who have been described as 'filthy and unkempt … [and] chafing at the unaccustomed strain and discipline of the classroom'.[76] Yet, while the Rule directed that the 'Order shall admit none into their schools but poor children', the majority of the boys did not come from abject poverty, but were drawn from the ranks of 'tradesmen, clerks, labouring classes, servants and a few shopkeepers'.[77] That said, in 1825, over half of them were unable to pay one penny per week towards their education and visitors to the schools noted that large numbers were barefoot and poorly dressed.[78] Moreover, in spite of the pious rhetoric about the inclusive nature of 'Ricean education', free schooling involved the stigma of poverty and this excluded boys who were, in Archbishop Murray's estimation, 'too proud to go to poor schools [but] too poor to go to high schools'.[79] Likewise, the colonial official, James Bicheno observed that 'the superior poor … [preferred] … a less meagre and abstinent course of education' than that provided by the Monks, who he crudely berated as 'the instructors of a potato-fed people, whose … intellectual appetites are on the lowest scale'.[80]

The Brothers' improvement extended to the physical appearance of the boys and each day began with a cleanliness inspection, as described above. Br Austin Grace argued that not only was 'cleanliness … essential to health', but that a 'neglect of it in childhood [was] the fruitful source of slovenly and filthy habits in life'.[81] Such sentiments became institutionalised in the *Manual* which directed masters to keep a 'watchful eye', since cleanliness was 'a mark of industry', just as nastiness was a sign of 'sloth and indolence'.[82] Significantly, when Richard Lovell Edgeworth visited the North Monastery in 1824, he noted that while many of the boys were dressed 'in very indifferent clothing … their faces and hands were cleaner than in most schools of the same sort'.[83] Twenty years later, Edward Caswall made a similar observation of the Presentation Brothers in Cork, noting how, among the boys, 'one of the best at Euclid' had no shoes or socks but that his hands were clean.[84]

This preparation for employment included training in diction, posture and deportment. Above all, the system sought to engender self-control, the quality most admired by the middle classes, in children who might otherwise have been running wild through the streets. In the Brothers' schools, children were socialised to behave with 'modesty and decorum'. 'Rude and disorderly conduct' was forbidden and teachers were to correct the boys' 'awkward and clownish habits'. They were taught to 'sit, stand, move, and address a person with the modesty, gracefulness, and propriety' which polite society expected.[85]

The school curriculum reflected a similar modernizing tendency in its ori-
entation towards the demands of an increasingly commercialised society
which required a literate workforce.[86] Exaggerated claims have been made for
the scope of the education offered by the first Brothers, as instanced by
Normoyle's assertion that 'Edmund Rice gave a graded teaching from the
lowest primary level to a complete secondary education'.[87] At one level this is
correct, but it requires qualification of the kind offered by John Kent whose
analysis demonstrates that the vast majority of students remained only a short
time at Rice's schools.[88] And even then, the Brothers' task was made more difficult by the irregularity with which boys attended school, due to the cycles of
the agricultural year and the counter-attractions of the city. The returns for
Hanover Street, for instance, cite the enrolment as 550 at the Dublin school,
yet 'counting those who are obliged to be frequently absent', the average daily
attendance was 480.[89] Added to this was the great challenge of creating habits
of regularity in undisciplined kids.

It is true that at exhibitions, like that held at the 'North Mon' in 1838, the
subjects examined included 'architectural drawing … hydrostatics, hydraulics
and the philosophy of heat'.[90] Likewise, successive official reports and scores of
visitors echoed the observations of Sir Thomas Wyse MP, who witnessed 'nav-
igation, mensuration and other portions of the mathematical science' being
taught in the Brothers' schools.[91] However, while these subjects were taught to
the higher classes, the vast majority of 'Mr Rice's scholars' did not advance
beyond the basics; as Br J.B. Duggan informed a Royal Commission in 1854,
'every boy does not go through the course'.[92] In 1825, for instance, an appeal for
the Hanover Street School outlined the boys' progression:

First School: 180 Boys taught alphabet and two syllable words.
Second School: 100 Boys taught to spell, read and write.
Third School: 120 Boys taught reading, writing and arithmetic.
Fourth School: 100 Boys taught reading, writing, arithmetic, English gram-
                 mar and maths useful to artificers, merchants and mariners.[93]

The essential point is that the Brothers acknowledged these realities and adapted
their teaching accordingly.

There were, of course malevolent critics like Bicheno who claimed that the
chief instruction given by the Brothers was 'bad writing, bad reading and toler-
able arithmetic' (1830).[94] Yet in his evidence before a Select Committee of the
House of Lords (1837), the Revd George Dwyer, rector of Ardrahan, hailed the

schools in Mill Street, Dublin, and Cork as the 'most perfect schools' he had ever been in. There he witnessed 'the most extraordinary progress ... made by children', but he was especially struck by the Brothers' flexibility, or what might be called child-centred curriculum, as reflected in their:

> Admirable adaptation of the information ... to the peculiar bent and genius and disposition of the child; a sifting and searching of what the future destination of the child was, and an application of Instruction to that destination ... [and] a most curious eliciting and drawing forth and development of the powers of the children.[95]

The rector's evidence was corroborated by Edward O'Flynn, a student at the North Monastery in the late 1840s, who recalled an equally pragmatic approach:

> In these times the master would always find out what a new boy's parents would want him to be, so as to get a suitable education, so as not to be wasting time on things he could do without, for it was uncertain when they would be taken away to business.[96]

The Halls, too, believed that the Brothers offered boys 'an education suited exactly to their condition in life'.[97] Such practicality was entirely consistent with the Brothers' original aim, which was, in Br Austin Grace's expression, the provision of 'a suitable education, to qualify [boys] for business and the various departments of commercial life'.[98] Furthermore, Edmund Rice's retention of a tailor at Mount Sion suggests a desire on his part not only to educate boys, but also to clothe them in advance of their employment by the shopkeepers, merchants and tradesmen of the city, as was the practice of Moylan's Cork Committee.[99] This was the vocational preparation required by the children of the poor; basic numeracy, literacy in English and the necessary social skills to function in an increasingly bourgeois society. The extent to which the Brothers satisfied this need was evident in the numerous testimonies to what the Revd Richard Ryland of Waterford lauded as 'the incalculable benefit' which Rice's schools had brought to the 'distressed and unemployed'.[1]

IV

Rice's primary ambition, however, was not simply the material improvement of his scholars, but rather his desire to see them 'godly'.[2] In McQuaid's expression, he worked and suffered to form the image of Christ on the heart of every boy he encountered.[3] Such sentiments were clearly articulated in his correspondence, while the Rule and teaching *Manual* were unambiguous in their definition of the Brothers' purpose. It was to sanctify their own souls and 'to be instrumental in the salvation of the children for whom Jesus Christ died'.[4] The original Presentation Rule was inspired by the spirituality of the Catholic Reformation and that same spirit defined the character of the Brothers' schools. At its simplest, the scheme which Edmund Rice outlined to Archbishop Bray of Cashel in 1810 was an attempt to adapt European Catholic pedagogy to the particular needs of the Irish Church. And just as the secular instruction in his schools sought to foster internalised self-discipline, so too, the catechesis was directed towards the formation of a religious disposition and commitment to the Catholic way of life. In the words of a lord mayor of Dublin, Rice's maxim, was to 'instruct the young in the way they should walk, and … they will not depart from it'.[5]

To this end, each school day began with an elaborate morning offering, which reflected not just the Brothers' Ignatian spirituality, but their desire 'to teach the children to offer themselves up to God from the first use of reason':

> Most Merciful Creator! I offer myself to thee this day, with all my thoughts words and actions, in union with the merits of my Lord and Saviour Jesus Christ. I firmly resolve, by the assistance of thy grace, to avoid sin above all things this day, especially those sins which I am most in the habit of committing. I humbly ask, through the sacred passion and death of my Divine Redeemer, and through the intercession of his immaculate Virgin Mother, for strength to fulfil this resolution. Receive, O Lord, all my liberty, my memory, my understanding, and my whole will; – thou hast given me all that I have, and all that I am, and I return all to thy divine will, that thou dispose of me. Give me only thy love and thy grace; with these I shall be rich enough, and shall have no more to ask. Our Father, Hail Mary, Creed, Glory be to the Father, &c. *Amen.*[6]

There were set times for prayer throughout the day: at noon the students recited the Angelus, and acts of Faith, Hope and Charity; at three the *Salve Regina* and the Litany of the Blessed Virgin were said, while the entire day was punctuated with the recitation of the Hail Mary on the strike of every hour, in keeping with the tradition of the continental orders.

6.3 Father William Gahan OSA. Engraving by
Patrick Maguire (1783–1820), NLI.

In Rice's schema, a half hour was set aside each day for formal catechesis. This he believed was 'the most salutary part of the system'. It was, he argued, 'the most laborious to teachers; however, if it were ten times what it is … we are amply paid in seeing such a Reformation in the children'.[7] During this period, Brothers taught Christian Doctrine, usually from Butler's Catechism but, just as in the secular subjects, this was adapted to the ability of the children and was usually memorised.[8] Moreover, the 'question and answer' style of the catechism was considered most appropriate since it actively engaged the children:

> It cannot be too often reiterated, that the manner of catechising should be simple and conversational; that the children should be made to speak as much as possible; and, that, anything like a consecutive discourse should studiously be avoided.[9]

Yet while this lesson was isolated for formal instruction, the entire day was run through with a Catholic ethos. Indeed Rice's concern for the whole man gave the system its 'mixed character', where religion and the secular subjects were integrated, and taught side-by-side, in contrast to the 'separate' instruction of the technically non-denominational National Schools. Even the singing, introduced to the schools as a refining influence, was directed towards the moral formation of the boys. It would, in Br Joseph Hearn's view, 'effect the disposition of the children', a sentiment which echoed those of the English educationalist and moral reformer, Mary Carpenter (1807–77), who observed that 'music may be made an important auxiliary in tranquilising and subduing the wild spirits we have to deal with'.[10] It would also serve to make school more enjoyable, contribute to the beauty of parish liturgies and provide an alternative to the popular ballads which offended bourgeois sensitivities.

The reading material, too, was carefully selected. Rather than using the chapbooks which were used in many of the Catholic pay-schools, Rice relied initially on Fr William Gahan's *History of the Old and New Testament*, which was an abridged version of Joseph Reeve's translation of *Le Bible de Royaumont* (1670). He also used Charles Gobinet's *Instruction of Youth in Christian Piety*, first published in Paris in 1665. These texts, however, became less important following the publication of the Brothers' elaborate readers, beginning in 1839. A further novelty of their schools was the existence of a lending library in the schools, which the boys were encouraged to read to their parents at night. Pious books were also supplied to apprentices in the town who, in return, were obliged to attend the sacraments once a month. Amongst the first expenses recorded for the North Monastery in Cork, was five guineas spent on a bookcase for the library.[11] By 1822, the lending library at Hanover Street, Dublin, contained 268 volumes, mostly catechisms, hagiography and devotional material, including Rice's favourites, *The Spiritual Combat* and the *Imitation of Christ*.[12] A decade later it had expanded to over one thousand books. There was still a preponderance of devotional material, but the scope was considerably broader and contained a significant historical section, including Charles O'Conor, Eugene O'Curry and Edward Hay. There was controversial material, too, including Burke's *Reflections on the Revolution in France* and William Corbett's *History of the Protestant Reformation in England and Ireland* (1829), while contemporary controversy was represented in James Warren Doyle (JKL), and the English Tractarians, Henry Edward Manning and Nicholas Wiseman. There were pedagogical materials, too, readers and practical manuals, including Michael Donovan's *Domestic Economy* (1830), which contained chapters on brewing and distilling, vital occupations in Dublin's inner city.[13]

The library catalogues reflected the focus upon the sacraments which was an integral part of Rice's system. It was not enough to teach the children Christian Doctrine; the Brothers sought to instil in their charges a devotion to the Church and its practices. This was no mean task, because contrary to the popular notion that Catholicism embraced the Irish of all classes, the poor were often alienated from the institutional Church. If, as Magray argues, 'Catholicism had to be taught aggressively to the majority of the population', the Brothers' system was designed to meet that challenge.[14] The Presentation Rule laid down that the Brothers should accustom the children to 'think and speak reverently of God and holy things'; they were not to be over-curious in their questioning, but rather to 'captivate their understanding in obedience to faith'.[15] The library was an important resource in this task, and the shelves contained classic Tridentine texts such Antoine Arnaud's treatise, *On Frequent Communion* (1643), and a Dublin edition of John Gother (*c.*1650–1704), *Instructions for Confession, Communion and Confirmation* (Dublin, 1825).[16]

The schools sought to foster an internalised obedience to the Church, and a disposition 'to receive instruction from those whom Christ has appointed to rule' it.[17] Children learned 'to honour and respect their parents and superiors', and the Brothers' emphasis on the special reverence due to priests attracted criticism that their system cultivated 'ready instruments for the priests' domination'.[18] They were also taught to examine their conscience in preparation for Confession, and Rice's system provided for the reception of the sacrament of Penance by the children four times during the school year.[19] The *Manual*, for instance, contained a pro-forma school register which included columns in which the boys' monthly Confession and Communion were to be recorded.[20] As the century progressed, preparation for First Communion and Confirmation assumed increasing importance and very often the sacraments marked the end of primary school and the beginning of pupils' working lives.[21] Hanover Street School had an average daily attendance of 480, yet the returns for 1837 indicate that 200 of the boys made their first Holy Communion each year (a figure which demonstrates the short stay of most pupils).[22] Yet, while religion appears to dominate the day, the focus was less intense than in many Protestant Bible schools where frequently the only reading allowed was from the Bible.[23] Nor did Rice's regime include the De La Salle and Presentation Sisters' practice of daily Mass.

In theory the Brothers' schools were open to all boys 'without religious distinction', but this was not the case in practice; the Halls observed in Mount Sion that all the pupils were Catholic.[24] This they attributed to the 'excellent schools for Protestants in the city', but, in Ireland at least, the overwhelmingly Catholic

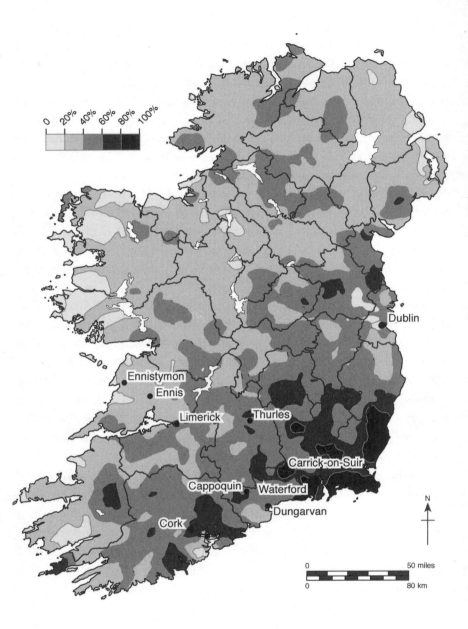

6.4 Mass attendance as a percentage of the Catholic population, 1834.
Source: David W. Miller, 'Mass attendance in Ireland in 1834', in Brown et al. (eds),
Piety and Power in Ireland. Map drawn by Matthew Stout.

nature of the syllabus at the Brothers' schools would not have attracted children of other faiths where alternatives were available. Indeed, it is more likely that the Brothers' emphasis upon the inclusive nature of their schools was a rhetorical assault on the proselytising schools which they bitterly opposed. In fact, the Brothers' schools were exclusive to the extent that Rice forbade his pupils to 'play or keep company' with boys from other schools.[25]

Inevitably, given these emphases, Edmund Rice's system was not without its critics. Few challenged his pedagogical method, but most rounded on the religious ethos of the schools and the perpetuation of 'popish superstition'. The traveller, Henry Inglis' observations were typical of many:

> The most important institution I visited [in Waterford] was a Catholic school at which upwards of 700 children were instructed ... [A]lthough I am far from questioning the motives of the founder Mr Rice or the young men who thus made a sacrifice of themselves, yet I cannot regard favourably an institution under such tuition. I know too much of Catholicism in other countries to doubt that intellectual training will be made very secondary to theological instruction ... I would rather not see a system of education extensively pursued in which the inculcation of popish tenets forms so chief a part.[26]

Writing in 1825, one observer condemned the Brothers' schools as 'the most intolerant and mischievous which any individual or society has attempted to mask under the disguise of Christian instruction':

> Nothing could be more hopeless, in a human sense, than the task of attempting to eradicate the peculiar impressions which are burned into juvenile feeling by the operation of the system. There are about 6,000 orthodox larvae in these poisonous receptacles, and the queen bee, it seems is still in vigorous operation.[27]

Bicheno, too, held up the Brothers' schools to demonstrate 'how little likelihood there was of Protestants and Catholics joining cordially in the cause of education' in Ireland.[28]

Such criticism was understandable, given the heightened sectarian tensions of the 1820s, but there were many Anglicans who were generous in their praise. At a critical point in the history of the Christian Brothers, in 1829, the liberal Member of Parliament for Waterford, Sir John Newport (1756–1843), led a spirited defence of their cause. In a petition signed by the lord mayor and sixty-seven of the most prominent citizens of the city he praised the schools established by Edmund Rice:

> To this date … [they] continue to afford every opportunity to hundreds of the poor children of this city to acquire a truly useful education, [and] have materially contributed to improve the morals of our youth, by the excellent system of instruction which is practiced in them, and to diffuse among our poor principles of integrity and social order. I have the highest possible opinion of the system of instruction pursued in Mr Rice's Waterford school, and have for many years witnessed with the most cordial satisfaction the infinite benefits resulting from it to the inhabitants of this city, in particular, and to the public generally.[29]

This transformation of the poor was due in no small degree to the system which Edmund Rice had fashioned and the extent to which he created what Bishop Dorrian later described in Presbyterian terms as the formative 'surroundings of education' in his schools.[30]

In England and Wales, Methodism has been described as 'the midwife of social and political progress' on account of the self-discipline, order and organisational skills it brought to the working classes.[31] Likewise in Ireland, the Brothers instilled in their pupils the virtues of discipline, hard-work and sobriety. From the very beginning Edmund Rice cultivated these values. Charles Bianconi, one of the first recipients of Rice's charity, was encouraged to be 'industrious', careful and sober.[32] These values were at the core of the Brothers' programme and were celebrated by contemporary commentators. Richard Ryland, in spite of his hostility to the 'unhappy' Catholic ethos of the schools, expressed satisfaction for the work of the Christian Brothers:

> They have already impressed upon the lower classes a character which hitherto was unknown to them: and in the number of intelligent and respectable tradesmen, clerks and servants which they have sent forth, bear the most unquestionable testimony to the public services of Edmund Rice.[33]

Such testimonies point to the inclusion of Edmund Rice and the first Brothers in the great modernisation process which swept the nineteenth-century world.

6.5 Father Theobald Mathew
(1790–1856), 'The Apostle of
Temperance'. NLI.

Thirty years ago Hugh Kearney published a seminal essay which celebrated
Fr Theobald Mathew (1790–1856) as 'the Apostle of Modernisation'.[34] He argued
that the temperance crusade was only intelligible within a transatlantic context,
beginning in New England in the 1820s and gradually spreading to Britain and
Ireland. In this sense, Mathew transplanted what had previously been an evangelical Protestant discipline to Ireland. Far from being simply a teetotal campaign, this was part of a wider process of reform which was linked with other
campaigns, including the abolition of slavery. The British novelist, Thackeray,
believed that, while Mathew 'avoided all political questions', no man seemed

> more eager than he for the political improvement of this country. Leases
> and rents, farming implements, reading societies, he was full of these
> and his schemes of temperance above all.[35]

His was a truly modernising campaign, in the sense that it represented a shift
from 'local' to 'cosmopolitan' values and an attempt by urban men to control
and reform rural society:

The urban thrust of the crusade, its emphasis upon such values as literacy, thrift, and insurance against illness and its involvement in politics in some areas link it to other movements which were attempting to
cope with the new problems of a changing world.[36]

These values were shared by the Christian Brothers and sobriety had been a constant theme in Rice's teaching. Of the few anecdotes which survive about him
one of the most substantial concerns a Waterford alcoholic and prostitute, Poll
McCarthy, who begged Rice for help. Instead of listening to her tales of woe, he
lectured her on her drinking. She promised that if he would help her, she would
go to Cork and take the pledge from Fr Mathew. There and then he brought her
to a draper and fitted her for the journey. She walked to Cork and back and 'her
life subsequently was as edifying as previously it had been notorious'.[37] Within
the schools, too, he encouraged temperance. Many of the *Memories* of Edmund
Rice recall his kindness to the children of alcoholics; how he took special care
of them, while at the same time seeking out their parents and urging them 'to
lead a better more sober life'.[38]

Edmund Rice and Fr Mathew were friends for over forty years; the friendship may have begun while the young Mathew was a pupil at St Canice's
Academy in Kilkenny, before he went to Maynooth in 1800. Both men shared
a common vision and desire to improve the lot of the poor. Education was
also a concern of the young Capuchin; shortly after arriving in Cork in
1814 he established a school in an effort to do for the south side what the
Brothers had done for the north. By 1824 there were 500 pupils in this school
and before the Brothers' school at Sullivan's Quay was completed in 1828,
classes were held in an old store at Cove Street, where Fr Mathew lived.[39] The
Brothers played a crucial part in Fr Mathew's temperance crusade. It is surprising, however, that Fr Mathew's recent biographers have largely neglected
the important part played by Edmund Rice in this campaign for 'temperance
and modernisation'.[40]

The first juvenile total abstinence society founded in Ireland was at the
North Monastery and Fr Mathew consciously cultivated contacts with the
Brothers. In June 1843, in North Richmond Street, he praised their work and
expressed his delight:

That the Christian Brothers had come forward as living examples of the
great lessons of total abstinence which they inculcated. He thanked God
that he had their active co-operation and that of their numerous pupils

whose example alone in taking the pledge was a vast gain for the cause of temperance.[41]

The identification of the cause of education and temperance found expression in Fr Mathew's numerous visits to the Brothers' schools. In 1843 alone, he made at least nine visits to their schools; in September of that year he delivered a charity sermon for the North Richmond Street school in Gardiner Street church which raised one hundred guineas.[42] The 'Liberator' was expected to attend that service, but declined on account of a 'Monster Meeting' at Clifden. His apology declared, 'the same hour at which your sermon is to take place … I expect to be addressing a million men on the heights of Connemara'.[43] Two years later, when O'Connell visited the North Monastery the hall was decorated with two large satin banners; one read *in hoc signo vinces*, while 'Temperance and happiness' was emblazoned on the other.[44]

Paul Townend has described Fr Mathew's temperance crusade as the 'most extraordinary social movement … in pre-famine Ireland'.[45] Yet the extent of what O'Connell called this 'moral and majestic miracle' depended upon the cooperation of like-minded agents of improvement.[46] That the Christian Brothers were vital collaborators in that revolution was reflected in the Capuchin's recollection of the day Edmund Rice took the pledge as the happiest day of his life:

> I was aware that when he and the other members of that illustrious body came forward from their mountain, a second Carmel, to diffuse the blessings of temperance as they had those of education, not only through Ireland, but also in England, the principles of the Society were placed on a sure basis, even on a rock which the breaking of the tempest could not shake.[47]

The Apostle of Temperance's faith in the Brothers was echoed by many of their peers. They were in John Shelly's words, 'no mere hirelings', but men of the world who had embraced the cause of regeneration and as such exercised an influence in society vastly disproportionate to their small numbers.[48]

Such sentiments were confirmed by the Endowed Schools Commission (1858), which acknowledged the 'special excellencies' of the Brothers' schools. These were enumerated as the 'extraordinary personal influence exerted by the teachers', the quality of their training, and the efficiency of their 'organisation and discipline'.[49] In his final summation, Frederick McBlain, the Assistant

Commissioner, attributed the superiority of the schools to the character of the Brothers, who 'devoted their lives to the cause of education, for no private or personal gain', but as 'a sacred and self-imposed duty'.[50] If further affirmation of the system was necessary, however, this was to be found in the numerous requests for communities which Rice and his successors received from bishops throughout Ireland and beyond.

CHAPTER 7

Expansion and union, 1802–22

EDMUND RICE'S MISSION EXPANDED RAPIDLY during its first years. The early Brothers had made a heroic response to the needs of the poor, setting aside the comforts of the middle class to educate the poorest sections of the community. Everywhere their schools were established the welfare of the poor improved, resulting in what the entrepreneur Charles Bianconi called 'a quiet revolution in the south of Ireland'.[1] The life of the Church, too, was greatly renewed by the participation of the previously alienated under-class which the Brothers introduced to the renewed discipline and devotion which characterised nineteenth-century Catholicism.

I

A great deal has been written about the Gaelic survival of south Leinster and east Munster. Under the sympathetic influence of Catholic or crypto-Catholic grandees the region was sheltered from the full rigors of the penal laws. Through a combination of collusion and connivance the Catholic interest was protected and extended. Beneath the sub-gentry, there was a layer of strong farmers and these developed a complex web of connections with their co-religionists in the towns. Increasingly, this aggressive, articulate, class supplied the leadership of the Catholic community. While the aristocratic influence of the Dillons, O'Conors and Taaffes had waned by mid century, the transformation was completed in 1791 by the ejection of Lord Kenmare and his associates from the leadership of the Catholic Committee. In their place, direction was provided by Edward Byrne, one of the largest merchants in Dublin – 'a sugar-baker, seller of wine and other commodities' – and John Keogh, 'a retailer of poplins in Dame Street'.[2]

The patterns of clerical leadership changed in parallel. The economic restrictions of the penal era favoured the promotion of financially independent-gentry candidates to the episcopacy. By the end of the century, however, bishops were drawn increasingly from the ranks of the middle-class: Thomas Hussey was a farmer's son; Archbishop Troy's people were merchants in Smithfield; Bishop James Lanigan was the son of a grocer in Carrick, while

Archbishop Thomas Bray's father had been a wine merchant in Fethard, County Tipperary. The religious founders of the late eighteenth and early nineteenth century came from similar backgrounds. Edmund Rice and Nano Nagle epitomise this group, whose numbers included the heiress, Catherine McAuley, the Dublin milliner Teresa Mullaly and Frances Ball, the first Loreto sister and daughter of a prosperous Dublin silk merchant.[3] These well-educated, confident founders were highly motivated and many in their close-knit circle were attracted by their values and vision.

Rice's first disciples emerged from the same social class as the clergy, and several had brothers who were priests; John Rice was an Augustinian, while Austin Grace's brother William was a Jesuit at Georgetown University.[4] The early Brothers were drawn largely from the ranks of the strong tenant farmer and merchant class. In Gillespie's expression, 'commercial men formed the backbone of the first generation', an evaluation which echoes Daniel O'Connell's observation that 'the community consisted principally of men who, after serving their time in trade, betook themselves to the Religious life, bringing into the general stock from £100 to £250'.[5] Rice's earliest followers were Callanmen, Patrick Finn and Thomas Grosvenor. In time they were joined by John Mulcahy, a former clerical student from Cappoquin, John Power, nephew of the bishop of Waterford, and Joseph Murphy, uncle of Margaret Aylward, the foundress of the Holy Faith Sisters.[6] The early group included two wine merchants, John Watson of Dublin and Thomas O'Brien from Waterford, who was 60 years old when he joined the Brothers. Something of the diversity of the group is reflected in the presence of the convert Benjamin Francis Manifold, who had served in the Wicklow militia, and the Callan cobbler, Thomas Cahill, the founder of the Thurles house, who had been flogged for his part in the 1798 rebellion.[7] Only one of the founding generation had any teaching experience. Patrick Ellis (1792–1859) is described as 'professor' of mathematics in St John's diocesan college, Waterford, but he was appointed at the age of 19 and held the position for a little over a year before he entered Mount Sion in 1812.[8] By that point, the social composition of the group had begun to change. While earlier recruits had brought property in the form of a dowry, neither of the Cork novices who joined in 1811 appears to have had personal property.[9] Instead, Jerome O'Connor and John Leonard brought £100 from Bishop Moylan's Charitable Society.[10]

Many of the early Brothers were inspired by Rice's enthusiastic example. Certainly, this was so in the case of Austin Dunphy (1785–1847), who recorded his first encounter, as a boy, with the charismatic merchant on the quay in Waterford in 1796:

He was above middle height, being about six feet, of sanguine complexion, with eyes large and expressive, and of a bright hazel colour. His frame of body was formed for active habits, and his intellectual powers were of a high order. He had broad and just views of life and its varied problems, and possessed great mental vigour and steadfastness of purpose. He was generous, warm-hearted, and most paternal.[11]

Yet while the hagiography suggests that his recruits were ready for any sacrifice in the cause, it appears that the attrition rate among the early Brothers was high; in Rice's lifetime over 140 Brothers tried their vocations and left.[12] Their departure was often not without consequence, as in the case of Francis Ryan who left the Mill Street community in Dublin, in 1841, taking desks and maps with him to set up his own pay-school.[13] It was clear, too, that the Brothers hoped that their schools would provide the best recruits. But the great obstacle to this avenue was the poverty of the boys and the inability of their parents to keep them at school.[14] Within this context, the possibility of establishing a juniorate was mooted as early as 1828. The general of the De La Salle Brothers encouraged this suggestion, observing that such an environment was essential, since 'the corruption of morals is so great today, that this is perhaps the only way remaining for us to secure pure and innocent souls'.[15]

Edmund Rice was able to tap into the enthusiasm and financial resources of the Catholic community, often in a dramatic fashion. This was the case in 1807 when William Barron of Faha left £1,000 to erect a school in Dungarvan. With the bishop's approval, John Mulcahy was sent to take charge of the venture which attracted two hundred students on its opening day. Not one of these boys had previously been at school.[16] Local response was the key element in the diffusion of the early schools. The erection and maintenance of even the most basic school houses required considerable resources and the creation of a system of schools was beyond the limit of Rice's personal fortune. Along with this, the competition for scarce resources within Catholic ranks was intense, and chapel building generally took precedence over the provision of schools. In this scenario, the stimulus for education often came, not from the clergy, but from the Catholic middle class. Where such financial support was available the nuns and the Brothers could be invited to open free schools. It is this factor which explains the initial diffusion of the Christian Brothers in the prosperous crescent running from Waterford to Limerick.[17] The circumstances surrounding the establishment of Rice's second school, at Carrick-on-Suir, illustrates many of these features.

In 1834 Henry Inglis described Carrick as 'distinguished in nearly equal proportions, by … exquisite opulence and soft beauty … and by the haggered misery, the squalid poverty … which characterises the great body of its population.'[18] Yet despite this poverty, the town experienced the wave of ecclesiastical renewal which characterised the province. A new chapel was built in Carrick in 1804 and two years later the parish priest built a new house for himself. The new chapel was an ambitious construction; a contemporary has left an account of its dimensions:

> It is 82 feet long by 62 feet wide, making it 5,004 square feet, which sat 2 feet to each person will accommodate 1,250 persons, and galleries 17 feet wide and quite round the house will accommodate 94 persons more.[19]

The scale of the chapel reflected the increased population of the town, but it was also an indication of more regular Mass attendance. The chapel was financed by general subscription and the surviving list of contributors supports our earlier observations. Once more, it was the mercantile class which promoted and financed this venture, while the vast majority of the population – the labourers, fishermen, factory workers – appear to have made no contribution whatsoever to the fund. This might be attributed to their poverty or perhaps a sense of alienation from the predominantly bourgeois Church.[20]

Similarly the school at Carrick was financed by the contributions of two substantial benefactors. The site for the school was bequeathed by a local man, James Doyle, and the costs involved were borne by public subscription. The monastery, built at a cost of £1,500, was financed by a donation made by one of Edmund Rice's friends and first disciples, the wine merchant Thomas O'Brien who was the oldest of the early Brothers. The school opened in January 1806 and was attended by sixty 'rude, ignorant and uncultivated' boys.[21] In the same year a free school was opened for girls. From the beginning there were close links between the parish and the Brothers. The parish priest, John McKenna, gave encouragement to the venture, visiting the school and celebrating Mass for the 'monks and scholars'. It is perhaps a measure of the efforts of the Brothers that 800 children were presented for Confirmation in July 1807, apparently the first time the sacrament had been administered in the parish since Dr Hussey's visitation in 1802. The most recent Confirmations before that were held in 1791.[22]

Wherever possible, Edmund Rice responded favourably to invitations to open schools. In reply to a request from Archbishop Bray of Cashel in 1810 he

7.1 Francis Moylan (1735–1815), bishop of Cork. Irish school (*c.*1800), NGI.

expressed a wish that his system would 'spread before long in most parts of the Kingdom'.[23] From the outset, however, Rice made it an essential precondition that the 'arrangements of the school and the mode of teaching the children' were left entirely to the Brothers.[24] There were, in addition, practical limitations which restricted his freedom to meet the many requests which came to him. Apart from the obvious financial considerations, the shortage of manpower was the greatest impediment to renewed expansion. Circumstances necessitated choices; Edmund Rice increasingly devoted his scarce resources to the provision of education in the cities where demand was greatest and where their innovative large schools were particularly effective. The early years of the nineteenth century witnessed an alarming increase in the population of Ireland; in the thirty years from 1792 numbers rose from four and a half million to almost seven million. This expansion fuelled the fear of a Malthusian check, but educationalists took solace in the notion that such a catastrophe could be averted by the exercise of what Malthus(1766–1834) had called 'restraint and foresight', the product of an education which would raise the condition of the poor and make them 'happier men and more peaceful subjects'.[25]

This rapid rise in the population meant that the proportion of children in society was unprecedented. Their educational needs were particularly pronounced in the cities where the streets were teeming with poor children. In Cork, for instance, the Catholic Poor Schools Committee expressed its concern at 'the alarming groups of idle boys who infest and disgrace the streets and public places' of the city.[26] The bishop of Cork, Francis Moylan, had made every effort to promote the education of the poor since his transfer from the diocese of Kerry in 1787. As a consequence, Catholic education was more advanced in the city than in any other location in Ireland. Moylan facilitated Nano Nagle's request for papal approval of her congregation and, in 1793, he supported the initiative of the merchants who founded the Committee. Established in the wake of the Catholic Relief Act of that year, the merchants sought to continue Nagle's work and to provide free education and material assistance to boys and girls in their 'little seminaries'. The Society was governed by a General Committee, composed of twenty-four merchants and chaired by the bishop, and a further five sub-committees which managed the schools in the particular districts.[27]

By 1799 the Committee had nine schools under its direction catering for the needs of 700 students from funds collected by subscription and through charity sermons.[28] These numbers were totally inadequate in a city of 80,000 people. The Committee established night schools, but these, too, were insufficient. While the decision to teach boys and girls on alternate nights allowed the Society to increase the numbers of children enrolled, only a fraction of the poor of the city could be accommodated in their schools.[29] Perhaps more ominously the inefficiency of the teachers meant that the future of these schools was in jeopardy. In January 1806, the subcommittee noted that 'the deficiency of some of their [teachers was] shamefully great. However, we cannot expect perfection when the annual salary cannot be said to be more than a pittance which no man of liberal education would accept.'[30] In the interim solution, the subcommittee recommended the adoption of Joseph Lancaster's educational methods, and voted that a teacher trained personally by Mr Lancaster be appointed, 'owing to the novel and mechanical' nature of his system.[31] The Committee also planned the construction of a 'large and commodious' central school which would be 'sufficient to embrace the population of the centre, south and west parts of the city'.[32] However, in the longer term, Bishop Moylan believed that the only solution to the city's education crisis was the introduction of a male religious institute like Rice's 'monks'.[33]

7.2 Monastery and schools, at Our Lady's Mount (North Monastery), Cork. The centre was first built in 1816. The wings were erected in 1850.

No member of the Waterford community could be spared. So, just as the Presentation Sisters in Cork had accepted the Power ladies into their Novitiate in 1796, Edmund Rice welcomed two candidates from Cork to Mount Sion. On Moylan's suggestion, Jeremiah O'Connor and John Leonard, both members of his Charitable Committee, travelled to Waterford in March 1810 to begin their novitiate and 'be fitted' for the establishment of a monastery in Cork.[34] In the following year they were professed before returning to Cork to assume responsibility for their first school, a small room in Chapel Lane, which had until this point been conducted by paid teachers.[35] They were joined by Br Patrick Joseph Leonard, the elder brother of Br John, who had been a bank manager in the city, and in 1814, the bishop's Committee voted £50 to allow the Brothers accept two more recruits who would allow the school to cater for an additional 120 boys.[36]

Before long the Brothers had initiated change in Cork, similar to the experience of Waterford. In his annual report of 1815, Fr John England, clerical superintendent of the Society and subsequently bishop of Charleston, South Carolina, made lavish claims for the transformation of Cork, 'a city of 100,000 inhabitants … unprotected by a stipendiary police' force. Crime had diminished, 'morality had improved and social order had been ameliorated' to a point where Cork enjoyed 'peace, regularity and good conduct' unequalled, he boasted, not only in the United Kingdom, but in Europe. This he attributed to the influence of education, but especial mention was made of the efforts of the Monks:

> The Committee had not at first been as successful as they could wish the description of persons who have lately undertaken the superintendence of the schools have succeeded beyond their most sanguine hopes. The gentlemen of the Monastery admitted into that Institute solely from their capability and zeal have even improved upon the plan of Mr Lancaster and vast progress made by the children since those gentlemen have taken charge is the best evidence of the benefits which have arisen from the change.[37]

In that same year Bishop Moylan died and left a substantial bequest of £600 to the Brothers, who he described as 'his successors'. The foundation of the 'North Monastery' was laid in 1814, but the school was not opened until 1818, because it was placed at the disposal of the Committee of Public Health during the typhus epidemic which devastated the city. During this crisis the Monastery served as a hospital, and two of the community, Jerome Ryan and Ignatius McDermott, died caring for the sick.

Similar conditions prevailed in Dublin, where commentators were struck by the poverty of the 'many thousand neglected but not useless beings' in the streets behind the elegant thoroughfares.[38] Indeed, one preacher referring to these striking contrasts described the city, in 1808, as 'very wealthy and very wicked, very gay and very dissolute'.[39] In the last quarter of the eighteenth century there were 48 Catholic schools in the capital and these had 1,300 boys on their rolls. Only eight of these were free schools and these could accommodate no more than 255 boys.[40] In the early years of the new century the Presentation Sisters opened a large school for girls at George's Hill and the distinguished Jesuit, Dr Thomas Betagh, opened a free boys' school in the Liberties of the city. In 1812, Daniel Murray, the coadjutor archbishop, invited the Christian Brothers to Dublin. Rice was in a position to grant this request and a community was established at Hanover Street, under the direction of his first disciple, Brother Thomas Grosvenor. With the community Rice sent funding of £387 to help the new foundation. In time this link with Dr Murray would prove of crucial significance to the development of the Christian Brothers. Education was the archbishop's priority and he made every effort to consolidate and extend the presence of the new teaching orders, male and female, in the diocese.

In Hanover Street, the Brothers continued the work which had established their reputation in Munster among the poor of the south docks. Referring to their achievement sixty years later, Fr Gregory Lynch reminded Cardinal Cullen of the critical role of the Brothers in the transformation of the Church in the capital and the extent to which they had introduced the urban poor to the new devotions of the age:

> All the pious sodalities, societies and all the teachers in the Sunday Schools, and even the ranks of the clergy, were mainly fed from the Hanover Street School. The holy and practical Catholics of the parish, and the regular ones at the confessional during the past twenty years, were all educated in their schools.[41]

Not surprisingly, the Brothers were invited to extend their work in Dublin. In 1818 a school was opened in Mill Street, where 500 boys were taught in four large rooms in the former city residence of the earl of Meath. The community, which in 1821 was composed of one professed Brother, three novices and a postulant, also operated a Sunday school, which was instituted for adults 'whose employment allows no daily instruction'.[42] On those occasions Brothers offered catechesis, but it was the norm to read from a source approved by ecclesiastical authorities since extempore preaching was forbidden. Mill Street flourished until 1838 when the lease expired. The community then transferred to Francis Street and subsequently to Synge Street which became the most distinguished of the Brothers' schools. In 1820 another school was established in James Street, where 200 boys were educated under the direction of Br Francis Manifold.

In Munster the expansion continued with the opening of a school in Thurles. As early as 1810 Dr Bray had requested a community for his diocese, but Rice was unable to meet this request. Then in 1815, two members of an existing lay community of 'monks' in Thurles travelled to Mount Sion to begin their novitiate. Following their profession they returned to establish a school in the town. Limerick, with a population of 45,000, had particularly pressing needs. A contemporary account described the poverty of the city which 'exceeded any other town in Ireland in the wretchedness of its inhabitants ... [it was] the very acme of those evils of starvation, disease and putridity'.[43] Bishop Touhy unsuccessfully requested a community in 1812, but Rice agreed to send three Brothers to the city four years later. Resources were particularly short. The diocese had no potential candidates for the congregation, nor had the bishop acquired suitable accommodation for the new school. Coupled with this, the initial response

7.3 Christian Brothers' School, Limerick, engraving by O'Driscoll, Cork (*c.*1850), CBGA, Rome.

to a charity sermon in aid of the venture was extremely poor and just £42 was collected instead of the £135 expected. Br Austin Dunphy attributed this disappointing response to the poverty of the city: 'the times are bad', he exclaimed, 'we must make allowances'.[44]

In those difficult circumstances the Brothers were forced to beg from door to door in order to raise the necessary funds to establish their school. On the opening day of their temporary school two hundred boys presented themselves for admission. In time these numbers grew and such was the level of defections from the nearby nondenominational Lancastrian School that it was forced to close. As had been the case in Mount Sion, the Brothers in Limerick distributed clothes to the poorer students. The usual donations were a coat, boots, a pair of pants or, for the very young boys, a dress. Records were kept of these donations and between January 1817 and February 1838 some 1,551 boys were clothed by the Brothers.[45] Significantly, too, many of the pupils in these urban schools were drawn from beyond the town. The Revd George Dwyer, in his evidence before a Select Committee of the House of Lords (1837), stated that many of the children travelled a distance of ten or fifteen miles to the schools. This he attributed to the 'peculiar reputation and sanctity' of the Brothers' schools.[46]

The real poor of Ireland, very often, were to be found not in Dublin or Cork, but in the slums of England. With the same generous spirit with which he had responded to the poor of Waterford, Edmund Rice sent communities to minister to this Irish diaspora. The first foundation in England was made in the industrial centre of Preston, Lancashire. Rice travelled to the city in 1825 and was so impressed by the educational needs there, that, in spite of a chronic shortage of manpower and funds at home, he immediately dispatched a community to England. Two Brothers, Joseph Murphy and Aloysius Kelly, took charge of 150 boys and their daily programme was tailored in response to specific instructions from the local clergy. Edmund Rice outlined their task:

> The duties to be performed in Preston … are as follows viz.:
> 1. Three hours school before noon.
> 2. Three hours afternoon.
> 3. Catechism and Religious Instruction twice a week from 6 to 7 o'clock in the evening for those who do not frequent the school.
> 4. Catechism and Religious Instruction twice a week from 8 to 9 o'clock for those employed in the factories.
> 5. Religious Instruction morning and afternoon on Sundays.[47]

Further schools were planned for Manchester, but the expectations of the local Catholic Board proved unacceptable, especially the request that the Brothers 'visit the sick and prepare them for the Sacraments'.[48] Twenty years of experience had taught Rice that such missionary activity was beyond the scope of his congregation. Accordingly, the Manchester Committee initiated discussions with the Patrician Brothers who accepted the invitation, but it appears as if the vicar apostolic of the district, Bishop Thomas Smith, chose to invite the Christian Brothers in spite of their preconditions. That said, once established, the Brothers contributed towards the evangelisation of the city. And just as their radical system at home had involved the boys in the education of their parents, so, too, in Manchester the students became agents of transformation. After Sunday School, the boys were sent out to the 'lofts in different directions' giving instruction to about 2,000 people each week. 'So numerous were the conversions', one Brother boasted, 'that the priests could not attend conveniently to all'.[49] In the same year, the Brothers took over a Catholic school in Soho, London, where the annalist of the congregation recorded 'no boy in the school had made his first communion between the year 1803 and the arrival of the first brother in 1826'.[50]

II

From their first profession the Brothers were a diocesan congregation. Each community, though united by a common vision, was an independent founda-

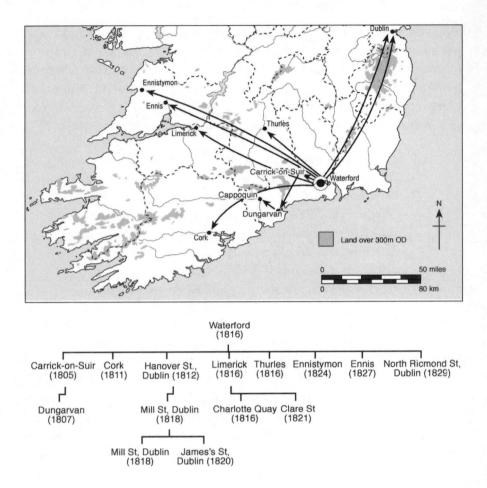

Waterford
(1816)

| Carrick-on-Suir (1805) | Cork (1811) | Hanover St., Dublin (1812) | Limerick (1816) | Thurles (1816) | Ennistymon (1824) | Ennis (1827) | North Ricmond St, Dublin (1829) |

Dungarvan
(1807)

Mill St, Dublin
(1818)

Charlotte Quay   Clare St
(1816)   (1821)

Mill St, Dublin   James's St,
(1818)   Dublin (1820)

7.4 Expansion of the Christian Brothers, 1802–30.
Map drawn by Matthew Stout.

tion subject only to the bishop of the diocese, to whom the Brothers professed their vows. In reality, while the local superiors looked to Edmund Rice for guidance and financial assistance, the society was a loose body with no official head. Each local superior was independent of every other superior and of the 'founder'. Rice had no control outside of Mount Sion, and even then his legal authority existed only as long as he was superior of the community.[51]

In time the practical weaknesses of this system became apparent. On one level, the financial needs of the various houses illustrated the desirability of a common fund where scarce resources could be pooled and managed more effectively. More fundamental, however, were the restrictions which the diocesan structures placed on the Brothers' freedom of response to the needs of the Church. This limitation had been clearly demonstrated following Bishop Murray's request for Brothers for Dublin and the understandable reluctance of Dr Power to release any Brothers from under his control in Waterford. It appears that there were informal ways around these restrictions, and Rice appears to have directed aspiring members towards communities where manpower needs were greatest, but these did not solve the problem.[52] The Dominican archbishop of Dublin, John Troy, appreciated the advantages which could be gained from the subjection of the Brothers to a single superior general. His coadjutor, Daniel Murray, was equally attached to the idea of centralisation and he, too, urged Edmund Rice to apply to Rome for approval of a Rule and constitutions which would enable him to transfer men from diocese to diocese. The essential point about this proposal is that it involved not just a change in canonical status, as the traditional historiography of the Christian Brothers suggests, but the creation of a new order in the Church from the amalgamation of the Presentation communities.

It is apparent, too, that there were voices calling for change within the ranks of the Brothers. Some were more radical in their expectations. Thomas Grosvenor, Rice's first follower and superior of the initial Dublin foundation, envisioned a sweeping restructuring of the congregation which would include the ordination of selected members to meet the pastoral needs of the boys. He communicated his thoughts on this scheme to Archbishop Murray in May 1815:

> Tho' the exertion of the members of the Institute are great to promote the moral improvement of their pupils, 'tis evident they have not within their power the means of doing so effectively until such time as one or two priests are attached to each establishment – such was the Rt Rev. Dr. Hussey's design under whom the Institute was first formed in Waterford. He proposed that they should have the care of delivering spiritual instruction to the children, hearing their confessions and giving Mass to the community. With them could not such persons be most usefully employed in visiting the sick and prisons as was the practice with some of the members of the Waterford community?[53]

Grosvenor's observation must be qualified in the light of his growing vocation to the priesthood, but it suggests a marked dissatisfaction with the Brothers' increasingly exclusive employment in the schools.

Apart from such practical considerations, the archbishop of Dublin had more immediate reasons for pressing for a change in the Brothers' canonical status. Politically the decision to subject the Brothers to the Rome alone was of great significance. From the last quarter of the eighteenth century attempts were made to subject episcopal appointments to a Royal veto; certainly prior to 1815, it appeared that full emancipation would only be conceded in return for this safeguard. Once they had recovered from the crisis on 1798, the Catholic hierarchy resisted this intervention from the state, and Rice had long expressed his determined opposition to such a measure, 'a wicked veto' which he believed would bring 'schism, and every other mischief'.[54] In these circumstances freedom from a potentially compromised episcopate was eminently desirable.

Archbishop Murray suggested that Rice's companions adopt the Rule of the De La Salle Brothers; in this sense the change of status was an episcopal initiative. On returning from Rome in January 1817, Dr Murray brought with him copies of the French Rule and the original papal brief of the institute of the Christian Schools (1680). These provided a model of the kind of central government the new institute needed and were accepted by representatives from each of the foundations, which Rice assembled at Mount Sion in August 1817.[55] No record of the discussion survives, but we may assume that the gathering was far from united in its appraisal of the desirability of the proposed changes. Br Thomas Grosvenor, for one, had previously mooted the value of placing the institute under the 'immediate direction of the bishops' as the best means of assuring that 'its rules [were] fiercely and strictly adhered to'.[56] However, following 'discussion and deliberation', the assembly voted to apply for constitutional change; it drafted thirteen articles to be presented to Rome and passed a number of resolutions, which called for consultation with the bishops and the professed Brothers.[57]

Responsibility for this process was entrusted to 'Br Ignatius [Rice] of Waterford' who drove the project single-handedly.[58] He consulted the Brothers, and summoned at least two gatherings of the professed members at Thurles, in 1818 and 1819. At these, too, he encountered stern opposition, and Br Patrick Corbett, one of the superiors present, recorded how Rice 'failed to secure any agreement among the Brothers'.[59] There is no evidence, either, that he engaged in any meaningful discussion with the hierarchy, with the exception of the archbishop of Dublin and his coadjutor who were the patrons of the project. They presented the adapted constitutions to Rome for approval, in the summer of 1818, along with a memorial 'on behalf of the Brothers' which contained just one signature, that of Edmund Rice.[60] In a letter which accompanied the application, Archbishop Troy was generous in his praise of the Brothers, who:

7.5 Portrait of John Thomas Troy (1739–1823), archbishop of Dublin, by Thomas
Clement Thompson, oil on canvas, NGI.

by means of their labours in promoting religion and the moral education of poor boys have done the greatest good for Religion not only in Dublin but also in other parts of this Kingdom. Furthermore I testify that the aforesaid rules of this Society are adapted to the conditions of this country and very suitable for the propagation of the Institute. The testimony of other Bishops in Ireland agrees with me in this matter.[61]

Yet in spite of Archbishop Troy's confidence, the Irish bishops were far from united in their enthusiasm for the proposed amalgamation. The untimely deaths of Bishop Power of Waterford (1816) and Dr Moylan of Cork (1815) not only deprived Rice of his closest supporters, but their successors led the opposition to the amalgamation.

The new bishops were understandably troubled at the prospect of the Brothers being removed from their jurisdiction by the formation of a Pontifical Institute. The fiercest opposition to the amalgamation came from Robert Walsh, bishop of Waterford. Walsh had succeeded to the diocese following a bitter interregnum and he attributed a great deal of the resistance to his candidacy to the influence of Edmund Rice. Indeed, Walsh's administration of the diocese proved so divisive and produced such 'deplorable evils', that Rice, with encouragement from Bishop Coppinger of Cloyne, promoted a petition among the laity of Waterford seeking redress from Rome.[62] Walsh and his circle were infuriated by this intervention. One of the bishop's correspondents, James Bernard Clinch, expressed their anger when he condemned 'that foolish antipope', Coppinger, who had:

> invited and encouraged by letter Edward Rice [*sic*] to debauch the fidelity and morality of [Walsh's] flock, into the atrocious crime of subscribing to lies, which they knew not, against their Bishop.[63]

Walsh refused to ignore such interference and complained to Rome of the bishop of Cloyne's action in fomenting sedition among the laity and 'discontented priests' which would serve only to encourage sedition against ecclesiastical authority. The same letter launched a broadside against Rice, 'once a butcher', and his 'good-for-nothing' brother the Augustinian.[64] Besides the business of the petition, Rice and the bishop were at loggerheads over the administration of his predecessor's will. Edmund Rice was Dr Power's executor and as such he opposed Walsh's attempts to divert the late bishop's estate, two-thirds of which was bequeathed for the education of the poor, for the upkeep of St John's College, his diocesan seminary.

There were serious clerical politics at play, too, not least of which were the heated debates about the appropriate form of episcopal nomination and appointment. Archbishop Troy was never simply a 'Roman hack', but from the outset it was clear that he had returned to Ireland in 1778, 'freighted with the prerogative doctrines of the Court of Rome'.[65] The death of Bishop Power, and the subsequent search for a successor, highlighted the radical contrast between the traditional method of nomination, in which Troy's recommendation had held enormous sway, and the concept of 'domestic nomination', which allowed greater say to the clergy of the vacant diocese.[66] The archbishop opposed the widening of the process, which he described as 'an intolerable abuse, productive of Cabals and democracy in the government of the Church, an act encouraging the Laity to meddle in Ecclesiastical affairs'.[67] Accordingly, he resisted this 'dangerous innovation', and in the course of a very complex selection process, he unsuccessfully attempted to block the appointment of Robert Walsh, the preferred candidate of the clergy of Waterford and Lismore.[68]

The archbishop's enthusiasm for a change in canonical status of the Brothers was clearly driven by a desire to remove them from the influence of such bishops. From Rice's perspective, too, the change would save the schools from clerical conflict by giving them the stability pontifical status would afford. More immediately, however, it would protect him from Bishop Walsh who was incensed by Rice's conspicuous interference and whose anger seriously threatened the future of the congregation. Ironically, Rice's prominent action was an example of the caballing which Troy sought to prevent and the bitterness of the interregnum served only to harden episcopal resistance to the Brothers' search for change. Bishop Kyran Marum, of Ossory, was enraged by Rice's meddling and communicated his fury to Austin Dunphy, Rice's superior at Mount Sion:

> I beg to state that in my opinion, the interference ascribed to Mr Rice could be warranted only by very extraordinary circumstances. Whether such circumstances … exist in the diocese of Waterford and Lismore it has not been in my power to ascertain, nor indeed my duty to enquire. But were I Mr Rice's superior in religion, I would certainly not sanction or permit the interference in question until it had been made appear to me with evidence, that the very rare but yet possible case had arrived when ordinary rules should be departed from and when the private sol-

7.6 St Patrick's Church, Dunmanway, County Cork, designed by
Brother Austin Riordan (1834). Courtesy of Praxiteles, archiseek.com.

dier may step forth from the ranks and, for the general welfare assume
the office of general.[69]

Within this context, Robert Walsh's opposition to the proposed amalgamation
of the Brothers' foundations was as much personal as principled and his campaign against the measure degenerated into an ugly assault on Rice's character,
the severity of which shocks, even at a distance of two centuries.

In a correspondence with Franciscan priest, Richard Hayes, Walsh rounded
upon Edmund Rice's meddling in clerical politics. Never before, he argued, had
there been 'smuggling' and 'scheming' like that of 'Rice and his juvenile class to
obtain mitres and crosiers and benefices for their friends'.[70] In a series of frantic
addresses to Propaganda Fide, too, he opposed the plan to give the Brothers
greater autonomy, suggesting, instead, that it would be better to impose a
vow of enclosure to 'restrict [them] as far as possible to their houses and
schools'.[71]

Indeed most of the Bishops of Munster have written to me deprecating
the conduct of some of the Monks, & protesting loudly against the idea
of having a perpetual chief or General among them … My object is, &
it is necessary, whereas they are thus unruly & not disposed to live subject to pastoral & clerical superiors, & in order to enforce regularity &
order among them if they absent themselves about the country for Days
without leave either of the Bishop or their respective Pastors, to order
that they do not receive the Sacraments—without adhering to their
original Discipline nothing can go on well—this unruly, foolish &
insubordinate conduct may yet bring the eye of our Protestant
Government on them, whom even the Laws as yet do not recognise as
a Body & this would be dangerous to us all. [72]

The bishop took his cause to the Vatican secretary of state. He described William
Coppinger as not merely 'wild' but 'mental', while Rice was damned as 'a
common butcher on the stalls and a public fornicator'.[73]

The bishop's letter was followed by similar objections, purporting to come
from 'Six Monks' of the congregation, which opposed 'the intention of some
of the Superiors to have Mr Rice', whom they considered as 'unfit and not
capable', elevated to the position of superior general. This letter, a blatant
forgery, was filled with inaccuracies, such as the inclusion of Clonmel (founded
1847), and Youghal (founded 1857) among the houses of the order.[74] In the
autumn, a further appeal was addressed to Propaganda Fide, in the name of
seventeen pastors of the diocese of Waterford and Lismore. This remarkable
letter echoed the vicious assault on Rice's reputation made by the bishop in his
correspondence:

It may not be amiss to give Your Eminence a brief outline of Rice the
Monk's life … This man sometimes was a Dealer in cattle and a
common Butcher in the streets of Waterford—Your Eminence will
judge from this, his Slaughtering profession of the savageness of his
nature and absence of tender sensibility and want of human feeling.
This impertinent intruder in the affairs of the sanctuary was of habits
irregular and of desires lustful, which to the prejudice of morality and
the scandal of the faithful he fully gratified—from his loins issued many
a bastard child, some of which breed and spurious progeny are still
living; reflecting on his unprincipled conduct—this is a truth we all
know and so do the laity of Waterford …—ashamed of his misfortunes,

he entered on a religious life, and how happy the change if he be truly repented and did not meddle in other people's concerns. Not still satisfied, this wretched man's ambition also is to become perpetual General of his institute and to lord it over the Priests and Bishops and be under no control.[75]

This letter, like the one from the 'Six Monks', was an obvious forgery and recognised as such by Propaganda Fide; modern analysis has attributed it to the bishop's closest collaborator, Patrick O'Meagher, parish priest of Dungarvan.[76] Emmet Larkin has studied the bitter clerical politics of the age, but none of the correspondence compares to the vitriol and unsubstantiated accusations made against the founder of the Christian Brothers.[77] This was not an informal clerical exchange, but the bishop's animus towards Rice was vented in official correspondence with the highest officials in the Roman curia.

Clearly, Rice could excite the range of emotions, from love to hate, but the irrationality of Walsh's rant undermined his cause, particularly as he embroiled the Presentation Sisters in an attempt to discredit the Brothers. In one frenzied petition to Propaganda, he referred to improper communications between the two groups, which implied the presence of Brothers in the Sisters' cells at night time. This he described as a 'scandal to the faithful'.[78] Such invective enraged Archbishop Murray, who rallied to the Sisters' defence. 'The Bishop of Waterford', he complained to Cardinal Fontana, 'speaks of dreadful suspicions … What crueler wound could even the heretics themselves inflict upon the honour of virgins?'[79] And Archbishop Troy, too, rallied to endorse the reputation of the Sisters whose 'exceptional piety and virtues … spread abroad everywhere an odour of sweetness'.[80]

Notwithstanding the collapse of Bishop Walsh's credibility, Rice's application for approval had to go through exacting procedures. As part of this process Cardinal Fontana requested further clarification of Troy's assertion that the application enjoyed the support of the hierarchy. This was a difficult task, especially as five of the eight communities in the proposed union were in the diocese of two bishops who fiercely opposed the move.[81] Troy, however, with characteristic tenacity circumvented his opponents and received the necessary confirmation indirectly, approaching the three archbishops, Curtis of Armagh, Everard of Cashel and Kelly of Tuam at a series of episcopal consecrations in the summer of 1819.[82] In the subsequent submission to Rome, which contained just Troy's signature, the archbishop informed the cardinal prefect that he had secured the approval of sixteen bishops to his proposal, but that they had recommended the addition of several new constitutions. The most serious of these amendments included the provision of an episcopal veto on the removal of Brothers from the diocese, a ban on Brothers visiting nuns, and the introduction of a vow to deliver 'gratuitous education'.[83]

The Brothers were fortunate in having Fr John Rice in Rome to handle the progress of their appeal. By now Rice's brother was assistant general of the Augustinians and he exerted considerable influence through his friendship with Dom Mauro Capellari, the future Gregory XVI, who was consultor to several pontifical congregations. Rice successfully argued that conceding an episcopal veto on transfers would make the effective government of the institute impossible, but he was unable to reverse the addition of the rule concerning visits to convents. However, this became a dead letter following Bishop Walsh's unfounded accusations against the Presentation Sisters, which exposed the folly of the clause which might encourage such malicious complaints.[84]

The insertion of a vow of 'gratuitous education' proved more problematic. The Rule of the Presentation Sisters included a vow to teach the poor gratuitously, but Rice and the early Brothers had not taken this vow in 1808, on the grounds that in the absence of a sufficient endowment it was unwise to rule out the acceptance of modest fees. Such arguments carried little influence in Rome, and the contentious vow remained in spite of a unanimous appeal from the first chapter of the Christian Brothers assembled in 1822.[85] The Brothers appealed again in 1827 and in 1839, but the prohibition against fees remained in place until the third superior general, Br Aloysius Hoare, obtained a Rescript in 1872 to charge pupils in comfortable circumstances.[86]

The decisive factor in securing papal approval for the new constitutions, however, was Rice's known hostility to proselytising schools. In 1818, the prefect of Propaganda Fide had rallied the Irish bishops in terms reminiscent of those employed by Thomas Hussey in his pastoral address of twenty years before. The cardinal outlined papal opposition to these schools and urged the pastors 'to watch, and carefully protect their flocks from the snares of wolves':

> Information has reached the ears of the Sacred Congregation that Bible Schools, supported by the funds of Catholics, have been established in almost every part of Ireland, in which, under the pretence of charity, the inexperienced of both sexes, but particularly peasants and the poor, are allured by the blandishments, and even gifts of the masters, and infected with the fatal poison of depraved doctrines.[87]

cere gratitude for his fatherly care of them. They then said that it was the interests of the Institute, and through it the interests of the Church in Ireland that induced them to take the step they had determined on. Then the bishop turned to Michael A[ugustine] Riordan and another who were very dear friends of his, he appealed to them to remain under his jurisdiction ... The two severed their connection with the Brothers of the North Monastery to the very great regret of the Community.[96]

The brothers under the leadership of Br Augustine Riordan remained a diocesan congregation under the jurisdiction of Dr Murphy and continued to live according to the original Presentation rule. The bishop provided them with a house on the south side of the city, and this foundation, known as the South Monastery, became the home of these 'Presentation Brothers'.

Bishop Murphy was particularly heartened by the resolve of Augustine Riordan (1783–1848) to remain under his jurisdiction, a decision which the Presentation annals attribute to his tenacious adherence to his first vocation.[97] However, the historian of the Presentation Brothers attributed Br Augustine's decision to a personal appeal from the bishop, who feared the loss of a close collaborator in the revival of Catholicism in the region.[98] Riordan's efforts extended beyond the schools, and it was principally his skills as an architect which set him apart from his confreres. He had worked in the architectural practice of Sir Thomas Deane's father and subsequently designed many of the principal churches and convents in the dioceses of Cork and Cloyne. The bishop's fear of losing such a vital 'subject' was understandable. In 1827, the Presentation Brothers took responsibility for the Lancastrian School in the city, thus effectively assuming the functions of Bishop Moylan's Charitable Society. Before long, Riordan was joined by able companions, most notably Paul Townsend, another architect who was the founder of the second and third schools of the Presentation Brothers, in the diocese of Kerry, at Killarney and Milltown. Before Augustine Riordan's death, in 1848, the 'Pres' Brothers had made their first tentative steps on the foreign missions with foundations in Pittsburgh, Pennsylvania, and Madras, India.[99]

Receipt of the papal brief gave the new congregation stability and permanence. In consequence, the change in canonical status has been celebrated by the Christian Brothers and described by Rice's biographer as a 'triumph'.[1] Certainly, as a political manoeuvre, the achievement of pontifical status warrants this appellation. The immediate context of the change was, of course, the imminent and ominous appointment of Robert Walsh as bishop of Waterford, but the desirability of independence from episcopal control had been apparent from the outset. While the conduct of Walsh, described as 'a man of the most dubious integrity and morality', is regularly contrasted with the benevolence of his predecessors, it is worth recalling that Rice's relations with the bishops of Waterford were never smooth.[2] In the first instance, the venture nearly failed in the face of Hussey's anger at Rice's development on the site of the former Faha chapel; only the Brother's humble submission averted a crisis. And Bishop Power, too, remembered as 'the best friend of the Brothers', threatened to close the school and disperse the Brothers of the Carrick community, during a financial crisis which undermined the establishment in January 1815.[3]

The irony of Rice's escape from episcopal control is that the initiative came from the archbishop of Dublin. The suggestion was occasioned not just because of the antipathy which existed between Troy and Robert Walsh, but also on account of the extent to which his predecessor had frustrated attempts to transfer Brothers to the capital.[4] Of course, as a Dublin initiative, the change was resented by the other bishops who had previously considered the various communities to be their 'subjects'. The newly appointed bishop of Waterford, Patrick Kelly, communicated this frustration to the Roman curia, arguing that 'what has been done in this place should not … have been done at all'.[5] Indeed, the presence of Bishop Murphy and two confreres in Rome, in the spring of 1828, convinced the Cork community that lobbying was underway to seek the withdrawal of the brief.[6] While such fears proved unfounded, there was no desire to repeat the process with the other teaching congregations. The Patrician Brothers remained a diocesan institute until 1888, while the status of the Presentation Brothers remained unchanged until the following year.[7] Paradoxically, the papal brief is celebrated in traditional histories as affording Edmund Rice the opportunity to realise his ambition of the congregation spreading throughout the kingdom.[8] Yet in reality episcopal resentment assured that this would not be so. Indeed, clerical reaction to the change was immediate. In Cork, for instance, it appears that the Charitable Committee had decided to place the Lancastrian School under the Brothers of the North Monastery, but this was effectively vetoed by the clergy, who insisted that it be entrusted to Br Augustine Riordan and 'two competent masters'.[9] Only two further establishments outside of the Dublin diocese were made in Rice's lifetime. And even these invitations, to Ennistymon (1824) and Ennis (1827), were received in the critical context of the 'Bible Wars', when the bishops turned in desperation to the Brothers for assistance.[10]

Rice's success in securing the assent of the majority of the Brothers to the amalgamation was a measure of his own determination. Prior to this, his legal authority was limited to Mount Sion, and it is unclear whether the Brothers in the other communities considered him to be their founder. Strictly speaking, Rice had 'founded' only one establishment, Mount Sion, and each of the other houses had its own 'founder'. In the house annals of Carrick-on-Suir, for example, that title is used explicitly in relation to the Waterford wine-merchant, Thomas [O']Brien.[11] The creation of the Christian Brothers was a corporate enterprise, not unlike like that of the foundation of the Jesuits by Ignatius and his companions in the sixteenth century, or indeed the establishment of Fr John Rice's Augustinian Order in the 'Great Union' of 1256.[12] In a real sense, there was not just *one* founder of the Christian Brothers, but eight. In Fitzpatrick's expression, to expect such men to be enthusiastic about the papal brief 'was equivalent to asking each to sign a self-denying ordinance'.[13] That said, the Brothers certainly regarded Rice as the founder of the Christian Schools movement in Ireland.

That seven of the Brothers' communities joined the union in 1822 was recognition that alternative forms of governance were necessary in a rapidly changing environment. Yet, while Rice's critics may have represented his orchestration of the amalgamation as the behaviour of a private soldier assuming the role of general, there was no sense in which his actions could be considered a coup.[14] In fact, having achieved agreement, Rice submitted to an election process at the congregation's first general chapter. It is significant, too, that the first history of the institute, 'Origin' written in the 1820s by Br Austin Dunphy, records that Rice was not elected unanimously, but by 'the majority' of the Brothers present.[15] Nor is there a suggestion that, having been elected, the new general attempted to assume the mantle of 'founder'. On the contrary, his characteristic reticence and obdurate refusal to pose for a formal portrait suggest a rejection of such presumptions. In any event, such vain ambition would have been futile given the increasing influence of the Cork brothers within the congregation and the particularity of their own foundation story.

From the outset Rice's companions had responded generously to the invitations to make new establishments, but only when the principle of 'exclusive superintendence' was agreed.[16] Securing the papal brief accentuated that desire for independence within the ranks of the Christian Brothers. In the longer term, the uncompromising defence of their autonomy may have restricted their apostolic effectiveness; it certainly contributed to the conflict with the National Board of Education, and the dramatic clash with the Irish bishops in the 1870s. In the short term, however, the mobility afforded by the change in canonical status allowed the Brothers to respond rapidly to the needs of the Church, within the context of the 'Bible Wars' which represented the greatest challenge to Irish Catholicism since the Protestant Reformation of the sixteenth century.

CHAPTER EIGHT

The new reformation, 1820–50

THE TIMING OF THE PAPAL RECOGNITION of the Christian Brothers is particularly significant and, placed within the context of the 'Second Reformation', it demonstrates the renewed confidence and the combative nature of Irish Catholicism. Within that dynamic environment, the Brothers not merely advanced the 'Tridentine surge', but were synonymous with the Counter-Reformationary zeal which became the hallmark of nineteenth-century Irish Catholicism. Like his patron, Rice saw education as critical to the process of renewal in the Church, but like Ignatius of Loyola, too, circumstances combined to give the efforts of his companions a militant character. Indeed, in that role he was celebrated by contemporaries as a second Ignatius, called 'to confront the hydra-headed Reformation and its spawn of ten thousand sects'.[1]

I

The excesses of 1798 revived sectarian tensions in Ireland. In the aftermath of the rebellion a concerted effort was made to represent the bloody events of that summer as a 'popish plot'. Richard Musgrave, the 'Orange baronet', sought to revive sectarian memories of 1641, while George Taylor, a Methodist missionary who had been held captive by the rebels at Gorey, County Wexford, published a history of the rebellion which claimed that 'none of the rebels were so bloodthirsty, as those who were most regular attendants at the popish ordinances'.[2]

Such attitudes fostered the notion among British Evangelicals that the Irish were no less attractive as targets for evangelisation than the heathens of Africa or India.[3] With this task in mind a plethora of missionary societies were formed in Ireland, the more important of which included the Hibernian Bible Society (1806), the Irish Society for Promoting the Education of the Native Irish through the Medium of their own Language (the Irish Society, 1818), and the Scripture Readers' Society (1822). These societies embarked on a vigorous campaign to convert Irish Catholics *en masse*, and they were successful to the extent that, by

1829, an apologist argued that 'the Reformation has progressed more in Ireland since the Act of Union than in any period of her former history'.[4]

Preachers were dispatched to Ireland laden down with Bibles and tracts, which they distributed to the poor. Many of these early missionaries were fluent Irish-speakers and regarded this skill as a crucial part of their armoury. This represented a novel development, especially from the perspective of the Church of Ireland which had previously been hostile towards the language. Although hardly representative, in 1787, Bishop Woodward of Cloyne had argued that Irish 'obstructs religion; embarrasses civil intercourse ... [and] prevents cordial union'.[5] Yet within the context of a missionary crusade the distinguished Ulster Methodist, Adam Clarke, declared: 'the Irish language is with the natives a sacred language ... they allow themselves to feel from that tongue, what they do not consider themselves obliged to feel from another'.[6] The British and Foreign Bible Society, which supplied these missionaries, considered making an Irish translation of the Bible, but were initially advised against the move on the grounds that the few Irish peasants, who could read, read in English. Daniel O'Connell, for instance, claimed that flooding the country with Bibles in Irish would serve little purpose; in his native Kerry there were not five people who could read Irish, and not more than thirty in the province of Munster.[7] After the formation of the Irish Society, however, the Evangelicals were persuaded of the value of such a translation.

The Methodists were among the first to enter the great crusade and the most successful. John Wesley made his first of twenty-one visits to Ireland in 1747, but Methodist efforts gained considerable momentum in the aftermath of the 1798 rebellion. In 1799 a nationwide mission to Irish Catholics was begun; in 1809 there were twelve Methodist missionaries working in six areas, while ten years later twenty-one missionaries worked in fourteen stations dotted around the country. Like many of the other missionaries, they believed their task was not simply one of conversion. This was an opportunity to civilize Ireland, to bring the Gospel to the deluded Irish peasantry and in so doing the problems of the island, drunkenness, lawlessness and rebellion could be resolved. In 1811, for instance, the satirical *Irish Magazine*, edited by the former United Irishman Watty Cox, published a skit entitled 'Essay on the Irish Crusade for the extirpation of Popery and Pike Making'.[8] Another contemporary, the Scottish evangelical, 'Captain' James Gordon of the London Hibernian Society, spoke of the 'substitution of the cross of Christ for the gibbet', in what Stewart Brown has recently described as a crusade to secure the Protestant United Kingdom through the conformity of the 'semi-barbarous Irish' to the Established Church.[9]

8.1 'Holy Invasion of Ireland by British Apostles', *Irish Magazine*,
May 1811, NLI.

Desmond Bowen has highlighted this connection between evangelicalism and imperialism; he cites the third Earl Grey, a former Colonial Secretary, who in 1853 described the British crown as:

> the most powerful instrument under Providence, of maintaining peace and order in many extensive regions of the earth, and thereby assists in diffusing among millions of the human race the blessings of Christianity and civilization.[10]

More than this, many Methodists, fuelled by millenarianism, looked upon Ireland as the centre of a world-wide conflict between heretical Catholicism and biblical Protestantism.[11]

From the outset, the Methodist campaign was marked by a militant anti-Catholicism.[12] Yet, as the historian of Irish Methodism, David Hempton, comments, 'for some peculiar reason Wesley and his followers have been treated with ecumenical kid gloves by a spectrum of twentieth-century writers'.[13] Little of this spirit of tolerance, however, could be found among contemporary Catholic commentators, who universally identified Methodism with intolerance and opposition. Writing in 1866, the Jesuit W. J. Amherst articulated these sentiments:

> The Wesleyan Methodists have always been among the most bitter enemies of the Church. Their founder was not only an enthusiast, but a firebrand. One of his first principles was, no toleration to Catholics; he inculcated it in his followers, and he urged it by actual persecution.[14]

Not that Catholics were willing to tolerate Methodism and what Cardinal Fontana described as 'the fatal poison of [its] depraved doctrines'.[15] At an elite level, there was a surprising degree of religious toleration and co-operation among the Christian Churches in the first decade of the nineteenth century; but, this evaporated in the wake of the sermon delivered by William Magee, at his inauguration as archbishop of Dublin in Christ Church cathedral in October 1822. Magee claimed that the Church of Ireland was the only legitimate ecclesiastical body in Ireland; he called his flock to renewal, but more significantly he urged them to bring the entire population, including Catholics and Dissenters, into its fold.[16] From this point the 'gloves were off'; the bishop's entry brought the Protestant crusade to a new level, and his charge drew immediate response from Catholic quarters, particularly from James Warren Doyle, who was the most articulate of a new generation of confident Catholic bishops.[17]

8.2 'Public debate between a Protestant clergyman and a Catholic priest',
Irish Church Mission (*c.*1840–69), NLI.

Sean Connolly has attributed this increased sectarianism to three factors:
the launch of the so-called 'Second Reformation', the emergence of a new style
of popular politics under Daniel O'Connell, and the more combative outlook
of the Catholic Church.[18] The confidence of the Catholic cause was also buoyed
by the rise of millenarianism and the expectations created by the miracles of a
German priest, Alexander Emmerich, Prince Hohenlohe, which appeared to
reinforce the moral authority of the Church. In an Irish context, too, the prophe-
cies of 'Signor Pastorini', the pseudonym of Charles Walmesley (1722–97), an
English Catholic bishop, predicted the extermination of all Protestants by 1825,
the year of the papal jubilee.[19]

Rivalry and conflict increasingly became the norm as resurgent Catholicism
clashed headlong with evangelical Protestantism, often in highly choreographed
public disputes. In January 1827 at Cavan, one such meeting organised by the
evangelical landowner, Lord Farnham, was told that 'Popery and slavery [are]
twin sisters', while in Limerick, Bishop Tuohy felt it necessary to refute the
calumny directed against the priesthood which had 'become the fashion … even
from the Christian pulpits of our Dissenting brethren'.[20] The Catholic clergy,

however, were not above such behaviour. As early as 1812, Fr Burke of Rosscarberry, County Cork, compared his English rulers unfavourably with the pagan Romans, while Fr Hayes in Cork condemned reformers such as Wycliff, Luther and Zwingli, by accusing them of intercourse with the devil.[21] Among the Catholic hierarchy, too, liberal Catholicism began to give way to ultramontanism. This process has become synonymous with Archbishop Paul Cullen of Dublin, who once boasted he had never dined with a Protestant. On another occasion, while still rector of the Irish College, Rome, the future cardinal rebuked Fr Theobald Mathew, for his misguided ecumemism:

> In some of the sermons preached by you, or attributed to you in the public papers, you appear to entertain sentiments too liberal towards Protestants in matters of religion. I suppose there is no real foundation for this complaint ... However, it is well to be cautious. We should entertain most expansive sentiments of charity towards Protestants but at the same time we should let them know there is but one true Church and that they are strayed sheep from the one fold. We should let them know this; otherwise we might lull them into a false sense of security in their errors and by doing so we would really violate charity.[22]

Yet, while a great deal of attention has been focused upon the changes in the fortunes of Irish Catholicism which produced such confidence, it is vital to recall that the religious revival that characterised the early years of the nineteenth century was not confined to the Catholic Church. Nor indeed was it simply an Irish phenomenon. This was part of a wider renewal which had swept Great Britain and Ireland, dramatically transforming the religious landscape in the process.[23]

Much of the religious rivalry was centred on the education question. Since their first arrival, the provision of schools had formed a vital part of the evangelical crusade: as Thomas Wyse, one of O'Connell's lieutenants in the Emancipation campaign put it, the era witnessed 'a battle fought in every school, under every hedge for the minds and feelings of the country'.[24] The Bible societies established schools in which free education was offered to all those who were prepared to accept religious instruction. These bodies established free schools in places which had previously lacked educational facilities and very often they enticed pupils away from nearby pay schools. By 1826, Rice's assistant, Br Austin Dunphy, complained that the country was 'infested with Protestant schools', funded to the tune of £72,000 by the Treasury.[25] The societies appear to have been most active in poorer counties, such as Cavan or Mayo, where the Catholic revival had not been so pronounced.[26] This trend was particularly evident in County Clare where the London Hibernian Society had over eighty schools with one thousand Catholic children on their rolls. According to Bishop James O'Shaughnessy of Killaloe, these Bible schools had been 'the cause of diminishing considerably the mutual harmony and friendship between Catholics and Protestants that had subsisted till the unfortunate period of their existence'.[27] Similar concern was expressed by the western bishops of Tuam, Ardfert and Galway.[28]

At the heart of the controversy was the use of scriptural texts in schools, since the Bible itself had become a weapon in the war. For Protestants the Word of God alone would be sufficient to convert. Indeed, in his evidence before the Commission of Irish Education Inquiry (1825), the Scotsman 'Captain' James Gordon stated that 'a great many instances have occurred in which children from reading the Scriptures have left the Roman Catholic Communion'.[29] Catholic ecclesiastics were, therefore, determined to prevent the exposure of children to scripture without adequate interpretation and opposed the use of the Authorised Version rather than the Douay Bible, which contained notes relating to the interpretation of the Eucharist, the Blessed Virgin, the Supremacy of St Peter and other doctrines. As Archbishop Troy remarked in 1818:

> Since the days of Luther the Catholic Church condemns the indiscriminate use of Scripture in vulgar tones without note or comment and permits it only to the learned or lettered laity.[30]

Such sentiments were not unreasonable within an environment where Scripture had become so highly politicised that, as Irene Whelan observes, the 'Bible without note or comment' had entered political culture, not just as a symbol of the triumph of Protestant Christianity, but 'as the standard under which British Protestantism would conquer the world'.[31] In the following decade, within this context, Leo XII reiterated Catholic teaching and delivered an aggressive broadside to the Bible societies, whom he accused of attempting through 'a perverse interpretation of the Gospel of Christ' to turn the Bible into a 'human Gospel, or, worse, into a Gospel of the Devil'.[32]

On the ground, these convictions were often manifest in crude proclamations from the pulpit, as the Catholic clergy became more assertive in the face of evangelical opposition. One witness before the 1825 Education Inquiry spoke of threats of excommunication and 'warnings from the Altar that if they read the Bible or took it into their houses, they should be damned; that the Devil was in the Bible'.[33] In relation to schooling, too, the clergy used all their influence to force parents to withdraw their children from the objectionable 'biblical schools'. They not merely refused the sacraments, but were known to have cursed recalcitrant parishioners as well. Yet while 'JKL' denied all knowledge of the 'priest's curse', witnesses before various enquiries attested to its power. James E. Gordon, who was admittedly violently anti-Catholic, alleged that:

> In many parts of Munster and Connaught, they believe that the priest is armed with powers of life and death; that he could strike them dead … in other parts they believe that he could afflict them with sickness, make their hair fall off, kill their cattle and blight their crops.[34]

Another witness, a Catholic inspector with the Kildare Place Society, confirmed such notions, referring to popular fear that such curses could 'bring down the vengeance of Heaven', in which event the victim would have 'neither Luck nor Grace'.[35]

II

It was at this point that the Irish hierarchy turned to Rice's band of Brothers for support. Crucially, Archbishop Troy's quest for an alteration in the Brothers' canonical status coincided with anxiety in Propaganda Fide about the dangers of the Methodist schools in Ireland, which aimed at 'seducing the young and … eradicating from their minds the truths of the orthodox faith'.[36] Troy assured Rome that the Brothers were most useful in the conflict against the evangelicals. 'As regards the Bible Schools', he wrote, 'the bishops and clergy … zealously … work against these by establishing Catholic schools under the direction of the Brother Monks'.[37] Propaganda welcomed their labours to 'preserve the youth', and sanctioned the changes requested by Rice with a haste unusual for the Roman curia, which reflected not merely the critical nature of the Irish situation, but Pius VII's contempt for the evangelical cause.[38] 'These [Bible] societies', he informed Poland's Archbishop Ignatius Raczynski, 'are abhorrent to me, they tend to the subversion of the Christian religion, even to its very foundation; it is a plague which must be arrested by all possible means'.[39] In an Irish context, the Christian Brothers were such an instrument.

Of course, Edmund Rice and his Christian Brothers were well disposed to join in this battle. The congregation had been conceived amid the controversy of a passionate debate, provoked by Thomas Hussey's pastoral address, which called priests to 'stand firm against all attempts ... to withdraw [their] flocks from the belief and practice of the Catholic religion', especially in 'those places of education where ... religious faith or morals are likely to be perverted'.[40] Rice's response to the pastoral, however, was not simply reactionary as it might be interpreted. His intention was not simply to counter the proselytising schools, but rather, in a pro-active way, to provide an alternative, Catholic education for children in Waterford. That said, the decision of the early Brothers to open schools in Dungarvan and Carrick-on-Suir, where the Methodist 'swaddlers' had been active since 1794, have been attributed to an attempt to forestall the establishment of biblical schools there.[41] Certainly, once the 'Second Reformation' began, the Brothers were not slow to defend the Catholic cause. It is essential, however, to recall that for all its social and political ramifications, the battles of the 'Bible Wars' were about the vital business of the salvation of souls. On the evangelical side, there was the belief that 'papists' were destined for eternal damnation, while from a Catholic perspective, Paul Cullen, in evidence before the Powis Commission (1869), compared proselytism to murder since it deprived the soul of life by killing its faith. 'What does it profit a man', he asked, 'if he gain the whole world but suffer the loss of his soul.'[42]

The Brothers' *raison d'être* was the salvation of souls; as Br T. J. Hearn paraphrased the Rule and *Manual*, 'the object of their vocation was, the greater glory of God, the sanctification of their own soul and ... those little ones whom the Redeemer has conferred to their care'.[43] However, since the terms of the papal brief, which committed the Brothers to the provision of gratuitous education, frustrated the scope of that mission, Rice made an urgent appeal to Rome for its amendment. That request contained striking echoes of Hussey's pastoral, written twenty years earlier, undermining recent attempts to deny the bishop's influence upon the Waterford merchant. Referring to his previous unsuccessful appeal, Rice reminded Pope Leo XII that:

> The Petitioners in the first instance drew attention to the rapid progress which irreligion was making every year because of non-Catholic education which the unfortunate children receive because of the efforts made by the Heretics to induce the parents to send their children to schools recognized by the Bible Societies, which schools are well paid by the Government, the sum this year amounting to the huge sum of £32,000, not one penny of which is given to our Christian Schools because these teachers use the Catholic Bible quite differently and in a diametrically opposite sense to that used by the Bible Schools ...

> Therefore the Petitioners are fully persuaded that when such per-
> mission [to charge fees] is given to them … they will be able to extend
> the Christian education of the Poor and even to face the horrible
> destruction which the Bible Society threatens, the sad consequences of
> which have already been experienced.[44]

These extreme sentiments were mirrored in the correspondence of other members of the leadership of the Christian Brothers. In 1826, Br Austin Dunphy
informed the assistant superior general of the De La Salle Brothers, in Paris, that
'Great efforts have been made by the English Government to pervert the
Catholic youth of this country':

> Vast sums of money have been given by the British Parliament to vari-
> ous Protestant Associations for the Education of the poor Catholic chil-
> dren of Ireland … This money is all put into the hands of Protestants
> in order to bribe the poor children, to seduce them from the Catholic
> faith. The country is infested with Protestant schools … We must rest
> our success on the assistance of Almighty God and on the excellence of
> our schools above theirs.[45]

And the leader of the Cork faction of the Brothers expressed bitter resentment
at the 'vicious' proselytism of the state supported 'Protestant Churchmen', but
he took solace in the Catholic response:

> In the midst of this poverty, of these injustices and insults, we have the
> consolation of holding on to the faith of our ancestors and seeing it
> grow everyday, while the religion which they try to spread by means of
> money and the sword, like that of Mahomet, is growing less day by day
> and has split into a thousand sects which slander one another: but when
> the question is of something Catholic, they unite to strip us of our
> goods and our character. The large sums of money at the disposal of
> the department of education enable them to seduce some of the
> Catholic children; and although these poor little ones do not become
> Protestants, they become bad Catholics. Wherever the Brothers open
> schools they arrest the progress of these departments.[46]

Leonard's reference to the effects of proselytism, and the creation of 'bad
Catholics', reflected the experience of his contemporaries, not merely Catholic

clerics, but Protestant evangelists. In evidence before the Commissioners of Irish Education (1825), for instance, one witness made a distinction between 'converts' and those who had not conformed in a formal sense.[47] Nevertheless, he argued that there were 'a great number of Roman Catholics who had received enough light to discover a discrepancy between ... the Scriptures and the tenets of their own Church'. These were lingering in 'the Pale' of the Catholic Church, but had not yet entered into any other communion. Such alienation created a category which one Commissioner described as 'quasi converts'.[48]

Of course, with their geographic restrictions lifted, in theory at least, the Brothers were frequently called on to stem such leakages, and to defend the interests of the Catholic community against militant Protestantism. In a battle which contemporaries characterised as 'a war of extermination', they became the cutting edge of the Counter-Reformation sword in Ireland.[49] Indeed, the Brothers became synonymous with that struggle. Frederick Lucas, journalist, Member of Parliament and convert to Catholicism, believed that, in the face of 'fanatical proselytism', the establishment of a Brothers' school was 'the first means which occurs to a Catholic mind ... [as] a bulwark against assault'. This he declared was the 'signal test' of the esteem in which the Christian Brothers of Ireland were held.[50]

III

The urgency of the issue is clearly illustrated in the case of Clare, one of the poorest and most densely populated counties in Ireland. There, too, the early years of the new century were marked by religious tolerance and a spirit of coexistence between the different faiths. This was reflected, not least, in the support which Bishop O'Shaughnessy gave to the establishment of a Lancastrian school in Ennis in 1812.[51] Relations, however, were tested by the activities of Gideon Ouseley (1762–1839), an exotic Methodist who preached and sang in Irish, to large crowds gathered at fairs and funerals across the county.[52] From his first appearance at Ennis in 1809, the preacher was met with violence and was pelted with stones and brickbats, but as an eccentric he posed little threat to the Catholic Church. Neither was the foundation of a branch of the Hibernian Bible Society in the town, in March 1813, considered particularly significant, nor indeed was the expansion of the number of schools in the diocese enjoying financial support from the Kildare Place Society, which insisted on the use of Scripture 'without note or comment'.[53]

8.3 Richard Mant, Church of Ireland bishop of Killaloe and Kilfenora
(1820–3). Engraved by Richard Smith, London, 1840, NLI.

The decisive change in ecumenical relations in the county occurred in 1820, with the appointment of Richard Mant as Church of Ireland bishop of Killaloe and Kilfenora. His *Charge* to the clergy of the diocese put the 'Bible War' on an official footing in the region. Mant called the clergy to remove 'the errors of the Romish Church' and to take their mission to the cabin door.[54] This, he argued, was their sacred duty to which their ordination had committed them: to 'abolish Roman superstitions … [to] rescue our deluded people from their blind teachers … delivering them from the arrogant domination of the Church of Rome'.[55]

The address aroused immediate outrage in Clare, and several attempts were made on the bishop's life. He removed his family, first to Dublin and then to England, but was forced to return by his patron, the prime minister, Lord Liverpool, who chastised him for fomenting such commotion.[56] Ironically, Mant was not an evangelical, and later in the decade he opposed evangelicalism in the Church of Ireland. Indeed, by the 1840s, while bishop of Down and Connor, he was being described as a crypto-papist because he was considered too sympathetic to both ecclesiology and Tractarianism.[57] Essentially his initial charge betrayed the Englishman's naivety and ignorance of Ireland rather than evangelical conviction. Yet, while Mant avoided controversial issues in his subsequent charges in Killaloe, the tenor of his initial address heightened sectarianism in the diocese, particularly within the realm of education, which the bishop identified as critical to the 'correction of error and diffusing knowledge of true religion':

> Education is so powerful an engine in its operation on the human mind … [and] if we be faithful in our ministry, it may please Him to open to our instructions the hearts of His now deluded people and to render us the blessed instruments of bringing into the way of truth many of those who have erred and are deceived … The education of the poor … ought to … be regarded as an instrument, not of political or civil, or merely moral improvement, but of religious improvement: our great and ultimate object in the furtherance of their education should be to establish our poor brethren in the knowledge, profession and practice of the Christian religion, pure and undefiled.[58]

Such assertions increased Catholic opposition to the London Hibernian Society, which by 1823 had 23 schools in the county.[59] Moreover, the provocative *Charge* appeared to confirm Daniel O'Connell and Professor John MacHale's criticism of the Kildare Place Society, which subsidized 42 schools in the diocese of Killaloe. The Catholic clergy had previously no difficulty in accepting grants from the Society, in spite of the scriptural requirements. Yet, in the radically altered environment, the KPS became synonymous with proselytism and their genuine attempt to provide nondenominational education foundered in the face of opposition from an increasingly assertive clergy.[60]

This was the context in which the Christian Brothers began their school at Ennistymon, in the diocese of Kilfenora.[61] The parish priest, Peter O'Loughlin, hoped to establish a school in a disused chapel and received a consignment of furniture from the Kildare Place Society for this purpose. It is unclear who was intended to teach the school, but the initial appeal to the KPS confirmed that Scripture would be used without 'note or comment', and that 'no catechism … or any book inculcating peculiar religious opinion' would be used in class.[62] However, before the school opened in the summer of 1824, O'Loughlin made a radical reversal and appealed to Edmund Rice, assuring him of the support of Bishop Edmund French, for two Brothers.[63] Rice's response was immediate and, given the critical nature of the mission, he dispensed with the usual financial preconditions upon which his foundations were established. Instead, he offered the school a subvention of £30 a year for the first two years.[64] Moreover, Rice chose the community carefully, sending two of his most trusted companions: Austin Grace, a fluent Irish speaker, and the convert Francis Manifold, who at six feet six inches tall had a commanding presence.[65] They possessed the requisite zeal and experience for the task. In his correspondence with Kildare Place, however, the parish priest remained vague about the management of his school, but withdrew his earlier commitments and expressed opposition to the indiscriminate use of scripture as 'a common school-book' in the hands of 'the rude and illiterate'.[66] Such deviations were clearly unacceptable to the KPS and, in August 1824, the parish priest severed all connections with the Society.[67]

Before long, the Brothers had three hundred boys in their thriving school at Ennistymon. Beyond the classroom, their ministry included the promotion of new devotions through catechesis and the introduction of various confraternities to the town. In this regard, Br Austin Grace was particularly useful, and each Sunday he would stand at the rear of the chapel, translating the sermons for those who understood no English.[68] Yet, in spite of their achievement, relations between the diocesan clergy and the 'Monks' were fraught. The project was dogged by financial difficulties, but the principal contention was the parish priest's objection to the Brothers' insistence on the 'exclusive superintendence' of the school which was at odds with his own ambition.[69] The future of the venture was clearly at risk. In June 1826, Francis Manifold informed Rice of the crisis in Clare:

> We have no school here but ours at present, thronged to excess, and as for the adults, they are still increasing. It is going so well now, to stop this great good would be a great evil.[70]

Rumours spread that the Brothers were about to quit, but several of the laity intervened and appealed to Edmund Rice directly. Attempting to compensate for what they described as a 'lack of support and encouragement from another quarter', they offered £42 towards the expense of the school.[71] The crisis, however, was not averted until the following year when the appointment of a new parish priest, Fr John Sheehan, brought a radical improvement in relations.

That the second foundation in Clare at Ennis was plagued by similar problems is ironic given the critical circumstances in which the school was established. From the outset, the parish priest of the town, Dean Terence O'Shaughnessy, and his uncle, Bishop James O'Shaughnessy, were uncompromising opponents of the 'biblical schools' in the county. The dean, who publicly burned proselytizing literature, did not confine his energy to opposition, but sought to offer alternative education to the poor of the town.[72] In 1821, he established a free school for boys, and within three years he had three schools catering for over four hundred pupils.[73] Yet as the evangelical effort intensified, and the numbers attending the 'bible schools' rose to 400, the dean and his uncle called on the Brothers for assistance.[74] In March 1826, the bishop made a series of deferential requests to Edmund Rice for a community of 'monks':

> My Dear Sir,
> I am requested by the very Rev. Dean O'Shaughnessy, P.P. of Ennis, to solicit at your hands as a most particular favour, in which I join myself, that you may have the goodness to send to the town ... two competent men of your Brethren, qualified for Religious and literary instruction. There is no town in all Ireland where two Gentlemen of this description could be of more utility, in every point of view ... I beg to hear from you by return of post and hope your answer will be as such as I anxiously wish it. The sooner they may with convenience arrive the better.[75]

Br Rice responded favourably to this appeal, and by December preparations were well under way to welcome the Brothers to Ennis. In that month Dean O'Shaughnessy addressed two letters to Rice. These demonstrate the extent to which the Brothers were perceived as the first line of defense against the evangelical crusade:

> ... I shall expect them in the first week of the New Year, lest the Biblicals who are endeavouring to make another effort may be in the field before me. Nothing will be left undone to make the place agreeable to whoever you send & both laity and clergy will feel ever grateful for your condescension in accommodating this town in preference to so many others equally anxious & entitled to your attention.[76]

When the Brothers arrived, they assumed responsibility for the dean's school in Murray's Lane, which was in keeping with Rice's determination not just to offer schooling where none existed.[77] In this instance, too, the Brothers chosen by Rice had considerable experience, especially Jerome O'Connor, who had been a member of Bishop Moylan's charitable committee and a founder of the North Monastery in Cork.[78] In Ennis, he taught alongside Br Ignatius Barry in a disused grain store. Approached through filthy laneways, conditions in the school were inadequate if not lethal, given the prevalence of cholera in the region. In 1832, a local physician described the thronged conditions of the 'school', where many boys spent the day standing with their backs against cold, damp walls.[79] Yet despite these challenges, the influence of the Brothers brought a considerable improvement to the town, as they had at other centres across Munster. O'Shaughnessy credited their school with instilling discipline in the boys, who had previously been notorious for their pitched battles on the street. More specifically, he rejoiced that by 1833 the biblical schools were 'eradicated out of the town of Ennis'.[80]

Yet, for all the effusion and flattery of the initial invitation to the town, once that danger had lifted, the dean's interest in the Brothers declined.[81] Just as in Ennistymon, the priests resented the arrogant independence of the Brothers, which it must be acknowledged the superior chose to flaunt, to a point where his presence jeopardised the establishment, and necessitated his eventual removal to Cork.[82] In many respects, however, the crisis which faced the Brothers was a consequence of the rapid pace at which the dean pushed the process of ecclesiastical renewal, particularly the pressures created by the campaign to build a cathedral at Ennis. This bitterly divided the town and resulted in a rampant anticlericalism and animosity which was vented at chapel meetings in the autumn of 1833. Bishop McMahon described the rancorous gathering as 'disgraceful to any parish', yet the *Clare Journal* attributed the prelate's anger, not just to his wounded pride, but because the meeting had exposed the painful reality:

> That the laity are beginning to check the domineering arrogancy [*sic*] of the priesthood and are not willing to be longer under the reproach of being the only slaves in the land of freedom.[83]

At the chapel meetings, sections of the laity, politicised in the O'Connellite campaign, were pointedly critical of what they perceived as clerical avarice and the crippling costs of maintaining the dean, his curates, two Franciscan friars and a community of 'monks' in the town.[84] This forced the dean to justify the 'greatest advantage' which the Brothers had brought to the town, by 'preventing the youth … from murdering each other with stones'.[85] The bishop subsequently assured Rice that, while 'there are restless spirits in the world, whom it is impossible to satisfy', he should take no notice of any complaint he should hear about the 'professors at Ennis'.[86]

As it happened the Brothers' presence in the town was prolonged by the influence of the bishop, Patrick MacMahon, and the bounty drawn down when the school affiliated with the National Board of Education (1831). Nevertheless, so concerned was Edmund Rice for the future of the establishment, that he had over one thousand Masses offered for the intentions of the Ennis community in the twelve months from October 1829.[87]

At another level, of course, clerical opposition in Clare augured badly for the future of his fledgling institute. While the two communities, at Ennis and Ennistymon, were the first to be established since the Brothers secured papal recognition, it is clear that the invitations were made in desperation rather than from any great admiration for the institute. It is apparent, too, in the case of Killaloe that the bishop and clergy lacked enthusiasm for religious orders *per se*, as was manifest in their opposition to the Franciscan decision to open a chapel at Ennis in 1830, and indeed, the dean's shabby treatment of both the Presentation and Ursuline Sisters .[88] In this scenario, the Brothers' pontifical status and the independence it afforded them, made them less attractive still. The Christian Brothers would not open another house in Killaloe diocese until 1874, when they began a school in Kilrush. Significantly, too, in the neighbouring diocese of Kilfenora and Kilmacduagh, Bishop Edmund French, who had welcomed the Christian Brothers' to the 'Bible War' at Ennistymon, chose the Patrician Brothers, a diocesan congregation, to open a school in Galway in December 1826.[89]

IV

Edmund Rice's antipathy towards the evangelical assault of the 'Second Reformation' was driven not merely by second-hand accounts, but by his experiences in Waterford. Great emphasis has been laid on the extent of Rice's friendship and collaboration with the Protestants of Waterford.[90] It may well be that he enjoyed good relations with citizens of 'all classes and creeds', but Waterford was a liberal county and moderate Protestants were as incensed by the 'biblicals' as Catholics were. Indeed, recent scholarship has suggested that the traditional focus on the polarisation of the period has obscured the extent to which the bitterness of the 'Bible Wars' led to the emergence of a liberal middle ground.[91] Moreover, even among Anglicans who were not opposed to the notion of converting Catholics, there was a sense that the conflict had retarded this prospect by placing Catholics on the defensive.[92] John Jebb, Church of Ireland bishop of Limerick, for one, condemned Richard Mant's *Charge* as:

> breathing theological warfare against the papists ... [which] may involve the south of Ireland in flames, and at the same time stop any

quiet progress that has been making towards an unsuspecting influence in the minds of our Roman Catholic population.[93]

Certainly, in the case of Waterford, the challenge of proselytism placed the city's Catholics on a defensive footing.

By 1820 an Auxiliary Bible Society, affiliated to the London Hibernian Society, was founded in Waterford to promote the use of scripture 'without note or comment'. It operated a book depository at Georges Street but it appeared to enjoy little support.[94] Before long, however, the situation changed dramatically. In 1824, six hundred attended the Society's annual general meeting, which was chaired by the dean of Waterford, Usher Lee. The presence of the dean, in itself, was an indication of the extent to which the crusade had been embraced by elements within the leadership of the Church in the region. And in the following year, the Revd William Frazer, curate of St Patrick's Anglican church, delivered a stirring exhortation to the clergy of Waterford which contained local echoes of both Mant and Archbishop William Magee of Dublin:

> If ever there was a period which imperatively called for the exertions of the Established Church, the present assuredly was the period, and while the Bible went forward … divested of notes and comments, it behoves the clergy … to follow it to the remotest recesses of the poorest possessor, teaching and expounding its sublime doctrines, bearing in their hands the most excellent liturgy of the Church, the articles, the homilies, the catechism; thus guarding against all perversion of sacred and pure doctrine.[95]

A Waterford auxiliary of the Church Missionary Society was founded, in 1824, and, in the same year, Dean Lee established a Sunday school in the city.

The Catholic clergy in the diocese sought to defend their interests in the crusade; the parish priest of Passage East was particularly effective in preventing the establishment of a Kildare Place School, which he characterized as 'a snare laid for the faith of the child'.[96] But the catalyst which galvanised the Counter-Reformation in Waterford was a proposal to establish a school by the London Hibernian Society in the city. In September 1824, two members of the Society, James E. Gordon and the Revd Baptist Noel, called a meeting in the City Hall to outline their proposals for the education of the lower orders. A large gathering of Catholics and Protestants assembled and admission was by ticket only for fear of disorder.[97] When the two visitors had finished their address, Fr

John Sheehan, the parish priest of St Patrick's, with whom Rice had collabo-
rated in the Bishop Walsh debacle, replied from the floor:

> Catholics were charged with being benighted and ignorant but we dis-
> proved the assertion, if desired, by sending for any three or four of the
> humble children educated in Mr Rice's extensive school, and he would
> fearlessly assert that any one of them would be found as fully informed
> of the nature of his duties towards God, his neighbour and himself as
> even the Hon. Gentlemen.[98]

These bitter exchanges at City Hall were a prelude to an assembly of the
Catholics of Waterford, held at the 'Great Chapel' in the city. At the end of that
meeting a vigilance committee, composed of the bishop, some clergy and leading Catholics, was formed to present a petition to parliament, calling for full
emancipation and denying the malicious allegations made against Catholic
schools. Edmund Rice was unanimously elected to this committee, an acknowl-
edgment not just of his status within the community, but of his well-known
antipathy towards the proselytising schools.[99] These city meetings, however, were
merely the opening salvos of a bitter struggle, which marked what Eugene
Broderick has described as a decisive 'turning point in Protestant–Catholic relations in Waterford'.[1]

Rice's Brothers were particularly effective in the cities, where their big
schools had an enrolment the equivalent to ten or twelve smaller schools.[2] In
Dublin, at Archbishop Murray's parish in Liffey Street, there were no fewer than
thirty-six Protestant free schools attended by upwards of one thousand Catholic
children. To counteract these, Rice opened a temporary school in Jervis Street
in 1828, which was the precursor to the celebrated O'Connell's Schools.[3] A similar role, of course, was performed by the teaching sisters in their inner city
schools, and there is evidence of practical collaboration between the male and
female religious orders. By the 1820s the Brothers had 'perfected' their system of
education, but in Dublin the Sisters of Charity faced a daunting task at their
new school in Gardiner Street, where the 'children were first subdued before
they were taught'.[4] Towards that end, Mary Aikenhead, foundress of the Irish
Sisters of Charity, sought assistance from Edmund Rice, who sent Br Bernard
Duggan, the principal of the Brothers' branch school in Jervis Street, to offer
'in-service' support to the Sisters. The convent annals record his efforts and present a vivid account of the Brother's frantic activity in the classroom, which was
a far cry from the impressions formed from a reading of the Christian Brothers'

8.4 Br James Bernard Duggan (1800–82), contributor to the *Manual of School Government* (1845).

Manual (1845) which he had written, with its emphasis upon the robotic silence of the master. The annalist remarked how Duggan, a small and frail brother, 'had to whistle and shout to secure' silence in the classroom, but that he soon took charge. By the time he withdrew from the school, several months later, the Sisters had secured 'perfect order'.[5]

Almost a century later, in 1923, the Sisters of Charity appealed to the Brothers for assistance once more. This time, Mother Agnes Morrogh-Bernard, foundress of the celebrated Foxford Woollen Mills in County Mayo, requested a community of Brothers to teach the mill workers. In her application she appealed to the historic memory of the Brothers:

> [Sister Mary Xavier Hennessy, foundress of Gardiner Street,] often told me of all we owed to the Christian Brothers for the admirable service they rendered to our Sisters in 1830 when Mary Aikenhead opened her first school. Our poor Sisters had no control over the children, who had been attending proselytizing schools and got strict injunctions from their parents to eat all they could get and take the clothes that were going, but to be sure to give plenty of trouble to the teachers. They did

so, not knowing how to distinguish between the Sisters of Charity and Mrs Smyly's [proselytizing] crowd, until Br Duggan came to the rescue and brought them to their senses.[6]

The tenor of this Foxford application, however, illustrates the extent to which the intensity of the 'Bible Wars' had been purged from the popular memory of the period. More specifically, it reveals the way in which triumphant Catholicism chose to ignore the scale of the defections to the 'biblicals', and the very real threat which the crusade had posed to the Church. There are, regrettably, few reliable statistics to illustrate the extent of the conversions.[7] However, on the Farnham estate in County Cavan alone, which John MacHale described as 'the strong citadel of the Reformation', over five hundred were reported to have conformed in the winter of 1826–27.[8] The *Dublin Evening Mail* reported in 1826 that the entire population of many Catholic parishes of the county was about to defect to the Established Church and so great was the threat that Archbishop Curtis and four other bishops descended on Cavan town in mid-December 1826 to stem the tide.[9]

The evangelicals enjoyed greatest success among the poor. In 1833, Rice informed his brother that the country had become 'worse every day, [with] people absolutely starving in the midst of plenty',[10] but in the city the Brothers were joined by the new communities of Sisters in the fight against proselytism. In Dublin, Catherine McAuley boasted to John Rice that her sisters in Baggot Street had 'restrained the New Lights in their attempts to pervert Catholic servants'.[11] But many of the isolated regions in which the 'Biblicals' were most effective lacked the ecclesiastical structures or resources which had brought the Brothers to other locations. Evangelical efforts in the 1830s were focused upon the Dingle Peninsula and Achill Island, where the Revd Edward Nangle established a colony, but there is no record of the Brothers being invited to establish schools in either region.

During the Great Famine (1845–50), too, the threat of conversion was keenly felt. In that context, the Brothers were particularly active in opposition to 'souperism' in the urban ghettos which became the refuge of the hungry poor from the countryside. The decision to establish a foundation at Francis Street, Dublin, in 1846 was a direct response to the 'perverters' who 'with meal and money bags … tempt[ed] the poor to forfeit their glorious birthright in Heaven for a mess of pottage'.[12] Similar motives brought the Christian Brothers to Dingle (1848), where, according to Fr Philip Dowley CM, the 'demon of heresy' had induced 'hundreds of the ignorant poor' to sell their souls 'to the devil by *outwardly* renouncing the faith of their Fathers'. There the Brothers worked not just in the school, but they also accompanied the Vincentian 'missioners' to the remote parts of the county, translating, catechizing and seeking out apostates.[13] During the celebrations to mark the centenary of Rice's death, a preacher at Tralee recalled their mission in florid terms:

> The Great Famine had brought the threat and the opportunity for pros-elytism [to Kerry] … weaklings went down for the bribe and the faith-less failed; the selfish sold their souls for gold and the hungry pawned their bodies for bread hoping to redeem it again when the potatoes grew again.
>
> The temptation was terrible and souperism had a local triumph for a while. A breach was made in the lines of the Church and the Christian Brothers were rushed to the front. The breach was sealed with their aid and the line has never been broken in Kerry.[14]

Such sentiments, reflect the notion of a 'temporary conversion' which had emerged before the Famine. The Ulster novelist William Carleton (1794–1869), himself a somewhat opportunistic convert to the Church of Ireland, used the con-cept of a 'loan' of Protestantism in his satirical novel *Valentine McClutchy, the Irish Agent* (1844).[15] There is, however, in this popular association of conversion and poverty an implicit slur on the veracity of the religious experience of those who conformed to the Reformed Churches. The Catholic establishment nurtured this association which deflected attention from the formidable threat posed to Catholicism by the evangelical crusade. Bishop MacHale, for one, dismissed the converts as 'miserable creatures, worthless vagrants, strolling beggars, prostitutes with their illegitimate children, idle schoolmasters, unemployed labourers … dis-guised Protestants pretending they were Catholics, ignorant and starving crea-tures'.[16] Daniel O'Connell, too, dismissed the converts as 'wretches', who were 'a disgrace' to the Biblicals, and 'no loss' to the Church which they had deserted.[17]

The poorest of the Irish, however, were to be found not on the island, but in bourgeoning English slums where families crowded into small rooms. Yet, while the institutional history of the Brothers perpetuates the notion that 'loy-alty to the Catholic faith was of the highest importance' to the Irish diaspora, many immigrants seemed unduly concerned about the faith of their fathers, at a formal level at least.[18] Perhaps unsurprisingly, the alienation from the institu-tional Church, which was prevalent among the poor in Ireland, transferred across the water. In 1842, for example, Paul Cullen was alarmed at the terrible spectre of Liverpool where less than half of the hundred thousand Catholics in the city were hearing Mass on Sundays.[19] Social reformers, too, were increasingly aware of the link between slum conditions and immorality, a reality borne out in the experience of one London parish priest who warned that 'the children [were] going to Hell by wholesale for the want of Brothers to instruct them'.[20]

The Brothers established a reputation for their evangelisation in these migrant conditions, branching out from their first foundation at Preston (1825) to Manchester (1826), London (1826), Sunderland (1836), Liverpool (1837), Leeds (1843), Salford (1844), Bolton (1844) and Birmingham (1845). Perhaps the most overtly 'Counter-Reformationary' of the schools opened in Br Rice's lifetime, however, was the foundation in Gibraltar. Founded in 1835, the school on the Rock was established for the express purpose of eliminating the Methodists' English language schools which had attracted large numbers of Spanish students.[21] Their success was eulogised by Frederick William Faber (1814–63), himself a convert member of the Oxford Movement. In a sermon entitled 'The Apostolic Character of the Destiny allotted by Providence to the Irish Nation', he condemned the 'horrors of proselytism', but noted anecdotal evidence that among Irish immigrants, 'those who were educated either by the Christian Brothers or the Presentation Nuns never abandoned their faith'.[22]

With such a reputation, Captain Gordon characterised the Christian Brothers as a 'fraternity ... as mischievous as it is well possible to conceive'.[23] It was not surprising, therefore, that the apostasy of one of their number became a *cause celebre* which delighted evangelicals on both sides of the Irish Sea. Br Philip Halley, a native of Waterford, was 33 years old when he renounced the Catholic faith in Preston Anglican church at Easter 1827. The excitement of the press reflects the joy of Protestants at so public a defection, while the private correspondence of the Brothers indicates their dismay at such a loss and scandal.[24] The *Preston Pilot*, an anti-Catholic print, gave a full account of the Brother's conversion to the Established Church:

> It is quite impossible for us adequately to express the feelings of gratification we experience in being able to announce that ... an event has occurred in this town which affords well grounded hope for believing that the Reformation which it has pleased the Divine Will should prosper so signally in Ireland, is already shedding its hallowed rays upon the benighted in this quarter of the Empire.[25]

The Irish papers also reported the news, and Waterford's evangelical *Mail*, which carried extensive coverage of Catholic conversions, delighted in Halley's abjuration.[26] For his part, Br Austin Grace, superior of the Preston community, was shattered by the young Brother's defection:

> It is quite impossible [he wrote] to describe the sensations of astonish-
> ment which this wretched act of apostasy excited throughout the coun-
> try, but particularly in this town where he had been so well known and
> remarked for his religious and edifying appearance.[27]

Rice was also distressed by the departure of Halley in whom he had placed con-siderable confidence, as demonstrated not just in his selection for the mission to Lancashire, but by his signature on several legal deeds, which included, iron-ically, those of the 'Counter-Reformationary' foundation at Ennistymon.[28] By coincidence, Rice was in Manchester when the Brother conformed, and although his instincts were to intervene, priests and other friends advised him to avoid involvement in so public a scandal.[29] Instead, he transferred Br Stephen Phelan from Dublin to Preston, with expectations that he might be able to reason with his friend. As it happened, Phelan found Halley 'quite hardened in the evil choice he had adopted', and held out little hope for his return. Significantly, he noted that the former Brother, dressed like 'a *dandy*', was being feted by the 'most inveterate enemies of the civil and religious rights of the Catholics'.[30] Clearly, within the context of the struggle for Emancipation, the spectacle of the Brother's apostasy was of great utility to the opponents of the cause; however Halley's spectacular return to Rome within ten weeks deprived the crisis of its political potential.

Rice welcomed the 'unfortunate Apostate' back but the description of Halley's highly choreographed recantation, where he 'was exhibited publicly on the Altar', suggests a comical conclusion to the episode.[31] If only the issues concerned were not so critical. The *Preston Pilot* sought to minimise the damage to the evangeli-cal crusade by the dramatic reversal, expressing pity for any 'idiot' who could 'tri-umph in the return of such a subject as Mr Halley'.[32] Rice's assistant, Br Patrick Ellis, welcomed 'poor Halley's return to the only saving faith', noting that his with-drawal from 'the biblicals' was 'in itself a great point gained for truth'.[33] In spite of this positive spin, however, the Brothers had no illusions about the scale of the crisis which had been averted, and the potential of the defection to devastate the reputation of the institute, and indeed the Catholic cause in the 'Bible War'. As it was, the apostasy retarded the growth of the institute not just in England but in Ireland, because in spite of numerous requests for new foundations, Rice was inclined to adopt a cautious approach in the wake of the crisis.[34]

8.5 'Oh! what will our pious Vicar say now?' Broadsheet celebrating the return of Brother Halley to the Catholic Church, Samuel Trott, Liverpool, 2 July 1827, Archivum Britannicum Societatis Iesu, Preston Scrapbook, 1799–1858, 4/4/2.

Ultimately, the 'Second Reformation' failed in its effort to complete the process of conversion begun in the sixteenth century. The march of the Reformation had been halted by the prompt response of the Catholic community, and rather than eradicating 'popish superstition' the movement had the effect of strengthening the Church. The 'Bible War' effected a polarisation in Irish society, but within the Catholic community it brought a radical transformation.[35] The fear of the penal era had given way to the confidence of the mid nineteenth-century, but perhaps more significantly, the liberal Catholicism of Troy, Murray and O'Connell had begun to yield to ultramontanism. Moreover, the Second Reformation brought about a further change, as the defensive instincts of the penal Church galvanised an alliance of priest and people to create a combative response in the face of protestant opposition, which has been described as 'an evangelical blitzkrieg'.[36] The Christian Brothers played a vital part in this process in which they were the Jesuits of Ireland's Counter-Reformation.

The Brothers were both agents of the reaction and affected by the experience. Edmund Rice's impetus had been to provide education for the poor, but his association with Bishop Hussey's condemnation of proselytism in Waterford predisposed his congregation towards reaction. In that contest, Rice's first biographer believed the Brothers were 'raised ... to meet the terrible crisis ... and baffle the *last effort* ... to seduce and pervert the children of St Patrick'.[37] So just as Ignatius' little company became synonymous with Counter-Reformation and reaction, so too, Edmund's Brothers became champions of 'Faith and Fatherland', which was not without cost to their initial vocation. Furthermore, while the 'New Reformation' aimed at the destruction of 'priestcraft', the rapid Catholic response had the opposite effect of consolidating the prominent role of the priest within Irish society. In consequence, the Irish Church became a more clerical institution in which there were diminishing opportunities for the kind of lay initiatives championed by pioneers like Edmund and the early Brothers.

CHAPTER NINE

Testing times, 1822–32

SHORTLY AFTER THE CHAPTER OF 1822 Edmund Rice undertook his first general visitation of the houses which made up the congregation. Immediately, it became clear to him that increased centralisation was necessary if the problems of the various foundations were to be overcome. Central to his planned renewal of the institute was the establishment of a new generalate in Dublin. Psychologically Mount Sion had enormous significance for the congregation: it was there Rice and his companions had begun their mission, and it was there, too, the first group of Brothers had made their religious profession. Nevertheless, as a generalate Mount Sion had its limitations.

The Brothers had enjoyed cordial relations with Bishops Hussey and Power, but their successors were openly hostile to the infant congregation. As it happened, Bishop Robert Walsh was hopelessly compromised, but his successor Patrick Kelly, who dismissed the Brothers as 'tailors and cobblers', proved a more menacing prospect.[1] In the Dublin diocese the Brothers had the protection of Daniel Murray, their greatest benefactor, and the establishment of a curia there would facilitate the administration of the order. Besides, prior to the amalgamation of the houses, each foundation had admitted and trained its own candidates. It was now Rice's hope to establish a single novitiate for the congregation and a model training school in connection with the generalate. This would give the order not only a recognisable focus, but it would promote unity and the uniform standards which were essential to their system of education.

Brother Rice met with the archbishop in July 1826 and outlined his plans for a new centre in Dublin. Murray was charmed by this proposal and invited the Brothers to his own parish of St Mary's, which had particularly pressing needs. Of the 3,000 Catholic children in the parish, 2,000 received no education whatsoever, while the remaining one-third attended Protestant schools.[2] The Catholic school in Liffey Street was totally inadequate, and, on Murray's invitation, a meeting of the combined parishes of the area established an Education Committee which hoped to fund the new venture. Rice's close friend Bryan Bolger, an architect in Dublin Corporation, was commissioned to secure a suitable site, but in the meantime the Committee acquired premises in Jervis Street, where the Brothers began their school in June 1827. As in the other locations, the three Brothers did not restrict their ministry to the school; they embarked on a wide range of apostolates, visiting patients at the nearby hospital and assisting the Sisters of Charity as they attempted to establish their school in Gardiner Street.

I

Politically these were exciting times. The campaign towards Emancipation gained a new momentum in February 1823 with the formation of the Catholic Association. This was an ambitious move in which Daniel O'Connell and Richard Lalor Shiel, leaders of rival factions during the Veto controversy, joined together to achieve a solution to Catholic grievances.[3] The new movement had enormous potential. At issue was not merely a proposal to present another petition to parliament in favour of emancipation, but, along with other complaints, the new Association opposed tithes, bias in the judiciary and the alleged proselytism of the Kildare Place Society.

In spite of its appeal, however, the Association made little popular impact and its survival appeared in doubt until January 1824 when O'Connell proposed the collection of what became known as the 'Catholic rent'. Previously membership of the Association was one guinea a year, but O'Connell proposed a new category of members, associates who would contribute as little as a penny per month. Apart from the vital financial considerations of such a move, which allowed the Association conduct a vigorous campaign, the associates would have personal commitment to the process, while the masses could be marshalled behind the banner of emancipation. This suggestion met with phenomenal success and resulted in the transformation of a relatively small middle-class campaign into a mass movement, which some consider the first truly popular, mass-democratic organisation in the modern world.[4] In assessing this phenomenon, John Jebb, Church of Ireland bishop of Limerick 1822–33, declared, 'In truth, an Irish Revolution has in a great measure been effected'.[5]

Moreover, the participation of the Catholic clergy gave the renewed campaign an apparently inexorable momentum. From the beginning, the Constitution of the Catholic Association had included the clergy as *ex officio* members, and O'Connell made brave promises to the Church when he announced the 'Catholic rent'. £5,000 would be set aside for the education of priests, £5,000 was earmarked for building of chapels and presbyteries, while a further £5,000 was provided for the use of Catholic schools and the purchase of

9.1 'The Liberator', Daniel O'Connell (1775–1847).
Engraving by Thomas McLean, London, July 1829, NLI.

books. The possibility of a positive clerical response to these overtures was now greater than ever: the bitter divisions surrounding the proposed royal veto on episopal appointments had been overcome, and O'Connell's deferential mani-festo achieved the desired response. Critically, as Bartlett has put it, 'by binding priest to people in a political/religious agitation, the "Catholic rent" could be seen as a shield against proselytism' within the context of the vicious Bible Wars.[6] The clergy threw their weight behind the 'Catholic rent' and the campaign for emancipation in 1824–9; as one Methodist pundit remarked, 'the Roman Catholic peasantry was not only deluded by the priesthood, but was now paying a penny a month for the privilege'.[7] Priests acted as agents for the Association, they organised local committees, addressed meetings, canvassed voters and headed processions to the polling booths. In 1828 one election banner announced that a vote for O'Connell was a 'Vote for Your Religion', illustrating the extent to which 'the Great Dan' could unite the worlds of high and popular politics, explicitly linking religious, political and economic grievances.'[8]

The year 1828 marked the culmination of the emancipation campaign, beginning with an enormous show of Catholic solidarity. O'Connell opened the year with 'simultaneous meetings' throughout the country; on 13 January ral-lies took place in 1,600 of 2,500 parishes in Ireland as a challenge to the gov-ernment. With an attendance of over one and a half million these presented an impressive demonstration of Catholic force and determination.[9] In the spring of that year Edmund Rice acquired a suitable site for his school at North Richmond Street. Initially he intended the archbishop of Dublin to lay the foun-dation stone, but Murray suggested instead that O'Connell, who had been a reg-ular collector at charity sermons for the Brothers' Hanover Street school, should perform the honours.[10]

The Liberator was more than enthusiastic about the prospect; it provided him with an opportunity to restate his commitment to Catholic education, while at the same time the occasion could be turned into a display of what he termed the 'moral force' of mass non-violent action. Following his discussion with Rice, O'Connell outlined the plans for Richmond Street to the Catholic Association. Apparently the Association intended building its own model train-ing school, but O'Connell suggested that this could be built in connection with the Brothers. Accordingly, the Association voted £1,500 towards the costs of the Richmond Street school and agreed that the laying of the foundation stone should become a demonstration of Catholic determination.

The event became another of O'Connell's political rallies, a 'monster meet-ing' which attracted a crowd of over 100,000, another example of what Richard

English has called 'the muscular application of extra-parliamentary pressure'.[11] A procession of the principal clergy and laity marched from the Corn Exchange, in the city centre, to the North Circular Road, where O'Connell addressed the crowd. There he outlined his hopes for the school, delivering a bitter assault to the 'Biblicals' in the process. In stark contrast, he described how this would be a school founded on 'liberal and not sectarian principles'; 'in this national seminary … no means would be adopted to proselytise the Protestant child, he would be educated and taught with as much anxiety as the Catholic, but with his religion there would be no intermeddling'.[12] O'Connell concluded his address with lavish praise for 'his dear and old friend, Br Edmund Ignatius Rice', who he flattered as 'the Patriarch of the Monks of the West'.[13] Two weeks after that great occasion, O'Connell announced his candidacy in the parliamentary by-election in Clare, which he subsequently won by 2,057 to 982 votes, thereby precipitating the constitutional crisis which delivered Catholic emancipation.

Years later, in 1844, when O'Connell was imprisoned in Dublin's Richmond Jail, following his controversial conviction on charges of conspiracy, he was visited by Br Austin Grace. During the visit, the Liberator recalled those great celebrations at the school which later bore his name:

> When that stone was laid, I had to stand on it and make a speech. What I said then I now repeat, namely that I expect much from that school and the teaching of your brotherhood … Education to be suited to this country must be Catholic and Irish in its tone, having for its motto 'Faith and Fatherland'. All engaged in the education of the young should remember that 'As the twig is bent, so the tree inclines'.[14]

Not all of the Brothers, however, were enamoured by O'Connell's style of politics nor the empty promises made to the Richmond Street school. In November 1828, Br Joseph Leonard, a future assistant general, complained that there was no hope of getting the grant promised by the Catholic Association. The 'Catholic rent' he dismissed as a strategy 'calculated to support the ambition, of perhaps a single man' and he pointed to the practice of every 'trick, chicane and a monopoly of power' in the Association.[15] That said, O'Connell remained a constant friend of the Brothers and their schools, frequently acting as a collector at charity sermons in Ireland and England. The last time he did so, was in 1844, amid the euphoria of his release from prison. On that occasion, he had to be provided with a second plate, such was the desire of the crowd to give their offerings to the Liberator.[16]

9.2 The triumphal procession following Daniel O'Connell's release from
Richmond Penitentiary (*c.*1844), NLI.

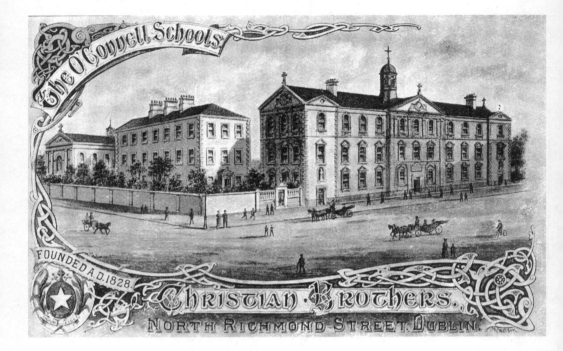

9.3 Monastery and O'Connell Schools, North Richmond Street, Dublin.
Established 1828.

Yet in spite of the initial enthusiasm and promises, the Brothers experienced many difficulties in establishing their school at Richmond Street. The project pushed the congregation to its limits, but it took an especially heavy toll on Edmund Rice who suffered a breakdown in November 1828.[17] Exact details of the illness are unknown, but it appears to have been a severe depression brought on by stress, or a minor stroke. This left him isolated and exposed, not just to challenges from without, but to opposition within his own order. Deprived of personal resources, either mental or physical, he turned instinctively to prayer. And just as in the earlier crisis at Ennis, this was manifest in an intense Eucharistic devotion; between October 1828 and May 1832 he had an incredible 2,773 Masses offered for the success of the North Richmond Street project.[18]

The principal obstacle facing the venture was financial. Not merely was Rice's personal fortune long since exhausted, but he was at the mercy of determined creditors. Moreover, as an unforeseen consequence of the papal brief, donors were less inclined to contribute to the Christian Brothers, which they perceived as a national charity, but chose instead to direct their funds to clearly identified local projects.[19] Neither, was there great enthusiasm among the clergy for the Brothers' projects, and Joseph Leonard believed that where 'such jealousy' existed, pressure was brought to bear to prevent the dying leaving their property to the institute.[20] In the early months funds flowed in to the O'Connell's project but then dwindled, and by 1829 all work on the site had ceased. Serious measures were called for: the Brothers approached the archbishop with a view to establishing a general appeal in Dublin. This was done and a published address called for the eradication of 'ignorance and vice' and the extension of the Brothers' 'virtuous and useful Education'.[21] Dr Murray headed the list of subscribers with a donation of £20. It was also agreed that Br Francis Thornton, superior of Limerick, would tour England in search of funding. This was a successful mission raising £500 which, together with £1,000 loaned by Bryan Bolger, was enough to complete the last phase of the building. Within this context, too, in March 1829, Rice visited each of the Dublin communities promoting great austerity and a reduction in the Brothers' already meagre diet. This was asking the impossible, and it appears that Brothers from several of the communities met in Dublin and resolved to place themselves under the authority of the archbishop unless Rice withdrew these instructions.[22]

The erection of the building was not the end of the Brothers' difficulties. One problem remained to be resolved: the provision of an adequate water supply. It was customary for Dublin Corporation to provide the service free to charitable institutions, but not alone was Rice's application to the Water Pipe Committee refused, but exorbitant fees were demanded for water facilities. After all their trials the Brothers were not to be deterred by this difficulty: a water diviner was employed and an adequate supply was discovered beneath the site. With everything in place, Edmund Rice, his two assistants and the novice master took up residence in North Richmond Street on 23 June 1831. Two weeks later the new school opened its doors to six hundred boys, almost five years after the Brothers had first discussed the project with Archbishop Murray.

II

The long-awaited Emancipation Bill passed both houses of parliament with comfortable majorities in April 1829. Catholics now enjoyed the right to sit in parliament, be members of any corporation or hold higher civil and military offices. In many respects, however, this was a hollow victory which offered little to the majority of Irishmen. More than this, the Irish Parliamentary Elections

Act which accompanied the Emancipation Bill actually deprived the forty-shilling freeholders of the right to vote, by raising the property qualification to £10. This move immediately cut the electorate to about one-sixth of its former size, but the measure was deemed necessary in order to defend the constitution against the forty-shilling freeholders which conservatives had characterised as pawns of their priests in the Waterford and Clare elections. Br Joseph Leonard resented the Liberator's part in this, and delighted in reporting that there was little love for O'Connell among 'radical' Catholics in London. Indeed, some argued that it would do 'much in favour of religion and Ireland if [his] ashes were scattered with his forefathers'.[23] In particular, they resented his failure to preserve the forty-shilling freeholders; 'with them' they lamented, 'Ireland lost its independence'.[24]

Not alone were O'Connell's foot soldiers made to pay the price for Emancipation, but the Catholic Association was suppressed and further penal restrictions were placed on congregations of male religious. One clause of the Bill, apparently aimed at diffusing the opposition of the 'ultra'-Protestants to the measure, declared that:

> Whereas Jesuits and members of Religious Orders, Communities or Societies of the Church of Rome, bound by Monastic or Religious Vows are resident within the United Kingdom, it is expedient to make provision for the gradual suppression and final prohibition of the same therein.[25]

The Bill made it a misdemeanour for religious orders to receive new members, while any person admitted to vows was liable to banishment for life, thereby removing the security which regulars had enjoyed as a consequence of the relief acts of 1778 and 1782. Whatever the intention of these penal clauses, and they may have been simply a sop to conservatives for the failure of the emancipation legislation to include the comfort of a royal veto on episcopal appointments, the news of their inclusion in the Relief Bill appeared as a death sentence to the religious orders in Ireland. During the Lords' debate on the measure, the prime minister, the duke of Wellington, declared:

> There is no man more convinced than I am of the absolute necessity of carrying into execution that part of the present measure which has for its object the extinction of the Monastic Orders in this country.[26]

Such sentiments convinced Br Joseph Leonard that the measure would 'prevent the[ir] development for posterity', since without recruits the orders would be doomed to extinction.[27]

As soon as it became known that the bill contained these provisions a meeting was called for 15 March 1829 of the religious superiors of Cork under the chairmanship of the Augustinian provincial, Fr Daniel O'Connor. At this meeting it was resolved to campaign against the legislation by means of memorials to parliament. Among the petitions presented was a generous endorsement of the Christian Brothers and their invaluable work from the Protestant gentry and inhabitants of the City of Waterford:

> If the members of this most useful body of men … should come within the meaning of the Act and thereby become suppressed, it would deprive thousands of poor destitute children of education and clothing, blessings so much wanted in this country.[28]

The Cork meeting was followed by one in Dublin where Fr O'Connor and the Dominican provincial, Pius Leahy, consulted the regular clergy at a gathering in John's Lane priory. At this meeting it was resolved that Fathers Leahy and O'Connor should travel to London to wait on the duke of Wellington and Robert Peel in an effort to plead their case.[29] John Rice joined the delegation in his capacity as assistant to the Augustinian provincial.

The Dominican historian, Reginald Walsh, believed that Edmund Rice was also a member.[30] If so, it was an indication of the esteem with which the religious superiors held him. That he agreed to be part of this deputation, given his illness and the fact that he shunned such public engagements, was a measure of the threat posed by the penal clause. It is clear, too, that the journey to London was delayed, as the team was forced to rest at Birmingham, because 'poor Mr Rice was so sick from fatigue'.[31] Yet, while it is tempting to place him among the delegation, archival sources name only John Rice, whose signature was added to the minutes of the various meetings. It is likely, therefore, that Walsh and subsequent commentators have been mistaken in their assumption of Edmund Rice's participation.[32] However, the Brothers in London played a vital role in the enterprise, and boys from their schools acted as runners, distributing printed resolutions to the homes of Members of Parliament.[33]

As it happened, the mission was unsuccessful in that the contentious articles remained; nevertheless it did serve to clarify the situation. Edmund Rice's long-term acquaintance, Henry Agar-Ellis, Viscount Clifden of Gowran, who had presented the Waterford petition to parliament, agreed that the contentious provisions were 'unreasonable', and ruined what was otherwise an 'excellent bill'; but he advised that raising a commotion might lead to the intensification of the restrictions, which were not likely to be enforced in any case, since they depended upon the attorney general for their implementation.[34] This interpretation was confirmed by Wellington and Peel in their meetings with the Irish delegation. They were certain that the provisions would not be enforced against the regulars, but 'Mr Rice', whose father had taken the Catholic oath of loyalty in 1779, was unsatisfied with this connivance. He argued with the duke that the measure cast a stigma on the loyalty of the religious orders: 'why', he asked 'should we be suppressed if we were not disloyal or obnoxious to the state?'[35] The Dominican provincial pushed the duke as to whether the religious orders had not been legalized by the relief acts of 1791 and 1793. Wellington said he thought not, but Rice insisted that he put the matter before the government.[36] There was no way the situation could be improved; there was considerable opposition to emancipation in England and George IV had lost all patience with the Catholic question. According to Pius Leahy, Peel had suffered an outburst from the king in which he shouted: 'Damn the Catholics! Damn the Protestants! Damn you all! I can't get a moments rest about this question.'[37]

The delegation returned to Ireland without satisfaction, before Edmund Rice travelled to Mount Sion to address a controversial 'general chapter', which he had reluctantly convened for 13 April 1829. When the chapter addressed the problematic clauses in the Relief Bill, Rice read O'Connell's legal opinion of the legislation, which he had given in his capacity as counsellor to the Franciscans:

> Though the law is insolent enough in its pretensions, it will be and must be totally inefficient in practice, it is almost impossible that any prosecution should be instituted at all: and it is quite impossible that any prosecution should be successful.[38]

O'Connell had also expressed a belief that the non-professed members could in due course take vows without fear of prosecution. There were at that time twelve Brothers who were eligible for final profession, and the chapter agreed that these could be admitted immediately to perpetual vows without the usual scrutiny.

The chapter also agreed that the Brothers would be registered in accordance with the requirements of the new law, but that the registration would be accompanied by a firm protest against the penal clause. Br Leonard's address from the Cork community was typical of the remainder:

> I hearby enter my protest against the Act, which requires free-born
> British subjects to submit to this mode of registering their names and
> professions in any office whatsoever. I deem it in every respect penal,
> and an infringement on the liberty and privilege of the subject, and I
> trust that a more enlightened Senate will erase it in common with every
> remnant of the penal code from the Statute Book. The persons in whose
> behalf this protest is made are not in orders; they are simply religious
> men who have voluntarily undertaken the gratuitous education of the
> poor neglected children of Cork.[39]

As a consequence of the clause, the Christian Brothers were technically an
illegal organisation. O'Connell's interpretation of the law was correct in the
sense that the law was intended. However, the Brothers suffered in consequence
of the law. As an illegal body every bequest to them was liable to be contested
and there were several instances where testators' wishes were overturned. The
most significant challenge concerned the bequest by Bryan Bolger of £10,000
to Edmund Rice and Michael (Br Bernard) Dunphy. The decision to leave the
money to the named individuals was taken on legal advice in an effort to evade
this penal clause. In spite of this, however, his nieces and nephews
unsuccessfully contested the will, but after prolonged litigation the bequest
frittered away to just £1,000.[40]

III

Closer to home, tensions among the Brothers posed a more significant threat
to the survival of the congregation. This was the context in which Rice called
the contentious 1829 'general chapter', in response to agitation, and what he
termed as extortion, from a faction led by Br Joseph Leonard.[41] The tensions
between the 'Founder' and the Cork Brothers were not helped by their delay in
joining the 'union' until 1826 and the belief that they were unrepresented in the
government of the institute. They had not participated in the first general chapter, nor was the composition of the general council altered in the wake of their
accession. Moreover, while the 'North Mon' had been an independent foundation, the Brothers now found themselves subject to a superior general, and his
two assistants, who had been chosen by the directors of the seven communities,
'the Heptarchy', which combined to form the institute in 1822.[42]

Their frustration was further exacerbated by a misunderstanding of the nature of the relationship between the Irish Brothers and the De La Salle Order. Br Leonard seems to have believed that the French constitutions had been extended to the Irish Brothers *in toto*. This was not so, but the assumption was not unreasonable.[43] The Cork Brothers had been part of the Society for just three years and were unclear of such constitutional issues, neither was Edmund Rice any clearer as his enquiries of the French general suggests. Moreover, Leonard's enthusiasm for the De La Salle regime increased following a visit to France, which afforded him an opportunity to observe the French system firsthand. He was enamoured by what he considered the 'parental Institute on which ours is grafted', and subsequently established a correspondence with the French superior general.[44]

Frère Guillaume assumed that Br Leonard enjoyed Rice's confidence. The Cork Brother made no attempt to disillusion him and their exchange was further confused by a parallel correspondence in which the Dublin leadership sought advice from the French Brothers.[45] It is likely, therefore, that Frère Guillaume believed that his letters to Ireland were being shared. A significant part of the Leonard–Paris exchange focused upon constitutional issues, the election, and composition of chapters and the number and function of the assistants to the general. Quite clearly, these queries were directed with a view to improving the representation of the Cork community. This agenda coloured the information supplied to the French Brothers and the spin which Leonard put on the responses received.

Throughout his correspondence, Br Leonard was careful to describe Rice in deferential terms, as 'our very dear Brother Ignatius', but at the same time he exploited the superior general's ill-health in a manner which presented him not simply as an 'imbecile' (a catch-all expression used to describe the full range of mental illness including depression), but as a tyrant:

> His mind is so disordered that he is completely incapable of applying himself to the business of the Institute … He was inclined to set himself against the views of the two Assistants in all matters concerning the welfare of the Institute. He even said to them very often that he would not listen to any remonstrance of theirs, and that he was not obliged to follow their advice, unless it agreed with his own opinions … It seems to me that his illness will be of very long duration. I am extremely grieved when I forsee the evil that will afflict the Institute if he continues in his present condition.[46]

The implication of Rice's ill-health was significant, on account of the legal pro-vision for the removal of a superior who had become mentally incapacitated. The French general, however, urged caution. If indeed Rice was 'deranged', then the Brothers were obliged to stand firm against him, since, in that case 'his opin-ion was of very little value'. However, Frère Guillaume was not convinced that Leonard had established Rice's inability to govern; in that case, he warned against the dangers of 'forming cabals and of rupturing union and charity'.[47] In parallel, Joseph Leonard maintained a forthright correspondence with Pius Leahy, superior at the Dominican convent of Corpo Santo, in Lisbon. As the authors of the *Positio* observe, the content and style of the Leonard–Leahy let-ters make a striking contrast with the 'unctuous approach and studied religious nature' of the communication with Paris.[48] Throughout this exchange, Leonard is scathing in his criticism of 'the governor', 'Rice and co.' and 'our taskmasters'; even Peter Kenney, the highly respected spiritual director of several of the newly founded Irish congregations, was dismissed as 'Peter the Jesuit'.[49]

Edmund Rice had been elected superior general at the chapter of 1822. Legally, therefore, no chapter was required until the end of his ten-year term. It had, however, been Rice's practice to hold consultative assemblies at significant moments, such as the series held in 1817, 1819 and 1821 in preparation for the application for the papal brief. By the winter of 1828–9, a critical confluence of circumstances warranted another such gathering. The four commissioners appointed by the first general chapter to draft rules were due to deliver their findings. In addition, the difficulties in Clare, the 'Second Reformation', the near-bankruptcy of the institute and the implications of the penal clauses, all convinced Rice to call the professed Brothers together. Yet while he assumed that the meeting would be merely consultative, and the inclusion of all thirty professed Brothers reflected this, Br Leonard had already informed Paris that the imminent assembly would be a 'general' chapter, with legislative functions to increase the representation at chapters and the number of assistant generals to four.[50] Among the *junior* Brothers, and this related not to age but years in the congregation, such an agenda had obvious attractions, since the composition of chapters was effectively restricted to directors. Not surprisingly, therefore, Joseph Leonard gained significant support beyond his immediate community for his reform agenda. In Rice's view, 'the rest of the professed Brothers got rather clamorous' to the point where he was forced to call a chapter.[51]

The Brothers assembled at Mount Sion on 13 April 1829, the day the Emancipation Bill received the royal assent. Very quickly, however, the gather-ing became a nightmare for Rice. Leonard and his cabal had extorted a full chapter from the general and they were prepared to push their victory to its logical conclusions. Rice was president of the chapter, but there was an attempt to deprive him of any influence, by removing from him the authority to propose or even amend proposals at the assembly.[52] This effort to reduce him to a neutral chair was reinforced by a move to make a majority vote of the assistants binding upon the superior general, 'whether he approved of the measures ... or not'.[53] This clearly amounted to a coup. Rice voiced his opposition and he subsequently requested clarification from the French general about this measure, which he believed was 'inconsistent with the nature of a Superior'.[54] Notwithstanding these objections, the chapter proceeded to elect two additional assistants, one of whom was Joseph Leonard, and decreed that these could live apart from the general, despite the fact that Frère Guillaume had explicitly declared such practices contrary to article 4 of the French constitutions.[55] In addition, the Brothers, in a move designed to break the rule of the existing oligarchy, voted that future chapters would be composed of directors and non-directors in equal numbers, in contravention of the papal brief of 1820.[56] In addition to these constitutional reforms, the chapter altered the Brothers' frugal lifestyle, diet, and their traditional simple dress, which was abandoned in favour of what Rice described as 'a more genteel and expensive sort of woollen cloth'.[57]

Rice was distressed by such innovations. In his opinion they served no purpose but threatened the destruction of the 'old and good order'.[58] More than this, he believed they sowed the seeds of independence and 'principles subversive of religious discipline'.[59] This latter observation was related, perhaps, not so much to the scale of the changes, but to the fact that they represented an overwhelming rejection of the austerity measures for which he had canvassed in the previous March. In this sense, he regarded the chapter's decision as a rejection of his own leadership. We can only speculate about his isolation at this juncture, especially as the opposition to his government was not simply the work of young hot-heads, but enjoyed the support of many of the older brothers.[60] Quite clearly, his position as superior general had become untenable. Accordingly, at the conclusion of the chapter, on 1 May, Rice knelt before the Brothers, and read his resignation.[61] This snap decision astonished the assembly, and while their actions had precipitated the crisis, they voted unanimously to request him to continue. Br Joseph Leonard, who must have been enraged by this dramatic reversal, described the moment with characteristic guile to the French general:

> At the conclusion of the Chapter our very dear Brother Ignatius edified us very much, begging us persistently to accept his resignation. For

9.4 Brother John Leonard.

seven and a half years he has retained his position and as his health has improved very much at present, we refused his resignation. May God give him his grace and health to accomplish his divine will.[62]

Yet while Rice accepted the Brothers' invitation, his instinct to resign was correct. Substantial difficulties remained; there were important challenges in the future and, as time would show, his health and temperament were insufficient for the task.

Not least of these challenges was the question of the legality of the 'chapter'. His advisor Peter Kenney SJ had cautioned against holding it in the first instance, but the French general advised that legal uncertainties could be clarified in subsequent appeals to Rome. However, the voice of experience urged Rice not to rush into any such application since the passage of time might demonstrate the wisdom of the chapter's reforms.[63] In the interim, he advised Rice to 'faithfully observe' the decisions of the chapter; 'the Superior', he advised, 'must be the first to give the example of submission'.[64] Frère Guillaume also made efforts to heal the divisions between Rice and his newly elected 'assistant', who accused him of attempting to reverse the decisions of the chapter. Yet while the French general instructed Br Leonard 'to act in a way as to win for [Edmund] … the esteem, reverence and obedience of all your Brothers', his behaviour continued as before.[65]

The extent of Br Leonard's hostility to Rice is most apparent in the Leonard–Leahy–Paris correspondence. The *Positio,* completed as part of Rice's canonization process, includes a comprehensive analysis of this material, which constructs a contrast between the troubled mind of Br Leonard and the 'tolerance … kindness and humility' of the Founder.[66] This tendency to demonise Br Joseph is repeated in Rice's most recent biography which refers to his 'obsessional antipathy' towards his superior.[67] Yet while the Cork Brothers were castigated for their 'eccentricity and imperiousness' by their opponents, the grievances they articulated were reasonable and enjoyed significant support within the congregation.[68] Moreover, while the *Positio* highlights the 'antagonism, bitterness and self-centredness' of Leonard's correspondence, many of the strong emotions it contains were entirely justified.[69]

In February 1830, for instance, Joseph Leonard recorded an altercation between his blood-brother, Br John Baptist Leonard, and the superior general:

> Rice … lectured him severely for nearly two hours … charged him and me with creating a rebellion in the Institute with several other base calumnies; peremptorily ordered him to leave the house next day, and [although John] asked with surprise, – must I leave in the snow and sleet in a bad state of health – the reply was – leave the house tomorrow. I would sooner pay coach-hire than you should spend another day here![70]

Edmund Rice was obviously no plaster-cast saint, nor was he simply 'a man of true grit', as a late twentieth-century Irish Education Minister, himself a former Christian Brother, described him.[71] He had amassed his fortune, not through compassion but in the unforgiving world of the marketplace. The malicious objections to Rice's application for papal approval, in 1818, were clearly overstated, particularly those of the 'Seventeen Pastors of Waterford' who complained of his savage nature, lack of sensibility and want of human feeling.[72] However, such defamation depends on at least a modicum of credibility. Edmund Rice had, after all, the ability to arouse a spectrum of emotions, from love to bitter hate. In this instance, Joseph Leonard was clearly incensed by Rice's harsh treatment of his ailing brother.

The critical point is that Rice fought his natural inclinations as he attempted to live the Gospel he proclaimed. This was apparent not just in this episode, but at other times in his long career when he promptly apologised for his sharp temper.[73] On this occasion, when Br Joseph Leonard learned of Rice's 'cruel conduct', he demanded an explanation. Significantly, he could later boast to have:

> completely turned the tables on Rice and C[o.]. The good old man wrote a long and valuable letter, full of charity – apologies and kindness.[74]

And having scored this point, Leonard looked forward to their next formal encounter, the general chapter scheduled for 1832; 'one week at lecturing our would-be task Masters is all I look for' he proclaimed.[75] That pleasure, however, was denied him, for he died from a painful lung hemorrhage on Palm Sunday 1831.[76] In responding to the news of Br Leonard's death, whom he had known in Paris, the newly elected general of the De La Salle Brothers described the 'great loss' suffered by the Institute as a result. 'I esteemed this Brother highly, for he seemed to me very zealous and resourceful and totally dedicated to his holy state'.[77] Yet in spite of Frère Anaclet effusive appreciation, Br Leonard's reputation among successive generations of Christian Brothers was such that his necrology has never been written. Joseph Leonard's death removed the focus for the opposition to Rice and brought a temporary halt to the open confrontation within the Institute. Serious tensions, however, remained. John Leonard continued to oppose Rice's administration under which he believed the institute was 'not only stationary but tottering' on the verge of collapse.[78] Perhaps of greater significance was the addition to the opposition camp of Br Paul Riordan, a former clerk who had become 'as furious' against Rice as his confreres in Cork.[79] His resistance to the 'despotism' of the 'governor' had painful consequence in the longer term, since he was elected superior general in succession to Edmund Rice in 1838.[80]

The 1830s brought further conflict. In the first instance, the irregularities of the 1829 'chapter' had introduced illegal novelties into the government of the Institute, most notably the election of the two additional assistant generals. As it happened, the death of Joseph Leonard went some way towards rectifying this, but the chapter decision to enlarge future assemblies caused more difficulties. This created especial confusion in the run up to the decennial chapter of 1832, where Rice initially called both directors and non-directors to the assembly, but was later forced to countermand his instruction in light of canonical advice.[81] This reversal, which limited participation in the chapter to directors, created 'great discontent' and it appears a majority of the Brothers in Ireland joined Br

John Leonard in a petition to Archbishop Murray, requesting an appeal to the Holy See for a revision of the Brief in order to accommodate a more representative chapter.[82]

Time did not allow for such an appeal, and when the chapter met in North Richmond Street in December 1831, it contained just fourteen of the forty-two professed Brothers. The mood among the assembly was fraught, especially as the principal task of the chapter was to elect a superior for the next decade. Brother John Leonard had already shared his intentions: 'I respect Mr Rice', he confessed, but 'I shall never sacrifice the interests of our little Order, by voting for an individual whom I consider *eminently* calculated to misdirect it.'[83] Rice's own spirits were low, and emotionally he had been dejected since the turmoil of the 1829 chapter. A spell at the English spa town of Cheltenham brought no improvement, but his supporters continued to stress his intellectual prowess in the face of persistent rumours to the contrary.[84] He had led the congregation for almost thirty years; he had attempted to resign in 1829, so a change of leadership might have been expected. Yet, when the vote was taken, he was returned to office, securing eleven of the fourteen possible votes. Surprisingly, or perhaps not given the way in which the chapter was 'stacked', there were no votes for Br Leonard; Francis Thornton received one vote, as did the novice master Patrick Ellis. The most unusual aspect of the election, however, was the vote cast in favour of Br Paul Riordan who was not a member of the chapter.[85]

The chapter then turned to the critical issues facing the congregation. Within itself it had the competence to address many of the concerns, but others had to be referred to the Holy See. These included the status of the 'serving' or lay-brothers [*Fratres Conversi*] and the extension of subsequent superior generals' term of office to life. Most critically, given the clamour among the Brothers, they requested a change in the composition of chapters, to include eight directors and eight 'ancients', or senior non-directors, to be elected by all finally professed Brothers. This, it was hoped, would address the democratic deficit within the institute.[86] Another issue the chapter addressed directly was the formal adoption of the new *Book of Common Rules*. Not alone were new statutes necessitated by the change in canonical status as a result of the papal brief, but the confusion and acrimony of the previous years were due in no small degree to the absence of structures and what Br Joseph Leonard had called 'the very imperfect system by which we are governed'.[87] The new rule was the fruit of a decade of reflection. Drafted by four commissioners appointed in 1822, it was an adaptation of the Brothers' original Presentation Rule, and reflected a range of influences including those of the Jesuits and the De La Salles who had pioneered the vocation of the lay brother within the Church.

The chapter devoted considerable attention to the establishment of a centralized novitiate for the congregation. This was part of Rice's vision for the North Richmond site, since the introduction of exacting standards for the formation of young Brothers was essential to the future of the institute. Prior to this, initial formation had been 'flexible', and novices were frequently dispatched prematurely from the novitiate to meet the pressing needs of the schools. As a result, many of the Brothers were ill-prepared, and perhaps theologically uninformed, so as to necessitate the introduction of a new regulation requiring the superiors of each community to hold monthly examinations on doctrinal and other prescribed material.[88] For the future, the chapter laid down that each novice would complete a minimum of one full spiritual year before being sent on the mission. This was to be directed by a novice master, whose sole responsibility was the care of the novitiate. It was in this context, too, that the chapter sent two Brothers on a reconnaissance mission to the De La Salle community in Paris. As Rice explained to Frère Anaclet, their task was to:

> Learn of your System of training your Novices, as well as to gain information from you upon other matters connected with your Institute, and which must be of the greatest importance to us.[89]

This visit allowed the Brothers to tap into a wealth of experience, which Rice deemed essential due to what he described, in terms reminiscent of Br Joseph Leonard's observations, as 'the deep feeling of our own deficiency and inexperience'.[90] However, the visit may have unwittingly perpetuated the notion which Rice and his canonical advisers sought to quash, that the Christian Brothers were a branch of the French Brotherhood, 'the parental institute' upon which the Irish Congregation was grafted.[91]

That aside, it would not be an exaggeration to conclude that the 1832 chapter was a triumph for Rice from which he derived particular satisfaction.[92] Against a background of conflict and confusion, he successfully steered a middle course through the chapter, carrying the divergent factions with him towards a resolution of the issues which had divided them so bitterly. Rivalries remained, and perhaps the order was 'tottering', but the chapter had approved a new Rule and placed the institute on a sound constitutional footing, providing a base upon which his successors would build. In this context, the chapter marked the end of the charismatic period in the history of the group, the point where the relative flexibility of the early years gave way to institutionalised structures. For Rice, too, the adoption of the rule and constitutions circumscribed his freedom of action and any inclination he had to dictate the direction of the institute.[93] However, it was a measure of his achievement, and the esteem in which he was held by his Brothers, that the chapter voted *unanimously* that he should sit for a formal portrait. With characteristic reserve, Rice curtly rebuked the Brothers: 'For what', he exclaimed, 'to have my portrait in front of you and my soul to be burning in Hell?'[94] He was inflexible on this as on so many other issues and resisted having his likeness painted until 1841, by which time he was in no position to resist.

CHAPTER TEN

Faith or fatherland? The Brothers and the National Board, 1831-6

IN RETROSPECT, IT SEEMS INCREDIBLE THAT the 1832 general chapter failed to discuss the great educational issue of the day; the establishment of the National Board of Education. However, this glaring omission created difficulties for the Brothers which endured until the foundation of the Irish Free State in 1922. By failing to assess the implications of the National scheme, the Brothers entered the project in a half-hearted fashion with little apparent understanding of its workings or its potential for development. Moreover, the failure to engage with the system assured that not only was their effectiveness as a teaching order seriously circumscribed, but as a consequence of their hasty withdrawal future generations lost sight of their driving principles which have been obscured by the myth of the Brothers' nationalism.

I

The 1820s brought the question of Catholic education to a head: as 'JKL' wryly remarked: 'there were not as many verse makers in Rome in the days of Horace, as there are writers and speakers on education now-a-days in a single assembly of ladies and gentlemen in Ireland'.[1] The 'Second Reformation' increased the sense of urgency with which the Catholic clergy viewed the education question and there was growing resentment at the levels of state funding for the Kildare Place Schools. Established in 1811, the Kildare Place Society aimed to provide a liberal education free from any imputation of proselytism. From its foundation, the Kildare Place Society received a government grant which rose to £30,000 by 1831. The Society intended to combine religious and secular knowledge and religious teaching consisted solely of scripture reading without 'note or comment'. As Fr Peter O'Loughlin's application from Ennistymon illustrated, all catechisms and books of religious controversy were banned from their classrooms during school hours.

Of all the educational societies, the liberal principles of the Kildare Place Society made it the most progressive. From the beginning it enjoyed a measure

10.1 Archbishop Daniel Murray (1768–1852). Engraving by Charles Fleming (*c.*1830), NLI.

of Catholic support, but in the sectarian tension of the 1820s the use of scriptural texts without comment became increasingly unacceptable to the hierarchy. The 'Biblicals' had made extensive use of scriptural texts in their proselytising schools, believing that the power of the Word of God alone would be sufficient to convert the Irish. In 1820, Archbishop Troy made a specific ruling that 'the scriptures, with or without note or comment were not fit to be used as a school-book'.[2] In the same year, John MacHale, in a series of letters under the name of *Hierophilos*, attacked Kildare Place for subsidising schools of the Biblical Societies. Daniel O'Connell brought these concerns to a general meeting of the KPS in February 1820, advocating a 'new-model' which would acknowledge the Tridentine formula, that the 'entire word of God has not been preserved in writing … [alone but also in] tradition'.[3] 'Every Catholic', he argued, 'is bound to assert this', but his proposal was rejected by 80 votes to 19.

The future of the Kildare Place Schools as the basis of a broad system of education was now obviously in doubt. Later that year O'Connell, the duke of Leinster, Lord Fingal and Lord Cloncurry resigned from the Society. In Hislop's expression, the Society was ultimately 'a doomed experiment in 'mixed' education which ignored the realities of denominational control of schools':

The hostility which the Kildare Place experiment encountered in the 1820s proved the principle on which the Society was founded was an unworkable compromise and that the Irish education question could be solved only if the realities of denominational control, and particularly Catholic denominational control were accepted.[4]

The Catholic hierarchy brought renewed pressure to bear on government for a solution to the educational question. In May 1824 the bishops presented parliament with a statement of the conditions under which they would accept a system of state-funded education. This pressure resulted in the establishment of a commission of inquiry to examine all aspects of educational provision in Ireland, but neither the composition of the board nor its report met with Catholic approval.

The commission reported in 1825 and recommended the government to discontinue its practice of channeling aid to education through voluntary agencies, such as the Kildare Place Society. Instead the commissioners advocated the establishment of a government board which would superintend a national state aided system of education. Similar recommendations were made by a parliamentary committee in 1828. The government accepted these suggestions and, in September 1831, the chief secretary, Edward Stanley, outlined a radical plan to provide Ireland with a national system of popular education, a full four decades before England.[5] In the following December a seven-member board of administration met for the first time. Two of the board were Catholic: Archbishop Daniel Murray and A.R. Blake; three were members of the Established Church: Dr Richard Whately, the liberal archbishop of Dublin, the duke of Leinster, and the Revd Francis Sadlier, provost of Trinity College; and two were Dissenters: the Revd James Carlile (Presbyterian) and Robert Holmes (Unitarian). The main features of the new system may be summarised as follows:

1. To unite in one system children of different creeds, while taking care not to interfere with the religious beliefs of any.
2. One or two days each week were to be set aside for separate religious instruction, as approved by the clergy of the different persuasions.
3. The applicants for the board's grants were given the power to appoint teachers.
4. A local contribution of not less than one third of the cost was required for building a school house. These were 'vested' schools, as opposed to 'non vested' or existing schools which joined the system.

5. The board was to have complete control over the books used – schools were free to use their own texts, provided the Board approved.[6]

Initially, the greatest opposition to the Board came from the Protestant denominations. The Church of Ireland held a meeting in the Rotunda, Dublin, in January 1832 as a result of which the primate and fifteen bishops signed a long protest at the Bill, a Whig measure, which they perceived as an assault on the Established Church's role in the provision of education.[7] Moreover, given the failure of the 'Second Reformation' and the grave constitutional implications of Emancipation, state support for 'mixed education', if not tantamount to the establishment of Roman Catholicism, was at the very least tolerance of popish superstition. As 'Captain' James Gordon, itinerant preacher turned Tory MP for Dundalk, exclaimed, 'It is one thing to tolerate an error, it is another to teach it'.[8]

Through the 1830s this opposition hardened, and in 1839 the Church Education Society was founded to promote an alternative educational system in which all its children, Catholic and Protestant, were required to read the Bible. The Presbyterians, too, had reservations about the system and the concessions made to Catholics, including objections to the inclusion of a bishop among the Commissioners, which manifested what Nigel Yates describes as 'the crudest feelings of militant anti-popery'.[9] They also wished to use the Bible at any point during the day, and many were inclined to exclude Catholic children while it was being read. Unlike the Church of Ireland, however, Presbyterians sought modifications rather than a complete overthrow of the system. Following pro-longed negotiations between the Synod of Ulster and the National Board, an agreeable solution had been reached by 1839, whereby Catholic clergy were no longer entitled to visit non-vested schools for religious instruction.

The initial reaction of the Catholic hierarchy to the National School system was one of quiet approval, but vocal opposition came from John MacHale, then coadjutor bishop of Killala, who slammed the system as 'narrow, bigoted and insulting'.[10] Nevertheless, by 1831 the Church had reached an educational crisis and was unable to meet the costs of providing the necessary schools, a reality clearly illustrated in the problems faced by Edmund Rice at North Richmond Street. The establishment of the Board seemed like an answer to prayer: the Commissioners were prepared to fund up to two-thirds of the capital costs and to provide texts, furniture and teachers' salaries. Besides, while Stanley had instructed the Commissioners to look with particular favour on joint applications from different Churches, he conceded to Archbishop Murray that such

10.2 John MacHale (1791–1881), archbishop of Tuam. Engraving by
John Corcoran, Dublin (*c.*1820–70) from an original by J.F. O'Kelly, NLI.

applications would not be necessary or even likely.[11] In effect, then, the flexibility
of the Commissioners assured that virtually all applications were initiated by the
local parish priest, and although he undertook to fulfill all the requirements laid
down by the Board, the schools became to all intents and purposes parish schools.
Indeed, the observation that the National system was 'the archetypal Irish solution
to an Irish problem' is borne out in Daly's analysis of the applications, which
illustrates a high degree of continuity between the clerically patronised schools
of the 1820s and the National Schools of the following decade.[12]

For all these concessions to the Catholic cause, the National system fell far
short of the scheme described by Edmund Rice to Archbishop Bray in 1810. Above
all, the introduction of designated periods of religious instruction was at total
variance with Rice's integrated approach where religion permeated the entire
school day. He was, therefore, inclined to remain independent of the National
system.[13] Indeed, from the outset Rice held many of the objections which MacHale,
John Cantwell and the younger generation of bishops developed at a later stage.[14]

It is worth recalling, however, that in 1831 the Irish hierarchy was still grateful for the recent 'gift' of emancipation and was reluctant to appear demanding.[15] By contrast, the Christian Brothers had developed an independent, uncompromising, character, which in time would become a general feature of Irish Catholicism. Moreover, the addition of the penal clauses to the Emancipation Act assured that there was no love lost between the Brothers and the London government. At a structural level, too, in contrast to the pragmatism of the clergy, as displayed in their previous willingness to work with the KPS, the Christian Brothers had very clearly defined guidelines regarding the exclusive management of their schools. On receiving an invitation to Preston (1825), for instance, Rice was at pains to assure that it was 'distinctly understood … that the arrangements of the school and the mode of teaching the children are to be left entirely to our Brothers'.[16] When invited to Liverpool (1837), too, he insisted that his confreres assumed responsibility for 'the entire internal management of the schools'.[17]

Still, in spite of these precedents, Edmund Rice applied for inclusion in the National system in 1831. The traditional history of the Christian Brothers asserts that the decision, against his inclinations, was made both from dire necessity and in response to a personal invitation from Archbishop Murray.[18] There is no archival evidence of this exchange, but this is not surprising, given that they met regularly in Dublin. Yet even then, Rice agreed merely to test the system in selected schools. At a practical level, of course, a refusal to participate in the scheme was never an option. Not alone were the Brothers' resources strained to the limit, but the parishes upon which they relied for support were increasingly incapable of financing the schools. This was most apparent in Clare, where at both Ennis and Ennistymon, the future of the schools was in jeopardy. Had Rice refused state support, the priests and people would certainly have sought other teachers to conduct the schools. Accordingly, seven of the Brothers' twelve schools joined the system: Richmond Street, Mill Street, Ennis and Ennistymon were affiliated in 1833; Waterford and Dungarvan joined in 1834. Neither Cork, Limerick, Thurles nor Carrick-on-Suir had any connection with the National Board.

More recently, however, an alternative interpretation has been offered by Kent and developed by McLaughlin which attempts to dispel the 'myth' that the Christian Brothers were reluctant participants in the National system. They argue to the contrary that Rice was, in fact, an enthusiastic supporter of the system, which he considered an 'authentic opportunity to provide his Catholic education for the poor'.[19] The thesis, which is well made, rests primarily on Rice's early application for inclusion, made on 12 September 1831, before the publication of the Bill. The implication is that Rice was 'clearly in the know' and that the architects of the scheme had given him assurances that the operation of the National Schools would be consistent with his educational philosophy.[20]

However, this interpretation fails to account for the decision of certain of the Brothers' schools to remain outside the system. The financial security of the Cork schools allowed them remain aloof, but the decision of the other communities cannot be simply attributed to either 'anti-Rice' sentiments or 'an energetic Catholic-nationalist pride' within the order.[21] McLaughlin, for instance, links the abstention of Hanover Street School to the director's nationalism and 'robust disaffection towards officious Protestant bureaucrats'.[22] Yet, at the Commission of Irish Education Inquiry (1825), Bernard Dunphy displayed no such inclination when, in an O'Connellite formulation, he described the Brothers as 'bound not only in duty, but gratitude' to teach loyalty and fidelity to their sovereign, King George IV.[23] Such sentiments were in excess of any required by the National Board. McLaughlin argues, too, that it was 'clear to any keen observer like Rice' that it was just a question of time before the proposed system would become a denominational one.[24] This is obvious in hindsight. But it was not apparent in 1831, and his citation of expressions of support, made by Paul Cullen in the following decade, create a misleading impression of circumstances which pertained at the launch of the state scheme.[25] Indeed, it was Evangelical pressure, and the rival Church Education Society, which ensured that the National Schools became *de facto* Catholic preserves in most parts of Ireland.[26]

Besides, the Brothers had not long to wait to see that the system was at variance with their ideal. Most objectionable was the restriction of religious instruction to one or two days per week: prayers were said furtively, and the removal of statues and the crucifix from class-rooms caused the Brothers distress. This latter prohibition, in time became an icon of all that Catholics found offensive about the system: the substitution of the lion and the unicorn for the Virgin and Child.[27] The catechisms and Gahan's devotional texts, of which so much of the daily reading consisted, were banished from the school. In their place the Brothers were expected to rely on texts which they regarded as objectionable. Most of the texts were written by James Carlile, a Presbyterian minister, who modelled them on those of the Catholic Book Society. These texts, however, were not in keeping with the sentiments of 'Faith and Fatherland', which O'Connell had identified as the essential elements of an Irish education. Of the sixty books published by 1858, only seventeen had been written by an Irishman, and of these only one, a book on gardening, was by an Irish Catholic.[28]

The texts scrupulously avoided any subjects which might provoke a nationalist spirit. In a long historical section of 130 pages in the *Fifth Book* the sole reference to Irish history was contained in a single line: 'It was towards the end of the century that Henry II of England invaded Ireland and obtained homage of the Irish kings'.[29] This ethos was again reflected in Carlile's geography lessons published in 1850. The section on the 'British Islands' begins:

> The island of Great Britain, which is composed of England, Scotland, and Wales and the island of Ireland, form ... the British Empire in Europe. The people of these islands have one and the same language (all at least who are educated), one and the same laws, and though they differ in their religious worship, they all serve the same God ... All this is enough to make them brethren, in spite of many disagreements and faults which history tells ... but a better knowledge of their duty will give future history better things to record.[30]

Apart from these philosophical objections however, it must be admitted that the National Board texts were of a very high educational standard and were well printed.[31] By the middle of the century these Irish school texts were the most popular in the British empire and in 1861 the Royal Commission on education admitted that they were the most widely used school books in England.[32] In their defence it is argued that the texts were neither anti-Irish nor anti-Catholic; in fact it was their neutrality which gave them such appeal across the empire. Of course, within the charged Irish environment, a neutral stance was unacceptable. Catholics condemned the texts as 'calculated to impress the children with the idea that their parents fell from the skies'.[33] Evangelical clerics criticised the system for failing to proselytise, while the Young Irelanders would later dismiss the readers of the National Board as 'sapless and un-Irish'.[34]

By 1836, it was clear that the Brothers' experiment with the National Board had taken its toll; in Br Paul Riordan's estimation, the system was fine for lay masters, but certainly not for religious Brothers.[35] Participation in the system had a demoralising effect on the congregation, as many believed their work had been undermined by their restricted freedom to impart an emphatically Catholic education. There were other objections too, particularly from the fractious Cork community who regarded the acceptance of state funding as a breach of their vow of gratuitous instruction. Whatever Rice's initial thoughts on the National system were, time had served to confirm his doubts. He had closely monitored the progress of the communities which had been affiliated to the scheme and in 1836 convoked an extraordinary general chapter to discuss the question of continued participation.

The chapter met in North Richmond Street on 27 December 1836. Participation in the National School system had many advantages to offer. Most of the Brothers' communities remained in dire financial circumstances; charitable donations were few and far between, while the Brothers' vows precluded them from charging even nominal fees. If nothing else, affiliation to the Board removed this difficulty. There were, however, more fundamental considerations which the chapter believed offset any possible advantages. The strongest opposition was directed against the prohibition of the integrated approach favoured by the Brothers. The separation of secular and religious instruction had made the latter appear of secondary importance, while the devotion to a full day each week to religion was generally regarded as impractical and educationally unsound. The essential contradiction between the two systems was subsequently outlined by Br Austin Grace in evidence before the Powis Commission (1868):

> The system of the National Board is based on a very different principle. It gives to secular instruction the first and chief place. The rules of the Board do not allow a religious emblem to be exposed in the school room, and the incidental teaching of Catholic doctrine is directly prohibited … It is for Patrons and Managers to determine whether any, and if any, what religious instruction should be given in the school room, and thus practically teaching the children that religion is a matter of secondary importance and may even be laid aside altogether at discretion.[36]

Regrettably, the 1836 chapter minutes contain just the decisions of the gathering and not a record of the discussions.[37] However, Br Joseph Murphy explained to Tobias Kirby, the vice-rector of the Irish College, Rome, and the most distinguished of the Brothers' past pupils, that the chapter had voted 'una voce condemning the Commission', on account of 'its inconsistency with our system'.[38] This account is compatible with the minutes, which record a unanimous rejection of the Board and a decision to sever their connection which would 'ultimately prove fatal to the religious as well as the professed object of the institute'.[39] The unanimity of that decision is significant, because whatever arguments may be posited to suggest Rice's initial support for the system, he voted with the entire chapter, the parliament of the congregation, to end participation in 1836. There were, however, serious financial restraints which made it impossible to withdraw all schools at once. Following an examination of the accounts of every foundation, Mount Sion, Richmond Street and Mill Street were withdrawn from the National system at Easter 1837. Dungarvan seceded in the following year, but it was some years before the poorer schools at Ennis (1840) and Ennistymon (1857) could be restored to their independence.

II

Despite Austin Grace's emphatic assertion that the two systems were incompatible, other teaching congregations had no such scruples. By 1838, the Presentation Brothers and as many as twenty-six convent schools were affiliated to the Board.[40] Their experience reflected the popular consensus that the only major restriction which the National system imposed was the limitation of religious instruction to the hours timetabled by the school manager. Indeed, during his visit to Ireland in 1835, the high-church Anglican, George Mathison, observed that the National Schools were *de facto* Catholic Church schools, attended only by Catholics and using only Catholic books.[41]

Moreover, in time, the Presentation Brothers made a virtue of the separation of religious and secular learning. In stark contrast to the testimony of Austin Grace, Br Paul Townsend, of the South Monastery, stated before Powis that he would never combine the two on the grounds that 'religious instruction was too solemn' to have it mixed up with secular education.[42] Such an assertion was a radical departure from the Catholic pedagogy of their founder. McLaughlin cites Nano Nagle's biographer to the effect that:

> Religious teaching could now [1837] be fitted into times before, intermediate with, or following secular instruction. In practice, therefore, the little acts of piety prescribed by the Presentation constitutions were retained. Morning and evening prayers were said, the Angelus at noon, the Hail Mary was said inaudibly at the hourly striking of the clock.[43]

He neglects to mention that the alteration of the regulations concerning religious instruction had been made to accommodate the Presbyterian Synod of Ulster only *after* Rice and his chapter voted to withdraw their schools. In a real sense, the Brothers' departure represented the first crack in the National system as designed by its architects.[44] Besides, the Brothers were obviously not alone among the religious orders in their opposition to the Board. The Presentation convent at George's Hill, Dublin, refused to join the National system until 1849, and their reluctance to compromise the Presentation tradition of education led to a cooling in their relations with Archbishop Murray, the great patron of female religious life in the city.[45] Perhaps the most vociferous in their criticism of the system were the Holy Faith Sisters. Their foundress, Margaret Aylward, whom Br Paul Riordan described as 'a great admirer of the Brothers of the Christian Schools', and her spiritual director, John Gowan CM, maintained a deep suspicion of the National Schools, their 'anti-Catholic books' and their Rules and Regulations which they believed were 'favourable to heresy'.[46] The Brothers' withdrawal had fuelled doubts about the system's integrity which forced the Commissioners to be more accommodating towards the demands of the various parties who remained within the system.[47] In this respect, the consequences of the Brothers' resolute opposition to this experiment of 'mixed education' determined the character of state-sponsored elementary education in Ireland which would endure until the first decades of the twenty-first century.

There is, too, a tendency to subject education history to the overarching narrative of Irish nationalism. Within this framework, Archbishop John MacHale, the 'Lion of the West', is pitted against Daniel Murray, who is simplistically portrayed as the accomplice of a malign anglicising regime.[48] In the context of the Christian Brothers and the National Board, however, it is more instructive to examine the tension from a theological or ecclesiological perspective. One of the ironies of the penal laws is that the Catholic Church in Ireland emerged from the eighteenth century as one of the freest churches in Europe. It was unlimited by the terms of any concordat, and the hierarchy went to great lengths to preserve its independence, opposing the imposition of a royal veto on episcopal appointments, despite papal recommendations to the contrary in 1815.[49] Moreover, the 1820s accentuated the status of the hierarchy which became increasingly assertive in the course of the 'Bible Wars'. The withdrawal of O'Connell and the Catholic leadership from the Kildare Place Society, too, marked an important milestone in that process, for it was clear from that point Catholics would participate in government-sponsored initiatives only on their own terms.[50]

While initially both the Church of Ireland and the Presbyterian Synod of Ulster expressed strident opposition to the National Board, they were forced by practical considerations to moderate their stance.[51] The opposite was the case among the Catholic clergy, who moved from their initial qualified acceptance towards open hostility to a system which they believed, fell far short of the ideal. By 1838 the hierarchy was bitterly divided upon the issue, but MacHale saw the struggle within a wider defence of clerical prerogatives, if not a contest for supremacy with the state:

> For the extraordinary powers now claimed by the state over mixed education, it would soon claim a similar despotic control over mixed marriages, and strive to stretch its net over all ecclesiastical concerns.[52]

That such sentiment echoed the indignation of the Established Church at the intervention of the Whigs into Irish education, with the creation of the National Board, illustrated the rise of Catholic ascendancy in nineteenth-century Ireland.

The essential issue at stake, therefore, was not the national question or anti-English sentiment, but rather the independence and status of the Catholic Church. Within the realm of education, this was manifest in the struggle for unfettered control of schooling. In 1812, when legislation regarding popular instruction appeared imminent, Bishop John Power, Rice's mentor, expressed a view to Francis Moylan of Cork that the Church 'may consent, for want of better to a school for reading ... but we must ever prefer, when we can, a school calculated to teach Catholic children Catholic principles'.[53] From the outset Edmund Rice and his Brothers offered such an uncompromising education and they were not prepared to surrender its superintendence to the Protestant state. Significantly, too, in an English context, the Tractarians opposed state control of education on similar grounds. In his defence of Church of England supremacy, Henry Edward Manning argued that Christian education concerned not merely intellectual or civic formation. It was about shaping inward character and conforming mankind to the image of its Saviour. And since Christ himself was the author and exemplar of this transformation, he argued that only the Church, as the depositary of his truth and grace, was competent to educate.[54] In an Irish context, this argument was made explicitly by the Holy Faith Sisters in 1861 to justify their refusal to subject their schools to the National Board; 'to the State is given the power to rule society, but to the Church God has given a commission to teach'.[55] It is instructive, too, to look at the rhetoric employed by the Irish hierarchy in the following decades in the context of university education, and their determined opposition to the 'godless colleges' offered by the state, which Pius IX condemned as 'harmful to religion'.[56]

In terms of their canonical status, too, securing the papal brief had given the Brothers an exemption from episcopal supervision. Having achieved a cherished independence they were unwilling to surrender to the regular inspections of a state agency like the National Board. Canonically, too, being subject only to the pope, the Christian Brothers represented 'a church within the church' in Ireland. As a consequence they displayed determined ultramontanist tendencies a generation ahead of their peers. Such sentiments appealed greatly to Paul Cullen who subsequently patronised the Brothers as archbishop of Dublin. Indeed, once the institutional Church gained the confidence and resources to confront the National system, he employed the Brothers in that task, as his predecessors had used them to repel the 'Biblicals' thirty years earlier.[57]

In the short term, however, rejection of the National Board alienated many friends and benefactors. Rice's initial decision to affiliate to the National system was due, in part, to respect for Archbishop Murray. When the difficult resolution was made to withdraw the schools, he wrote informing the archbishop and concluded that 'If this step should be disagreeable to Your Grace I shall be very sorry for it.'[58] Murray, who possessed the patience of a saint, was particularly displeased by the Brothers' action. He was, after all, a member of the Board; he had invested in Catholic education in his diocese and had been a long-time benefactor of Rice's schools. Along with this, the archbishop may have been aggrieved at the Brothers' failure to inform him of their decision before they communicated it to the Commissioners. Initially, Murray expressed his dissatisfaction with the withdrawal of his annual donation of £40 to the Hanover Street School.[59] By 1840, however, his temper had cooled. He allowed charity sermons, once more, and, in the following year, apologised that 'unexpected disappointments' had left him 'without the means' to make a personal contribution to the appeal.[60] At a practical level, too, withdrawal from the system had severe consequences for the Brothers' schools. In Dublin, at the struggling O'Connell Schools, for instance, the loss of the annual grant of £60 forced the closure of two school-rooms, the redeployment of two Brothers and the consequent reduction of student numbers by two hundred.[61] Significantly, Charles Bianconi, himself an ardent supporter of the National Board, realized the financial consequences of the Brothers' withdrawal. It appears that it was in this context, that he began to send an annual donation and suits of clothes as a gesture of solidarity with his first benefactor, Edmund Rice.[62]

As a precedent, however, the frustrating flirtation with the Board provided the Brothers with 'a precautionary training for the future', as described by Br Joseph Hearn, assistant to the second superior general:

> If at any time yet to come, the Christian Brothers may be induced to accept state aid … they may learn a lesson from these demands and prudently adopt such measures as will prevent any one from swindling them out of their principles or compromising the … object of their vocation.[63]

This formative experience, however, accentuated the Brothers' sense of isolation within the Church. For without state funding they were less attractive to bishops and other prospective patrons who increasingly failed to appreciate the principle of their abstention from the system. Ironically, the Brothers were punished

10.3 Charles Bianconi (1786–1875), 'King of the Irish Roads' (c.1840).

for defending the principles which the prelates preached. However, as the National Schools evolved into a system of denominational education, the Brothers' continued abstentionism appeared increasingly unreasonable. It was not so much that the Brothers left the system, but their resolute failure to consider a return cast them as uncompromising zealots. In addition, the Brothers' cherished independence hardened in the experience to become almost a fetish which placed them on a collision course with the Catholic hierarchy and disinclined them to co-operate with successive state initiatives, up to and including the Vocational Education Act (1930), and indeed the Community School enterprise of the 1970s. Moreover, the financial restraints created by the rejection of the system, predisposed the Brothers to embrace the Intermediate Education Act (1878), which inaugurated a system of payment by results. In the longer term this had very significant repercussions for the system of education designed by Edmund Rice.[64]

CHAPTER ELEVEN

The comfort of friends, 1838–44

RICE'S EXIT FROM THE NATIONAL BOARD has been eulogised as 'the crown-ing glory of his heroic life', but the turmoil of the decade brought his frag-ile body to breaking point.[1] In his own expression, he reached a 'very delicate state of health' which necessitated his resignation as superior general in 1838.[2] Yet while biographers have described a graceful retirement at Mount Sion, 'his dear old home', surrounded by all the consolations that 'love … and gratitude could provide', the reality was quite the contrary.[3] Rather than enjoying the peaceful preparation for death which is the stuff of hagiography, Rice's last years were blighted by bitter acrimony and recrimination in what became for him a purgatory on earth.

I

The historiography of the Christian Brothers celebrates the acceptance of the papal brief (1822) and the rejection of the National Board (1836) as the great tri-umphs of Rice's administration.[4] In truth, however, the rapid progress of events in Ireland undermined the value of both resolutions which, in the short term at least, appeared ill-considered. Few in 1822 could have predicted the outcome of the 'Bible Wars', yet once the tide had turned in favour of the Catholic cause the rationale for the controversial change in the Brothers' canonical status was forgotten. Ironically, therefore, the measure which the pope had intended to increase the mobility of the congregation had the opposite effect, since episco-pal opposition to the Brothers' autonomy stunted its expansion. Archbishop Michael Slattery of Cashel, for one, admitted that the bishops of Munster were unwilling to sanction further establishments in the absence of a measure of cler-ical control.[5] Similarly, the Brothers' rejection of the National Board appeared not just as arrogant folly, but as counterproductive since the rejection of Treasury funds frustrated the task of educating the poor. Their existing schools were placed under intolerable financial burdens, while few bishops could afford the luxury of establishing a new community when the state would fund an effec-tive alternative. Significantly, too, many of the prelates who could support the

Brothers chose instead to divert the scarce resources towards the chapel-build-ing projects which characterised the age.

Paradoxically, then, these defining resolutions determined that Rice's earli-est recorded wish, that the institute would spread throughout the Kingdom of Ireland, was never realised.[6] Nevertheless, the last years of his administration brought a litany of requests for new foundations abroad, fuelled by sentiments similar to those of the Benedictine William Ullathorne, who sought to woo the 'monks' to New South Wales. 'The Christian Brothers would be worth every-thing to us here', he proclaimed; 'these are the men we want to form model schools, not men who have become schoolmasters because they can do noth-ing else'.[7] To Rice's despair, however, a shortage of manpower dictated that the majority of these invitations were refused, but there were a number of excep-tions. He sent a community to Sunderland (1836) in response to the pleas of an Irish pastor, Fr Philip Kearney, whose persistence proved irresistible.[8] In the fol-lowing year, new communities were established at Liverpool and Wapping, while plans were afoot to open an English novitiate in Preston.[9]

At this time, too, Rice acceded to an invitation from Rome to send Brothers to the Rock of Gibraltar to teach Catholic children of the garrison there. This short-lived mission discussed above, foundered in the face of political intrigue and clerical rivalry, but Daniel Murray attributed its ultimate failure to a lack of piety among the people and zeal among the clergy.[10] Details of the mission, however, demonstrate important aspects of the congregational dynamics and its *modus operandi*. Br Patrick O'Flaherty led the venture. As a young man he joined a lay community, teaching in a school at Harcourt Road in Dublin. Like Rice's own 'novitiate' at St Patrick's chapel in Waterford forty years earlier, this circle gave religious instruction in local churches and attended daily Mass at the Carmelite friary on Clarendon Street. It was there he met Rice. The young teacher was impressed by Rice's charisma, especially the candour of his invita-tion to him to join the Brothers: 'Come and see.'[11] Significantly, too, the abortive mission to Gibraltar was undertaken in response to the alarming success of a Methodist school, which attracted eighty Catholic boys.[12] In Ireland the Brothers had been prominent in the Counter-Reformationary assault, and they proved no less effective on the Rock. There they brought the patterns perfected in the 'Bible Wars' to bear, forcing 'the swaddling pedagogue' to close his school and cross the border into Spain.[13]

Circumstances in England and the colonies were radically different from those in Ireland. There was no equivalent of the National Board in those parts. Neither were bishops as protective of their prerogatives, but they were anxious to secure the assistance of the Brothers, for the valuable educational services they could provide. In time, relationships abroad changed, too, as these missions became institutions, or when crises were averted, as in the case of Gibraltar, but the contrasts between the fortunes of the Brothers at home and abroad were striking. As the president of St John's College, Waterford, observed, 'everywhere [the Brothers] are prized but in Ireland'.[14] Such stark realities convinced Rice that the future of his congregation lay not in Ireland, but overseas.[15]

That said, Rice's reflections on the experience in Gibraltar suggested a possible solution to the stalemate at home. Not alone had the Brothers rescued poor children from proselytism, but, as he explained to his brother John, they had established 'pay-schools':

> where the rich received an education suitable to their situation in life, and the poor by that means supplied with all things necessary for a religious and literary education.[16]

Such a two-tiered model was eminently suited to Ireland, and Rice had argued this point since the early 1820s.[17] The establishment of fee-paying schools would generate income to subsidise the poor, but perhaps of greater significance was the possibility of extending the Brothers' mission to a new constituency of boys who were excluded by the social stigma attached to the acceptance of free schooling. The introduction of modest fees could remove this prejudice and encourage children of what Rice called 'shopkeepers and decent tradesmen'.[18] To his business mind, the attractions of this innovation were obvious, but from a pastoral perspective a change in traditional practice was imperative for the survival of his floundering institute.

Once more, however, the restrictive clauses of the papal brief, particularly the addition of an unnecessary vow of 'gratuitous education', posed an obstacle to the realisation of Rice's plan. The Brothers had unsuccessfully appealed the clause to Rome in 1823, twice in 1824 and again four years later, but in 1838 Rice laid out a cogent argument in favour of the establishment of pay-schools. This he circulated to the professed Brothers in preparation for a general chapter which would adjudicate on the matter:

> After serious consideration on the depressed state of some of our houses particularly this [Nt. Richmond Street], and the impossibility of supporting others of our houses without the painful dissipating and dangerous alternative of perpetual begging even against the wish or

rather at the unpleasant expense of incurring the displeasure of Priests, and even Bishops also, the injurious effect such a system must have on our schools, by having some of their best conductors absent from them on this begging mission. Contemplating the impossibility of deserving support from this system on account of the Poor Law Tax which will fall heavily on the class of people who now contribute to our support and consequently will absorb all they can spare, or are inclined to give, add to this the impossibility of extending our Institute, or even adding one school [class] to the few already established in Ireland from the circumstances of our not being in connection with the Board of Education now patronised by Bishops, Priests and Catholic Laity.

These and other such considerations lead me and other Brothers of our Institute to the conclusion that there is but one alternative left for the support of some of the houses already established, and the further propagation of our Institute on a permanent and independent footing in Ireland, that is the gradual establishment of pay-Schools for the education of the children of shop-keepers and decent tradesmen, a class who scarcely ever receive a religious Education, the proceeds of such schools would enable the Brothers to educate the poor in greater numbers, and thereby counteract the effects of a system now so popular, and which scouts religious education.

There may be some objections to what I here propose for your consideration and in order to know the sentiments of all the professed Brothers on a matter of so much importance to our Institute, I wish to know your and their opinion without being influenced by any person. Another matter that strikes me and which I wish to submit to your consideration is, the introduction of the Bible into the National Schools, which will render it quite impossible for the houses now in connection with the Board of Education to continue that connection. I contemplate calling a General Chapter in order to determine on a matter of such importance to the Institute, but I wish beforehand to be directed by your unbiased opinion in conjunction with those of the other professed Brs.

> I remain, My very dear Br ...
> Your affect. Br.,
> Edmd. I. Rice.[19]

Rice's rhetoric differs little from the arguments made in the first appeal to Rome in favour of pay-schools.[20] The crucial difference, however, was the extent to which the climate within which the Brothers worked had changed. If there ever had been a 'penal consensus' among Irish Catholics, it had clearly evaporated by 1838; the education debate was polarised on the issue of the National Schools, while the Brothers faced challenges for their very survival. Rice's priorities, however, remained steadfast. He began his mission in 1802 to offer an *alternative* 'Catholic education'. In 1838 his ambition was to extend his care to 'a class who scarcely ever receive a *religious* Education', to children who the archbishop of Dublin believed were 'growing up in the most appalling ignorance with regards to the truths of religion'.[21] Significantly, too, the changes which he advocated were intended to 'counteract the effects of a system now so popular … which scouts religious education'.[22] Whatever uncertainty there may have been about Rice's attitude towards the National Board at its inception these had long vanished by 1838.

While awaiting the opinion of the Brothers, Rice drew up his will and entrusted his financial affairs to three of his closest collaborators, Brothers Francis Thornton, Joseph Murphy and Austin Dunphy. The terms of the will were simple; his entire estate was left for the benefit of the work and charities to which he had devoted his life. The notable omission from the will, however, is any allowance for the care of his 'delicate' daughter Mary.[23]

II

In February 1838, Rice retired to Mount Sion. His health was poor and he was unable to administer the affairs of the institute. Accordingly, he wrote to the various houses convoking a general chapter which would appoint his successor. Preparations were made, delegates chosen and, following a preparatory retreat, the chapter opened on 24 July 1838. Edmund Rice presided over the opening proceedings and when the formalities were out of the way he addressed the Brothers and tendered his resignation. Nine years earlier the assembled Brothers had persuaded their founder to withdraw his resignation, but this time all were struck by the finality of his decision.

The choice of a successor would not be easy. Rice had led the Brothers for thirty-six years; many of the congregation had joined with the specific intention of following his example. The cult of his personality and his renowned holiness all contributed to make the choice of successor exceedingly difficult. The correct choice was imperative since, according to the terms of rescript granted to the institute by Pope Gregory XVI in 1832, the new superior general would serve for life. The Brothers had never before been in the position of having to choose a superior general; they were unfamiliar with procedures, while the existence of two factions within the congregation added further complications. Moreover, through a combination of ignorance and inexperience, the chapter degenerated into farce. The first and second votes produced no absolute majority, and since the constitutions contained no provision for this eventuality, the Brothers made an impromptu decision to adopt a process of elimination following successive ballots until a new superior was elected. This innovation delivered a result, and Paul Riordan was chosen on the fifth ballot, but, as subsequent legal opinion confirmed, these irregular proceedings rendered the election process 'absolutely invalid'.[24]

The transfer from founder to successor is inevitably difficult. In the case of the Irish Christian Brothers it was a particularly acrimonious affair. The new superior general, a native of Cahir, was born in the year of the French Revolution (1789). Before joining the institute he was employed as a clerk in the counting house of a Cork silk merchant. He entered the North Monastery where remained there until his election as superior general sixteen years later. Consequently, his experience of the congregation was very limited. Nor, indeed, had he a sense of Edmund Rice as 'founder', since he had joined the community in the critical interim, between the receipt of the papal brief and Cork's reluctant union with the Christian Brothers four years later. In this sense, Riordan's critics were justified in their charge that he had not served a novitiate in '*this* Institute'.[25] Furthermore, during this period, the 'North Mon' was an independent institution, in which the raw recruit came under the influence of Br Joseph Leonard, 'founder' of the Cork schools and leader of the opposition to Rice's leadership.

Perhaps the election of Br Austin Dunphy, Rice's natural heir, would have made the transition of power more agreeable, but the choice of a vocal critic augured badly for the future, particularly as he retained Br John Leonard as his assistant. Yet while the historiography of the Brothers accentuates the tensions between Rice and his successor, Riordan enjoyed Rice's confidence to the extent that he had appointed him director of the Cork community in 1836. This in itself was a measure of his trust, but it is especially pertinent since the appointment assured his presence at the next chapter and the possibility of his election as Rice's successor. Nor was there any hint of personal acrimony between the two at the general chapter. On the contrary, there was a moving episode on the evening Riordan was elected, when Rice humbly surrendered his seat at table to his successor. This gracious act of fealty was recorded by Stephen Carroll, a young novice at Mount Sion:

> The same day when the bell rang for dinner I was present in the dining room and the ex-Superior was one of the first to enter, and he stood right by the side of his chair which he filled for many a long year. As the newly elected walked in the ex-Superior said to him, 'This, Sir, is your seat.' I heard him say so, and obliged him to sit therein, then and there.[26]

Within days of the election, however, as the chapter began to discuss the agenda outlined in Rice's circular, chaos descended on the assembly when one of the capitulants challenged the superior general's authority and the legality of his election. Amid the confusion, one Brother called for his resignation, another ruled out that possibility, while a third opinion suggested applying to Rome for a *sanatio*, a papal dispensation which would heal any irregularity relating to the election.[27] Riordan put the latter motion to a vote. Its acceptance by an emphatic majority of 17 to 2 was, if not a vote of confidence in the general, at very least an indication that the chapter wished him to proceed.

Moreover, that the successful memorial to Rome was drafted by Austin Dunphy, the defeated candidate, suggests a desire for unity among the Brothers. But the moment was lost, however, to resolve the critical issues which faced the congregation – the proposed pay-schools and the continued participation in the National Board. Of the two, the latter was the least contentious. The chapter renewed its condemnation of the system and outlined an exit strategy for the remaining schools.[28] Debate on the pay-school issue, however, was more protracted and involved four sessions of the chapter. The arguments in favour of the motion were well rehearsed, but important considerations were offered by the opposition. Certainly the objections recorded by Br T.J. Hearn, admittedly an adversary, were not inconsiderable. These included fears that the better teachers would be employed in the pay-schools; that class-distinctions would emerge among the Brothers and that it would become more difficult to move teachers in and out of the parallel systems.[29] These arguments had been articulated a decade before by Br Joseph Leonard, who had been particularly concerned by the spectre of proselytism, and the fear that 'the poor children would be abandoned to the ravishing wolves, who use money and trickery to pervert the unfortunates from the faith of their ancestors'.[30]

The chapter was bitterly divided on the point, with the greatest resistance to the plan coming from Paul Riordan and the Brothers of the North Monastery.

11.1 Brother Michael Paul Riordan (1789–1862),
second superior general of the Christian Brothers.

Normoyle argues that all of the capitulants were committed to the education of
the poor as their principal duty, but that their attitude towards fee-paying
schools depended to a large extent on the financial position of the houses in
which they lived. The Brothers in England, for instance, had free accommodation, heating and an average stipend of £50 per annum. The North Monastery,
Br Riordan's community, lived equally securely on the proceeds of a substantial
bequest made to the school in 1835 by the Cork physician Dr John Barry.[31] The
outcome of the debate was inconclusive and the chapter stopped short of a
definitive adjudication on the issue. By way of a compromise, it declared its
opposition *in principle* to pay-schools, but on account of dire necessity agreed
to allow the Brothers at Mill Street and Hanover Street charge nominal fees, subject to Roman approval, in an experiment to be reviewed at the next chapter.[32]
This represented no more than a weak fudge which rather than stemming divisions gave them space to fester.

III

Paul Riordan lacked the charisma of the founder, but he was an effective leader. He had been 'a clerk', an accountant, and as superior general he behaved as such. Austere and grave, he seldom laughed, but as a quintessential administrator, he was perfectly equipped to effect the transition the troubled Institute required.[33] At the time of his succession, the order was tottering, in danger of collapse, but by his death in 1862 he had given it permanence and stability. 'Permanence' is perhaps the antithesis of the prophetic, but that is what was required to salvage Rice's dream. In the words of his obituary, 'Mr Rice's name symbolized the infancy and the struggles; Mr Riordan's the strength and success of the Order'.[34]

Relations with Archbishop Murray were strained following the Brothers' rejection of the National system, but the chapter's failure to support the principle of pay-schools increased tensions. In the following year, Riordan removed the generalate from Dublin, first to Cork and later to Mount Sion (1841), ostensibly on account of the precarious financial state of North Richmond Street, but there is little doubt that he sought to put distance between himself and the archbishop.[35] Br Austin Grace returned from England to take charge of the O'Connell's Schools, a task he likened to the rescue of a 'sinking ship'.[36] Certainly, the foundation was in trouble; two of the large schoolrooms lay idle, the community funds were reduced to shillings, creditors coveted the property while the Brothers were forced to rely upon the pennies of the boys and the sale of vegetables from the monastery garden.[37] These conditions were replicated in the schools at Hanover Street and Mill Street on the south side of the city, while in Limerick things were little better. In those circumstances, Br Alphonsus Hoope, who later founded the Artane Industrial School, was 'overpowered and overworked' to the point where 'he could do little for his own sanctification and less for the boys'.[38]

There were, all the same, some signs of encouragement. Not least of these was the decision of the celebrated playwright Gerald Griffin (1803–40), author of *The Collegians*, reckoned the best nineteenth-century Irish novel, to enter the Brothers' novitiate in 1838.[39] This choice was made against the advice of family who at first considered the 'simple task' of instructing the poor as 'degrading and most unworthy' of their brother's 'abilities of the highest order'.[40] Griffin rejected this pressure, and his choice in preference to the priesthood was a public endorsement of the work of the Brothers, described in his obituary as 'a humble and most useful brotherhood'.[41] Yet while 'Brother Joseph', enjoyed happiness in his new-found state, the conditions he encountered in the school spoke volumes:

11.2 Souvenir of Brother Gerald Griffin – Irish poet and novelist
(c.1897–1923). Guy, Cork, NLI.

> I was ordered here [to Cork] … last June, and have been since enlight-
> ening the craniums of the wandering Paddies of this quarter, who learn
> from me with profound amazement and profit that O X spells ox: that
> the top of the map is the north and the bottom is the south, with vari-
> ous other branches, as also that they ought to be good boys, and do as
> they are bid, and say their prayers every morning and evening, &.[42]

The timing of Griffin's arrival in Cork was fortunate, too, as it coincided with
the launch of what might be considered Br Riordan's legacy project – the publication of the Christian Brothers' textbooks.

Having rejected the National Schools, not least on account of their objectionable texts, the new general launched an ambitious project to equip his
schools with a home-produced alternative. The bulk of the writing was carried
out in Cork; Riordan assumed the lion's share of the work, but Griffin assisted

in compiling the first edition of the *Literary Class Book* and a series of scriptural lessons.[43] While the design and production values were no match for those of the National Board, the Brothers' texts were acclaimed by liberal commentators. The *Cork Reporter* highlighted the absence of 'sectarian bigotry or gross misrepresentation' in the readers, while the *Nation* contrasted them with the 'studious suppression and distortion' which characterised the National School books.[44] The tenor of the Brothers' texts was unapologetically Catholic and Irish. This patriotism appealed to the cultural nationalism of the Young Irelanders, who applauded the extent to which the readers 'infused everything that can make their pupils proud and fond of their country'.[45] In the longer term, too, as patriotism gave way to separatism, the texts were particularly influential. They were not subversive, as unionists claimed, but their spirit nurtured the cultural philosophy of Irish nationalism.[46]

From the Brothers' perspective, the great advantage of the texts was the opportunity they provided for the removal of the notorious chapbooks from their schools; objectionable texts such as *Freney the Robber* and *Irish Rogues and Rapparees* which hawkers pedalled through the country could now be banished.[47] A downside of the new readers, however, was their cost which placed an additional burden on poor parents. Nevertheless, the advent of their own texts allowed increased standardisation across the Brothers' schools, an essential boon in the age before effective teacher training. In Austin Grace's estimation:

> One great blessing will attend these publications, that they will be the means in a great measure of establishing uniformity in all our schools … and enable our young Brothers to manage the classes better. Heretofore, wherever a Brother was located he had to almost learn the books he had to teach in each place, whereas now, having but precisely the same books everywhere … he will always be prepared from the time he leaves the noviceship.[48]

In 1843, too, Br Riordan, accompanied by Joseph Murphy, spent time studying the celebrated De La Salle schools in Le Havre, Rouen and Paris. What they saw there appealed greatly to the general's ordered mind. It was 'well worthy of … imitation', and many 'improvements' were made as a result.[49] At Mount Sion, a new building was planned along the lines of the school at St Laurent; classroom would be smaller than before, and the weakness of the monitorial system was implied in Riordan's observation that 'the boys could be better taught [in the De La Salle system]'.[50] As a result, the Irish were 'attempting to imitate the

MANUAL

OF

SCHOOL GOVERNMENT;

BEING A COMPLETE

Analysis of the System of Education

PURSUED IN THE

CHRISTIAN SCHOOLS.

Designed chiefly for the Junior Members of the Society.

BY

THE CHRISTIAN BROTHERS.

DUBLIN:

PRINTED BY WILLIAM POWELL,

68, THOMAS-STREET.

1845.

11.3 Title page of the Christian Brothers' *Manual of School Government* (1845).
Brother Allen Library, Dublin.

[French Brothers'] plan as nearly as' they could.[51] That inspection preceded the publication the *Manual of School Government* (1845), which represented a further step towards the achievement of uniformity across the Brothers' schools. The *Manual* established standards, while the publication of the texts assured the content of the lessons. Through an application of the two the Brothers could offer a credible alternative to the National system, but only if they could heal their own differences.

IV

Edmund Rice, meanwhile, had remained in Waterford following the general chapter. Relieved to have passed on the burden of leadership, the Brothers noted a marked improvement in his health and humour.[52] As his spirit returned, he began to visit the neighbouring communities at Dungarvan and Carrick-on-Suir, renewing acquaintances and enjoying the sea air at his favourite place, Annestown, one of the locations suggested as the home of his late wife.[53] This respite, however, was short-lived, as he was beset with a myriad of trials, the unfinished business of his term in office.

At the heart of the difficulties of Rice's latter years was the rumbling dissatisfaction on the pay-school issue. While the general chapter of 1838 had adopted an interim measure, Paul Riordan was troubled by the implications of that decision. Whether due to personal scruples about the breach of a solemn vow, or simply due to his own antipathy, he disregarded the will of the chapter and called an immediate halt to the preparation of the schoolrooms at Hanover Street and Mill Street. Riordan, however, had seriously misjudged the mood of the community there, and the angry backlash was such that he was forced to rescind these orders.

Two pay-schools opened at the trial sites as planned in September 1838. Students paid £1 per quarter in advance and the curriculum was similar to that of the other schools. However, a notice in the *Catholic Directory* emphasised the exclusivity of the schools, noting that 'the Seminary is altogether apart from the Free-Schools'. In fact the notice went even further, announcing that the timetable of the school was constructed in such a way as 'to preclude all possibility of intercourse' between the pupils of the two establishments.[54] The director of Mill Street, however, had no qualms about such social segregation, but rather boasted of the success of the enterprise:

> Our schools are doing admirably – Free Schools and Pay Schools; the
> latter has been opened about two months, and has at present 43 boys.
> Some of the boys express the happiness they feel at being in a Catholic
> School, in which religion is taught, as all the other schools in which they
> had been were mixed schools – Protestants and Catholics. Indeed the
> pay-schools have quite surpassed our expectations … The funds avail-
> able from the school have nearly supported the House from the day it
> was opened … Dr Murray has expressed his peculiar pleasure in
> patronizing it, and his happiness that provision was now made for that
> hitherto destitute class, and that he always considered our system defec-
> tive without Pay Schools. The clergy are equally delighted at its success.[55]

Yet, for reasons unknown, Br Riordan had delayed in applying for the necessary
papal permission to open these schools until July 1839, almost a year after they
had opened their doors. And even then, the general couched his petition in
terms which effectively determined Rome's adjudication against the venture:

> The petitioner believes that the Chapter departed not only from the
> spirit of the Brief, but also that the same Chapter usurped an authority
> which it did not possess when it gave permission to open pay schools.
> In the opinion of the Petitioner … this measure was an innovation con-
> trary to the letter and spirit of the intention which they had when they
> embraced the Institute … the free teaching of the very poor and desti-
> tute boys absorbs all our attention.[56]

Having secured papal condemnation, in August 1839, it might have been
expected that Riordan would close the schools, but he tarried once more.
Nevertheless, his indecision produced a power struggle within the congregation
in which the pay-school faction attempted not merely to save their venture, but
to remove the superior general from office.

Rice's part in these machinations is unclear. The historiography of the
Christian Brothers, from the 1970s at least, presents this struggle in terms of a
Riordan–Rice conflict, which was the successor to the battles between the
founder and the Cork Brothers of the previous decade.[57] The issues involved,
however, were too complex to be explained in simple terms of personal animosities. The directorship of Mill Street is a case in point, since the general's
appointment of Br Patrick O'Flaherty, a vocal opponent of the pay-school, is
usually interpreted as farther evidence of Riordan's malicious intent.[58] Yet of all

the Brothers, O'Flaherty was particularly close to Edmund Rice and was described by one contemporary as 'a man after the founder's own heart'.[59]

William Gillespie has described the conflict in broader terms, not just as a clash of personalities but as a power struggle within the institute.[60] But if this was so, the principal protagonist was not the enfeebled Br Rice, but Bernard Dunphy (1788–1843), whom Riordan identified as 'the head and front' of divisions within the congregation.[61] A native of Callan, Dunphy's reputation among the Brothers was such that he was chosen to represent the congregation before the 1825 Commission of Irish Education Inquiry. As director of Hanover Street, from 1821, he faced an uphill battle to restore discipline to the school, but his principal difficulties were financial. Weekly collections proved entirely inadequate, but as the reputation of the schools improved under his direction, he abandoned these in favour of a subscription from the wealthier members of the parish. This cleared the school's debt, but unrelenting financial worries convinced him of the value of the 'pay-school' model.[62] As time progressed, his support for the initiative assumed the character of a personal crusade, which intensified with the onset of a terminal illness.

It was Dunphy who first challenged the legality of Paul Riordan's election as superior general.[63] Significantly, his blood-brother, Br Austin Dunphy, had been Rice's assistant, and it was he, according to the anti-pay-school faction, who had drafted the 1838 circular on the issue.[64] Yet while he was Rice's preferred successor, and an advocate of the pay-schools, disappointment did not affect him as it did his younger brother. On the contrary, as the congregation senselessly tore itself asunder, Br Austin attempted to reconcile the parties. In August 1840, for example, when tensions were at their height he wrote to Br Francis Thornton, Riordan's assistant, in an effort to bring the factions together:

> I am fully convinced unless an effort be speedily made to adjust the differences which have unhappily existed for a considerable time back in the Society, these differences will lead to very disastrous results ... the sooner they are made up the better. It strikes me, if the Brothers immediately involved in these differences were to meet, and in a spirit of peaceful deliberation talk upon these matters, something good might be expected ... I now speak my own individual opinion, for I have no communication with any brother upon the subject. However, of this, you are the best judges yourself. I pray Almighty God to direct all to what is right and with affectionate regards to Brs Paul [Riordan] and Baptist [John Leonard].[65]

By that juncture, however, divisions had become irreconcilable, and Dunphy had been drawn in to the maelstrom to an extent which rendered his conciliatory role untenable. That said, he continued to restrain the pay-school faction, urging caution at every turn, particularly against hasty memorials to Rome, which he believed would serve only to discredit the Brothers and the institute.[66]

Rice's declining mental health was a decisive factor in the escalating conflict, particularly as it reached its denouement in July 1840, the most critical month in his long life.[67] Although his assistants had consistently refuted rumours, there had been lingering doubts about his mental capacity since the late 1820s when he was reported to have been in 'a very pitiable condition'.[68] The young novice, Stephen Carroll, noted that Rice's 'mind and frame ... were telling against him' as he approached his eightieth year, but others were less charitable in their charge that he had suffered 'imbecility' for some years before leaving office.[69] What they meant by this is unclear, but Rice confessed that his head had 'gone to pieces' in the Spring of 1839.[70] That his signature was notarized on legal documents after this date suggests that he was not senile. It is clear, however, that there were intermittent interruptions in his mental functioning, during which Paul Riordan feared that Brothers had taken advantage of 'poor old Mr Rice' to sign legal documents.[71]

It is doubtful that Rice had Alzheimer's or a similar degenerative disease, because, without medication, it is improbable that he would have survived the sixteen years since its first manifestation. However, Brothers noted that financial difficulties and 'temporal embarrassments [had] considerably depressed his spirits and injured his health'.[72] We may assume that this was another bout of the profound depression which had afflicted him in the 'Chapter' crisis of 1829. This diagnosis is consistent with his frustration, digestive problems and the irritability which was noted by his carers at Mount Sion.[73] Whatever the case, Br Joseph Murphy was certain that 'painful and troublesome' trials had 'contributed to abridge [Rice's] valuable life'.[74]

Riordan's anxiety about the exploitation of these episodes were well founded. Throughout his life, Rice had acted as an executor of wills and as trustee for a host of charities. Several of these duties resulted in litigation, particularly those which involved the irascible Commissioners of Charitable Donations and Bequests. Critics noted Rice's litigious character and some of the Brothers protested that he was too 'frequently engaged in law suits'.[75] Daniel Murray agreed, but with the important caveat that he initiated those cases reluctantly, and only then in defence 'of the institute ... the poor or his wards'.[76] However, on leaving office in 1838 Rice failed to divest himself of his legal obligations as trustee and executor of the various bequests. Moreover, he had not sold his property to fund his mission, but chose instead to finance the institute through a labyrinthine series of investments and mortgages. These were never surrendered to the Order, but had this property and other legal responsibilities been assigned to Brother Riordan, who was after all an accountant, the transfer of authority would have been less fractious. But this omission aggravated existing animosities, particularly as Rice added a codicil to his will, in July 1840, to ensure that any debts he had acquired in connection with the institute would be honoured in full. In Riordan's view, this left the Order dangerously exposed, particularly as the executors named in the codicil were his opponents Bernard Dunphy and Ignatius Kelly.

The implications of this action became immediately apparent in the context of the contested Bryan Bolger bequest, which was complicated by the loan of £1,000 which the architect had extended to Edmund.[77] Lawyers advised the Brothers that the only means of securing their position and providing for the legal claims of the legatees was to mortgage the Richmond Street property.[78] Paul Riordan was not indifferent to the plight of the O'Connell's Schools, on the contrary he had levied a tax on each house of the institute and urged the Brothers to 'strive every nerve for its support'.[79] However, he rejected this legal advice, and wrongly assumed that a mortgage would necessitate the sale of the school. This set him at odds with the executors of the Bolger estate, Brothers Edmund Rice, Bernard Dunphy and Ignatius Kelly. The scene was now set for a direct confrontation between the leaders of the pay-school faction and the general who strictly forbade them under their vow of obedience from proceeding with their plan. A similar warning was extended to Brs Patrick Ellis and Austin Dunphy, the legal owners of the North Richmond Street Schools, in fear that the property would be sold from under the Brothers.

It is curious that in this crisis of conscience Rice did not turn to his mentor Peter Kenney SJ for counsel, but sought advice instead from Fr R.J. Colgan the distinguished Carmelite. It was his opinion that 'no subject was bound to obey his superior commanding anything sinful or contrary to justice'. Since the repayment of debts was involved, Rice felt obliged to proceed with the proposal and, on 7 July 1840, together with Austin Dunphy he mortgaged the premises.[80] Riordan was naturally enraged by this act of defiance and charged the Brothers involved with formal disobedience before a meeting of the general council.[81] Rice, who was not present at that 'trial', was nevertheless troubled by the decision to defy his superior, and later explained to Archbishop Murray that 'I have done no more in this affair than justice called upon me to do'.[32]

11.4 Father Peter Kenney SJ (1779–1841), spiritual director of Edmund Rice and counsellor of the early Christian Brothers.

At this juncture Riordan laid the business before Father Kenney for his adjudication, an ironic turn of events given the traditional antipathy of the Cork Brothers towards Rice's spiritual director.[83] Riordan's explanation of events was inaccurate and partisan to the extent that it determined that Kenney's ruling was in his favour. Nevertheless, the Jesuit attributed the crisis not to any malicious intention, but rather to a series of faults and misconception which were 'entitled to charitable indulgence'.[84] But Kenney's personal reaction to the debacle and its implications for Rice's standing within the institute was particularly astute:

> I would give all the money at stake in this business to have prevented one of the obligators [Edmund Rice] from signing the mortgage. I feel too strongly the influence of that act on the high reputation of him to whom you are all so much indebted.[85]

Yet while Kenney called for harmony, the same month brought further trials which would complete the destruction of Rice's reputation. In this instance, however, Rice was the victim of an elaborate fraud perpetrated by Br Bernard Dunphy and his associates.

On 23 July 1840, at the height of mortgage affair, the pay-school faction drafted an appeal to the prefect of Propaganda Fide, requesting authorisation for the maintenance of their controversial schools.[86] Evidence suggests that this address was never presented. There is no record of it in the archives of Propaganda, while the version preserved in the Dublin Diocesan Archive, including the names of the appellants, Edmund Rice, Bernard Dunphy, Ignatius Kelly and five other Brothers, is in the hand of a draftsman. Furthermore, within a week, the same group addressed a second memorial to Rome, containing a venomous assault on the character of Paul Riordan, the illegality of his election, and his arbitrary style of government, which they described as contrary to 'justice, charity and the laws of the State'. In summary, the petitioners sought the deposition of this 'Stone of Scandal' and his replacement with Br Austin Dunphy, 'the oldest Associate of the Founder'.[87]

Forensic examination has identified the signature of Edmund Rice on the petition as a forgery, but this was not known to his contemporaries.[88] Rome sought direction from Archbishop Murray, who in turn deferred to Fr Kenney's knowledge of the Christian Brothers. He rejected the appeal, describing it as 'unworthy' of all concerned.[89] Murray, too, declared for Riordan, informing Paul Cullen that he was 'inclined to lean to the side of authority'. It was, he suggested, 'much better that some slight inconveniences or even hardships' should be suffered by 'a few individuals', than insubordination introduced into 'a useful body of men'.[90] Accepting this, however, the archbishop advised the prefect of Propaganda Fide to sanction pay-schools for the preservation of the institute and the extension of its work to a class ' who are not really poor not yet rich'. This request was granted and a papal rescript issued to the effect in February 1841.[91]

What disillusioned Peter Kenney most about the Brothers' appeal to Rome was the part played in it by Edmund Rice. 'I know not', he lamented, 'if I ever felt for anything not done by myself, as I feel to see the name of B[rother] Rice to that unworthy document.'[92] Moreover, this uncharacteristic act served to confirm the Jesuit's anxiety about Rice's irrational behaviour:

> I found that my conscientious conviction forced me to disapprove of the very men who were my own greatly revered friends and old acquaintances. I have been in close habits of sacred friendship with good Mr Rice for nine and thirty years, and the part he has taken with the memorialists is the only fault I had ever to complain of.[93]

What, he asked, would result from the success of such a petition: a schism or a dissolution of the institute? Yet as if suspecting that the ailing Rice had been duped into signing the address he concluded starkly, 'this is the honour that the *seven* Brothers would procure for their Founder'.[94]

11.5 Hanover Street Monastery and School, Dublin. Opened 1812. Closed 1844. Guy, Cork [ca. 1897–1923], NLI.

Even without the deposition of Br Riordan, this was the inclination of the congregation. Morale was at an all time low: public estimation of the Brothers was poor; excellent candidates were discouraged from entering, while senior members of the Thurles community, including its 'founder' and a former novice-master, sought to leave the Order and place themselves under the archbishop of Cashel.[95] In Dublin, several of the recalcitrant Brothers mooted subjection to Dr Murray, while another two were poised to join a Carthusian monastery in Rome.[96] And of those who remained? The province was riven between a vocal minority who attacked Riordan's administration and the majority, who castigated the dissidents as a 'worldly, money-making' faction hell bent on persecuting the superior general.[97] The papal rescript, too, which Murray had secured caused further divisions, and there were farcical accounts of Brothers lampooning the 'Bull' by setting it to rhymes and airs.[98] Senior clergy, too, had taken sides in the dispute and their intervention threatened the unity, if not the survival of the congregation.

At a personal level, Edmund Rice paid a heavy price for the criminal actions of Br Bernard Dunphy and those who masqueraded as his allies in this act.

Having been projected in so prominent a fashion as the leader of dissent, he was forced to endure the wrath of angry Brothers. There was one particularly petty incident, during the mortgage crisis, when he visited the community at Hanover Street. The Brothers there had no spare bed and requested one for their founder from the generalate at Richmond Street. In spite of the many beds available in that house, which he had built and furnished himself, Edmund Rice suffered the humiliation of having this simple request refused.[99]

In the following year, too, he endured the further indignity of being turned away from the door of the Brothers' general chapter. Explanations for his exclusion have been greatly influenced by the traditional 'pro and anti-Rice' interpretation of the conflict and the consequent demonisation of Br Riordan. Yet in this instance, too, simple dualities do no justice to the complexity of the issues involved. Rice, it seems, believed he had a right to attend the chapter as an *ex-officio* member, but the majority of the capitulants rejected this view, voting eleven to eight to exclude him.[1] That vote was influenced, no doubt, by the legal advice offered by Fr Peter Kenney, although serious doubt has been cast on the authenticity of the Jesuit's written opinion.[2] McLaughlin described the Kenney letter as 'a forgery', part of 'an immoral move by Riordan's supporter's to exclude Rice' from the chapter.[3] Yet while this may be so, the votes did not align on crude party lines; Joseph Murphy, a 'Riordan man', favoured his admission, while several 'Rice men', including Austin Grace and Patrick Corbett, voted to exclude him.[4] It seems, rather, that having suffered the consequences of illegality at two previous chapters, 1829 and 1838, the Brothers had become sensitised to the importance of keeping to procedures.[5]

It is also possible that the vote of exclusion was influenced by Rice's depression or mental incapacity. Certainly, when the chapter discussed the financial legacy of the 'ex-Superior' no effort was made to introduce him as a witness, even though he was at Mount Sion throughout the assembly. And in their discussions of the celebrated mortgage affair, too, the chapter, in its desire to 'bury the whole matter in oblivion', accepted that both Austin Dunphy and Ignatius Kelly had acted conscientiously. But no such pardon was extended to Edmund Rice.[6] In this instance, too, his absence from the record is perhaps a measure of the extent to which he was considered no longer *compos mentis* by his confreres. Indeed, Riordan implied as much in his subsequent correspondence with Dr Paul Cullen:

> I do not by any means censure the Ex-Supr. for the part he has taken in these disedifying matters, as he had been labouring imbecility of mind for some time before he went out of office and has been ever since.[7]

And as if by way of obituary, the chapter directed Brothers who had known Rice to record their recollections of 'the Founder and the history of the different houses of the Institute'. Sadly there is no record of this instruction being ful-filled, although a portrait of Edmund Rice was commissioned towards the end of that year.[8]

It is, of course, likely that Rice's exclusion from the chapter was a consequence of his 'signature' on the appeal for Riordan's deposition. As an apparently irrational leader of dissent within the congregation, his attendance was perhaps unwelcome at a chapter intent on reconciliation. Neither were any of the other signatories of the Roman Appeal elected to the chapter, although it is assumed that Bernard Dunphy would have been in attendance but for his failing health.[9] As it happened, the chapter voted 16 to 3 to reject the papal rescript which had sanctioned the maintenance of pay-schools. This signified the official end of the experiment, although divisions remained until after the death of Br Bernard Dunphy from cancer in February 1843 and the closure of Hanover Street in the following year. In retrospect, however, Br Patrick O'Flaherty believed that the chapter would have decided otherwise had Rice been present to influence the debate.[10] If this was so, and Rice had displayed considerable powers of persuasion in the 'Union' debates, it is ironic to speculate that the pay-school venture could have been saved but for the fraudulent Roman Appeal. Moreover, the chapter marked an important mile-stone in Riordan's leadership, for it was there he managed to establish his author-ity within the congregation. As Ray English has observed, it was 'at this chapter that Riordan came into his own as superior general'.[11]

V

It was not the opposition of a vindictive Brother Riordan which killed Rice's reputation within the institute, but rather the misguided actions of his friends which left him isolated in his old age. Throughout his life the defining charac-teristic of Edmund Rice's spirituality had been his unwavering trust in Divine Providence. During one legal battle he confided to a Brother, 'the Lord gave and the Lord taketh away, so blessed be his name for ever and ever. This should be our motto'.[12] The trials of his old age severely tested that faith, yet away from the politics and bickering he lived out his last days at Mount Sion in a pious prepa-ration for death. Age, however, had not dimmed his interest in the school, and while he was able to move about he would visit the class rooms to encourage both masters and boys. Indeed, it is perhaps paradoxical that while there are no records of him teaching in the prime of his life, there are many recollections of his visits to the school in the troubled years of his retirement.

Many of the memories of this period recall his kindness as he passed through the school. At least one past-pupil recalled him making these visits in the company of Br Riordan.[13] One of the Brothers later described such visits:

> When he entered my school it was my custom to get a seat for him, and he would sit down and look at the work with great pleasure. He would speak in his own kindly and affable manner to the groups of reverent youngsters who would invariably try to get as near as possible to him whom they loved as a father and revered as a saint. They would come to present him their writing copies, and go away delighted with a word of approbation. His pleasure in hearing the little ones say the prayers and answer the catechism was delightful to observe.[14]

The pupils had equally fond memories of these visits. Years later, Patrick Browne recalled his childhood in Mount Sion in the 1830s, and how the 'boys had such a veneration for Brother Rice that they regarded it even as a privilege to get a look at him'.[15] Another, remembered him as a 'homely … fatherly man', while John Flynn described his paternal care for the boys:

> He was very affectionate and kind to the children. Rich and poor were equally dear to him. When leaving school the boys shook hands with him. Next morning if they had been beaten by their parents they would show him the place to make it well.[16]

This is particularly poignant observation, given the unenviable reputation for harshness which his Brothers subsequently acquired.

Accompanied by a Brother he would walk through the grounds of Mount Sion. Inevitably, he would encourage his young helper to greater devotion to the Blessed Virgin. One of these helpers, Br Aloysius Hoare, a future superior general, remembered the advice he was given: 'Have great devotion to Our Blessed Lady; say in her honour the *Memorare* and she will take care of you and obtain for you the crowning grace of final perseverance.'[17] Rice retained his interest in spiritual reading, too, particularly the Bible which he read each day, and the life of St Teresa of Avila.[18] Other accounts recall his humour, his amusement at the stories of the children and his enjoyment of the community gatherings. One specific recollection identifies 'Oh had we some bright little isle of our own', a romantic melody by Ireland's national poet, Tom Moore, as his favourite song.[19]

Saints, of course, are not angels, and there were memoirs, too, which recall manifestations of his depression and irritability, like when he snapped at a novice for failing to help a lay brother set his fire.[20] On another occasion he fell from his wheelchair, and when another helper was obtained for him, he retorted nervously 'he looks too flighty'.[21]

At Christmas 1841 his health again failed and there seemed to be no hope of recovery. Br Riordan notified the various communities of their founder's condition:

> With feelings of pain and sorrow I have to inform you that our most dear Br. Ignatius Rice has been unusually ill since Christmas Eve. He has no pain or uneasiness, but great weakness, which confines him to his bed, and will, it is feared, end in his dissolution. I request you will have the prayers of the community offered, to beg for him the grace of a happy death.[22]

Contrary to expectations he rallied for a short while and was able to attend to his personal correspondence. The long-term indications, however, were not good and before long he was confined to his room. In time his mental faculties began to fail and he lived his last days in a semi-coma; from May 1842 he required the constant attention of a nurse.[23] So regular had the pattern of prayer been through his life that, even though he appeared unaware of what he was saying, his first words on awakening each morning were 'Praise be to you, O Christ'.[24]

In August 1844 Rice's health showed signs of rapid deterioration. On the morning of 28 August he was anointed by his confessor and the Brothers joined in prayerful vigil around his bedside. Among those present was a young novice, Br Stanislaus Hyland, who was one of those who had contemplated leaving the order in the pay-schools dispute.[25] He treasured the memory of his last meeting with Edmund Rice which he recorded it in a stylised fashion:

> I was sent to Mount Sion, Waterford, in 1844 to prepare for Profession, and there was the Founder, my revered Superior, fast drawing to an end. Mine was the last hand, I think, that he shook in friendship on this earth.
>
> I had just returned from St Patrick's branch school, and I at once ran up to see him. He clasped my hand in his, now clammy before death. I noticed his clasp growing unconsciously closer, and a doze seemed to come on. His eye was glassy. I was expecting the bell to ring for dinner, and I said aloud to him: 'Good bye, Sir; the bell will soon ring.' I disengaged my hand from his grasp, and he awoke and said to me: 'Good bye, and God bless you, my child'.[26]

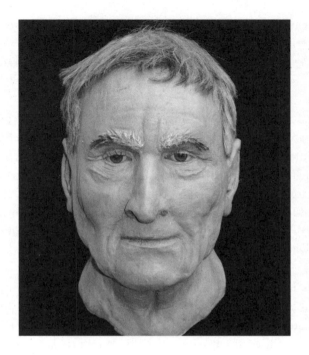

11.6 Edmund Rice (1762–1844). Forensic reconstruction of his skull,
© Edmund Rice Centre, Mount Sion, Waterford.

Rice died the following morning, 29 August. Describing the late general, Br
Joseph Murphy, superior of Mount Sion, wrote: 'his life was a long series of sufferings, labours and contradictions under which he manifested a greatness of
soul which betokened sublime virtue'.[27]

In the absence of Paul Riordan, who was on visitation in England, Br
Murphy notified the various communities of his passing:

> We have the sorrowful duty of announcing to you the death of our most
> dear Father, Founder, and Brother, Ignatius Rice, who died at eleven
> o'clock this morning after having received the Last Sacrament.
>
> We trust he is gone to receive the reward of his labour for the poor,
> for the Congregation, and for us all.[28]

Rice's body was dressed in the simple habit of the congregation, with beads and
a crucifix in his hands, and placed in the small oratory at Mount Sion. The
Brothers prayed by his side and a great number of people came to pay their last
respects. The mayor and the leading citizens of the city, together with parents

and pupils, came and knelt beside the remains of the great benefactor of the poor of Waterford.

The *Waterford Mail* announced Rice's death and described him in glowing terms as:

> A venerable, a good, and, in the best sense of the word, a great man … A man of vast knowledge of human nature, of a comprehensive grasp of intellect, of indomitable energy, of irresistible perseverance, of unbending integrity, of profoundest piety, of boundless charity, Edmund Rice, the Founder of the Christian Brothers, is dead – the herald of a new age to Irishmen in education, the harbinger of virtue and of blessings, and the benefactor of his fellow-men in every country where his brothers have been established.[29]

Bishop Nicholas Foran, who had visited Edmund regularly during his illness, presided at the Solemn Requiem Mass and final obsequies at Mount Sion, on Saturday, 31 August. He was joined on the altar by twenty-nine priests, and the small oratory was filled to capacity with Christian Brothers and the leading citizens of Waterford. After the Mass, his remains were interred in the cemetery of the monastery grounds and the spot was marked by a simple stone cross.

The restricted capacity of the oratory at Mount Sion made the exclusion of the public from the obsequies unavoidable, but the bishop of Waterford set aside October 1, the 'Month's Mind', for a great public thanksgiving for the life of Edmund Rice. This occasion was marked by a High Mass in the city's cathedral, where the seats were removed to accommodate the thousands who crowded 'the church … as in a festival'.[30] Dr Foran presided at the ceremony and was joined on the altar by fifty priests, including Theobald Mathew who travelled from Cork for the occasion. Among the Christian Brothers who assembled to pay their respects to their Founder were thirty-five members of the congregation from the schools in England. The oration was delivered by Fr Richard Fitzgerald, chaplain to Mount Sion, who paid tribute to the great achievement of Edmund Rice:

> Need I say that he stands not in need of the genius of the sculptor or the painter; for as long as gratitude shall find a place in the Irish heart, as long as religion shall be prized, as long as sterling patriotism shall be accounted a virtue, the name of Edmund Ignatius Rice shall be held in benediction.[31]

Conclusion

THERE WAS A CYCLICAL QUALITY TO Edmund Rice's life. John Charles McQuaid referred to the 'character of initial failure and mighty renaissance which strikes one' in considering his life.[1] Yet for Rice, death occurred at the bottom of a cycle when there were few signs of the recovery which would come only with his successor. Indeed, a close confrere characterised Rice's life as 'a long series of suffering, labour and opposition'.[2] More recently, a theological report to the Congregation for the Causes of Saints noted that 'a man can be patient when there is nothing to drive him to anger ... We can all thank God for the weather when the sun is shining and the birds are singing. Yet for Edmund Rice, it is not clear that the birds were ever singing in the balmy sunshine; it seemed to be mostly gales and hail and rain.'[3]

At his death, there were eleven communities of Brothers in Ireland, twelve in England and one in Sydney educating between them 8,000 boys.[4] This represented a tiny fraction of the Irish population of eight million, and was small even when compared to the 100,000 children who attended the schools conducted by the Church of Ireland Education Society.[5] In spite of their numbers, however, the seventy Christian Brothers exercised an influence which was entirely disproportionate to their numbers. It was their exceptional reputation as teachers, and the quality of their lives, which inspired the eulogies of Edmund Rice and placed him alongside Daniel O'Connell and Theobald Mathew as the great men of nineteenth-century Ireland.[6]

12.1 Brothers in vows

1808	1815	1825	1835	1845	1855
8	26	38	64	103	153

Contemporaries praised the incalculable benefit which his schools had brought to the poor. While the penal code failed in its intention to banish Catholic schoolmasters, the operation of the laws frustrated the creation of an effective system of Catholic schooling. This produced what *The Nation* described as a 'lamentable gap' between the hedge schoolmasters and the proselytising schools.[7] Edmund Rice sought to fill that lacuna and, for his work in Waterford alone, the Halls believed he should be numbered high among 'the benefactors of mankind'.[8] His Brothers were pioneers in establishing the foundations of universal elementary instruction in Ireland, and the elimination of tuition fees which had restricted Catholic access to education. The methodologies which Rice perfected were ideally suited to the employment needs of nineteenth-century Ireland. With their uniform standards and emphasis upon 'work-discipline', his large schools were to education what the factories were to the industrial age.

This revolution in education facilitated the modernisation of Irish society, as the Brothers instilled bourgeois 'Protestant' values and formed a disciplined, literate workforce from the ranks of the 'rough' masses. This achievement was celebrated by contemporaries, who lauded the extent to which the 'Monks' had 'withdrawn multitudes from the dangers of idleness and vice', promoting instead 'the pursuit of useful knowledge and the habits of virtuous and honourable industry'.[9] For this 'moral elevation' Rice was praised as Ireland's De La Salle.[10] At his centenerary, too, preachers would hail him as the island's Don Bosco.[11] More recently, he was beatified by Pope John Paul II in 1996.

Among the urban poor the Christian Brothers and the teaching Sisters played a vital part in widening the base of the institutional Church. Through their teaching and catechetical instruction the Brothers advanced the process of 're-Christianisation', introducing the poor to the new forms of devotion which became the hallmark of nineteenth-century Catholicism. The effect of this teaching was to bring a previously alienated class within the ranks of the Church, which in time provided the backbone of the emerging Catholic Ireland. In the context of the 'Bible Wars', too, the Brothers were particularly effective. And if, as the recent scholarship suggests, this was not in fact a 'Second Reformation', but the conclusion of the sixteenth-century crusade, the intervention of this second Ignatius, Br Rice, in an Irish context, was as significant, as his patron's had been in the earlier continental conflict. Indeed, if as Aidan Clarke suggests, it was not that the Reformation failed in Ireland, but that the Counter-Reformation succeeded, then the Christian Brothers must claim some credit for the final outcome.[12]

In ideological terms, too, the uncompromising pedagogy of the Brothers' schools effected a radical transformation of Catholic culture. Their philosophy of 'Faith and Fatherland' represented a logical development of aspects of the Jacobite ideology of an earlier period. Their patriotic texts informed a process through which Irish and Catholic became synonymous, and nurtured the notion of the Catholic Irish as an elect, a people set apart by their fidelity to the Church.[13] If this was so, then the Brothers personified and perpetuated that sense of martyrdom. This ideology was particularly powerful among the Irish diaspora, where the presence of the Brothers supported the advance of an 'Irish episcopal imperialism'.[14]

The patriotism of the schools, however, produced a formidable challenge to another empire. In the long term, the schools were perceived as seminaries of sedition, but more immediately the educational opportunity they afforded advanced a meritocracy which undermined the existing social ascendancy. 'Millions upon millions of our countrymen', claimed John A. Blake (1826–87), the merchant and Liberal MP for Waterford , 'both at home and abroad, wherever the English language is spoken, have reason to bless [Rice's] name, for enabling them to fight the battle for life, and rise to prosperity'.[15] Most recently, Taoiseach Bertie Ahern celebrated Rice as 'a key figure in the story of Ireland' on account of 'the foundations of ... [Irish] freedom and prosperity' which he laid.[16]

Deliverance became the dominant theme of the obituaries of Edmund Rice, whom the patriot, Thomas Francis Meagher (1823–67), eulogised as 'the preceptor, the patriarch and the prophet'.[17] Alongside O'Connell, he was celebrated as 'a benefactor of his race ... not only of the present generation but of the future'.[18] This was Rice's achievement. It was not the remarkable accomplishments of his troubled life which signalled his greatness; it was rather what the great project promised for the future. He was not the liberator, but a prophet, 'the herald of a new age of Irishmen'.[19]

Appendix 1

The Will of Robert Rice, Westcourt, Callan, Co. Kilkenny. 21 September 1787. (CBGA. 0308/005)

In the name of God, Amen. I, Robert Rice of Westcourt in the County of Kilkenny Farmer being weak in body but of sound mind memory and understanding thanks be to God for the same and knowing the uncertainty of this transitory life – do make publish and declare this to be my only true last will and testament hereby revoking and making null and void all other former will or wills by me heretofore at any time made – first and principally I commend my soul to Almighty God and my body to the earth hoping forgiveness for all my past sins and wickedness through the merits of my Redeemer and as to such worldly substance wherewith it hath pleased God to bless me to leave and bequeath the same as is hereafter mentioned.

Ordering that my just and lawful debts shall be first paid thereout by my executors herein after named together with my funeral expenses and requesting my said executors to collect in my several debts of what nature and kind soever due and owing unto me and it is my will and I do hereby order that my said executors shall immediately on recovery or payment of the whole principal debt and interest due to me from Thomas Candler deceased and pay discharge the residue of the legacies left by the will of my Uncle Patrick Rice to Joan Rice and Mary Brennan otherwise Rice.

Secondly I leave and bequeath unto my nephew Michael Croak of Gragaugh son of John Croak deceased the sum of twenty pounds sterling.

I leave and bequeath unto my nephew Patrick Rice son of Michael Rice of the City of Waterford Victualler the sum of ten pounds sterling.

I leave and bequeath unto my nephew Robert Rice second son of Michael Rice the sum of ten pounds sterling.

Thirdly my will is and I do hereby order that at any time after my decease when my executors shall think most convenient my stock of cows sheep and horses shall be sold by public cant in order to clear off all rent and arrears of rent that shall be then owing and due of me to my several and respective land-

255

lords and the residue of the money of said sale if any there be I leave and bequeath unto my sons Patrick William Edmund Richard John and Michael Rice to be equally divided between them share and share alike at the discretion of my said executors.

And likewise my will is and I hereby order that immediately after said sale my farm in Westcourt in the said County of Kilkenny shall be advertised to be set to the best and highest bidder for such term of years as my said executors shall think proper and my will is that the profit rent accruing from and out of said farm shall be divided equally among my said sons Patrick William Edmund Richard John and Michael Rice equally share and share alike as my said executors shall think most proper and if any of my said sons should die without issue during the term of years then on my decease to come and unexpired that then and in such case the share or shares of him or them so dying without issue as aforesaid shall go to and be divided between the survivors of my said sons being subject nevertheless and my will further is that my dearly beloved wife Margaret shall have and receive during her life an equal dividend out of the profits of said farm provided she shall convert her share or proportion thereof to such use or uses as shall be most advantageous to her as my said executors shall think proper.

Fourthly I leave and bequeath unto my eldest son Thomas Rice of Callan Publican the sum of two shillings and eight pence halfpenny and no more.

Fifthly I leave and bequeath unto my step daughters Jane and Joan Murphy the sum of two shillings and eight pence halfpenny each and no more.

And lastly I do hereby nominate constitute and appoint my brother Michael Rice of the City of Waterford Victualler and my son Edmund Rice of the said City Victualler and my cousin Maurice Rice of the City of Kilkenny dealer Executors of this my last will and testament.

In witness thereof I have hereunto set my hand and seal this twenty-first day of September in the year of Our Lord one thousand seven hundred and eighty seven.

Robert Rice [seal]

Signed sealed published and declared by the Testator Robert Rice in the presence of us who in his presence at his request and in the presence of each other have subscribed our names as witnesses hereto.

John Foley, P.P.   Patrick Larisy

Appendix 2: Edmund Rice to Archbishop Bray of Cashel

My Lord,

I should have sent the enclosed regulations of our schools to Yr. Grace before now, but waiting for an opportunity of some person going to Thurles, – Yr. Grace I hope will be able to select something out of them for to save the school of Thurles. The half-hour's explanation of the Catechism I hold to be the most salutary part of the system. It is the most laborious to the teachers; however, if it were ten times what it is, I must own we are amply paid in seeing such a Reformation in the Children – Drs Moylan & McCarthy have sent two young men to serve a Noviceship for the purpose of establishing our Institute in Cork. I trust in the goodness of God that it will spread before long in most parts of the Kingdom – indeed it would give me particular satisfaction to see it prosper in Thurles—May God give Your Grace life to see this effected. Anything in our power to serve this purpose Yr. Grace can freely command.

I am, My Lord
Your Grace's Most Obt. & Humble Servant
Edmd. Rice.
Waterford 9 May 1810.

Enclosure

Our schools open at nine o'clock in the morning at which time the business of the Masters who attend immediately commences. The boys whom we instruct are divided. Those who are advanced, so as at least to be able to read tolerably well, with others who are taught arithmetic, etc., occupy an upper room. The lower room is for such as are taught spelling, reading and writing on slates. In the upper room the boys are arranged as much as may be, according to their degrees of improvement, at double desks 12 on each. Over each desk a monitor or superintendent is appointed, who keeps an account of the conduct of those committed to his care – that they are at school in due time, diligently attend their school duties, etc. The desks are divided into different districts each of which is committed to the care of a master.

In the morning, the monitors of the several districts prepare the copy books of the boys under their care, and bring them to their respective masters, top have copy lines written or pieces to write from – pens prepared for writing, etc. While the boys wait for the copy books they are employed in looking over the tasks for the day. The writing of the copies usually commences as much as may be at the same time, that the masters may visit their respective desks, and give particular instructions relative to writing properly, and according to approved methods.

After the copies are written, Reading Lessons commence, the boys of each desk coming up according to their turn. The books made use of are Gahan's *History of the New and Old Testament*. Comments are made, and familiar moral instructions are given the class in the course of the lesson by the master. Whilst one class reads and hears instruction, the other desks are employed at sums, etc. At a convenient time the monitors question the boys of their desks in spelling and catechism tasks and make reports to the masters accordingly.

At the half hour before twelve o'clock the bell rings for giving general moral instructions, at which time one of the masters whose turn it is, having the boys all assembled about him, explains the Catechism or out of *Gobinet*, or other books that are deemed fit, gives instructions suited to the capacity of the children.

When the clock strikes twelve the Angelus and Acts of Faith, Hope and Charity with a few other devotional prayers are recited, after which the boys are dismissed and the school closes until one. At one, school opens again and from that to three the exercises are similar to those of the morning as nearly as time will admit. At three, the Litany of the Blessed Virgin, Salve Regina and a few other prayers are recited, when the boys are dismissed and school closes for the day. They are not allowed to play or keep company with any other boys but those of the school when out of it.

The children in the lower school are arranged in classes according to their degree of improvement as in the upper room. Those who write on slates at desks, the others on forms or other convenient seats. The desks are single, seven boys range at each and every boy provided with a slate to write on. Monitors are appointed for the desks as before mentioned whose duties are similar. Such assistants in fact are found so necessary that they are made use of even down to the lowest classes.

The masters who attend, commence the business of the morning by writing copies for the classes committed to their care. The copyline for the boys of a desk is the same, they being arranged, as before remarked, so that those who are nearly equal in improvement and abilities are kept together.

Each class writes the copy set them 4 or 5 times over without getting the copyline changed and always when finished requests the master to inspect them, and according to his decision inflict slight punishments on each other for defects in their writing – a permission given them for the purpose of stimulating one another to proper exertions. The masters give instructions in spelling, reading etc., occasionally, so that the boys may at least get two lessons; they are besides questioned in spelling and Catechism tasks by the master or the monitor if found fit.

Familiar moral instructions are given occasionally at the time of reading or otherwise by the masters who attend this school, suited to the weak capacity of those under their care. But no general instructions as in the upper room; the time appointed for that purpose being employed in teaching prayers and Catechism to the most ignorant. At twelve the Angelus etc., as above, after which they are dismissed till one. From one till three the exercises are the same as in the morning.

N.B. The slates that the boys write on, are ruled on one side with a sharp pointed piece of iron so that an impression is thereby made on the slate, and that thus when they have an occasion to blot out or deface any letter that they wish to improve, or the entire copy, the ruling remains. The other side is left for sums, etc., and of course is not ruled.

General examinations of the copies, sums, etc., are made twice a week in the upper school room, and rewards and punishments dealt out accordingly. More general ones are held two or three times a year, and such as are found most deserving receive gifts proportioned to their merit. Each boy reads about a page and a half, while the others of his desk stand with him when necessary. The half hour for instruction is given on Fridays for a general examination of the Catechism. Unless for some faults which rarely occur whipping is never inflicted.

A boy who has the care of about one hundred and fifty pious books, most of which are numbered, on every Friday evening distributes them among the monitors of each desk, of which he makes an entry; and they are obliged to return them to the boy giving a choice to the most deserving of which he also takes an account, by this regulation we seldom lose a book. We also supply the boys who are bound out to apprentices, with pious books, who are in general obliged to go to Sacraments once a month; and some are allowed by their Confessor to go more frequent.

The confessions of all the children are heard every year on 15th July, 15th Oct., 15th Jan., and 15th April, provided nothing interfered on those days to prevent it in which case it is deferred to another day. The boys read books for their parents at night, and on Sundays and Holydays, and instruct them otherwise when they can do it with prudence, from which we find much good to result.

We have a clock in the school, the better to direct them in the regulating the time, and every time it strikes, silence is observed all over the schools, and every boy blesses himself, says the Hail Mary, and makes some short pious aspirations which continues about a minute when they bless themselves again and resume their business.

Source: Cashel Diocesan Archives, Bray Papers 1810/21.

Appendix 3: Edmund Rice's Obituary

Cork Examiner,
9 September 1844

DEATH OF EDMOND IGNATIUS RICE
(from the *Tipperary Vindicator*)

The Waterford papers announce the death of a venerable, a good, and, in the best sense of the word, a great man – a man of powerful mind – of vast knowledge of human nature – of a comprehensive grasp of intellect – of undaunted courage – of irrestible perseverance – of unbending integrity – of pure piety – of immense charity – Edmond Rice, the founder of Christian Schools – the herald of a new age of Irishmen in the way of instruction – the harbinger of virtue and of blessings – the benefactor of his species, not only in Ireland but in whatever quarter of the globe the present generation of the humbler classes of our fellow countrymen have penetrated, because to Mr. Rice is mainly attributable the credit of whatever intellectual training they enjoy. We regret our Waterford contemporaries have confined their notice of the loss of this inestimable man to a simple paragraph. – The following are the words of the announcement in the *Mail* and the *Chronicle*:–

'At Mount Sion, in this city, in the 87th year of his age, the venerable Brother Edmond Ignatius Rice, founder of the Brothers of the Christian Schools in Ireland and England. The health of this venerable man has been declining for nearly three years. He bore his protracted illness with patience and resignation to the Divine will. In this city he founded his first establishment for the gratuitous education of boys in the year 1803, which has since branched out to the principal towns in this country and England. He was a man of indefatigable zeal and charity, endowed with great prudence, energy, and perseverance. He resigned the office of superior-general of his institute in the year 1838, in order to give his undivided attention to the concerns of his immortal soul. The city of Waterford particularly has lost in him one of its best benefactors.'

262 EDMUND RICE AND THE FIRST CHRISTIAN BROTHERS

We regret that those who are on the spot have not been able to contribute more particulars of the life and exertions of this truly excellent man. We have had opportunities of knowing and appreciating his exalted work – of witnessing in some degree the extent and value of his labours – of being partially acquainted with the strength and depth of the magnificent edifice which he raised for the instruction of the children of the poor of his native city in the first instance, and of Ireland, almost universally, afterwards. We have had some means of judging of the vast advantages conferred upon society by his ceaseless toils. We would endeavour, therefore to supply the void left by our Waterford contemporaries, to whom we should have looked for the minutest particulars connected with the subject.

Mr. Rice, as appears from the paragraph above given, had arrived at the middle period of life before he founded the Christian schools, he was in fact forty six years of age at the time. But for some years before he was engaged in planning the system, whose maturity he enjoyed the gratification of witnessing, and whose triumph is one of the most remarkable features in the modern history of Ireland. In 1803 he commenced an establishment in Waterford, for the gratuitous instruction of youth in literature and Christian piety. He was joined in the undertaking by two young men, desirous of devoting their lives to the same laudable purposes. In May, 1804, during the episcopacy of the Right Rev. John Power, a prelate whose memory is held in deserved reverence to this day in Waterford, the schools were opened. We are not exactly informed of the causes that operated on the mind of Mr. Rice to take this step. It was a new – it must have been a hazardous one just then. The great mass of the people were utterly unacquainted with even the rudiments of learning. The country had been suffering from the effects of the rebellion of 1798 – the mad rebellion of the unfortunate Emmett only broke out. The achievements of Napoleon were attracting universal concern, and causing general alarm. We believe that Mr. Rice's early life had not given promise of that religious seriousness which he now began to display. He had been engaged in trade – if we be not incorrect, it was in the provision trade – then one of the principal branches of business in Waterford, where, though the export of beef is annihilated, that of bacon, even at this day, is greater than from any other port of Ireland. His avocations brought him into immediate contact with the working classes. He perceived that, in many instances, irreligion proceeded from their ignorance –and that to its prevalence much of the crime that abounded could also be traced. He lived in a part of the city where vice and ignorance prevailed to a greater extent than elsewhere. En passant, we may observe that about this time also Mr. Rice had a brother in Cadiz who occasionally lived in San Lucia de Barrameda and Seville, and who was also engaged in trade; he, too, abandoned the desk for the cloister. He became an Augustinian friar, and by his abilities, energy, and piety, did vast service to his order in Ireland; he lived for many years in Callan, and died some years ago in Malta, to which place he went from Rome on business connected with his order. Mr. Rice having once embarked in the cause he undertook was resolved to persevere; he did not mind the difficulties that opposed his progress – every obstacle tended but to give him more nerve – he was determined to work out the great achievement on which he had set his heart. He and his associates, few, but zealous, proceeded success – fully in their good work. Daily augmentations were made to the numbers that flocked to their schools. They could have had no better cradle for their infant instruction than Waterford, where the purest piety and unbounded charity have always been known to exist, and where a princely magnificence on the part of the citizens in forwarding every benevolent object has always been known to prevail. It was but a few years before, and just when they were permitted by law, that the citizens erected one of the noblest edifices ever raised in this country to the worship of God, and one which has not since been surpassed in Ireland … Mr. Rice and his companions attracted the attention of pious and benevolent citizens. Paul Carroll – a name which shall never be forgotten in Waterford – aided their incipient efforts, as he knew how to do. Thomas O'Brien, an eminent wine merchant – one of the good old times – a gentleman in the purest acceptation of the term, appreciated the good they performed, founded a school and establishment at his own expense in Carrick-on-Suir, of which town we believe he was a native, and this with the approbation of Dr. Power.

The school was finished in 1807, and is now one of the best of the description in Ireland, presided over for many years by a truly religious and good man, who has done material service to the community. In the same year, Dungarvan participated in a similar advantage. The school in Dungarvan had been for many years situated outside the town, at a place called Shandon; it was too small for the numbers that flocked to it; but the present truly Apostolic Bishop of Waterford, the Right Rev. Dr. Foran, when parish priest of Dungarvan, built a magnificent schoolhouse, and a residence for the Christian Brothers at his own expense; and there are no buildings in Ireland belonging to the order superior to them. In Cork the next foundation was laid; this was in 1811 – and when we say that it was there that Gerald Griffin ended his days, we have said almost sufficient in praise of the noble institution of which that city boasts, and which is known as the Peacock Lane schools – presided over by a gentleman of the most extensive acquirements, and of the most solid piety and purest benevolence. In 1812 an establishment was founded in Dublin, where the order made unexampled progress, and where Mr. Rice lived for years, at the house in Townsend Street.

In 1815 the Most Rev. Dr. Bray introduced the order to Thurles, where the establishment flourishes admirably, doing incalculable service. The Right Reverend Dr. Tuohy introduced the order in Limerick in 1816, and on the 5th of September, 1820, the bull of Pope Pius VII was issued confirming the institute as a religious order. Mr. Rice was elected to the office of superior-general on the 12th of January, 1822, after a retreat conducted by the late distinguished, learned, and apostolic Dr. Peter Kenny, S.J., whose family resided in Waterford, where his brother was for many years at the head of one of the most respectable medical establishments in the south of Ireland. At the end of ten years the Pope's brief having provided that a general chapter should be held at the end of every ten years, and that the superior-general should govern for ten years only, Mr. Rice was re-elected to the high office he had held, in January, 1833[1832], at a chapter convened at the house of the order, North Richmond Street, Dublin. This establishment is one of the principal of the society, and may be said to have been the offspring of the Catholic Association – the foundation stone having been laid by the illustrious O'Connell in June, 1828, surrounded by a vast multitude, who walked in procession from the Corn Exchange to witness the ceremony. This house, from its opening in 1831, became the principal residence of Mr. Rice for the remainder of his official life, and if anything more than wanting to add to its celebrity as an educational establishment, it would be found in the fact—that it was to this retreat of society and learning that Gerald Griffin repaired in 1838, and entered as a novice among the Christian brothers.

In July, 1838 Mr. Rice resigned his office of superior, years and infirmities pressing hard upon him; and we may say that since that period he withdrew himself almost entirely from the cares in which he had been so long engaged, and devoted himself with pious assiduity to those more sublime concerns to which he ever attended; and of the necessity of which his life was a constant example to others. There are eleven houses of the order in Ireland, twelve in England, one in Sydney, and the applications for their extension to the colonies and other parts of Great Britain and Ireland are constant and unremitting. We have thus hastily sketched an imperfect outline of the life of this great and good man. Mr. Rice enjoyed the intimate friendship of many of the Catholic prelates of Ireland and England, and of the leaders of the Catholic body in both countries. He and the Liberator were always on terms of the most sincere esteem and respect. His masculine mind – his undaunted energy – his integrity and perseverance, were qualities which won admiration at the hands of all who came into contact with him. He was trustee of several charities. The bequests left to his own institution were numerous and munificent; and there can be no doubt but that the best possible use has been made of them. Well may he say –

'Exegi monumentum aere perennius.'

He first laid the foundation of an educational system for the children of the Catholic poor of Ireland. On many and many a man, born in poverty, and who might have been brought up in crime, has he been instrumental of, not only, rescuing from peril, but affording the means of arriving at eminence in the mercantile world, and perhaps, in the learned professions. To his order he was a solid example of every virtue – to the community at large he was the same. On all hands he was a Christian man in the most perfect sense of the word. The city which gave him birth has given the same to other illustrious men; but there is not one among the roll, perhaps, more conspicuous for public usefulness than Edmond Ignatius Rice, who has just been called, in the fullness of venerable years, to receive the reward of his labours in that kingdom after which he long sighed. His remains are laid in the cemetery at Mount Sion, Waterford, and may he rest in peace.

Notes

Introduction

1   D. Blake, *A man for our times: a short life of Edmund Rice* (Dublin, 1994); J.D. Fitzpatrick, *Edmund Rice* (Dublin, 1945); D. Keogh, *Edmund Rice, 1762–1844* (Dublin, 1996); [M. McCarthy,], A Christian Brother, *Edmund Ignatius Rice and the Christian Brothers* (Dublin, 1926); J.A. Houlihan, *Overcoming evil with good; the Edmund Rice story* (New York, 1997); D. McLaughlin, *The price of freedom; the education charism of Edmund Rice* (Brisbane, 2007); M.C. Normoyle, *A tree is planted: the life of Edmund Rice* (Dublin, 1976); N. Ó Gadhra, *Éamann Iognáid Rís, 1762–1844* (Dublin, 1977); A.L. O'Toole, *A spiritual profile of Edmund Rice*, 2 vols (Bristol, 1984).
2   R.E. Burns, 'The Irish penal code and some of its historians', *Review of Politics*, 21:1, II (Jan. 1959), 276–99; Maureen Wall, *The penal laws, 1691–1760* (Dundalk, 1976); T.P. O'Neill, 'Discovers and discoveries', *Dublin Historical Record*, 37 (Dec. 1983), 2–13; L.M. Cullen, 'Catholics under the penal laws', in *Eighteenth-century Ireland*, 1 (1986), 23–37; David Dickson, 'Catholics and trade in eighteenth-century Ireland', in T. Power and K. Whelan (eds), *Endurance and Emergence; Catholics in Ireland in the eighteenth century* (Dublin, 1990), pp 57–84; S.J. Connolly, *Religion, law and power: the making of Protestant Ireland, 1660–1760* (Oxford, 1992); C.I. McGrath, '"Securing the Protestant interest": the origins and purpose of the Penal Laws of 1695', *IHS*, 30 (1996), 25–46; J. Kelly, 'The ascendancy and the penal laws' in J.R. Bartlett and S.D. Kinsella (eds), *2000 years of Christianity in Ireland* (2006), pp 133–54.
3   B.M. Coldrey, *Faith and fatherland: the Christian Brothers and the development of Irish nationalism, 1838–1921* (Dublin, 1988).
4   Conor Cruise O'Brien, *Ancestral voices: religion and nationalism in Ireland* (Dublin, 1994), p. 10.
5   T. Bartlett, *The fall and rise of the Irish nation: the Catholic question, 1690–1830* (Dublin, 1992).
6   T. Power and K. Whelan (eds), *Endurance and emergence: Catholics in Ireland in the eighteenth century* (Dublin, 1990).
7   J.G. Kohl, *Travels in Ireland* (London, 1844), p. 107.
8   D.W. Miller, 'Mass attendance in 1834', in S.J. Brown and D.W. Miller (eds), *Piety and power in Ireland* (Notre Dame, 2000), pp 158–79.
9   W. Coppinger, *Nano Nagle* (Cork, 1794), p. 4.
10 J.W. O'Malley, *Trent and all that: renaming Catholicism in the early-modern era* (Cambridge, MA, 2000); E. Larkin, *The historical dimension of Irish Catholicism* (Dublin, 1984).
11 J.E. Kent, 'The educational ideals of Edmund Rice, founder of the Christian and Presentation Brothers' (MEd., UCC, 1988), p. 108.
12 Edmund Rice to Mother Patrick Keeshan, n.d. [1836], CBGA, 007/0062.
13 Eugene Boylan, *Centenary souvenir on the death of Edmund Ignatius Rice* (Dublin, 1944), p. 104.
14 Recollection of Eliza Murphy (1912), in Normoyle (ed.), *Memories*, p. 200.
15 Br Austin to Kees Van Hoek, May 1944, CBGA, 191/2134.
16 David Fitzpatrick, *CBER* (1960), 1011.
17 Edmund Rice to Thomas Bray, 9 May 1810, CDA, 1810/21.
18 T.J. Walsh, *Nano Nagle and the Presentation Sisters* (Dublin, 1959).
19 Br E.A. Dunphy to Br Austin Grace, 21 June 1846, CBGA, 025/0293.
20 General Chapter Minutes (1910), CBGA, Rome; M.C. Normoyle (ed.), *Memories of Edmund Rice* (Dublin, 1979).

21 [M. McCarthy], A Christian Brother, *Edmund Ignatius Rice*; McLaughlin, *The price of freedom*.
22 See P. Burke, 'How to become a Counter-Reformation saint', in D.M. Luebke (ed.), *The Counter-Reformation* (Oxford, 1999), pp 129–42.
23 *Positio*, p. 382.

Chapter 1 The context: the Church in the Catacombs?

1   Edmund Rice to Thomas Bray, 9 May 1810, CDA, Bray Papers, 1800/21.
2   For the most recent discussion of the penal laws, see Kelly, 'The Ascendancy and the penal laws'.
3   W.P. Burke, *Irish priests in penal times* (Waterford, 1914), pp 164–5.
4   William King, *The state of the Protestants of Ireland under the late King James's government* (Dublin, 1691), p. 292.
5   Connolly, *Religion, law and power*, p. 263.
6   7 William III c. 4.
7   P.J. Corish, *The Catholic community in seventeenth and eighteenth century Ireland* (Dublin, 1981), p. 73.
8   Connolly, *Religion, law and power*, p. 273.
9   L.M. Cullen, 'Catholic social classes under the penal laws', in T.P. Power and K. Whelan (eds), *Endurance and emergence: Catholics in Ireland in the eighteenth century* (Dublin, 1990), p. 56.
10 Ibid.
11 Cullen, 'Catholics under the penal laws', pp 29–31.
12 Connolly, *Religion, law and power*, p. 311; idem, *Priests and people in pre-Famine Ireland* (Dublin, 1981), p. 27; Dickson, 'Catholics and trade in eighteenth-century Ireland', in Power and Whelan (eds), *Endurance and emergence*, pp 85–100; Cullen, 'Catholic social classes', pp 57–84.
13 R.E. Burns, 'Irish popery laws; a study of eighteenth-century legislation and behaviour', *Review of Politics*, 24:4, (1962), 485–508; Maureen Wall, 'Penal laws', in G. O'Brien and T. Dunne (eds), *Catholic Ireland in the eighteenth century; the collected essays of Maureen Wall* (Dublin, 1989), p. 8.
14 Corish, *The Catholic community*, p. 74.
15 J.G. Simms, 'The bishops' Banishment Act of 1697', in *IHS*, 17 (Sept. 1970), 185–99.
16 Kelly, 'The Ascendancy and the penal laws', p. 139.
17 Hugh MacMahon, *Relatio Status* (1714) cited in Henry A. Jefferies, 'The early penal days: Clogher under the administration of Hugh MacMahon (1701–1715)' in Henry A. Jefferies (ed.), *History of the diocese of Clogher* (Dublin, 2005), p. 147; L.J. Flynn, 'Hugh MacMachon, bishop of Clogher (1707–15) and archbishop of Armagh (1715–37)', in *Seanchas Ard Mhacha*, 7 (1973), 109–73.
18 MacMahon, *Relatio Status* (1714).
19 Richard English, *Irish freedom: the history of nationalism in Ireland* (London, 2006), p. 84.
20 7 William III c 14(1695).
21 See Kelly, 'The Ascendancy and the penal laws', pp 137–8.
22 Hugh Boulter to Duke of Newcastle, 7 May 1730, *Letters written by … Hugh Boulter D.D. …* (Dublin, 1770), ii, 11–12; see K. Milne, *The Irish Charter Schools, 1730–1830* (Dublin, 1997).
23 Thomas Wyse, *Speech of Thomas Wyse … on moving leave to bring a bill for the establishment of a board of national education …* (Dublin, 1835), p. 15.
24 Cited in Connolly, *Religion, law and power*, p. 288.
25 James McCaffrey, 'Report on the State of Popery, Ireland, 1731', in *Archivum Hibernicum*, 1 (1912), 11.
26 Nigel Yates, *The religious condition of Ireland, 1770–1850* (Oxford, 2006), p. 25.
27 Ibid., p. 25; in this context the penal legislation encouraging priests to convert to the Established Church was also renewed, 31: Geo. II c. 9 (1759).
28 Patrick Rogers, *The Irish Volunteers and Catholic emancipation, 1778–93: a neglected phase of Irish history* (London, 1934), p. 18.
29 Kelly, 'The Ascendancy and the penal laws', p. 147; Rogers, *The Irish Volunteers*, p. 2.
30 K. Whelan, 'The regional impact of Irish Catholicism, 1700–1850', in W. Smyth and K. Whelan (eds), *Common ground: essays on the historical geography of Ireland* (Cork, 1988), p. 254; H.J. Schroeder, (ed.), *The canons and decrees of the Council of Trent* (Rockford, IL, 1978).

31 S. Meigs, *The Reformation in Ireland* (Dublin, 1997), p. 73.

32 Alison Forrestal, *Catholic synods in Ireland, 1600–1690* (Dublin, 1998); see Alexandra Walsham, 'Translating Trent? English Catholicism and the Counter-Reformation', *Historical Research*, 78:201 (August, 2005), 288–310.

33 P.J. Corish, *The Irish Catholic experience: a historical survey* (Dublin, 1985), p. 131.

34 C. O'Dwyer (ed.), 'Archbishop Butler's visitation book', *Arch. Hib.*, 12 (1946), 1–90, and 34 (1977), 1–49; W.H.G. Flood (ed.), 'The diocesan manuscripts of Ferns during the rule of Bishop Sweetman (1745–86)', *Arch. Hib.*, 3 (1914), 113–23.

35 Hugh Fenning, 'The archbishops of Dublin, 1793–1786', in J. Kelly and D. Keogh (eds), *History of the Catholic diocese of Dublin* (Dublin, 2000), p. 210; see T. Wall, 'Archbishop Carpenter and the Catholic Revival' in *Repertorium Novum* (1955), 178–9; J.W. O'Malley, *Trent and all that*, p. 67.

36 M.J. Curran, 'Instructions, admonitions, etc. of Archbishop Carpenter, 1770–86', in *Repertorium Novum*, 2:1 (1958), 148–71.

37 John Carpenter, 'Address to the pastors assembled in Francis Street, 1770', in M.J. Curran, 'Instructions …', p. 152.

38 Ibid., p. 152.

39 Ibid., p. 154.

40 Emmet Larkin and Herman Freudenberger (eds), *A Redemptorist missionary in Ireland: memoirs of Joseph Prost* (Cork, 1998), p. 58.

41 P. Plunket, 1780 Visitation diary, in A. Cogan, *The diocese of Meath ancient and modern* (Dublin, 1870), iii, 27.

42 Ibid., p. 28.

43 Ibid., p. 38.

44 Ibid., p. 27.

45 M. Brennan, 'The Confraternity of the Christian Doctrine in Ireland', *Irish Ecclesiastical Record* (1934), pp 560–77.

46 M.V. Ronan, *An apostle of Catholic Dublin: Fr Henry Young* (Dublin, 1944), p. 124.

47 Fenning, 'The archbishops of Dublin', p. 213.

48 See Ciarán MacMurchaidh, 'Dr James Gallagher, alumnus Kilmorensis: Bishop of Raphoe (1725–37) and Kildare and Leighlin (1737–51)', in *Breifne*, 10:40 (2004), 219–37.

49 Fenning, 'The archbishops of Dublin', p. 213.

50 Hugh Fenning, *The undoing of the friars of Ireland* (Louvain, 1972), p. 193.

51 Plunket, 1780 Visitation diary, p. 42.

52 M. Mullet, *Catholicism in Britain and Ireland, 1558–1829* (London, 1998), p. 187.

53 J. Troy, 'Schema for the diocesan clerical conference for 1790', DDA Troy Papers/1790.

54 Liam Swords, *A hidden church: the diocese of Achonry, 1689–1818* (Dublin, 1997), pp 370–1.

55 Br Joseph Leonard to Fr Pius Leahy, 17 Feb. 1830, CBGA, Rome, 25/296.

56 Larkin, *The pastoral role*, p. 44.

57 Ibid., p. 9.

58 'Return to the Queries proposed by His Majesty's Ministers to the Roman Catholic Prelates of Ireland, relative to the present state of their Church', 29 Nov. 1800, in Charles Vane (ed.), *Memoirs and correspondence of Viscount Castlereagh* (London, 1849), iii, 441–5.

59 S.J. Connolly, *Priests and people in pre-Famine Ireland* (Dublin, 1981), pp 32–3.

60 Larkin, *The pastoral role*, p.9.

61 John Troy, *Relatio Status*, Dublin 1800, DDA, Troy Papers/1800.

62 Cited in J. Bossy, 'The Counter-Reformation and the people of Catholic Ireland, 1596–1641', *Historical Studies*, VIII (1971), p. 164.

63 Connolly, *Priests and people*, p. 162.

64 Corish, *The Irish Catholic experience*, p. 135: see: Gearóid Ó Crualaoich, 'The merry wake', in J.S. Donnelly and K. Miller (eds), *Irish popular culture, 1650–1850* (Dublin, 1998), pp 173–200.

65 Diarmaid Ó Gioáin, 'The pattern', in Donnelly and Miller (eds), *Irish popular culture, 1650–1850*, pp 201–22.

66 John Troy, *Pastoral Address to the Clergy of Ossory* (1782), CDA, Bray Papers.

67   H. Fenning (ed.), 'Some eighteenth-century broadsides', *Collectanea Hibernica*, 12 (1969), 56.
68   M. McGrath (ed.), *The diary of Humphrey O'Sullivan* (Dublin, 1936), ii, 183.
69   Pastoral Address of John Troy, *Dublin Chronicle*, 23 June 1787.
70   Mary Peckham Magray, *The transforming power of the nuns: women, religion, cultural change in Ireland, 1750–1900* (Oxford, 1998), p. 5.
71   *Freeman's Journal*, 27 Aug. 1866: Fergus D'Arcy, 'The decline and fall of Donnybrook Fair; moral reform and social control in nineteenth-century Dublin', *Saothar*, 13 (1988), 7–21.
72   For the fullest discussion of this issue see Larkin, *The pastoral role*, pp 137–86.
73   Whelan, 'The regional impact of Irish Catholicism', p. 7.
74   Charles Smith, *The ancient and present state of the county and city of Waterford* ... (Dublin, 1746), p. 181.
75   See Anne Dillon, 'Praying by number; the confraternity of the Rosary and the English Catholic community, *c.*1580–1700', in *History*, 88:291 (2003), 451–71.
76   Hugh Fenning, 'A time of reform; from the penal laws to the birth of modern nationalism, 1691–1800', in B. Bradshaw and D. Keogh (eds), *Christianity in Ireland* (Dublin, 2002), p. 143.
77   D. Keogh, 'John Thomas Troy, 1786–1823', in Kelly and Keogh (eds), *History of the Catholic diocese of Dublin*, p. 227.
78   Samuel Lewis, *Topographical dictionary of Ireland* (London, 1837), p. 692.
79   E. McParland, *Public architecture in Ireland, 1680–1760* (New Haven, 2001), p. 37.
80   A. McAuley, *Septennial parliaments vindicated* (Dublin, 1766), cited in Patrick Rogers, *Irish Volunteers and Catholic Emancipation 1778–93* (London, 1934), p. 5.
81   K. Whelan, 'The Catholic Church in Tipperary, 1700–1900' in W. Nolan and T. McGrath (eds), *Tipperary: history and society* (Dublin, 1985), pp 225–7.
82   P.J. Duffy, *Exploring the history and heritage of Irish landscapes* (Dublin, 2007), p. 118.
83   Cashel Provincial Statutes (1828), cited in Yates, *The religious condition of Ireland*, p. 203.
84   K. Whelan, 'The Catholic parish, the Catholic chapel and village development in Ireland' in *Irish Geography* (1983), 1–16.
85   See D. Keogh, '*The French disease': the Catholic Church and Irish radicalism, 1790–1800* (Dublin, 1993), pp 12–13: Corish, *The Irish Catholic experience*, p. 160.
86   William Carrigan, *The history and antiquities of the diocese of Ossory* (Dublin, 1905), iii, p. 318.
87   P. Power (ed.), 'A Carrickman's (James Ryan's) diary 1786–1809', *Waterford Arch. Soc. Jn.* (1913), 19.
88   Larkin, *The pastoral role*, pp 189–259.
89   Corish, *The Irish Catholic experience*, p. 134.
90   *Waterford Chronicle and Advertiser*, 2 Aug. 1845.
91   *Cork Examiner*, 9 Sept. 1844.

Chapter 2   The Rices of Callan

1   See Donal Blake, *St Mary's Marino: Generalate and Teacher College* (Dublin, 2005).
2   *Juverna*, 3 (1 May 1903), p. 41.
3   *Juverna*, Souvenir Brochure, July 1903 [unpaginated].
4   Patrick Walsh, 'Daniel Corkery's *The Hidden Ireland* (1924) and revisionism', *New Hibernia Review*, 5:2 (Summer, 2001), 27–44; L.M. Cullen, 'The hidden Ireland: reassessment of a concept' in *Studia Hib.*, 9 (1969), 7–47.
5   F. Ó Fearghail, 'The Catholic Church in County Kilkenny' in W. Nolan and K. Whelan (eds), *Kilkenny: history and society* (Dublin, 1990), p. 229.
6   L. Ó Cáthnia, 'Edmund Rice and his social milieu', in S. Carroll (ed.), *A man raised up: recollections and reflections on Venerable Edmund Rice* (Dublin, 1994), p. 13.
7   W. Tighe, *Statistical observations relative to the county of Kilkenny made in 1800 and 1801* (Dublin, 1802), p. 515.
8   Ó Fearghail, 'Catholic Church in County Kilkenny', p. 240; Normoyle, *A tree is planted*, p. 13.
9   Ibid., p. 229.

10 Ibid.

11 Carrigan, *The history and antiquities of the diocese of Ossory* (Dublin, 1905), 3, 318.

12 Ó Fearghail, 'Catholic Church in County Kilkenny', p. 229; T.C. Butler, *The Augustinians in Callan, 1467–1977* (Kildare, 1977).

13 Carrigan, *Ossory*, iii, 315.

14 T. Power, 'Converts', in Power and Whelan (eds), *Endurance and emergence*, pp 101–29; M. Brown et al. (eds), *Converts and conversion in Ireland, 1650–1850* (Dublin, 2005).

15 Thomas Power, *Land, politics and society in eighteenth century Tipperary* (Oxford, 1993), p. 149.

16 K. Whelan, 'Gaelic survivals' , *Irish Review*, 7 (1989), 140.

17 *Positio*, p. 24; L.M. Cullen, 'The social and economic evolution of Kilkenny in the seventeenth and eighteenth centuries', in Nolan and Whelan (eds), *Kilkenny*, p. 280.

18 Normoyle, *A tree is planted*, p. 2.

19 M.C. Normoyle (ed.), *Memories of Edmund Rice* [henceforth *Memories*] (Dublin, 1979), p. 218.

20 Normoyle, *A tree is planted*, p. 2.

21 Carrigan, *Ossory*, iii, 315.

22 *Positio*, p. 12.

23 See pp 255–6.

24 Normoyle (ed.), *Memories*.

25 Ibid., p. 281.

26 [Mark McCarthy], *Edmund Ignatius Rice*, p. 52.

27 Tighe, *Statistical observations*, p. 385.

28 [McCarthy], *Edmund Ignatius Rice*, p. 51.

29 William Healy, *History and antiquities of Kilkenny, city and county* (Kilkenny, 1905), i, 118.

30 [McCarthy], *Edmund Ignatius Rice*, p. 49.

31 Fitzpatrick, *Edmund Rice*, p. 44.

32 Ciarán Ó hÓgartaigh and Margaret Ó hÓgartaigh, '"Sophisters, economists and calculators": pre-professional accounting education in eighteenth-century Ireland', *Irish Accounting Review*, 13:2 (2006), 63–73: [McCarthy], *Edmund Ignatius Rice*, p. 475.

33 [McCarthy], *Edmund Ignatius Rice*, p. 49.

34 J. Kennedy, 'Callan – a corporate town 1700–1800', in Nolan and Whelan (eds), *Kilkenny*, pp 289–304.

35 James Kelly, *Henry Flood; patriots and politics in eighteenth-century Ireland* (Dublin, 1998), p. 40.

36 R. Chetwood, *A tour through Ireland in several entertaining letters* (Dublin, 1748), pp 146–9

37 *Parliamentary Gazetteer of Ireland, 1844–45* (Dublin, 1845), i, 298.

38 *Positio*, p. 11.

39 McGrath (ed.), *Diary of Humphrey O'Sullivan*, i, 45.

40 Tighe, *Statistical observations*, pp 457, 460, 464.

41 Ibid., p. 480.

42 E. Burke to G. Nagle, 25 Aug. 1778, George Gutteridge (ed.), *The correspondence of Edmund Burke* (Cambridge, 1961), iii, 18–20; T. Wyse, *Historical sketches of the late Catholic Association of Ireland* (Dublin, 1829), i, 101.

43 See T. Bartlett, 'The origins and progress of the Catholic question in Ireland', in Power and Whelan (eds), *Endurance and emergence*, pp 1–21.

44 Bartlett, 'The origins and progress', p. 8.

45 Yates, *The religious condition of Ireland*, pp 214–48.

46 Carrigan, *Ossory*, iii, 348.

47 Registry of Deeds, Will of Robert Rice, 1787; Tithe Applotment Book, Parish of Callan, 18/6/1827, applotment nos 358, 363, 364.

48 Normoyle (ed.), *Memoirs*, pp 114, 138, 253.

49 Ibid., p. 253.

50 D. Allen, *The Presentation Brothers* (Cork, 1993), p. 2.

51 J.S. Donnelly, 'The Whiteboy movement, 1761–65', *IHS* (1978), pp 20–54.

52 S.J. Connolly (ed.), *The Oxford companion to Irish history* (Oxford, 1998), p. 510; W.P. Burke, *History of Clonmel* (Waterford, 1907), pp 360–405.

53 Cited in W.G. Neely, *Kilkenny; an urban history, 1391–1843* (Belfast, 1989), p. 159.

54 P. Wallace, 'Archbishop James Butler II' in W. Nolan (ed.), *Thurles: the cathedral town* (Dublin, 1989), pp 47–54.

55 Kennedy, 'Callan', p. 293; J. Burtchaell and D. Dowling, 'Social and economic conflict in county Kilkenny 1600–1800' in Nolan and Whelan (eds), *Kilkenny*, pp 251–73.

56 John Troy, *Pastoral and excommunication* (Kilkenny, 1779).

57 John Brady (ed.), *Catholics and Catholicism in the eighteenth century press* (Maynooth, 1965), pp 191–2.

58 J.D. Fitzpatrick, 'The Rice Family', *CBER* (1969), p. 2.

59 John Troy to Bishop Fallon, 14 Sept. 1778, DDA, Troy Letters.

60 Bishop Conway, Limerick, to Archbishop Butler, July 1786, CDA.

61 P. Power (ed.), 'A Carrickman's (James Ryan) diary, 1786–1809', *Waterford Arch. Soc. Jn.* (1913), p. 80.

62 Bishop Conway, Limerick, to Archbishop Butler, July 1786, CDA.

63 O'Toole, *A spiritual profile of Edmund Ignatius Rice* (Bristol, 1984), i, 3.

Chapter 3 The Waterford Merchant, 1779–1802

1 See J.E. Carroll, 'From charism to mission to ministry: Edmund Rice and the founding years of the Christian Brothers' in *Edmund*, 10 (Rome, 1991), 19–43.

2 C. Smith, *The ancient and present state of the county and city of Waterford* (Dublin, 1746), p. 195.

3 Thomas Hussey to Edmund Burke, 9 May 1797, *Burke Corr.*, ix, 444–6.

4 S. Lewis, *Topographical dictionary of Ireland* (London, 1837), p. 687.

5 E. Wakefield, *An account of Ireland, statistical and political* (London, 1812), ii, 624.

6 Normoyle (ed.), *Memories*, pp 120, 175.

7 *Positio*, p. 12.

8 Fitzpatrick, *Edmund Rice*, p. 55; Fitzpatrick later rejected the notion that John Rice had gone to Spain, *CBER* (1969), p. 8.

9 L.M. Cullen, *The emergence of modern Ireland, 1600–1900* (Dublin, 1981), p. 126.

10 Whelan, 'Regional impact', pp 258–62.

11 Br E.A. Dunphy to Br Austin Grace, 21 June 1846, CBGA, 25/093.

12 Normoyle (ed.), *Memories*, p. 184.

13 Ibid., p. 34.

14 Ibid., pp 23, 26, 34.

15 John Shelly, 'The founder of the Christian Brothers schools in Ireland', *The Victorian* (Sydney), 30 May 1863, cited in *Positio*, p. 28.

16 [McCarthy], *Edmund Ignatius Rice*, p. 58; see P.J. Daly, *Furnace of love, from the Irish of Tadhg Gaelach Ó Súilleabháin* (Dublin, 2002).

17 *Dublin Evening Post*, 17 Jan. 1789; *Freeman's Journal*, 17 Jan. 1789; *Faulkner's Dublin Journal*, 17 Jan. 1789; *Hibernian Journal*, 19 Jan. 1789.

18 Indeed, a cynic might ask if the 'Mr Rice' referred to was our subject or one of his Rice cousins in Waterford.

19 Sandra M. Schneiders, 'Edmund Rice and religious charism', unpublished paper delivered at Christian Brothers general chapter, Rome, 2002.

20 Diarmuid Ó Murchu, *Reframing religious life* (London, 1998), p. 28.

21 Edmund Rice to Mother M P. Keesham, n.d. [1836?], CBGA, 007/0062.

22 [McCarthy], *Edmund Ignatius Rice*, p. 55.

23 Daire Keogh, 'Our Boys, de Valera's Ireland and the European crisis', in Mary Shine Thompson and Valerie Coghlan (eds), *Divided worlds: studies in children's literature* (Dublin, 2007), p. 130.

24 [McCarthy], *Edmund Ignatius Rice*, p. 55.

25 Normoyle (ed.), *Memories*, p. 224; Liam Ó Caithnia, 'The death of Mrs Edmund Rice', in P.S. Carroll (ed.), *A man raised up: reflections and recollections on Venerable Edmund Rice* (Dublin, 1994), p. 76.

26   J. O'Neill, *A Waterford miscellany* (Waterford, 2004), p. 135.
27   Br W.B. Cullen to Br David Fitzpatrick, 7 Oct. 1949, CBGA Rome, 0012/137.
28   Br W.B. Cullen to Br John E. Carroll, 22 Sept. 1970, CBGA Rome, 0012/137.
29   Margaret Ó hÓgartaigh, 'Edward Hay (c1761–1826)', *Dictionary of Irish biography* (forthcoming).
30   I am grateful to Dr James Quinn, editor of the *Dictionary of national biography*, for advice on this question.
31   Ó Caithnia, 'The death of Mrs Edmund Rice', p. 77.
32   Yates, *The religious condition of Ireland*, p. x.
33   See D. Keogh, 'The Christian Brothers and the Second Reformation in Ireland', *Éire-Ireland*, 1&2 (Spring/Summer 2005), 42–59.
34   McLaughlin, *The price of freedom*, p. 50.
35   *Tipperary Vindicator*, 4 Sept. 1844.
36   McLaughlin, *The price of freedom*, p. 51.
37   Ibid.
38   I am grateful to Jack Burtchael for this information.
39   Kevin Whelan, 'The Catholic community in eighteenth-century county Wexford', in Power & Whelan (eds), *Endurance and Emergence*, p. 147.
40   J. Kelly, 'The abduction of women of fortune in eighteenth-century Ireland', *Eighteenth-Century Ireland*, 9 (1994), 7–43.
41   Normoyle, *A tree is planted*, p. 25.
42   Ó Caithnia, 'The death of Mrs Edmund Rice', pp 67–79.
43   Dorothea Herbert, *Retrospections, 1770–1806* (London, 1929), p. 203.
44   Br Mark Hill to T.C. Whitty, 19 May 1913, CBGA Rome.
45   17 Pastors of the Diocese of Waterford, to Propaganda Fide, 11 Sept. 1818, APF, SCRI, vol. 21, f. 513.
46   Normoyle (ed.), *Memories*, pp 38, 42.
47   Br M.I. Kelly to Br T. Hearn, 2 April 1850, GBGA Rome, 25/294.
48   Br W.B. Cullen to Br John E. Carroll, 22 Sept. 1970, CBGA Rome, 0012/137.
49   Ó Caithnia, 'The death of Mrs Edmund Rice', p. 76.
50   Normoyle, *A tree is planted*, p. 27.
51   Cullen surmises that Mary Rice's carer was a married D'Alton cousin; Br W.B. Cullen to Br John E. Carroll, 22 Sept. 1970, CBGA Rome, 0012/137. A monument was erected to mark her grave at Carrigbeg following Rice's beatification in 1996.
52   Extracts from the Account Books of the congregation, listing payments made for the maintenance of Edmund Rice's daughter, CBGA Rome, 0012/137.
53   *Positio*, p. 31.
54   Br M.I. Kelly to Br T. Hearn, 2 April 1850, CBGA Rome, 025/0294.
55   Ó Caithnia, 'The death of Mrs Edmund Rice', p. 77.
56   E. Rice to M.P. Keeshan, n.d. [1836] 007/0062.
57   Yates, *The religious condition of Ireland*, p. 244.
58   H. Outram Evennett, 'Counter-Reformation spirituality', in D.M. Luebeck (ed.), *The Counter-Reformation* (Oxford, 1999), pp 47–65.
59   J.W. O'Malley, *The first Jesuits* (Cambridge, MA, 1993), p. 139.
60   Larkin, *The pastoral role*, p. 185.
61   O'Toole, *A spiritual profile of Rice Ignatius Rice*, i, 58.
62   O'Malley, *The first Jesuits*, p. 266.
63   Lorenzo Scupoli, *Spiritual combat: how to win your spiritual battles and attain peace* (New York, 2002).
64   O'Toole, *A spiritual profile of Edmund Rice*, i, 87.
65   Carroll, 'From charism to mission to ministry', p. 21.
66   Normoyle (ed.), *Memories*, p. 138.
67   W. Coppinger to Bishop Laffan, 11 Oct. 1824 in Dickson, 'Catholics and trade in eighteenth-century Ireland', pp 92–3.
68   Carroll, 'From charism to mission to ministry', p. 21.
69   Edmund Rice to Brian Bolger, 10 Aug. 1810, in Normoyle (ed.), *Companion*, p. 7.

70   Garrett Connolly to E. Rice, 6 Feb. 1820, in Normoyle (ed.), *Companion*, p. 55.
71   Fitzpatrick, *Edmund Rice*, p. 59; The St Vincent de Paul Society was introduced to Ireland in 1844.
72   Philip Woodfine, 'Debtors, prisons, and petitions in eighteenth-century England', *Eighteenth-Century Life*, 2 (Spring 2006), 1–31.
73   M.J. O'Connell, *Charles Bianconi, 1786–1875* (London, 1878), p. 15.
74   Samuel Smiles, *Men of invention and industry* (London, 1884), p. 227.
75   M. O'Connell, *Bianconi: king of the Irish roads* (Dublin, 1962), pp 36–7.
76   N. John Hall, *Trollope* (London, 1991), p. 95.
77   O'Connell, *Charles Bianconi*, p. 15.
78   O'Connell Bianconi, *Bianconi*, p. 167.
79   A. O'Neill, 'Nuns and monks at Hennessy's Road', in Carroll (ed.), *A man raised up*, pp 79–96.
80   [McCarthy], *Rice Ignatius Rice*, p. 64.
81   T.W. Tone, *Journals*, cited in Keogh, '*The French disease*', pp 55–6.
82   R. Dudley Edwards (ed.), 'The minute book of the Catholic Committee, 1779–92', *Archivum Hibernicum*, 9 (1942), 157–60.
83   *Waterford Herald*, 8 May 1792.
84   *Waterford Herald*, 10 Apr. 1793; 31 Jan. 1795; cf. G.C. Bolton, *The passing of the Irish Act of Union* (Oxford, 1966), pp 138, 150–1.
85   New Ross Account Books, Augustinian Provincial Archives, Ballyboden, Dublin.

Chapter 4   'The Summons of Grace'

1   John Shelly, 'The founder of the Christian Schools in Ireland', *The Victorian* (Sydney), 30 May 1863.
2   *Irish Times*, 3 Nov. 1975.
3   Cited in Michael Viney, 'The Christian Brothers', in *CBER* (1969), 125.
4   J. D. Fitzpatrick, 'The Rice family', in *CBER* (1969), 8.
5   Nicholas Atkin and F. Rank Tallett, *Priests, prelates and people: a history of European Catholicism since 1750* (London, 2003), p. 33.
6   O'Malley, *The first Jesuits*, p. 265.
7   Keogh, *Edmund Rice, 1762–1844*, p. 40.
8   O'Toole, *A spiritual profile*, i, 42–5.
9   Elder Mullan (ed.), *The Spiritual Exercises of St Ignatius* (Rome, 1914), p. 12.
10   [McCarthy], *Edmund Ignatius Rice*, p. 70.
11   Ibid.
12   See J.D. Fitzpatrick, 'A lost chapter in the life of Edmund Rice' *CBER* (1950), 110–21.
13   'Origin', CBGA, 006/0053; F.R. Hickey (ed.), 'The first history of the congregation', in *CBER* (1982), pp 5–30.
14   Ibid., p. 7.
15   See Dáire Keogh, 'Archbishop Troy, the Catholic Church and radicalism in Ireland, 1791–3' in D. Dickson et al. (eds), *The United Irishmen; republicanism, radicalism and rebellion* (Dublin, 1993), pp 124–34; see Nigel Aston, *Christianity in Revolutionary Europe, 1760–1830* (Cambridge, 2002).
16   I.R. McBride, '"When Ulster joined Ireland': anti-popery, Presbyterian radicalism and Irish republicanism in the 1790s"', *Past and Present*, 157 (Nov. 1997), 63–93; D.W. Miller, 'Irish Christianity and revolution', in Jim Smyth (ed.), *Revolution, counter-revolution and union: Ireland in the 1790s* (Cambridge, 2000), pp 195–210.
17   Keogh, *Edmund Rice 1762–1844*, p. 34.
18   Denis McLaughlin, 'The founding of the Irish Christian Brothers; navigating the realities through the myths', *Australian E-Journal of Theology*, 5 (August 2005), 1–41.
19   Hickey (ed.), 'The first history', p. 7.
20   E. Rice to Frère Guilluame, 19 August 1826, DLSGA, ER 411/1/1/6.
21   P.J. Dowling, *Hedge schools of Ireland* (Dublin, 1933).
22   T. Corcoran, 'Enforcing the penal code on education', *Irish Monthly*, 40 (1931), 149–54.
23   Antonia McManus, *The Irish hedge school and its books, 1695–1831* (Dublin, 2002).
24   *The Nation*, 18 Dec. 1847.

25 E. Cahill, 'The native schools of Ireland in the penal era', *Irish Ecclesiastical Record* (1940), 21.

26 *Speech of Thomas Wyse … on moving leave to bring in a bill for the establishment of a board of national education …* (Dublin, 1835), p. 15.

27 H. Fenning (ed.), 'John Kent's report on the state of the Irish mission, 1742', *Arch. Hib.* (1966), 59–102.

28 H. Fenning, 'From the penal laws to the birth of modern nationalism', in Bradshaw and Keogh (eds), *Christianity in Ireland*, p. 137.

29 I. Murphy, *The diocese of Killaloe in the eighteenth century* (Dublin, 1991), p. 156.

30 Cahill, 'The native schools', p. 22.

31 M.E. Daly, 'The development of the National School system, 1831–40' in A. Cosgrove (ed.), *Studies in Irish history presented to R. Dudley Edwards* (Dublin, 1979), pp 150–63.

32 Ibid., p. 154.

33 Michael Quane, 'Waterford School in the opening decades of the nineteenth century', *Journal of the Royal Society of Antiquaries of Ireland*, 101, pt 1 (1971), 141–5.

34 Kent, 'The educational ideals', pp 56–7.

35 Ibid., p. 46.

36 Analysis of 1841 Census, in Kent, 'The educational ideals', p. 56.

37 Fitzpatrick, *Edmund Rice*, p. 95.

38 Ibid., p. 85.

39 Keogh, 'Thomas Hussey', pp 403–26.

40 Desmond Bowen, *History and shaping of Irish Protestantism* (New York, 1995), pp 186–7.

41 See Keogh, 'Thomas Hussey', pp 182–201.

42 *Morning Register*, 27 Jan. 1826.

43 W.G. Murphy, 'The life of Dr Thomas Hussey (1746–1803), bishop of Waterford and Lismore' (MA, UCC, 1968), p. 145.

44 T. Hussey to E. Burke, 9 May 1797, Earl Fitzwilliam (ed.), *Burke Corr.*, iv (London, 1844), pp 444–6.

45 T. Hussey, *A pastoral letter to the Catholics of the united dioceses of Waterford and Lismore* (Waterford, 1797).

46 Hussey, *Pastoral*, p. 3.

47 T. Tickle, *A letter to the Rev. Dr Hussey* (Dublin, 1797), p. 1.

48 P. Duigenan, *A fair representation of the present political state of Ireland* (London, 1799), p. 20.

49 T.L. O'Beirne to Castlereagh, 27 April 1799, in Charles Vane (ed.), *Memoir and correspondence of Viscount Castlereagh* (London, 1850–53), ii, 283.

50 J. Troy to T. Bray, 15 April 1797, CDA.

51 John Carroll to John Troy, 12 Nov. 1798, DDA, Troy Papers.

52 Fitzgerald, 1 October 1844 in J. Shelly, *Edmund Ignatius Rice and the Christian Brothers* (Kilkenny, 1863), p. 42.

53 Fitzpatrick, *Edmund Rice*, p. 85.

54 McLaughlin, 'The founding of the Irish Christian Brothers', p. 11.

55 Cited in Dáire Keogh, 'O'Connell and Irish Catholic Education', in Kevin Whelan (ed.), *Daniel O'Connell* (Dublin, 2002), p. 38.

56 Kent, 'The educational ideals', p. 4.

57 Hickey (ed.), 'The first history', p. 7.

58 Larkin, *The pastoral role*, pp 48–52.

59 McLaughlin, 'The founding of the Irish Christian Brothers', p. 16.

60 Hickey (ed.), 'The first history', p. 7.

61 Statement of Br Bernard Dunphy before the Commissioners of the Primary Education Inquiry, 1825, App 252; Normoyle, *A tree is planted*, p. 39.

62 Eamon Duffy, *Saints and sinners: a history of the popes* (New Haven, 2006), p. 259.

63 Cited in Mary Peckham Magray, *The transforming power of the nuns* (Oxford, 1998), p. 26.

64 Basil O'Connell, 'The Nagles of Ballygriffin and Nano Nagle', *Irish Genealogy*, 3 (1957), 67–73.

65 Walsh, *Nano Nagle*, pp 23–34.

66 W. Coppinger, *The life of Miss Nano Nagle, as sketched … in a funeral sermon preached in Cork on the anniversary of her death* (Cork, 1794), p. 8.

67   Coppinger, *Nano Nagle*, p. 8.
68   [McCarthy], *Edmund Ignatius Rice*, p. 70.
69   Walsh, *Nano Nagle*, p. 43: Coppinger, *Nano Nagle*, p. 8.
70   Coppinger, *Nano Nagle*, p. 8.
71   Nano Nagle to Miss Fitzsimons, 17 July 1769, cited in Walsh, *Nano Nagle*, p. 345.
72   Rosemary Raughter, 'Nano Nagle', *Oxford DNB* (Oxford, 2004).
73   Presentation Annals, cited in Walsh, *Nano Nagle*, p. 99.
74   Peckham Magray, *The transforming power*, p. 17.
75   David Dickson, *Old world colony; Cork and South Munster, 1630–1830* (Cork, 2005), p. 454.
76   Cited in Peckham Magray, *The transforming power*, p. 17.
77   Laurence Lux-Steritt, *Refining female religious life; French Ursulines and English Ladies in seventeenth century Catholicism* (London, 2006).
78   R. Po-Chia Hsia, *The world of Catholic renewal, 1540–1770* (Cambridge, 2005), p. 38.
79   Susan E. Dinan, *Woman and poor relief in seventeenth century France; the early history of the Daughters of Charity* (London, 2006), p. 20.
80   Peckham Magray, *The transforming power*, p. 17.
81   Elizabeth Raply, *The dévotes; women and church in seventeenth-century France* (Montreal, 1990), p. 119.
82   Peckham Magray, *The transforming power*, p. 27; *Positio*, p. 20.
83   *Positio*, p. 20; Asumpta O'Neill, 'Nuns and monks at Hennessy's Road', in P.S. Carroll (ed.), *A man raised up*, p. 86.
84   W.A. O'Hanlon, 'The early Brothers of the Society of the Presentation', *CBER* (1979) 3–148: McLaughlin, 'The founding of the Irish Christian Brothers', p. 19.
85   Fitzgerald, 1 October 1844 in Shelly, *Edmund Ignatius Rice*, p. 41. In one letter to Rome, the archbishop of Dublin commented, 'The Brother Monks … did … the same work for poor boys which the nuns were doing for girls. Hence they are sometimes called the Monks of the Presentation', Daniel Murray to Cardinal Fontana, 24 Mar. 1821, APF, SORCG, 1820, Vol. 923, Pt. 2, F. 465–6.
86   See [Mc Carthy], *Edmund Ignatius Rice*, pp 60–1; Normoyle (ed.), *Memories*, pp 267–8.
87   J.D. Fitzpatrick, 'Our venerable founder's practice of the virtue of faith', *CBER* (1961), 31.
88   O'Toole, *A spiritual profile of Edmund Rice*, i, 152–3.
89   Walsh, *Nano Nagle*, p. 139.
90   McLaughlin, 'The founding of the Irish Christian Brothers', p. 19.

Chapter 5   'Poor Presentation monks', 1802–22

1   Edmund Rice to Peter Kenney, 11 May 1814, Clongowes Wood Archive, cited in Normoyle (ed.), *Companion*, p. 18.
2   Bishop John Power, Relatio to the Holy See, 24 Oct. 1814, APF, SCRI, 1811–15, Vol. 19, F. 179–182.
3   Dickson, *Old world colony*, pp 147–8.
4   Registry of Deeds, Dublin, 715, 145, 489080 in Normoyle, *A tree is planted*, pp 437–8.
5   J.D. Fitzpatrick, 'The finances of our venerable founder', in *CBER* (1969), p. 13.
6   Br E.A. Dunphy to Br Austin Grace, 21 June 1846, CBGA, 0025/0293.
7   L.M. Cullen, 'Rebellion mortality in Wexford in 1798', *Journal of the Wexford Historical Society*, 17 (1998–9), 9.
8   *Faulkner's Dublin Journal*, 5 Nov. 1799.
9   William Power to John Troy, 6 Jan. 1800, DDA, Troy Papers/1810.
10   Keogh, '*The French disease*', p. 176.
11   Thomas Hearn to Thomas Hussey, Sept. 1799, Waterford Diocesan Archive.
12   Carroll, 'Charism to mission', p. 23.
13   Normoyle (ed.), *Memories*, p. 253.
14   Bishop Robert Walsh to Cardinal Fontana, 18 March 1818, APF, SCRI, 1818, Vol. 21, F. 18–20.
15   Normoyle, *A tree is planted*, p. 268.
16   Normoyle (ed.), *Memories*, p. 197.
17   [McCarthy], *Edmund Ignatius Rice*, p. 80.

18 Registry of Deeds, No. 553–315–368721, Normoyle, *A tree is planted*, p. 46.

19 Walsh, *Nano Nagle*, pp 95–6.

20 *CBER* (1891), 447.

21 17 Pastors of the Diocese of Waterford and Lismore to the Holy See, 11 Sept. 1818, APF, SCRI, Vol. 21, F. 513.

22 J.D. Fitzpatrick, 'The greatness of Edmund Rice as a founder of a religious congregation', *CBER* (1953), pp 13–14.

23 Luke Concanen, Rome, to Thomas Hussey, 26 Jan. 1803, Waterford Diocesan Archive.

24 *CBER* (1891), p. 447.

25 T. Hearn to Lord Donoughmore, TCD, T3459/D34/1.

26 Will of Thomas Hussey in *Arch. Hib.*, 3 (1914), 201: 'Memo of the funds of the founder', Jan. 1842, CBGA, 0006/51.

27 Thomas Hussey, *Relatio Status*, 29 June 1803, APF, S.C.R.I., 1802–1810, vol. 18, fol. 125.

28 Will of Thomas Hussey in *Arch. Hib.*, 3 (1914), 201.

29 *Rules and Constitutions of the Society of Religious Brothers* (Dublin, 1832).

30 Br J. Nugent, 'The Annals of Thurles' (1888), CBGA, 006/49; see R. Po-Chia Hsia, *The World of Catholic renewal*, pp. 26–43; Richard L. DeMolen (ed.), *Religious orders of the Catholic Reformation: essays in honor of John C. Olin on his seventy-fifth birthday* (New York, 1994); Querciolo Mazzonis, 'A female idea of religious perfection: Angela Merici and the Company of St Ursula (1535–1540)', *Renaissance Studies*, 18:3 (2004), 392–411; Jaroslav Pelikan, *The Christian tradition: a history of the development of doctrine* (Chicago, 1984), iv, 284–7.

31 See D.S. Blake, 'John Austin Grace (1800–86), educator' (PhD, University of Hull, 1986), p. 36.

32 Hussey, *Pastoral*, p. 3.

33 Fitzpatrick, *Edmund Rice*, p. 151.

34 Normoyle (ed), *Memories*, p. 13.

35 *Dublin Pilot*, 23 Mar. 1836.

36 Blake, 'John Austin Grace', p. 37.

37 Edmund Rice to Frère Guillaume, 4 May 1832, DLSGA, EN 411/1/7/3; Edmund Rice to Mother Austin McGrath, Dungarvan, 12 June 1832, CBGA, Rome; Limerick House Registry, CBGA, 040/0458; Normoyle, *Companion*, p. 403; see H. Fenning, 'Cholera epidemic in Ireland 1832–33', *Arch. Hib.* (2003), 77–125.

38 Manuscript biography of Br Baptist Leonard, CBGA, 006/48; North Richmond Street Annals, Apr. 1849, p. 111; *Cork Examiner*, 12 Mar. 1847.

39 Hussey to Propaganda Fide, 29 June 1803, APF, SRCI, 1802–10, Vol. 18, F. 125.

40 John Power to Francis Moylan, 26 June 1804, *Collectanea Hibernica*, 15 (1972), 69.

41 *CBER* (Dublin, 1891), 447.

42 Fitzpatrick, *Edmund Rice*, p. 160.

43 Normoyle, *A tree is planted*, p. 70.

44 Bartlett, *Fall and rise*, pp 289ff.

45 M.A. Connolly, *The story of Edmund Rice* (private publication, Rome, 1996), p. 8.

46 Hickey (ed.), 'The first history', p. 9.

47 F.R. Hickey, (ed.), 'The Presentation Rule', in *CBER* (1981), p. 182.

48 Memorial to Holy See in Favour of the Institute founded by Edmund Rice, 21 Jan. 1809, SRCI, 1808–09, Vol. 18, F. 45 Propaganda Fide to Dr Power, 21 Jan. 1809, APF, LDSC, 1806–13, Vol. 294, F. 94–5.

49 Hickey, (ed.), 'The Presentation Rule', pp 160–98.

50 H. Outram Evennet, *The spirit of the Counter-Reformation* (Notre Dame, 1968), pp 23–43.

51 *Positio of Nano Nagle* (Rome, 1994), I, p. 556.

52 O'Toole, *A spiritual profile of Edmund Rice*, p. 164.

53 Hickey (ed.), 'Presentation Rule', p. 196.

54 O'Toole, *A spiritual profile of Edmund Rice*, p. 165.

55 *History of the Institute*, i, 392.

56 Hickey (ed.), 'Presentation Rule', p. 170.

57 O'Malley, *The first Jesuits*, p. 162.

58   Hickey (ed.), 'Presentation Rule', pp 171–2.
59   Ibid., pp 172–3; David C. Steinmetz, 'The Council of Trent', in David Bagchi and D.C. Steinmetz (eds),
     The Cambridge companion to Reformation theology (Cambridge, 2004), pp 233–48; H. Denzinger and
     A. Schonmetzer, *Enchiridion Symbolorum: definitionum et declarationum de rebus fidei et morum*
     (Rome, 1976), pp 387–90.
60   Denzinger and Schonmetzer, ibid., p. 401.
61   Outram Evennett, *The spirit of the Counter-Reformation*, p. 37.
62   Hickey (ed.), 'Presentation Rule', p. 173.
63   Ibid., pp 180–1.
64   Larkin and Freudenberger (eds), *Memoirs by Joseph Prost*, p. 38.
65   Hickey (ed.), 'The Presentation Rule', p. 168.
66   Ibid., pp 166–8.
67   Ibid., p. 168.
68   Ibid., p. 166.
69   Ibid., p. 168.
70   'History of the Institute', *CBER* (1895), 102.
71   Br Bernard Dunphy, Notebook (1832), CBGA, 003/0021.
72   Hickey (ed.), 'Presentation Rule', p. 165.
73   Ibid., p. 165.
74   Br Joseph Leonard to Frère Guillaume, 14 Dec. 1829, DLSGA, EN 411/1/4/12.
75   Ibid.
76   Ibid.
77   Edmund Rice to Frère Guillaume, 16 Oct. 1829, DLSGA, EN 411/1/4/8.
78   Ibid.
79   Edmund Rice to Frère Guillaume, 19 Oct. 1831, DLSGA, EN 411/1/6/2.
80   *CBER* (1901), 532.
81   Fitzpatrick, *Edmund Rice*, p. 292.
82   W.B. Cullen, 'The spirit of our founder', *Edmund Ignatius Rice* (Cork, 1969), p. 16.
83   Br Joseph Leonard to Frère Guillaume, De La Salle, 14 Sept. 1829, DLSGA, EN 411/1/4/6.
84   *Rules and Constitutions of the Society of Religious Brothers* (Dublin, 1832), p. 10.
85   Hickey (ed.), 'The first history', p. 8.
86   Kent, 'The educational ideals', p. 8.
87   Christian Brothers, *Manual of school government* (Dublin, 1845), p. 7.
88   'Memorial of John Power … to the Sacred congregation … in favour of Edmund Rice' (n.d. [1808?]),
     APF, SC, Irlanda, vol. 18, f. 495.

Chapter 6   The Brothers' schools, 1802–45

1   Pedro de Ribadeneira to Philip II, 14 Feb. 1556, cited in O'Malley, *The first Jesuits*, p. 209.
2   Kent, 'The educational ideas', p. 46.
3   Hickey (ed.), 'The Presentation Rule', p. 161.
4   Walsh, *Nano Nagle*, p. 42.
5   Joseph Lancaster to John Foster, 1 Mar. 1805, cited in Timothy Corcoran (ed.), *Education systems in
     Ireland* (Dublin, 1928), pp 104–5.
6   Irene Whelan, *Bible War in Ireland; the 'Second Reformation' and the polarization of Protestant-
     Catholic relations, 1800–1840* (Dublin, 2005), pp 53–86.
7   *Waterford Freeman*, 10 Sept. 1845.
8   Edmund Rice to the Holy See, n.d. [Autumn 1819], APF, SORCG, Vol. 926, F. 146–48.
9   'The Presentation Rule', p. 161; Edmund Rice, North Richmond Street Appeal, n.d. [1829?], APF, S.C.,
     Irlanda, 1828–34, vol. 25, f. 748.
10   Edmund Rice, North Richmond Street Appeal, n.d. [1829?], APF, S.C., Irlanda, 1828–34, vol. 25, f. 748.
11   Edmund Rice to Thomas Bray, 9 May 1810, CDA, Bray Papers 1800/21; Br Thomas Grosvenor to Fr
     Joseph Dunn, 24 June 1814, CBGA, 07/0064.

12 Harold Hislop, 'The 1806–12 Board of Education and non-denominational education in Ireland', *Oideas, Journal of the Department of Education*, 40 (Spring 1993), 48–61.

13 Mr and Mrs S.C. Hall, *Ireland: its scenery and character*, 3 vols (London, 1841), i, 305.

14 Corcoran, *Education systems of Ireland*, p. xxi.

15 Outram Evenett, *Counter Reformation*, p. 86.

16 Sarah A. Curtis, *Educating the faithful: religion, schooling and society in nineteenth-century France* (DeKalb, IL, 2000), p. 84.

17 Br E.A. Dunphy to Frère Guillaume, 8 May 1826, DLSGA, EN 411/1/1/1/1.

18 Br Hubert Gerard FSC, Aug. 1963, DLSGA, EN 411/2/1/1.

19 Blake, 'John Austin Grace', p. 45.

20 Br E.A. Dunphy to Frère Guillaume, 8 May 1826, DLSGA, EN 411/1/1/1/1.

21 Blake, 'John Austin Grace', p. 45.

22 Mary Sturt, *The education of the people: a history of primary education in England and Wales in the nineteenth century* (London, 1967), pp 24–35.

23 Cork Poor Schools Committee, 10 Jan. 1806, PBGA, Charitable Soc. Minute Book, E 32.

24 Kent, 'The educational ideas', pp 87–90; Curtis, *Educating the faithful*, p. 97.

25 Cork Poor Schools Committee, 18 July 1815, PBGA, Charitable Soc. Minute Book, 85B.

26 [M.P. Riordan, T.J. Hearn, J.B. Duggan], *A manual of school government; being a complete analysis of the system of education pursued in the Christian Schools. Designed chiefly for the junior members of the society* (Dublin, 1845).

27 William Gillespie, *The Christian Brothers in England, 1825–1880* (Bath, 1975), p. 26.

28 Kent, 'The educational ideals', p. 91.

29 Ibid., p. 189; *The Catholic School*, 2:1 (Aug. 1850), 48 cited in Gillespie, *The Christian Brothers in England*, p. 29.

30 Br P.J. Murphy to Frère Leon, DLSGA, EN 411/1/12/1. I am grateful to Br Peter Gilfedder FSC for this insight.

31 *Manual*, p. 3.

32 *Manual*, p. 4.

33 Curtis, *Educating the faithful*, p. 96.

34 Edmund Rice to Thomas Bray, 9 May 1810, CDA, Bray Papers, 1810/21; E. P. Thompson, 'Time, work-discipline, and industrial capitalism', *Past and Present*, 38 (Dec. 1967), 56–97.

35 *Manual.*, p. 7; J. D. Fitzpatrick, 'Edmund Rice: religious instructor of the poor', in *CBER* (1958), 58.

36 John F. Murray, cited in *Testimonies to the efficiency and excellence of Roman Catholic schools conducted by religious teachers ...* (London, 1849), p. 46.

37 Br P.J. Leonard to Frère Guillaume, 29 Oct. 1829, DLSGA, EN 411/2/2/3; *Manual*, p. 13.

38 *Liverpool Journal*, 28 Jan. 1843, cited in Gillespie, *The Christian Brothers in England*, p. 31.

39 *Manual*, p. 13.

40 Edmund Rice to Thomas Bray, 8 May 1810, CDA, Bray Papers 1810/21.

41 Kent, 'The educational ideals', p. 82.

42 Br J. Hearn to Br Austin Horan, 28 Mar. 1858, CBGA, 05/0042.

43 Frère Guillaume to Br E.A. Dunphy, 9 Aug. 1826, DLSGA, EN 411/1/1/15; Malcolm Seabourne, *The English school: its architecture and organization, 1370–1870* (London, 1971), pp 131–61.

44 *Manual*, pp 10–11.

45 *Manual*, p. 9; Michel Foucault, *Discipline and punish: the birth of the prison* (New York, 1977).

46 David Hogan, 'The market revolution and disciplinary power: Joseph Lancaster and the psychology of the early classroom system', in *History of Education Quarterly*, 29:3 (1989), 408.

47 Br Thomas Grosvenor to Fr Joseph Dunn, 24 June 1814, CBGA, 07/0064.

48 *First Report of the Commissioners of Irish Education Inquiry*, H.C., 1825 (400), XII. I, 16–20.

49 Br Thomas Grosvenor to Fr Joseph Dunn, 24 June 1814, CBGA, 07/0064; Edmund Rice to Thomas Bray, 9 May 1810, Cashel Diocesan Archive; Bruce Curtis, '"My Ladie Birchely must needs rule": punishment and materialization of moral character from Mulcaster to Lancaster' in Kate Rousmaniere et al. (eds), *Discipline, moral regulation and schooling* (New York, 1997), pp 19–42.

50　Br Thomas Grosvenor to Fr Joseph Dunn, 24 June 1814, CBGA, 07/0064; Edmund Rice to Thomas Bray, 9 May 1810, CDA, Bray Papers 1800/10.

51　Barry Coldrey, '"A most unenviable reputation": the Christian Brothers and school discipline over two centuries', in *Oideas*, 38 (1992), 114–33; Blake, 'Austin Grace', p. 47.

52　Richard Lovell Edgeworth, cited in P.J. Hennessy, *A century of Catholic education* (Dublin, 1916), p. 26.

53　Edward Caswall Journal, 1 July 1846, Birmingham Oratory Archives, cited in Dermot Fenlon, 'Edward Caswall, Newman and the people of Catholic Ireland', in Howard Clarke and J.R.S. Phillips (eds), *Ireland, England and the Continent in the Middle Ages: essays in memory ... of F.X. Martin OSA* (Dublin, 2006), p. 316.

54　*Manual*, p. 187.

55　Br P. Ellis to Br T. J. Hearn, 27 Nov. 1855, GBGA, Rome, 06/0044.

56　John Lawson and Harold Silver, *A social history of education in England* (London, 1973), p. 243.

57　Cork Poor Schools Committee, 26 Jan. 1812, PBGA, Charitable Soc. Minute Book, 69A.

58　Br P. Ellis to Br T.J. Hearn, 27 Nov. 1855, GBGA, Rome, 06/0044.

59　Br Austin Dunphy to Frère Guillaume, 28 July 1826, DLSGA, EN 411/1/1/3.

60　Edward O'Flynn, cited in W.A. O'Hanlon, 'Brother Thomas John Wiseman and his contemporaries', *CBER* (1980) p. 147.

61　Curtis, *Educating the faithful*, p. 100.

62　Ibid.

63　Br Bernard Dunphy, Notebook (1832), CBGA, 003/0021.

64　O'Connell's Schools Annals (1842), CBGA.

65　Normoyle, *Memories*, p. 37.

66　*Manual*, p. 15.

67　McLaughlin, *The price of freedom*, p. 323.

68　W.A. O'Hanlon, 'Br Thomas John Wiseman', p. 148.

69　1841 General Chapter decrees, CBGA, 058/644.

70　M.P. Riordan, Circular Letter, 1856, CBGA, 058/0644.

71　*Saunders Newsletter*, 11 May 1855.

72　Coppinger, *Nano Nagle*, p. 29.

73　David Hogan, 'The market revolution', p. 408.

74　Mr and Mrs Hall, *Ireland*, i, 306.

75　*Manual*, p. 15.

76　[A Presentation Brother], *Brother Ignatius Rice and the Presentation Brothers* (Cork, 1963), p. 21.

77　Hickey (ed.), 'Presentation Rule', p. 162; Br P. Ellis to Br T. J. Hearn, 27 Nov. 1855, GBGA, Rome, 06/0044; *First Report of the Commissioners of Irish Education Inquiry*, H. C. 1825 (400), xxii, p. 85; Blake, 'John Austin Grace', p. 45.

78　Fitzpatrick, *Edmund Rice*, p. 299.

79　Dr Murray on Pay Schools, Aug. 1841, CBGA, 058/0644; Michael Quan, 'Waterford schools in the opening decades of the nineteenth century', *Journal of the Royal Society of Antiquaries of Ireland* (1971), 141–3.

80　J. Ebenezer Bicheno, *Ireland and its economy: a tour through the country in the autumn of 1829* (London, 1830), p. 280.

81　Austin Grace (1828) cited in Blake, 'John Austin Grace', p. 107.

82　*Manual*, pp 206–7.

83　Richard Lovell Edgeworth, cited in [McCarthy], *Edmund Ignatius Rice*, pp 217–18.

84　Edward Caswall Journal, 1 July 1846, Birmingham Oratory Archives, cited in Fenlon, 'Edward Caswell', p. 317.

85　*Manual*, pp 16–17; 206–7.

86　Cullen, *Emergence of modern Ireland*, p. 236.

87　Normoyle, *A tree is planted*, p. 55.

88　Kent, 'The educational ideals', p. 50

89　Hanover Street Returns (1837), DDA, 33/5/55.

90　*Cork Southern Reporter*, cited in [McCarthy], *Edmund Ignatius Rice*, p. 462.

91 *Report of the Select Committee on the state of the Poor, together with minutes of evidence*, 626, H.C., 1830 (667.) VII. I.

92 *Report on the Endowed schools in Ireland* (Kildare); 79, H.C. 1857–8 (2336–I.) XXII, pt. i, I, cited in Kent, 'The educational ideas', p. 50.

93 *Dublin Morning Register*, 4 Jan. 1825.

94 *Report on the State of the Poor*; 385, H.C., 1830 (667.) VII.I.

95 *Report of the Select Committee of the House of Lords on the Plan of Education in Ireland; with minutes of evidence*; H.L. 1837 (543–I.), VIII, 1245.

96 Cited in Kent, 'The educational ideas', p. 51.

97 Mr and Mrs Hall, *Ireland*, i, 306.

98 John Grace, 1828, Preston Scrap Book, Jesuit Archives English Province, cited in Donal Blake, 'John Austin Grace', p. 107.

99 Mr and Mrs Hall, *Ireland*, i, 306; Cork Poor Schools Committee, 26 Jan. 1812, PBGA, Charitable Soc. Minute Book, 69A.

1   R.H. Ryland, *The history, topography and antiquities of the county and city of Waterford* (London, 1824), p. 188.

2   Stephen Curtis, *Waterford Freeman*, 10 Sept. 1845.

3   John Charles McQuaid, Foreword to Fitzpatrick, *Edmund Rice*, p. xii.

4   *Manual*, p. 7; Hickey (ed.), 'Presentation Rule', p. 161.

5   John Reynolds, lord mayor of Dublin (1850–2), *Tablet*, 21 Sept. 1850.

6   Hickey (ed.), 'Presentation Rule', p. 162; *Manual*, p. 17.

7   Edmund Rice to Thomas Bray, 9 May 1810, CDA, Bray Papers 1810/21.

8   Hickey (ed.), 'Presentation Rule', p. 164.

9   Gillespie, *The Christian Brothers in England*, p. 35; *Manual*, pp 146–69.

10 Br Joseph Hearn to Br Austin Horan, 12 March 1858, CBGA, 005/42; [Mary Carpenter]. *Ragged schools: their principles and mode of operation* (London, 1850), pp 47–50, cited in Mary Hilton, *Women and the shaping of the nation's young; education and public doctrine in Britain, 1750–1850* (London, 2007), p. 190.

11 Cork Poor Schools Committee, 23 Dec. 1812, PBGA, Minute Book, 69A.

12 List of Books purchased for Hanover Street School Library, 1821–22, DDA, 33/5/1.

13 List of Books purchased for Hanover Street School Library, 1832–37, DDA, 33/5/5.

14 Peckham Magray, *The transforming power of the nuns*, p. 3.

15 Hickey (ed.), 'Presentation Rule', p. 162.

16 List of Books purchased for Hanover Street School Library, 1832–37, DDA, 33/5/5.

17 Hickey (ed.), 'Presentation Rule', p. 162.

18 Ibid.; J.C. Colouhoun (Cheltenham, 1838), p. 64.

19 Edmund Rice to Thomas Bray, 9 May 1810, CDA, Bray Papers, 1810/21.

20 *Manual*, p. 181.

21 Curtis, *Educating the faithful*, p. 92.

22 Hanover Street Returns, 1837, DDA, 33/5/5.

23 Donal Blake, 'John Austin Grace', p. 46.

24 Mr and Mrs Hall, *Ireland*, i, 307.

25 Edmund Rice to Thomas Bray, 9 May 1810, CDA, Bray Papers 1810/21.

26 H.D. Inglis, *Ireland in 1834: a journey through Ireland, in the spring, summer and autumn of 1834* (London, 1834), ii, 65–6.

27 W. Phelan and M. O'Sullivan, *Practical observations on the First Report of the Commissioners on Irish Education* (London, 1826), p. 33.

28 Bicheno, *Ireland and its economy*, p. 280.

29 Sir John Newport to Lord Melbourne, 1829 CBGA.

30 Bishop Patrick Dorrian's evidence to *Royal Commission of Inquiry, Primary Education, Ireland* (Powis) H.C. (1870), 28 (III) 351.

31 David Hempton, *The religion of the people: Methodism and popular religion, c.1750–1900* (London, 1996).

32   Smiles, *Men of invention and industry* (London, 1884), p. 227.
33   Ryland, *History*, pp 187–8.
34   H.F. Kearney, 'Fr Mathew: apostle of modernisation' in Art Cosgrove and Donal McCartney (eds), *Studies in Irish history presented to R. Dudley Edwards* (Dublin, 1979), pp. 164–75.
35   Thackeray, *Irish sketch book*, cited in M. Lysaght, *Fr Theobald Mathew: the apostle of temperance* (Dublin, 1983).
36   Kearney, 'Fr Mathew', p. 175.
37   Fitzpatrick, *Edmund Rice*, p. 280
38   Recollection of Mary Flynn (1912), Normoyle (ed.), *Memories*, p. 111.
39   Fr Augustine, *Fr Mathew and Edmund Rice*, p. 11.
40   C. Kerrigan, *Father Mathew and the Irish temperance movement, 1838–1849* (Cork, 1992). Lysaght, *Fr Mathew*, p. 32: John F. Quinn, *Father Mathew's crusade* (Amherst, 2002); Paul A. Townend, *Father Mathew, temperance and Irish identity* (Dublin, 2002).
41   Fr Augustine, *Fr Mathew and Edmund Rice*, p. 20.
42   *Freeman's Journal*, 18 Sept. 1843.
43   O'Connell's School Annals, 1843, CBGA Rome.
44   Fr Augustine, *Fr Mathew and Edmund Rice*, p. 29.
45   Townend, *Fr Mathew*, p. 1.
46   Cited in Fr Augustine, *Footprints of Father Mathew* (Dublin, 1947), p. 107.
47   Fr Augustine, *Fr Mathew and Edmund Rice*, p. 23.
48   John Shelly, *Edmund Ignatius Rice*, p. 132.
49   *Endowed Schools Report* (1858), Appendix, p. 11.
50   Ibid.

Chapter 7   Expansion and union, 1802–22

1   Charles Bianconi cited in Smiles, *Men of invention and industry*, p. 254.
2   J.A. Froude, *The English in Ireland in the eighteenth century* (New York, 1888), iii, 54.
3   See M.C. Sullivan, *Catherine McAuley and the tradition of mercy* (Dublin, 1995); D. Forristal, *The first Loreto Sister* (Dublin, 1994); Seamus Enright, 'Women and Catholic life in Dublin, 1766–1852', in Kelly and Keogh (eds), *History of the Dublin diocese*, pp 268–93.
4   Blake, 'John Austin Grace', p. 361.
5   Gillespie, *The Christian Brothers in England*, p. 14.
6   Fitzpatrick, *Edmund Rice*, p. 156.
7   Annals of Thurles, CBGA, 006/49.
8   'Brother Patrick Ellis', *CBER* (1892), 108.
9   Kent, *The education ideals*, p. 144.
10 Ibid.
11 [McCarthy], *Edmund Ignatius Rice*, p. 67; CBGA, 25/093.
12 Connolly, *The story of Edmund Rice*, p. 22.
13 Book of Changes (1832–43), CBGA, cited in Blake, 'Austin Grace', p. 44.
14 Br P.J. Leonard to Frère Guillaume, 28 Apr. 1828, DLSGA, EN 411/1/3/5.
15 Frère Guillaume to Br P.J. Leonard, 31 May 1828, DLSGA, EN 411/1/3/7.
16 Fitzpatrick, *Edmund Rice*, p. 158; Seán P. Farragher, *Edward Barron, 1801–54* (Dublin, 2004).
17 Whelan, 'Regional impact', p. 269.
18 Henry Inglis, *A journey throughout Ireland* (London, 1835), p. 74.
19 Power (ed.), 'Carrick Man's diary' (1913), p. 26.
20 Kevin Whelan, 'The Catholic Church in County Tipperary', in Power and Nolan (eds), *Tipperary: history and society*, p. 231.
21 Christian Brothers House Annals, Carrick-on-Suir; Normoyle, *A tree is planted*, p. 68.
22 Power, 'Carrickman's diary' (1913), p. 75.
23 E. Rice to Bray, 9 May 1810, CDA, Bray Papers 1810/21.
24 Edmund Rice to Fr Trappes, Preston, 24 June 1825, Normoyle (ed.), *Companion*, pp 118–20.

25 T.R. Malthus, *Essay on population* (1798), iii, 203–4, cited in H.C. Barnard, *A history of English education from 1760* (London, 1966), pp 47–8.

26 Cork Poor Schools Committee, 10 Feb. 1811, PBGA, Charitable Soc. Minute Book, 57B.

27 Cork Poor Schools Committee, PBGA, Charitable Soc. Minute Book, 103A: T.J. Walsh, *Nano Nagle*, pp 188–95.

28 Timothy MacAuliffe to David Nagle, 15 Mar. 1799, PBGA, Charitable Soc. Minute Book, 22A.

29 Cork Poor Schools Committee, 14 Feb. 1808, PBGA, Charitable Soc. Minute Book, 40A.

30 Cork Poor Schools Committee, 10 Jan. 1806, PBGA, Charitable Soc. Minute Book, E 24.

31 Ibid., E38.

32 Cork Poor Schools Committee, 31 July 1807, PBGA, Charitable Soc. Minute Book, 40A.

33 Walsh, *Nano Nagle*, p. 192.

34 Cork Poor Schools Committee, 25 Feb. 1810, PBGA, Charitable Soc. Minute Book, 51B.

35 [McCarthy], *Edmund Ignatius Rice*, p. 104.

36 *History of the Institute*, i, 23; Cork Poor Schools Committee, 19 May 1814, PBGA, Charitable Soc. Minute Book, 75A.

37 Cork Poor Schools Committee, 15 July 1815, PBGA, Charitable Soc. Minute Book, 85B.

38 John Whitelaw, *An essay on the population of Dublin, being the result of an actual survey taken in 1798* (Dublin, 1803), p. 65.

39 W. Meagher, *Notes on the life and character of … Daniel Murray* (Dublin, 1853), p. 8.

40 Ibid., p. 146.

41 Rev. Fr Gregory Lynch to Paul Cullen, 1864, *History of the Institute*, i, 34.

42 Henry Young, *The Catholic directory* (Dublin, 1821), p. 16.

43 *The Parliamentary Gazetteer of Ireland*, vol. 3, p. 644.

44 'Memoir of Brother Edward Austin Dunphy', *CBER* (1909), 54.

45 Normoyle, *A tree is planted*, p. 158.

46 *Report of the Select Committee of the House of Lords on the Plan of Education in Ireland …*, H.L., 1837 (543–1), VIII, 1246.

47 E. Rice to Fr Dunn, Preston, 24 June 1825, Normoyle (ed.), *Companion*, pp 116–17.

48 Gillespie, *The Christian Brothers in England*, p. 20.

49 Br P.J Murphy to Tobias Kirby, 10 Mar. 1843, PICR, Archives, Kirby/173.

50 Gillespie, *The Christian Brothers in England*, pp 21–2; *CBER* (1894), 469.

51 W.A. O'Hanlon, 'Development of our rules; 1802–1966', *CBER* (1968), 66.

52 Edmund Rice to Br Joseph Hogan, 24 May 1814, in Normoyle (ed.), *Companion*, p. 21.

53 Thomas Grosvenor to Daniel Murray, 27 Mar. 1815, DDA, 35/5.

54 Edmund Rice to Peter Kenney, 11 May 1814, Normoyle (ed.), *Companion*, p. 17.

55 Waterford Resolutions, 27 Aug. 1817, CBGA, Rome, in Normoyle (ed.), *Companion*, pp 35–6; W.A. O'Hanlon, *The early Brothers of the Society of the Presentation* (Dublin, 1979), p. 109.

56 Thomas Grosvenor to Daniel Murray, 27 Mar. 1815, DDA, 33/5.

57 Hickey (ed.), 'The first history', p. 18

58 *Positio*, p. 236.

59 Br Patrick Corbett, House Annals, Carrick-on-Suir cited in Normoyle, *A tree is planted*, p. 117.

60 Edmund Rice to the Holy See, [n.d. June 1818?], APF, SORCG, Vol. 926, F. 146–8.

61 John Troy to Cardinal Litta, [13 June 1818], APF, SORCG, 1821, Vol. 926, Pt. 2, F. 146–8.

62 Citizens of Waterford to Cardinal Fontana, 1 Oct. 1819, APF, SCRI, 1819, Vol. 22, F. 290–3.

63 J.B. Clinch to Robert Walsh, Oct. 1819, APF, SORCG, 1820, Vol. 923, F. 425. Clinch was Professor of Rhetoric at Maynooth and had written several of Archbishop Troy's published defences in 1798.

64 Robert Walsh to Cardinal Fontana, n.d (1820), APF, SORCG, 1820, Vol. 923, F. 97.

65 John Troy to Thomas Fallon, 15 May 1778, DDA, Troy Letter Book.

66 See Larkin, *The pastoral role*, pp 63–137.

67 John Troy to Cardinal Litta, 16 Mar. 1816 cited in Larkin, *The pastoral role*, p. 97.

68 Larkin, *The pastoral role*, p. 104.

69 Kyran Marum to Br E.A. Dunphy, 18 Mar. 1816, CBGA, 025/0293.

70 Robert Walsh to Richard Hayes, 25 Nov. 1817, cited in Ignatius Fennessy, 'Bishop Robert Walsh, the Friars and Edmund Ignatius Rice, 1817', *Collectanea Hibernica*, 38 (1996), 162.

71 Robert Walsh to Cardinal Fontana, 18 March 1818, APF, SCRI, 1818, Vol. 21, F. 18–20.

72 Walsh to Propaganda, 30 July 1818, APF, SRCI, Vol. 21, F. 354–5.

73 Robert Walsh to Cardinal Consalvi, APF, Rubrica, Vol. 280, F. 33–46 – Waterford 280/21.

74 Objection of Six Monks, 1 Aug. 1818, APF, SRCI, 1818, Vol. 21, F. 414.

75 17 Pastors of the diocese of Waterford, 11 Sept. 1818, APF, SRCI, 1818, Vol. 21, F. 513; B. Coldrey, *Faith and fatherland* (Dublin, 1988), p. 24.

76 Fitzpatrick, *Edmund Rice*, p. 182; *Positio*, pp 243–4.

77 Larkin, *The pastoral role*, pp 102–11.

78 Robert Walsh to Monsignor Pedicini, 24 Mar. 1821, APF, SORCG, 1820, Vol. 923, Pt. 2, F. 495–6.

79 Dr Murray to Propaganda Fide, 7 May 1821, APF, SORCG, 1820, Vol. 923, Pt. 2, F. 465–6.

80 Dr Troy to Cardinal Fontana, enclosure in Dr Murray to Propaganda Fide, 7 May 1821, APF, SORCG, 1820, Vol. Pt. 2, F. 465.

81 J.D. Fitzpatrick, 'The Brief – a triumph of failure', *CBER* (1952), 216.

82 John Troy to Cardinal Fontana, 10 Jan. 1820, APF, SC Irlanda, 1820–22, Vol. 23, F. 66–67.

83 Fitzpatrick, 'The Brief', p. 218.

84 See O'Toole, *A spiritual profile of Edmund Rice*, ii, 161–73.

85 Edmund Rice to Pius VII, 24 Jan. 1823, APF, SCRI, Vol. 24, F. 23–24.

86 Fitzpatrick, 'The Brief', p. 223.

87 Cardinal Fontana to John Troy, 18 Sept. 1818, APF, LDSC, 1819, Vol. 300, F. 642–3.

88 Daniel Murray to Edmund Rice, 3 Oct. 1820, Normoyle (ed.), *Companion*, p. 66.

89 Thurles Resolutions, DDA, 33/5/1; *Brother Ignatius Rice and the Presentation Brothers* (Cork, 1963), p. 40.

90 Hickey (ed.), 'The first history', p. 19.

91 *Brother Ignatius Rice and the Presentation Brothers* (Cork, 1963), pp 41–2.

92 Donal Blake, *A man for our time: a short life of Edmund Rice* (Dublin, 1994), p. 13; W. A. O'Hanlon, 'Development of our rules; 1802–1966', *CBER* (1968), 62–80.

93 J.M. Feheney, 'Edmund Rice and the Presentation Brothers', in J.M. Feheney (ed.), *A time of grace* (Dublin, 1996), p. 28.

94 Yates, *The religious condition of Ireland*, p. 102.

95 *Brother Ignatius Rice and the Presentation Brothers* (Cork, 1963), p. 43.

96 *Presentation Record* (1918), in D. H. Allen, *The Presentation Brothers* (Cork, 1993), p. 51; E. Rice to P. Kenney, 11 May 1814, Normoyle (ed.), *Companion*, p. 17.

97 Presentation Annals, 1818, PBGA, 20/1/1, p. 2.

98 J. Matthew Feheney, *Gentlemen of the Presentation* (Dublin, 1999), p. 12.

99 Allen, *The Presentation Brothers*, pp 91–101.

1 Fitzpatrick, 'The Brief', pp 203–25.

2 Gillespie, *The Christian Brothers in England*, p. 12.

3 [McCarthy], *Edmund Ignatius Rice*, p. 126; House Annals, Carrick-on-Suir, cited in Normoyle, *A tree is planted*, p. 151.

4 David Fitzpatrick to Br Pius Noonan, 18 June 1951, CBGA, 36/0416.

5 Patrick Kelly to Cardinal Consalvi, 5 July 1824, cited in J.F. Prior, 'Bishop Kelly of Richmond and of Waterford; hostility to Edmund Rice', *CBER* (1988), 78.

6 Br P.J. Leonard to Frère Guillaume, 28 Apr. 1838, DLSGA, EN, 411/1/3/4.

7 Ironically, the Presentation annals celebrate the receipt of papal status as the fruit of 'the heavenly inspired agitation for self-government'. Presentation Annals, 1889, PBGA, 20/1/1, p. 24.

8 E. Rice to Bray, 9 May 1810, CDA, Bray Papers 1810/21.

9 Poor Schools Committee, 1 Nov. 1827, PBGA, Charitable Soc. Minute Book, 103A.

10 Bishop John O'Shaughnessy, Killaloe, to Edmund Rice, 31 Mar. 1826, Normoyle (ed.), *Companion*, p. 136.

11 House Annals, Carrick-on-Suir cited in Normoyle, *A tree is planted*, p. 117.

12 Balbino Rano, *The Order of Saint Augustine* (Rome, 1975).

13 Fitzpatrick, 'The Brief, p. 209.
14 Kyran Marum to Br E.A. Dunphy, 18 Mar. 1816, CBGA, 025/0293.
15 Hickey (ed.), 'The first history', p. 30.
16 Gillespie, *The Christian Brothers in England*, p. 25

Chapter 8 The new reformation, 1820–50

1   Obituary for Br Thomas Bernard Aylward, *Kilkenny Journal*, Nov. 1861, cited in Shelly, *Edmund Ignatius Rice*, p. 127.
2   Richard Musgrave, *Memoirs of the different rebellions in Ireland* (Dublin, 1802); George Taylor, *A history of the rise, progress and suppression of the rebellion in the county of Wexford in the year 1798* (Dublin, 1800), p. 99; Jim Smyth, 'Anti-Catholicism, conservatism, and conspiracy: Sir Richard Musgrave's *Memoirs of the different rebellions in Ireland*', *Eighteenth-century Life*, 22 (Nov 1998), pp 62–73.
3   Joseph Leichty, 'The popular reformation comes to Ireland; the case of John Walker and the foundation of the Church of God 1804', in R.V. Comerford (ed.), *Religion, conflict and co-existence in Ireland* (Dublin, 1990), pp 159–87.
4   H. Newland, *An apology for the Established Church in Ireland* (Dublin, 1829), p. 82, cited in Yates, *Religious condition*, p. 167.
5   Richard Woodward, *The present state of the Church of Ireland* (Dublin, 1787), p. 53 cited in Yates, *Religious condition*, p. 141.
6   Cited in D. Hempton and Myrtle Hill, *Evangelical Protestantism in Ulster society, 1740–1890* (London, 1992), p. 53.
7   *Morning Register*, 25 March 1826.
8   *Irish Magazine*, May 1811.
9   J.E. Gordon, *The Church of Ireland considered in her ecclesiastical relation to the Roman Catholic part of the population* (Dublin, 1848), p. 3; Stuart Brown, 'The new reformation movement in the Church of Ireland, 1801–29' in Stuart Brown and David W. Miller (eds), *Piety and power in Ireland, 1760–1960: essays in honour of Emmet Larkin* (Notre Dame, 2000), pp 180–208; *The national churches of England, Ireland and Scotland, 1801–46* (Oxford, 2001), pp 99–100.
10 Earl Grey, *Colonial policy of Lord John Russell's administration* (London, 1853), ii, 13–14, cited in Desmond Bowen, *The Protestant Crusade in Ireland, 1800–70* (Dublin, 1978), xii.
11 David Hempton, 'The Methodist crusade in Ireland, 1795–1845', in *IHS* (1980), 36.
12 Yates, *Religious condition*, p. 262.
13 Hempton, 'Methodist crusade', p. 33.
14 W.J. Amherst, *The history of Catholic emancipation, 1771–1820* (London, 1886), i, 147.
15 Cardinal Fontana to John Troy, 18 Sept. 1818, APF, LDSC, 1819, Vol. 300, F. 642–3.
16 William Magee, *A charge delivered at his primary visitation in St Patrick's Cathedral*, Dublin (Dublin, 1822).
17 Whelan, *Bible War*, pp 153–87.
18 S.J. Connolly, *Religion and society in nineteenth century Ireland* (Dundalk, 1985), pp 25–30.
19 Thomas McGrath, *Politics, interdenominational relations and education in the public ministry of Bishop James Doyle ...* (Dublin, 1999), pp 109–15: J.S. Donnelly, 'Pastorini and Captain Rock: millenarianism and sectarianism in the Rockite movement of 1821–4', in Samuel Clark and J.S. Donnelly (eds), *Irish peasants: violence and political unrest, 1780–1914* (Madison, 1983), pp 102–39.
20 *Report of the proceedings of a meeting in Cavan ... January 1827 to form a society for promoting the Reformation in Ireland* (Cork, 1827), p. 17: *Dublin Evening Post*, 3 July 1824.
21 Fr Burke to Edward Hay, 10 January 1812, DDA, Catholic Board Papers, 390/1/file vii; 'A Protestant citizen of Cork to ——', 13 March 1816, Home Office 100/189/229, cited in Thomas Bartlett, *Fall and rise*, p. 320.
22 Paul Cullen to Theobald Mathew, cited in I. Murphy, 'Some attitudes to religious freedom ...', p. 104
23 Cf D.W. Bebbington, *Evangelicalism in modern Britain: a history from the 1730s to the 1980s* (London, 1989).

24　Thomas Wyse, *Education reform of the necessity of a National System of Education* (London, 1836), p. 18.

25　Austin Dunphy to Frère Guillaume, 8 May 1826, DLSGA, EN 411/1/1/1.

26　Mary Daly, 'The development of the National Schools system', in A. Cosgrove and D. McCartney (eds), *Studies in Irish history presented to R. Dudley Edwards* (Dublin, 1979), p. 154.

27　*Dublin Evening Post*, 27 April 1824.

28　Murphy, 'Attitudes', p. 101.

29　*First Report of the Commission of Irish Education Inquiry.* H. C. 1825 (400), XII.I, 716.

30　John Troy to Dr Trench, 28 Jan. 1818, cited in *First Report of the Commission of Irish Education Inquiry.* H.C. 1825 (400), XII.I, 47.

31　Whelan, *Bible War*, p. 135.

32　Ibid., p. 298; Atkin and Tallett, *Priests, prelates and people*, pp 102–3.

33　*First Report of the Commission of Irish Education Inquiry.* H.C. 1825 (400), XII.I, 51.

34　Ibid., 718.

35　Ibid., 50.

36　Cardinal Fontana to John Troy, 18 Sept. 1818, APF, LDSC, 1819, Vol. 300, F. 642–3.

37　John Troy to Cardinal Fontana, 10 Jan. 1820, APF, SCR, Irlanda, 1822–23, Vol. 23, F 66–7.

38　Propaganda Fide to John Troy, 22 Apr. 1820, APF, SCR, Vol 301, F 301.

39　Pius VII cited in Whelan, *Bible War*, p. 134.

40　Hussey, *Pastoral address*, p. 3.

41　B.M. Coldrey, 'The charism of Edmund Rice: opposition to Protestant proselytism', *CBER* (1989), 14; P. Power (ed.), 'Carrickman's diary' (1913), p. 23.

42　Jennifer Ridden, 'The forgotten history of the Protestant crusade: religious liberalism in Ireland', *Journal of Religious History*, 31:1 (March 2007), 95; *Royal Commission of Enquiry into Primary Education, Minutes of Evidence*, 25 Feb. 1869, p. 1177.

43　T.J. Hearn Notebook (1841–51), CBGA, 05/0041; Christian Brothers, *Manual* (1845), p. 7.

44　Edmund Rice to Pope Leo XII, 22 May 1824, APF, SC Irlanda, 1825–27, v. 24, f. 101.

45　Br E.A. Dunphy to Frère Guillame, 8 May 1826, DLSGA, EN 411/1/11.

46　Br P.J. Leonard to Frère Guillame, 15 Feb. 1827, DLSGA, EN 411/1/2/2.

47　Evidence of J.E Gordon, London Society, *First Report of the Commission of Irish Education Inquiry.* H.C. 1825 (400), XII.I, 714.

48　Ibid.

49　*Blackwoods Magazine*, May 1827, p. 582.

50　Frederick Lucas, *The Tablet*, Sept. 1854.

51　Ignatius Murphy, *The diocese of Killaloe, 1800–1850* (Dublin, 1992), pp 37–8.

52　David Hempton, 'Gideon Ouseley: rural revivalist, 1791–1839', *Studies in Church History*, 25 (1989), 203–14.

53　Murphy, *The diocese of Killaloe, 1800–1850*, pp 38–9.

54　Richard Mant, *A charge delivered to the clergy of Kilalloe* (Dublin, 1820), pp 25–6, 34–7.

55　Mant, *Charge*, p. 43.

56　Bowen, *The Protestant crusade*, pp 85–6.

57　I am grateful to Nigel Yates for these insights.

58　Mant, *Charge*, p. 40.

59　Murphy, *The diocese of Killaloe, 1800–1850*, p. 40.

60　Harold Hislop, 'The 1806–12 Board of Education and Non-Denominational Education in Ireland', *Oideas*, 40 (Spring, 1993), 48–60.

61　*Monastery Boys: celebrating 175 years, Ennistymon CBS 1824–1999* (Ennistymon, 1999), p. 15.

62　Peter O'Loughlin to Secretary, KPS, [n.d.], *First Report of the Commission of Irish Education Inquiry.* H.C. 1825 (400), XII.I, 590

63　Blake, 'John Austin Grace', p. 59.

64　Ibid., p. 60.

65　Ennistymon Annals, cited in Blake, 'John Austin Grace', p. 64.

66　Peter O'Loughlin to Secretary, KPS, 7 July 1824, *First Report of the Commission of Irish Education Inquiry.* H.C. 1825 (400), XII.I, 590.

67 Peter O'Loughlin to Secretary, KPS, 26 Aug. 1824, ibid.
68 Normoyle, *A tree is planted*, p. 181.
69 Blake, 'John Austin Grace', p. 66.
70 Br Francis Manifold to Edmund Rice, 3 June 1826, Normoyle (ed.), *Companion*, pp 141–3.
71 Frank Daly to Edmund Rice, 10 July 1826, Normoyle (ed.), *Companion*, p. 147.
72 [McCarthy], *Edmund Ignatius Rice*, p. 249.
73 Murphy, *The diocese of Killaloe, 1800–1850*, p. 41.
74 *Clare Journal*, 31 Oct. 1833.
75 James O'Shaughnessy to Edmund Rice, 31 March 1826, Normoyle (ed.), *Companion*, p. 136.
76 Dean Shaughnessy, Ennis, to Edmund Rice, 26 Dec. 1826, in Normoyle, *Companion*, p. 164.
77 Kent, 'The educational ideals', p. 56.
78 [McCarthy], *Edmund Ignatius Rice*, pp 248–9.
79 Dr Silver quoted in Murphy, *Diocese of Killaloe, 1800–1850*, p. 141.
80 *Clare Journal*, 31 Oct. 1833.
81 Normoyle, *A tree is planted*, pp 205–8.
82 Bishop Patrick Kennedy to Edmund Rice, 16 Nov. 1836, Normoyle (ed.), *Companion*, p. 482.
83 *Clare Journal*, 31 Oct. 1833.
84 Ibid.
85 Ibid.
86 Dr MacMahon to Edmund Rice, 2 Nov. 1831, cited in *CBER* (1895), 105.
87 Normoyle, *A tree is planted*, p. 206.
88 Ibid.
89 James Casserly, *The Old Mon: the story of the Patrician Brothers' School, Lombard Street, Galway* (Galway, 1996), p. 9.
90 McLaughlin, 'The founding of the Irish Christian Brothers', pp 27–8.
91 Ridden, 'The forgotten history', pp 80–1.
92 Yates, *The religion and condition of Ireland* (Oxford, 2006), p. 256.
93 John Jebb to Archbishop Broderick, 16 Oct. 1820, cited in Ridden, 'The forgotten history', p. 86.
94 Eugene Broderick, 'Waterford's Anglicans: religion and politics, 1819–1872' (PhD, NUI, Cork, 2000), pp 84–5.
95 *Waterford Mail*, 13 Dec. 1826, cited in Broderick, 'Waterford's Anglicans', p. 86.
96 Dean Hearn to the Secretary, Kildare Place Society, 8 May 1822, Waterford and Lismore Diocesan Archive, cited in Broderick, 'Waterford's Anglicans', pp 91–2.
97 *Waterford Mail*, 25 Sept. 1826.
98 Cited in Normoyle, *A tree is planted*, p. 61.
99 J.D. Fitzpatrick, 'Our Venerable Founder's practice of the virtue of the faith', p. 56.
 1 Broderick, 'Waterford's Anglicans', p. 93.
 2 Coldrey, 'The charism of Edmund Rice', p. 15.
 3 D.V. Kelleher, ''A timely restorer of faith and hope in Ireland', in Carroll (ed.), *A man raised up*, p. 108.
 4 Peckham Magray, *Transforming power*, p. 97.
 5 Annals of the congregation, 1828–30, SOC/M, cited in Peckham Magray, *Transforming power*, p. 97; [A member of the congregation], *The life and works of Mary Aikenhead* (Dublin, 1924), p. 106.
 6 Sr Agnes Murrogh-Bernard to Br P.J. Hennessy, 29 Sept. 1923, CBGA, 189/2111.
 7 Larkin, *The pastoral role*, p. 215.
 8 Brown, *The national churches*, p. 123.
 9 *Dublin Evening Mail*, 4 Dec. 1826; Brown, *The national churches*, p. 123.
10 Edmund Rice to Fr John Rice, 10 Dec. 1833, APF, S.C. America Settentrionale, Vol. 3, F. 197.
11 Catherine McAuley to Fr John Rice, 8 Dec. 1833, APF, S.C. America Settentrionale, Vol. 3, F. 197.
12 *The Tablet*, 14 Sept. 1854; *Synge Street Annual, 1946–7* (Dublin, 1947), p. 4.
13 'Proselytism in Dingle – measures to counteract it', Undated Broadsheet [1849?], CBGA, 035/0406; Br P.J. Murphy to Tobias Kirby, PICR, Achives, Kirby Papers/721; Philip Dowley CM, 30 Nov. 1846, cited in Emmet Larkin, 'The parish mission movement, 1850–1880', in Bradshaw and Keogh (eds), *Christianity in Ireland*, p. 197.

14   Sermon of Mgr Donal Reidy, St John's Tralee, 29 Aug. 1944, CBGA, 192/2139.

15   Brown, *The national churches*, p. 133.

16   Ibid., p. 124.

17   Daniel O'Connell to Mary O'Connell, 22 Mar. 1827, M. O'Connell (ed.), *Correspondence of Daniel O'Connell*, iii, 302.

18   Gillespie, *The Christian Brothers in England*, p. 15.

19   Paul Cullen to Tobias Kirby, 25 June 1842, PICR, Archives, KIR/1842/ 98.

20   P.J. Murphy to Tobias Kirby, 10 Mar. 1843, PICR, Archives, KIR 1843/173; cf. Heather Shore, *Artful Dodgers: youth and crime in early nineteenth-century London* (London, 1999).

21   Fitzpatrick, *Edmund Rice*, p. 336.

22   F.W. Faber, Charity Sermon for O'Connell's Schools, 19 Sept 1852, O'Connell's Schools Annals, CBGA, Rome.

23   J.E. Gordon, cited in Normoyle, *A tree is planted*, p. 62.

24   Gillespie, *The Christian Brothers in England*, pp 49–54.

25   *Preston Pilot*, 14 Apr. 1827.

26   *Waterford Mail*, 25 Apr. 1826.

27   Preston House Annals, 1827, cited in Blake, 'John Austin Grace', p. 100.

28   Normoyle, *A tree is planted*, p. 181.

29   Br Austin Dunphy to Br Patrick Corbett, 29 Apr. 1827, CBGA, 007/061.

30   Ibid.

31   Edmund Rice to Br Patrick Corbett, 4 July 1827, CBGA, 007/061.

32   *Preston Pilot*, 30 June 1827.

33   Br Patrick Ellis to Br Patrick Corbett, 1 July 1827; same to same, 4 July 1827, CBGA, 007/061.

34   Br P.J. Leonard to Frère Guillaume, 29 Oct. 1827, DLSGA, EN 411/1/2/3.

35   Bowen, *Protestant Crusade*, p. xii.

36   Whelan, *Bible War*, p. 86.

37   *Kilkenny Journal*, Nov. 1861, cited in Shelly, *Edmund Ignatius Rice*, p. 127.

Chapter 9   Testing times, 1822–32

1   Patrick Kelly to Propaganda Fide, 5 Jul. 1824, APF, SC Irlanda, 1823–27, v. 24, f. 256.

2   D. O'Herlihy et al. (eds), *To the cause of liberality: a history of the O'Connell Schools and the Christian Brothers, North Richmond Street* (Dublin, 1995): p. 16

3   Bartlett, *Fall and rise,* p. 329.

4   Richard English, *Irish freedom*, p. 128.

5   John Jebb (1824), cited in D.M. Hempton, *Religion and political culture in Britain and Ireland* (Cambridge, 1996), p. 80.

6   Bartlett, *Fall and rise, p.* 332.

7   Cited in Hempton, 'Methodist crusade', p. 39.

8   Connolly, *Religion and society*, p. 28.

9   Oliver MacDonagh, *O'Connell: the life of Daniel O'Connell* (London, 1991), p. 247.

10   Normoyle, *A tree is planted*, p. 212.

11   English, *Irish freedom*, p. 135.

12   *Freeman's Journal*, 10 June 1828.

13   [McCarthy], *Edmund Ignatius Rice*, p. 269.

14   Letter of Br Austin Grace, 13 July 1875 cited in Normoyle, *A tree is planted*, p. 214.

15   Br P.J. Leonard to Fr Pius Leahy, 21 Nov. 1829, CBGA, 0025/0216.

16   O'Connell's Schools Annals (1844), CBGA, Rome.

17   Br P.J. Leonard to Frère Guillaume, 28 Mar. 1829, DLSGA, EN 411/1/4/2.

18   Normoyle, *A tree is planted*, p. 215

19   Br P.J. Leonard to Frère Guillaume, 28 Apr. 1828, DLSGA, EN 411/1/3/5.

20   Ibid.

21   'Appeal to the General Public on behalf of North Richmond Street Schools', Normoyle (ed.), *Companion*, pp 262–4.

22 Br P.J. Leonard to Frère Guillaume, 14 Dec. 1829, DLSGA, EN 411/1/4/12.
23 Br P.J. Leonard to Pius Leahy, 30 June 1829, IDA, Letters, 30/6/1829.
24 Ibid.
25 10 George IV c. 7, XXVI–XXXVII.
26 Hansard, *House of Lords*, 2 April 1829, p. 56.
27 Br P.J. Leonard to Frère Guillaume, 28 Mar. 1829, DLSGA, EN 411/1/4/2.
28 *History of the Institute*, i, 141.
29 R. Walsh, 'A list of the regulars registered in Ireland pursuant to the Catholic Relief Act of 1829', *Arch. Hib.*, 3 (1914), 36.
30 Ibid.
31 Fr Pius Leahy to Fr Bat. Russell, 26 March 1829, IDA, Letters, 26/3/1829.
32 Fitzpatrick, *Edmund Rice*, pp 209–15; Keogh, *Edmund Rice*, p. 77.
33 Fr Pius Leahy to Fr Bat. Russell, [29] March 1829, IDA, Letters, 26/3/1829.
34 Lord Clifden to Edmund Rice, 10 Apr. 1829, Normoyle (ed.), *Companion*, pp 234–5.
35 Fr Pius Leahy to Fr Bat. Russell, 31 March 1829, IDA, Letters, 31/3/1829; R. Walsh, 'A list of the regulars', p. 48.
36 Ibid.
37 Fr Pius Leahy to Fr Bat. Russell, [29] March 1829, IDA, Letters, 29/3/1829.
38 O'Connell to H. O'Meara, 18 March 1829, *History of the Institute*, i, 139.
39 Br P.J. Leonard, 15 Sept. 1829, cited in Fitzpatrick, *Edmund Rice*, p. 223.
40 O'Connell's Schools Annals (1834), CBGA, Rome.
41 Edmund Rice to Frère Guillaume, 16 Oct. 1829, DLSGA, EN 411/1/4/8.
42 Br John Leonard to Fr Pius Leahy, 9 Sept. 1831, IDA, Colman Letterbook, Vol. 1, p. 295.
43 Normoyle, *A tree is planted*, p. 221.
44 *Positio*, p. 381.
45 Br P.J. Leonard to Frère Guillaume, 15 Feb. 1827, DLSGA, EN 411/1/2/2.
46 Br P.J. Leonard to Frère Guillaume, 29 Dec. 1828, DLSGA EN 411/1/3/7.
47 Frère Guillaume to P.J. Leonard, 22 Jan. 1829, DLSGA, EN 411/1/3/1.
48 *Positio*, p. 382.
49 Leonard–Leahy correspondence, in Normoyle (ed.), *Companion*, pp 309–31.
50 Br P.J. Leonard to Frère Guillaume, 29 Oct. 1827, DLSGA, EN 411/1/2/6.
51 Edmund Rice to Frère Guillaume, 16 Oct. 1829, DLSGA, EN 411/1/4/8.
52 Br P.J. Leonard to Frère Anaclet, 9 June 1829, DLSGA, EN 411/1/4/3.
53 Edmund Rice to Frère Guillaume, 16 Oct. 1829, DLSGA, EN 411/1/4/8.
54 Ibid.
55 Ibid.
56 Normoyle, *A tree is planted*, p. 233.
57 Edmund Rice to Frère Guillaume, 16 Oct. 1829, DLSGA, EN 411/1/4/8.
58 Ibid.
59 Ibid.
60 Br P.J. Leonard to Frère Guillaume, 14 Sept. 1829, DLSGA, EN 411/1/4/6.
61 Normoyle, *A tree is planted*, p. 234; Br P. J. Leonard to Frère Guillaume, 14 Sept. 1829, DLSGA, EN 411/1/4/6.
62 Br P.J. Leonard to Frère Guillaume, 9 June 1829, DLSGA, EN/1/4/3.
63 Frère Guillaume to Edmund Rice, 18 Jan. 1830, DLSGA, EN 411/1/5/1.
64 Ibid.
65 Frère Guillaume Br P.J. Leonard, 19 Jan. 1830, DLSGA, EN 411/1/5/2.
66 *Positio*, p. 400.
67 McLaughlin, *The Price of Freedom*, p. 358.
68 Br Bernard Dunphy to Daniel Murray, 26 Nov. 1840, DDA, 35/5.
69 *Positio*, p. 382.
70 Br P.J. Leonard to Fr Pius Leahy, 15 Feb. 1830, CBGA, 025/0216.
71 Richard Burke, *Irish Weekly Examiner*, 14 Sept. 1978.

72 Letter to the Holy See from '17 Pastors of the Diocese of Waterford and Lismore', 11 Sept. 1818, APF, SCRI, Vol. 21, F. 513, Normoyle, *Roman correspondence*, p. 29.

73 Memoir of Br Stephen Carroll, *Memories*, p. 40.

74 Br P.J. Leonard to Fr Pius Leahy, 15 Feb. 1830, CBGA, 025/0216.

75 Br P.J. Leonard to Fr Pius Leahy, 16 Feb. 1830, CBGA, 025/0216.

76 Frère Guillaume to Br P.J. Leonard, 19 Jan. 1830, CBGA, EN 411/1/5/2.

77 Frère Anaclet to Br John Leonard, 3 Nov. 1831, DLSGA, EN 411/1/6/4.

78 Br John Leonard to Fr Pius Leahy, 9 Sept. 1831, IDA, Colman Letterbook, Vol. 1, p. 295.

79 Br P.J. Leonard to Fr Pius Leahy, 16 Feb. 1830, CBGA, 025/0216.

80 Ibid.

81 *Positio*, pp 492–4; Edmund Rice to Br Austin Grace, 14 Nov. 1831, Normoyle (ed.), *Companion*, pp 387–8.

82 Fr Bat. Russell to Fr Pius Leahy, 6 Jan 1832, IDA, Letters, 6/1/1832.

83 Br John Leonard to Fr Pius Leahy, 9 Sept. 1831, IDA, Colman Letterbook, Vol. 1, p. 265.

84 *History of the Institute*, i, 147.

85 Normoyle, *A tree is planted*, p. 250; *Positio*, p. 497.

86 Decrees of the 1832 General Chapter, CBGA, 058/0644.

87 Br P.J. Leonard to Frère Guillaume, 14 Dec. 1829, DLSGA, EN 411/1/4/12.

88 Normoyle, *A tree is planted*, p. 251.

89 Edmund Rice to Frère Ancalet, 20 Feb. 1832, DLSGA, EN 411/1/7/1.

90 Ibid.

91 Br P.J. Leonard to Frère Guillaume, 28 Feb. 1828, DLSGA, EN 411/1/3/1.

92 Normoyle, *A tree is planted*, p. 252.

93 Br P.J. Leonard to Frère Guillaume, 15 Feb. 1829, DLSGA, EN 411/1/5/3.

94 Recollection of Br Alphonsus Collins (1841–1921), in Normoyle (ed.), *Memories*, p. 60.

Chapter 10 Faith or fatherland? The Brothers and the National Board, 1831–6

1 'J.K.L.', *Letters on the state of Ireland* (Dublin, 1825), p. 19, cited in Hempton and Hill, *Evangelical Protestantism*, p. 55.

2 Speech of Daniel O'Connell to the AGM of the Society for the Promotion of the Education of the Poor in Ireland, 24 February 1820, cited in A. Hyland and K. Milne (eds), *Irish educational documents* (Dublin, 1987), i, 89.

3 Daniel O'Connell, *Report of General Meeting* of KPS, 1820, in Corcoran (ed.), *Education systems in Ireland*, p. 129.

4 H. Hislop, 'The 1806–12 Board of Education and non-denominational education in Ireland', *Oideas* (1993), 48–61.

5 Cf E.G. Stanley to Duke of Leinster, Oct. 1831, in Corcoran (ed.), *Education systems in Ireland*, pp 164–70; D.H. Akenson, *The Irish education experiment: the National system of education in the nineteenth century* (London, 1970), p. 5.

6 For this and subsequent discussion of the System I rely on Daly, 'National System'; I. Murphy, 'Primary education', *A history of Irish Catholicism*, v, 1–33 and John Coolahan, 'The daring first decade of the Board of National Education, 1831–41', *Irish Journal of Education*, 17:1 (1983), 35–54.

7 Yates, *The religious condition of Ireland*, p. 57.

8 James E. Gordon, *Six letters on the subject of Irish education* … (London, 1832), p. 41, cited in Brown, *The national churches*, p. 159.

9 Yates, *The religious condition of Ireland*, p. 59; James Carlile, *A letter from the Revd. James Carlile of Dublin, one of the Commissioners of the Board of Education … containing some remarks on a speech of Capt. J. E. Gordon* (Dublin, 1832), pp 12–13.

10 *Freeman's Journal*, 9 May 1832, cited in Murphy, 'Primary Education', p. 13.

11 Stanley to Murray, 25 Feb. 1831, DDA, 33/3/42.

12 Hislop, 'Board of Education', p. 48; Daly, 'National Schools', p. 156.

13 Edmund Rice to Thomas Bray, 9 May 1810, CDA, Bray Papers 1810/21; Blake, *Short life*, p. 17.

14   Paul Connell, *The diocese of Meath under Bishop John Cantwell, 1830–66* (Dublin, 2004).

15   Akenson, *The Irish education experiment*, p.4.

16   Edmund Rice to Fr Trappes, 24 June 1825, in Normoyle (ed.), *Companion*, p. 119.

17   Edmund Rice to Fr Francis Murphy, n.d. [1837], cited in Gillespie, *The Christian Brothers in England*,
     p. 68.

18   *History of the Institute*, i, 193.

19   Kent, 'The educational ideas', p. 4; McLaughlin, *The price of freedom*, p. 267.

20   Minutes of the Board Meeting of Commissioners of National Education, Ireland, Vol. 1, NLI, MS
     5529, p. 20, cited in McLaughlin, *The price of freedom*, p. 263.

21   McLaughlin, *The price of freedom*, p. 265.

22   Ibid.

23   *First Report of the Commissioners of Irish Education Inquiry*, 1825 (400), XII, 1, 755.

24   McLaughlin, *The price of freedom*, p. 264.

25   Ibid., p. 266.

26   Bowen, *The Protestant crusade*, p. 76.

27   Shelly, *Edmund Ignatius Rice*, p. 129.

28   *CBER* (1895), p. 411.

29   *Fifth Book of Lessons* (Dublin, 1836), p. 199.

30   *Fourth Book of Lessons* (Dublin, 1850), pp. 52–6. See R.J. Scally, *The end of hidden Ireland: rebellion,
     famine and emigration* (Oxford, 1995).

31   Cf J.P.L. Walsh, 'A comparative analysis of the reading books of the Commissioners of National
     Education and the Christian Brothers, 1831–1900' (MA, UCD, 1983).

32   D.H. Akenson, 'Pre-university education, 1782–1870' in W.E. Vaughan (ed.), *New history of Ireland*,
     v, 532.

33   *Kilkenny Journal*, November 1861, cited in Shelly, *Edmund Ignatius Rice*, p. 129.

34   *The Nation*, 18 Dec. 1847.

35   Br Paul Riordan to Frère Ancalet, 5 Feb. 1838, DLSGA, EN 411/1/9/1.

36   *Powis Commission Report*, 1870 (C. 6111.), XXVIII, Part. III, p. 83; Letter of Br J. A. Hoare, Normoyle,
     A tree is planted, pp 280–1.

37   Minutes of 1836 General Chapter, CBGA, 92/1063.

38   Joseph Murphy to Tobias Kirby, 17 Sept. 1841, PICR, Archives, KIR/80; Michael Olden, 'Tobias Kirby;
     the man who kept the letters', in Dáire Keogh and Albert McDonnell (eds), *The Irish College, Rome,
     and its world* (Dublin, 2008), pp 131–48.

39   Minutes of 1836 General Chapter, CBGA, 92/1063.

40   Walsh, *Nano Nagle*, p. 215.

41   Akenson, *The Irish education experiment*, p. 224; [G.F. Mathison], *Journal of a tour in Ireland during
     the months of October and November 1835* (printed for private circulation, London, 1836), pp 5, 47–
     8, 90 cited in James Pereiro, 'Tractarians and National Education, 1838–1843' in Sheridan Gilley (ed.),
     Victorian churches and churchmen: essays presented to Alan McClelland (London, 2005), p. 253.

42   Feheney, *Gentlemen of the Presentation*, p. 29.

43   Laughlin, *The price of freedom*, p. 278; Walsh, *Nano*, p. 215.

44   Akenson, *The Irish education Eexperiment*, p. 131.

45   Walsh, *Nano Nagle*, p. 215; Roland Burke Savage, *A valiant Dublin woman* (Dublin, 1940) p. 237.

46   Paul Riordan to Frère Leon, 22 July 1845, DLSGA, EN 411/1/12/23; St Brigid's Orphanage, *Eleventh
     Annual Report* (1867), p. 16, cited in Prunty, *Margaret Aylward*, p. 105.

47   Deirdre Raftery and Susan Parkes, *Minerva or Madonna? Female education in Ireland, 1700–1900*
     (Dublin, 2007), p. 35.

48   Donal Kerr, 'Dublin's forgotten archbishop; Daniel Murray 1768–1852', in Kelly and Keogh (eds),
     History of the Catholic diocese of Dublin, p. 256.

49   Alvin Jackson, *Ireland, 1798–1998* (London, 1999), p. 29.

50   Whelan, *Bible war*, p. 120.

51   Yates, *The religious condition of Ireland*, p. 58.

52   *Dublin Evening Post*, 24 Nov. 1838.

53   Bishop John Power to Francis Moylan, 4 Jan. 1812, CBGA, 23/276.
54   H.E. Manning, *A sermon preached in the cathedral of Chichester on behalf of the Chichester Central Schools* ... (London, 1838) cited in James Pereiro, 'Tractarians and National Education', p. 262.
55   St Brigid's Orphanage, *Fifth Annual Report* (1861), p. 12, cited in Prunty, *Margaret Aylward*, p. 106.
56   John Coolahan, *Irish education*, p. 115.
57   T.J. Hearn Notebook, 30 July 1860, CBGA, 05/0041.
58   Rice to D. Murray, 4 June 1837, DDA, 35/5/6.
59   Joseph Murphy to Tobias Kirby, 17 Sept. 1841, PICR, Archives, KIR/80.
60   Daniel Murray to M.I. Kelly, 4 Sept. 1841, CBGA, 25/094; Fitzpatrick, *CBER* (1958), 60.
61   O'Connell's School Annals, 1873.
62   O'Connell, *Charles Bianconi*, p. 181.
63   T.J. Hearn Notebook, 1831–56, CBGA, 05/0041.
64   Blake, 'John Austin Grace', p. 145.

Chapter 11   The comfort of friends, 1838–44

1   J.D. Fitzpatrick, 'The founder's dream comes true', *CBER* (1964), 73.
2   Edmund Rice, Convocation of the General Chapter, 21 May 1838, Normoyle (ed.), *Companion*, p. 256.
3   Fitzpatrick, *Edmund Rice*, p. 323.
4   Idem, 'The brief', pp 203–25.
5   Michael Slattery to Paul Cullen, 6 July 1841, PICR Archives, Cull/1841/657.
6   Edmund Rice to Thomas Bray, 9 May 1810, CDA, Bray Papers, 1810/21.
7   Rev. Thos. Hempenstall, Acton, to Michael Paul Riordan, 23 Dec. 1839, CBGA Rome, 003/019.
8   Recollection of Br Stephen Carroll, 1888, in Normoyle (ed.), *Memories*, p. 37; Sunderland was unique among the Brothers' schools in that the majority of the students were non-Catholics; cf. Gillespie, *The Christian Brothers in England*, p. 66.
9   Gillespie, *The Christian Brothers in England*, pp 67–73.
10   Daniel Murray to Paul Cullen, 5 Dec. 1837, PICR Archives, Cul/390.
11   Recollection of Br Alphonsus Collins (1841–1921), in Normoyle (ed.), *Memories*, pp 61–3; Normoyle, *A tree is planted*, p. 290.
12   *History of the Institute*, i, 220.
13   *London and Dublin Orthodox Journal*, 111, 17 Sept. 1836, cited in Normoyle, *A tree is planted*, p. 291.
14   Fr James Patrick Cooke to Tobias Kirby, 11 Apr. 1842, PICR Archives KIR/1842.
15   *History of the Institute*, i, 271; J. Murphy to Tobias Kirby, 10 Mar. 1843, PICR Archives KIR/1843.
16   Edmund Rice to Fr John Rice, Aug. 1837, CBGA, 007/062.
17   Edmund Rice to Pius VII, 24 Jan. 1823, APF, SCRI, Vol. 24, F. 23–24.
18   Circular Letter of Edmund Rice, 22 Jan. 1838, Normoyle (ed.), *Companion*, pp 515–16.
19   Ibid.
20   Edmund Rice to Pius VII, 24 Jan. 1823, APF, SCRI, Vol. 24, F. 23–24.
21   Br Austin Dunphy, 'Private diary of the 1841 General Chapter', CBGA, 006/0048, p. 18.
22   Circular Letter of Edmund Rice, 22 Jan. 1838, Normoyle, *Companion*, pp 515–16.
23   Edmund Rice, 'Last Will and Testament with two codicils', 26 Feb. 1838, in Normoyle (ed.), *Companion*, pp 520–3; Normoyle, *A tree is planted*, p. 311.
24   Fr Peter Kenney to Daniel Murray, 31 Dec. 1840, DDA, 35/5/15.
25   Petition to the Holy See against Br Riordan, 30 July 1840, APF, SCRI, 1839–42, Vol. 27, F. 267–8.
26   Memoir of Brother Stephen Carroll, Normoyle (ed.), *Memories*, p. 42.
27   Fr Peter Kenney to Daniel Murray, 31 Dec. 1840, DDA, 35/5/15.
28   Normoyle, *A tree is planted*, p. 321.
29   Memoir of Br T.J. Hearn, CBGA, 0093/2196; Given the experience of the Industrial Schools in the following century, and the emergence of a class of 'Institutions men' within the ranks, such apprehensions were well founded.
30   Br P.J. Leonard to Frère Guillaume, 29/12/1828, DLSGA, EN 411/1/3/7.

31 Normoyle, *A tree is planted*, p. 32.
32 Gillespie, *The Christian Brothers in England*, p. 146.
33 Necrology, *CBER* (1907), p. 139.
34 *Catholic Telegraph* cited in Shelly, *Edmund Ignatius Rice*, p. 64.
35 Blake, 'John Austin Grace', p. 175.
36 O'Connell's Schools Annals, (1839), CBGA, Rome.
37 Blake, 'John Austin Grace', p. 176.
38 Br T.J. Hearn, Notebook, 23 Dec. 1841, CBGA, 0039.
39 G. Eckley, 'Gerald Griffin, 1803–1840', in R. Hogan (ed.), *Dictionary of Irish literature* (1996), i, 501–3.
40 Daniel Griffin, *Life of Gerald Griffin* (London, 1843), p. 365.
41 Shelly, *Edmund Rice*, p. 113; *Southern Reporter*, 20 July 1840.
42 Gerald Griffin, Oct. 1839, cited in 'Gerald Griffin as a Christian Brother', *CBER* (1891), 309.
43 Ibid., p. 313.
44 *Cork Reporter*, 27 July 1842; *The Nation*, 18 Dec. 1847.
45 *The Nation*, 18 Dec. 1847.
46 Coldrey, *Faith and fatherland*, p. 138.
47 Niall Ó Ciosáin, *Print and popular culture in Ireland, 1750–1850* (London, 1997), pp 96–7.
48 Br J.A. Grace to Br T.J. Hearn, Nov. 1840, cited in Blake, 'John Austin Grace', p. 368.
49 Br P.J. Murphy to Tobias Kirby, 28 Nov. 1843, PICR, Archives, KIR/1843/241.
50 Br P.J. Murphy to Frère Leon, 10 Dec. 1843, DLSGA, EN 411/1/10/4.
51 Ibid.
52 Br J.V. Cronin to Br J. Hearn, 4 Dec. 1838, cited in *History of the Institute*, i, 270.
53 Fitzpatrick, *Edmund Rice*, p. 323.
54 *Catholic Directory* (1841), p. 444, cited in Normoyle, *A tree is planted*, p. 328.
55 Br Ignatius Kelly to ——, 27 Nov. 1838, *History of the Institute*, i, 337.
56 Br M. P. Riordan's Petition to the Holy See, 11 July 1839, SCRI, 1839–42, Vol. 27, F. 112–13.
57 McLaughlin, *The price of freedom*, pp 310 ff; Gillespie, *The Christian Brothers in England*, p. 146 ff; Normoyle, *A tree is planted*, pp 328–41.
58 Gillespie, *The Christian Brothers in England*, p. 147.
59 Recollection of Br Edward Alphonsus Collins (1841–1921), in Normoyle (ed.), *Memories*, p. 63.
60 Gillespie, *The Christian Brothers in England*, p. 179.
61 'Memoir of Br Michael Bernard Dunphy', *CBER* (1909), 67.
62 'Ibid., p. 65.
63 Br J. Murphy to Tobias Kirby, 17 Sept. 1841, PICR, Archives KIR/1841.
64 Ibid.
65 Br Austin Dunphy to Br Francis Thornton, 1 Aug. 1840, CBGA, 025/0293.
66 Br Austin Dunphy, 'Private diary', CBGA, 006/0048, p. 5.
67 Br P. J. Murphy to Tobias Kirby, 17 Sept. 1841, PICR, Archives, KIR/1841
68 Br P.J. Leonard to Frère Guillaume, 29 Dec. 1828, DLSGA, EN 411/1/3/7.
69 Recollection of Br Stephen Carroll (1888), in Normoyle (ed.), *Memories*, p 42.
70 Edmund Rice to Br Austin Dunphy, 10 Feb. 1839, in Normoyle (ed.), *Companion*, p. 533.
71 Br M.P. Riordan to Tobias Kirby, 20 Aug. 1842, PICR, Archives, KIR/1842.
72 Br Joseph Murphy to Tobias Kirby, 17 Sept. 1841, PICR, Archives, KIR/1841.
73 Recollection of Br John Norris (1823–1912), in Normoyle (ed.), *Memories*, p. 214.
74 Br P.J. Murphy to Frère Leon, 16 Aug. 1845, DLSGA, EN 411/1/12/1.
75 Br Laurence Knowd, 20 Jan. 1832, SCRI, 1828–34, Vol. 25, F. 518–9, cited in Normoyle, *A tree is planted*, p. 184.
76 Daniel Murray to Propaganda Fide, 28 July 1832, APF, SCRI, 1828–34, Vol. 25, F. 51.
77 J.D. Fitzpatrick, 'An unwritten chapter in the life of Edmund Rice', *CBER* (1951), 102–27; Normoyle, *A tree is planted*, pp 342 ff.
78 Ibid., p. 347.
79 Paul Riordan, Circular, December 1839, cited in Blake, 'John Austin Grace', p. 175.

80 Normoyle, *A tree is planted*, p. 348.

81 Ibid., p. 350.

82 Edmund Rice to Daniel Murray, 14 Sept. 1840, DDA. 35/5.

83 Br Joseph Leonard to Pius Leahy, 15 Feb. 1830, CBGA, 025/216.

84 Opinion of Peter Kenney [1840], CBGA Rome; Normoyle, *A tree is planted*, p. 352.

85 Ibid.

86 Memorial in Favour of Pay Schools, 23 July 1840, DDA, 35/5/7.

87 Petition to the Holy See against M. P. Riordan, 30 July 1840, APF, SCRI, 1839–42, Vol. 27, F. 267–8.

88 *Positio*, p. 643.

89 Peter Kenny to Daniel Murray, 21 Jan. 1841, DDA, 35/5/15.

90 Daniel Murray to Paul Cullen, 21 Sept. 1841, PICR, Archives CUL/1841/682.

91 Daniel Murray to Propaganda, 11 Jan. 1841, in Normoyle (ed.), *Roman Correspondence*, p. 214.

92 Peter Kenny to Daniel Murray, 31 Dec. 1841, DDA, 35/5/15.

93 Ibid.

94 Ibid. The emphasis is mine.

95 Brs Patrick Ellis and Joseph Cahill to Pope Gregory XVI, 22 June 1841, Normoyle (ed.), *Companion*, pp 221–3.

96 Br P.J. Murphy to Tobias Kirby, 17 Sept. 1841, PICR, Archives, KIR/1841/56; Dean Meyler to Paul Cullen, 10 Feb. 1842, PICR, Archives, CUL/1842.

97 Br P.J. Murphy to Tobias Kirby, 17 Sept. 1841, PICR, Archives, KIR/1841/56.

98 Br P.J. Ryan to Daniel Murray, 21 Mar. 1841, DDA, 35/5/38.

99 Normoyle, *A tree is planted*, p. 333; this is a curious episode since Austin Grace, a 'Rice man', was director of North Richmond Street.

1   Br Austin Dunphy, 'Private diary', CBGA, 006/0048.

2   Thomas Morrissey, *As one sent: Peter Kenney, 1779–1841*, pp 421–2.

3   McLaughlin, *The price of freedom*, p. 309.

4   Br Austin Dunphy, 'Private diary', CBGA, 006/0048.

5   Morrissey, *As one sent*, p. 421.

6   Normoyle, *A tree is planted*, p. 367.

7   Paul Riordan to Paul Cullen, 12 Nov. 1842, PICR, CUL/1842.

8   *Positio*, p. 651.

9   Normoyle, *A tree is planted*, p. 363.

10 Br P.F. Ryan to Dr Murray, August 1841, DDA, 35/5/38.

11 Br Ray English, 'Br Michael Paul Riordan (1789–1862)', unpublished paper, p. 22.

12 Edmund Rice to Br Patrick Corbett, 3 July 1835, cited in *CBER* (1897), 89.

13 Recollection of Walter McGrath (1912), in Normoyle (ed.), *Momories*, p. 185; Recollection of John Caulfield (1912), in Normoyle (ed.), *Memories*, p. 55.

14 [McCarthy], *Edmund Ignatius Rice*, p. 416.

15 Recollection of Pat Browne (1912), in Normoyle (ed.), *Memories*, p. 16.

16 Recollection of Cornelius Dempsey (1912), ibid., p. 78; Recollection of John Flynn (1912), ibid., p. 110.

17 Normoyle, *A tree is planted*, p. 407.

18 Ibid.

19 Blake, 'John Austin Grace', p. 49.

20 Recollection of Br Stephen Carroll (1888), in Normoyle (ed.), *Memories*, p 40.

21 Recollection of Br John Norris (1823–1912), in Normoyle (ed.), *Memories*, p. 214.

22 Paul Riordan, Circular, 31 Dec. 1841, *History of the Institute*, i, 392.

23 Memoir of Br T.J. Hearn, CBGA, 005/42.

24 Recollection of Br Thomas Drislane (1825–1915), in Normoyle (ed.), *Memories*, p. 87.

25 Normoyle, *A tree is planted*, p. 404.

26 [McCarthy], *Edmund Ignatius Rice*, p. 418.

27 Br Joseph Murphy to Commissioners of Charitable Donations, 11 Sept. 1844, cited in Normoyle, *A tree is planted*, p. 413.

28 *History of the Institute*, i, 394.

29 Carried in the *Tipperary Vindicator*, 4 Sept. 1844.
30 *Kilkenny Journal*, 5 Oct. 1844.
31 Oration cited in [McCarthy], *Edmund Ignatius Rice*, p. 429.

Conclusion

1   J. C. McQuaid, Foreword, Fitzpatrick, *Edmund Rice*, p. x.
2   Br Joseph Murphy to Frere Philippe, 3 Sept. 1844, DLSGA, 411/1/11/14.
3   Cited in Keogh, *Edmund Rice*, p. 102.
4   Fitzpatrick, *Edmund Rice*, p. 333.
5   Akenson, *Irish education experiment*, pp. 187–202.
6   *Waterford Freeman*, 10 Sept. 1845; George Foxcroft Haskins, *Travels in England, France, Italy and Ireland* (Boston, 1865), p. 276.
7   *The Nation*, 18 Dec. 1847.
8   Mr and Mrs Hall, *Ireland*, i, 305–6.
9   *Waterford Chronicle*, 29 June 1816.
10 Shelly, *Edmund Ignatius Rice*, p. 20.
11 *Edmund Rice Centenary Souvenir* (Dublin, 1945).
12 Aidan Clarke, '"Varieties of uniformity":The first century of the Church of Ireland', *Studies in Church History*, 24 (1989), 105.
13 Whelan, *Bible Wars in Ireland*, p. 272.
14 See Colin Barr, '"*Imperium in Imperio*": Irish episcopal imperialism in the nineteenth century', *English Historical Review* (forthcoming).
15 J.A. Blake, Speech at Town Hall, Waterford, February 1864, cited in *Testimonies in favour of the Christian Brothers and their schools* (Dublin, 1877), p. 36.
16 Speech of Taoiseach Bertie Ahern at Mount Sion, 8 Feb. 2008.
17 *Waterford Freeman*, 10 Sept. 1845.
18 *Waterford Chronicle*, 16 Oct. 1844.
19 Maurice Lenihan, *Tipperary Vindicator*, 9 Sept. 1844.

Select bibliography

PRIMARY SOURCES

MANUSCRIPTS

Christian Brothers General Archive, Rome.
Superior General Correspondence.
Christian Brothers Ireland.
European Provincial Archives, Dublin.
Presentation Brothers General Archive, Cork.
Minutes of the Cork Charitable Society, 1798–1811.
Presentation Brothers' Annals.
Irish College Rome.
Papers of Tobias Kirby.
Papers of Paul Cullen.
De La Salle Brothers General Archive, Rome.
Irish Christian Brothers Correspondence.
Dublin Diocesan Archive.
Papers of John Troy.
Papers of Daniel Murray.
Cashel Diocesan Archive.
Papers of Thomas Bray.
Waterford Diocesan Archive.
Papers of Thomas Hussey.
Papers of John Power.
Irish Dominican Archive Tallaght, Dublin.
Coleman Letterbook.
Correspondence of Fr Pius Leahy.

PRIMARY SOURCES: PRINTED

Christian Brothers' Education Record (1891, in progress).
Denzinger, H., and A. Schonmetzer, *Enchiridion Symbolorum: definitionum et declarationum de rebus fidei et morum* (Rome, 1976).

Normoyle, M.C. (ed.), *A companion to a tree is planted: the correspondence of Edmund Rice and his assistants, 1810–1842* (Dublin, 1977).
——, *The Roman Correspondence: treating of the early years of the Institute of Edmund Rice, 1803–1844* (Dublin, 1979).
——, *Memories of Edmund Rice* (Dublin, 1979).

PARLIAMENTARY PAPERS

Reports of the Commissioners of the Board of Education in Ireland: Fourteen Reports; H.C. 1821 (744.) XI. 143. (Published originally as H.C. 1812–13 (21.) V. 221 and reprinted as H.C. 1813–14 (47.) V. 1.
Abstract of Answers and Returns for taking an account of the population of Ireland in 1821; H.C. 1824 (577.) XXII. 1.
First Report of the Commission of Irish Education Inquiry; H.C. 1825 (400.) XII. 1.
Second Report of the Commission of Inquiry. (Abstract of Returns in 1824 from the Protestant and Roman Catholic clergy of Ireland, of the state of Education in their respective parishes); H.C. 1826–27 (12.) XII. 1.
Report from the Select Committee to whom the Reports on the Subject of Education in Ireland were referred; H.C. 1828 (341.) IV. 223.
Report of the Select Committee on the state of the poor together with the Minutes of Evidence; H.C. 1830 (667.) VII. 1.
Report of Select Committee to inquire into the extent, causes and consequences of the Prevailing Vice of Intoxication among the Labouring Classes; H.C. 1834 (559.) VIII. 315.
Second Report of the Commissioners of Public Instruction (Ireland); H.C. 1935 (47.) XXXIV. 1.
Report on Foundation Schools and Education in Ireland (Wyse Report); H.C. 1836 (630.) XIII. 1.
A Report of the Select Committee of the House of Lords on the Plan of Education in Ireland; with Minutes of Evidence; H.L. 1837 (543 – I.) VIII. part i. 1.
Minutes of Evidence taken before the Select Committee of the House of Lords on the Plan of Education in Ireland; H.L. 1837 (485.) IX. 1.
Report of the Select Committee to inquire into the Progress and Operation of the new Plan of Education in Ireland; H.C. 1837 (485.) IX. 1.
Report of the Commissioners appointed to inquire into the endowments, funds and actual conditions of all schools endowed for the purpose of education in Ireland (Kildare); H.C. 1857–58 (2336–I.) XXII. 1.
Royal Commission of Inquiry, Primary Education, Ireland (Powis); H.C. 1870 (C.6) XXVIII. pt.i. 1.
——, *Reports of Assistant Commissioners;* H.C. 1870 (C.6 – I) XXVIII. pt ii. 1.
——. *Minutes of Evidence taken before the Commissioners, from March 12th to October 30th, 1868;* H.C. 1870 (C.6 – II) XXVIII. pt iii. 1.

SECONDARY SOURCES

Akenson, D.H., *A Protestant in Purgatory: Richard Whateley archbishop of Dublin* (Hamden, CN., 1981).

——, *The Irish education experiment: the National system of education in the nineteenth century* (London, 1970).

Allen, D.H., *The Presentation Brothers* (Cork, 1993).

Atkinson, N., *Irish education: a history of educational institutions* (Dublin, 1969).

Augustine, Fr, *Edmund Ignatius Rice and Theobald Mathew* (Dublin, 1944).

Bagchi, D. and D.C. Steinmetz (eds), *The Cambridge companion to Reformation theology* (Cambridge, 2004).

Bartlett, J.R. and S.D. Kinsella (eds), *Two thousand years of Christianity and Ireland* (Dublin, 2006).

Bartlett, T., *The fall and rise of the Irish nation: the Catholic question, 1690–1830* (Dublin, 1992).

Bew, Paul, *Ireland: the politics of enmity, 1789–2006* (Oxford, 2006).

Blake, D., *A nan for our times: a short life of Edmund Rice* (Dublin, 1994).

Bossy, J., 'The Counter-Reformation and the people of Catholic Europe', *Past and Present*, 47, (May, 1970), 51–70.

Bowen, D., *The Protestant crusade in Ireland 1800–70: a study of Protestant–Catholic relations between the Act of Union and Disestablishment* (Dublin, 1978).

Bradshaw, B., and D. Keogh (eds), *Christianity in Ireland* (Dublin, 2002).

Brown, Stewart J., *The national churches of England, Ireland and Scotland 1801–56* (Oxford, 2001).

Broderick, Eugene, 'Waterford's Anglicans: religion and politics, 1819–1872' (PhD dissertation, NUI, Cork, 2000).

Burtchael, J. and D. Dowling, 'Social and economic conflicts in county Kilkenny, 1600–1800' in W. Nolan and K. Whelan (eds), *Kilkenny: history and society* (Dublin, 1990), pp 251–72.

Cahill, E., 'The native schools of Ireland in the penal era', *Irish Ecclesiastical Record* (1940), 16–28.

Carroll, J.E., 'From Christian mission to ministry: Edmund Rice and the founding years of the Christian Brothers' in *Edmund* (Rome, 1991), pp 19–43.

Carroll, M.P., 'Rethinking popular Catholicism in pre-Famine Ireland', *Journal for the Scientific Study of Religion*, 34:3 (Sept. 1995), 354–65.

Carroll, P.S. (ed.), *A man raised up: recollections and reflections on Venerable Edmund Rice* (Dublin, 1994).

Châtellier, Louis, *The Europe of the devout: the Catholic reformation and the foundation of a new society* (Cambridge, 1989).

——, *The religion of the poor: rural missions in Europe and the formation of modern Catholicism, 1500–1800* (Cambridge, 1997).

Clear, C., *Nuns in nineteenth century Ireland* (Dublin, 1985).

Coldrey, B.M., *Faith and fatherland: the Christian Brothers and the development of Irish nationalism, 1838–1821* (Dublin, 1988).

——, 'The charism of Edmund Rice; opposition to Protestant proselytism', *CBER* (1989), 10–16.

Comerford, Kathleen M. (ed.), *Early modern Catholicism: essays in honour of John W. O'Malley* (Toronto, 2001).

Connolly, S.J., *Religion and society in nineteenth-century Ireland* (Dundalk, 1988).

——, *Religion, law and power: the making of Protestant Ireland 1660–1760* (Oxford, 1992).

——, 'Religion, work, discipline and economic attitudes; the case of Ireland', in T.M. Devine and D. Dickson (eds), *Ireland and Scotland, 1600–1850* (Edinburgh, 1983), pp 235–47.

Coolahan, J., 'The daring first decade of the Board of National Education, 1831–41', *Irish Journal of Education*, 17:1 (1983), 35–54.

Corish, P., *The Catholic community in the seventeenth and eighteenth centuries* (Dublin, 1981).

Cullen, L.M., 'Catholics under the penal laws' in *Eighteenth-Century Ireland* (1986), pp 23–36.

——, 'The hidden Ireland: reassessment of a concept' in *Studia Hib.*, 9 (1969), 7–47.

——, *The emergence of modern Ireland, 1600–1900* (Dublin, 1983).

Cunningham, Hugh, *Children and childhood in western society since 1500* (London, 1995).

Curtis, Sarah A., *Educating the faithful; religion, schooling and society in nineteenth-century France* (DeKalb, IL, 2000).

Daly, M., 'The development of the National School system, 1831–40', in A. Cosgrove and D. McCartney (eds), *Studies in Irish history presented to R. Dudley Edwards* (Dublin, 1979), pp 150–63.

DeMolen, R.L., *Religious Orders of the Catholic Reformation* (Fordham, 1998).

Dickson, D., 'Catholics and trade in eighteenth-century Ireland', in T. Power and K. Whelan (eds), *Endurance and emergence* (Dublin, 1990), pp 185–200.

Dowling, P.J., *A history of Irish education: a study in conflicting loyalties* (Cork, 1971).

English, Richard, *Irish freedom: the history of nationalism in Ireland* (London, 2006).

Feheney, J.M., *Gentlemen of the Presentation: brief biographies of twenty-five Presentation Brothers (1762–1999)*, (Dublin, 1999).

Fitzpatrick, J.D., *Edmund Rice* (Dublin, 1945).

Gilley, S., 'Catholicism in Ireland', in H. McLeod and W. Ustorf (eds), *The decline of Christendom in Western Europe, 1750–2000* (Cambridge, 2003) pp 99–112.

Gulliver, P.H. and M. Silverman, *Merchants and shopkeepers; a historical anthropology of an Irish market town, 1200–1991* (Toronto, 1995).

Hempton, D., 'The Methodist crusade in Ireland, 1795–1845', *Irish Historical Studies* (1980), 33–48.

—— with M. Hill, *Evangelical Protestantism in Ulster society, 1740–1890* (London, 1992).

——, *Religion and political culture in Britain and Ireland, from the Glorious Revolution to the decline of empire* (Cambridge, 1996).

Hilton, Mary, *Women and the shaping of the nation's young; education and public doctrine in Britain 1750–1850* (London, 2007).

Hislop, H., 'The 1806–12 Board of Education and non-denominational education in Ireland', *Oideas* (1993), 48–61.

Houlihan, J.A., *Overcoming evil with good; the Edmund Rice story* (New York, 1997).

Jefferies, H.J. (ed.), *History of the diocese of Clogher* (Dublin, 2005).

Kearney, H.F., 'Father Mathew: apostle of modernisation', in A. Cosgrove and D. McCartney (eds), *Studies in Irish history presented to R. Dudley Edwards* (Dublin, 1979), pp 164–75.

Kelly, D.A., 'Pro Deo et pro Patria; the contribution of Bl. Edmund Ignatius Rice and his Christian Brothers to the philosophy and structure of nineteenth-century Irish education' (PhD, Dublin University, 1999).

Kelly, J., The Ascendancy and the penal laws', in J.R. Bartlett and S.D. Kinsella (eds), *Two thousand years of Christianity and Ireland* (Dublin, 2006), pp 133–54.

Kennedy, J., 'Callan – a corporate town 1700–1800' in W. Nolan and K. Whelan (eds), *Kilkenny: history and society* (Dublin, 1990), pp 289–305.

Kent, J.E., 'The educational ideals of Edmund Rice, founder of the Presentation and Christian Brothers' (MEd., UCC, 1988).

Kerrigan, C., *Father Mathew and the Irish temperance movement, 1838–1849* (Cork, 1992).

Keogh, D., '*The French disease*': the Catholic Church and radicalism in Ireland 1790–1800 (Dublin, 1993).

——, 'Thomas Hussey, bishop of Waterford and Lismore, 1797–1803' in W. Nolan et al. (eds), *Waterford: history and society* (Dublin, 1992), pp 403–26.

——, *Edmund Rice, 1762–1844 (Dublin, 1996).*

——, and Albert McDonnell (eds), *The Irish College, Rome, and its world* (Dublin, 2008).

Larkin, E., *The pastoral role of the Roman Catholic Church in pre-Famine Ireland, 1750–1850* (Dublin, 2006).

Liechty, J., 'The popular reformation comes to Ireland: the case of John Walker and the foundation of the church of God 1804' in R.V. Comerford et al. (eds), *Religion, conflict and co-existence in Ireland* (Dublin, 1990), pp 159–87.

Luebke, D.M. (ed.), *The Counter-Reformation* (Oxford, 1999).

Lysaght, M., *Fr Theobald Mathew: the apostle of temperance* (Dublin, 1983).

[McCarthy, M.], A Christian Brother, *Edmund Ignatius Rice and the Christian Brothers* (Dublin, 1926).

MacCulloch, Diarmaid, *Christian history: an introduction to the western tradition* (London, 2006).

McGrath, T.G., 'The Tridentine evolution of modern Irish Catholicism, 1565–1962: a re-examination of the '"Devotional Revolution" thesis' in R. O'Muiri (ed.), *Irish church history today* (Armagh, 1990), pp 84–100.

——, *Politics, interdenominational relations and education in the public ministry of Bishop James Doyle* ... (Dublin, 1999).

McLaughlin, Denis, *The price of freedom; the education charism of Edmund Rice* (Brisbane, 2007).

McManus, A., *The Irish hedge school and its books, 1695–1831* (Dublin, 2003).

Mullet, M., *Catholics in Britain and Ireland, 1558–1829* (London, 1998).

Murphy, I., 'Some attitudes to religious freedom and ecumenism in pre-emancipation Ireland, *Irish Ecclesiastical Record* (1966), 93–104.

——, *The diocese of Killaloe in the eighteenth century* (Dublin, 1992).

Neely, W.G., *Kilkenny: an urban history, 1391–1843* (Belfast, 1989).

Normoyle, M.C., *A tree is planted: the life and times of Edmund Rice* (Dublin, 1976).

Ó Gadhra, N., *Éamann Iognáid Rís 1762–1844* (Dublin, 1977).

O'Herlihy, D. (ed.), *To the cause of liberality: a history of the O'Connell schools and the Christian Brothers, North Richmond Street* (Dublin, 1995).

O'Malley, J.W., *Trent and all that: renaming Catholicism in the early-modern era* (Harvard, 2000).

——, *The first Jesuits* (Cambridge, MA, 1993).

O'Sullivan, M., *Charles Bianconi: a biography 1786–1875* (London, 1878).

O'Toole, A.L., *A spiritual profile of Edmund Rice*, 2 vols (Bristol, 1984).

Parkes, S., *Irish education in the British Parliamentary Papers in the nineteenth century* (Cork, 1978).

Peckham Magray, M., *The transforming power of the nuns: women, religion and cultural change in Ireland, 1750–1900* (Oxford, 1998).

Prunty, Jacinta, *Lady of Charity, sister of faith: Margaret Aylward, 1810–1889* (Dublin, 1999).

Pereiro, James, 'Tractarians and National Education, 1838–1843' in Sheridan Gilley (ed.), *Victorian churches and churchmen: essays presented to Alan McClelland* (London, 2005), pp 249–78.

Quane, M., 'Waterford schools in the opening decades of the nineteenth century', *Royal Society of Antiquaries of Ireland* (1971), 141–5.

Raftery, Deirdre and Parkes, Susan, *Muse or Madonna: female education in Ireland, 1700–1900* (Dublin, 2007).

Ridden, Jennifer, 'The forgotten history of the Protestant crusade: religious liberalism in Ireland', *Journal of Religious History*, 31:1 (March 2007), 78–102.

Rushe, D. *Edmund Rice: the man and his times* (Dublin, 1981).

Shelly, J., *Edmund Ignatius Rice and the Christian Brothers: a compilation* (Kilkenny, 1863).

Sullivan, M. C., *Catherine McAuley and tradition of mercy* (Dublin, 1995).

Walsh, R., 'A list of the regulars registered in Ireland pursuant to the Catholic relief act of 1829' in *Arch. Hib.* (1914).

Walsh, T.J., *Nano Nagle and the Presentation Sisters* (Dublin, 1959).

Whelan, I., *The Bible War in Ireland; the 'Second Reformation' and the polarization of*

Protestant-Catholic Relations, 1800–1840 (Dublin, 2005).

Whelan, K., Review article, 'Gaelic survivals', in *Irish Review* (1989), 139–43.

_____, 'The regional impact of Irish Catholicism, 1700–1850' in W. Smyth and K. Whelan (eds), *Common ground: essays on the historical geography of Ireland* (Cork, 1988), pp 253–77.

_____, *The tree of liberty: radicalism, Catholicism and the construction of Irish identity, 1760–1830* (Cork, 1995).

Witteberg, P., *The rise and fall of Catholic religious orders; a social movement perspective* (New York, 1994).

Yates, N., *The religious condition of Ireland, 1770–1850* (Oxford, 2006).

Index

Compiled by Brad Morrow

Page numbers in italics refer to illustrations